COMPENSATION: EFFECTIVE REWARD MANAGEMENT

Compensation: Effective Reward Management

RABINDRA N. KANUNGO

MANUEL MENDONCA

McGill University
Faculty of Management

Butterworths

Toronto and Vancouver

Compensation: Effective Reward Management

Printed and bound in Canada by John Deyell Company Limited.

The Butterworth Group of Companies

Canada
Butterworths Canada Ltd., 75 Clegg Road, MARKHAM, Ont. L6G 1A1 and 409 Granville St., Ste. 1455, VANCOUVER, B.C. V6C 1T2

Australia
Butterworths Pty. Ltd., SYDNEY, MELBOURNE, BRISBANE, ADELAIDE, PERTH, CANBERRA and HOBART

Ireland
Butterworth (Ireland) Ltd., DUBLIN

New Zealand
Butterworths of New Zealand Ltd., WELLINGTON and AUCKLAND

Puerto Rico
Equity de Puerto Rico, Inc., HATO REY

Singapore
Malayan Law Journal Pte. Ltd., SINGAPORE

United Kingdom
Butterworth & Co. (Publishers) Ltd., LONDON and EDINBURGH

United States
Butterworth Legal Publishers, AUSTIN, Texas; BOSTON, Massachusetts; CLEARWATER, Florida (D & S Publishers); ORFORD, New Hampshire (Equity Publishing); ST. PAUL, Minnesota; and SEATTLE, Washington

Canadian Cataloguing in Publication Data

Kanungo, Rabindra N., 1935-
Compensation

Includes bibliographical references and index.
ISBN 0-409-89778-7

1. Compensation management. I. Mendonca, Manuel.
II. Title.

HF5549.5.C67K3 1992 658.3'142 C91-095718-5

Sponsoring Editor: Craig Laudrum
Editor: Julia Keeler
Cover Design: Brant Cowie
Production: Kevin Skinner
Typesetting: The Alger Press Limited

To our parents

for the invaluable lesson that
"it is more blessed to give than to receive"

To Minati and Rita

for their enduring patience, encouragement, and warm and generous support

To managers

committed to the full development of the human potential

Preface

The writing of this book was prompted by just one major consideration: the absence of a textbook that adequately addresses the issue of managing rewards within organizations in a coherent manner, properly integrating motivational theories and management practices. Managing people in an organization requires an understanding of how to motivate employees through a well-designed reward or compensation system. We have provided in this book an approach to the design and management of organizational rewards that is both practical and consistent with the accumulated findings of motivational research into work attitudes and behaviour. Specifically, the book accomplishes three objectives. First, it provides an understanding of the real nature of organizational rewards, why they work, and the circumstances under which they are most effective. Second, it presents a coherent framework of concepts and ideas — a framework that is critical to putting together into an integrated reward system the content, techniques, and processes inherent in a reward system. Finally, it recommends a diagnostic procedure for evaluating the effectiveness of a reward system in the light of an organization's philosophy and objectives.

The book is different from other existing textbooks in three ways. First, the book achieves a coherent integration of theory and practice through a unifying model. The model will force students and practising managers alike to take a good look at reward systems from a motivational perspective and to determine if there is a rational basis for the techniques and practices that prevail in an organization. Second, the book advocates the use of an innovative diagnostic procedure for evaluating the effectiveness of each reward item of an organization's compensation system. This procedure will enable an organization to determine if it is, indeed, getting the intended motivational effectiveness from its enormous compensation expenditures. If it is not, then the diagnostic procedure has the capability of identifying the specific reward item, policy, practice, or technique that needs to be addressed, and of proposing concrete and practical remedial interventions. Finally, the book deals with unique Canadian issues, legislation, and practices related to compensation management.

As a college text both at the undergraduate and graduate levels, this structured logical guide to compensation theory and practice will provoke students to experiment and to test the conclusions of the model. The book thus serves to promote deductive and inductive approaches to learning that are invaluable to the educational experience of both students and researchers in the field. Furthermore, practicing managers, compensation specialists, and management consultants will find the textbook to be a valuable resource in their effort to understand the reward-motivation phenomenon, and to design and administer reward policies and systems.

We would like to thank the Jaico Publishing House, Bombay, for permission to reprint an excerpt from the *Panchatantra*.

We would like to express our appreciation to all those who have helped us during the preparation of this book. We are thankful to our students and management trainees whose scepticism went a long way in persuading us to prepare this volume. We are grateful to Jean Hepworth for typing the manuscript with meticulous care, and to Julia Keeler, whose perceptive editorial queries and comments helped to clarify many an unclear thought and example.

Contents

Preface vii
List of Figures xvii
List of Tables xix

Chapter 1: An Introduction to Compensation 1

- Chapter Synopsis 1
- Learning Objectives 1
- The Nature of Compensation 1
- Classification of Compensation: Economic and Non-Economic Rewards 5
- The Economic Compensation System 7
  - Cash Payments 7
  - Benefits 9
- The Non-Economic Compensation System 10
- Objectives of the Reward System 11
- Effective Reward Management: A Compensation Model 12
- Summary 16
- Key Terms 17
- Review and Discussion Questions 17
- Case: The Tinkerman Corporation of Montreal 18

PART I: THE STRATEGIC INFLUENCE OF ENVIRONMENT 19

Chapter 2: The External and Internal Environments 21

- Chapter Synopsis 21
- Learning Objectives 21
- The Environment and the Compensation System 21
- The External Environment 22
  - Economic Conditions 22
  - Technological Changes 24
  - Government Regulations 24
  - Union Expectations 25

Sociocultural Environment 25
The Internal Environment 27
Internal Work Culture 27
Business Strategies 29
Product Life Cycle 32
Summary 36
Key Terms 36
Review and Discussion Questions 36
Case: Tandoori Burgers Limited 38

PART II: THEORETICAL APPROACHES TO COMPENSATION DESIGN AND MANAGEMENT 41

CHAPTER 3: THEORETICAL FOUNDATIONS: CONTENT THEORIES APPROACH 43

Chapter Synopsis 43
Learning Objectives 43
Introduction 44
Motivation and Motives 45
Theories of Motivation 45
Content Theories of Work Motivation 46
The Scientific Management Movement 47
The Human Relations Movement 48
Herzberg's Two-Factor Theory of Reward Classification 49
The Intrinsic-Extrinsic Reward Classification 51
A Critique of the Intrinsic-Extrinsic Dichotomy in Rewards Management 52
Summary 56
Key Terms 57
Review and Discussion Questions 58
Exercise 3.1: Preferences for Pay and Other Job Outcomes 59
Exercise 3.2: The Intrinsic-Extrinsic Approach to Rewards Classification 61

CHAPTER 4: THEORETICAL FOUNDATIONS: PROCESS THEORIES APPROACH 63

Chapter Synopsis 63
Learning Objectives 63
Process Theories of Work Motivation 64
Equity Theory 65
Expectancy Theory 66

The Elements of Expectancy Theory 67
The Determinants of the Elements of Expectancy Theory 68
The Process of Expectancy Theory 74
Empirical Support for the Expectancy Theory Model 77
Implications of the Expectancy Theory Model for Reward Management 80
Summary 82
Key Terms 83
Review and Discussion Questions 84
Exercise: The Practical Implications of Expectancy Theory 86

CHAPTER 5: SATISFACTION WITH PAY AND NON-ECONOMIC OUTCOMES 93

Chapter Synopsis 93
Learning Objectives 93
Introduction 94
Satisfaction with Pay 95
Determinants of Pay Satisfaction 96
Consequences of Pay Dissatisfaction 103
Practical Guidelines for Enhancing Pay Satisfaction 107
Satisfaction with Non-Economic Outcomes 109
Theoretical Approaches to Job Design 110
The Process of Job Design 114
Implications for Reward Management 117
Summary 117
Key Terms 118
Review and Discussion Questions 118
Case: Star Wars 120

PART III: PROCESSES AND TECHNIQUES IN DESIGNING THE COMPENSATION SYSTEM 123

CHAPTER 6: THE STRATEGIC AND PROCESS ISSUES IN COMPENSATION 125

Chapter Synopsis 125
Learning Objectives 125
Introduction 125
The Strategic Issues 129
Compensation Philosophy 129
Balancing the Mechanistic and Process Issues 131

The Choice of a Job-Content-based or a Person-based Evaluation System ... 134
The Compensation System as an End or as a Means to an End ... 136
The Choice of Internal or External Equity ... 137
The Choice of External Labour Markets for Salary Surveys ... 138
Centralization versus Decentralization ... 139
Performance versus Seniority ... 140
The Choice of the Compensation Mix ... 141
The Process Issues ... 142
Communicating the Compensation System ... 142
Involving Employees in Decision Making ... 145
The Role of the Strategic and Process Issues in Compensation Design and Administration ... 150
Summary ... 151
Key Terms ... 152
Review and Discussion Questions ... 152
Exercise: Deciding on Strategic and Process Issues in Compensation System Design ... 154

CHAPTER 7: PROMOTING ORGANIZATIONAL MEMBERSHIP BEHAVIOURS ... 155

Chapter Synopsis ... 155
Learning Objectives ... 155
Introduction ... 155
How Can Rewards Be Used to Reduce Absenteeism? ... 156
Problem and Effects of Absenteeism ... 156
Factors Related to Absenteeism ... 157
Reasons for Absenteeism ... 158
Methods of Controlling Absenteeism ... 163
How Can Rewards Be Used to Reduce Tardiness? ... 168
How Can Rewards Be Used to Reduce Turnover? ... 169
Why Employees Stay With or Leave an Organization ... 169
Methods of Controlling Turnover ... 173
Summary ... 174
Key Terms ... 175
Review and Discussion Questions ... 175
Case: Intexpro Inc. Meets Absenteeism Head-On ... 177

CHAPTER 8: PERFORMANCE-BASED PAY: PERSONAL EQUITY I ... 179

Chapter Synopsis ... 179
Learning Objectives ... 179

Introduction 180
Job Performance Behaviours 180
Objectives of Performance-based Rewards 182
The Role of Pay in Increasing Job Performance 183
Issues in Performance-based Pay 185
Rewarding Employees on the Basis of Individual, Group, or Organizational Performance 186
The Number of Performance-based Pay Plans 191
Merit Pay as a Salary Increase or a One-Time Bonus Payment 193
The Appropriate Amount of Merit Pay 194
Subjective versus Objective Measures of Performance 195
The Length of the Payout Periods 196
Employee Involvement in Designing and Administering Merit Pay 197
The Role of Performance Appraisal in the Administration of Performance-based Rewards 198
The Performance Appraisal Process 199
Essential Preconditions for Effective Performance Appraisal 202
Summary 203
Key Terms 205
Review and Discussion Questions 205
Case: Carpenter Creations Limited 207

Chapter 9: Incentive Systems and Gain-sharing Plans: Personal Equity II 211

Chapter Synopsis 211
Learning Objectives 211
Introduction 211
Individual Incentive Plans 212
Piece-Rate Plan 212
Standard-Hour Plan 213
Sales Commissions and Bonuses 215
Conditions that Favour the Effectiveness of Individual Incentive Plans 216
Group Incentive Plans 220
Critical Issues in Organization-wide Gain-sharing Plans 221
Types of Gain-sharing Plans 223
Scanlon Plan 224
Rucker Plan 227
Improshare Plan 229
Conditions That Favour Gain-sharing Plans 231

Summary 232
Key Terms 233
Review and Discussion Questions 233
Case: The Elusive Reward 234

CHAPTER 10: JOB ANALYSIS AND JOB EVALUATION: INTERNAL EQUITY I 237

Chapter Synopsis 237
Learning Objectives 237
Introduction 238
Internal Equity 238
What Is Internal Equity? 238
The Role of Internal Equity in the Design of a Compensation System 239
Tools and Processes for Ensuring Internal Equity 240
Job Analysis 241
What Is Job Analysis? 241
The Procedure and the Methods of Job Analysis 241
Interview 242
Observation 242
Questionnaire 243
Diary/Log 243
The Position Analysis Questionnaire (PAQ) 243
Job Description and Job Specifications 245
Job Evaluation 247
What Is Job Evaluation? 247
Methods of Job Evaluation 247
Ranking 247
Classification 248
The Factor Comparison and Point Methods 250
The Four Methods: Similarities and Differences 261
Administering the Job Evaluation Programme 262
Developing a Job Structure 263
Summary 264
Key Terms 264
Review and Discussion Questions 265
Exercise 10.1: Determining the Appropriateness of Job Analysis Methods 266
Exercise 10.2: Job Evaluation 268

CHAPTER 11: PAY EQUITY LEGISLATION: INTERNAL EQUITY II 273

Chapter Synopsis 273

Learning Objectives 273
Introduction 273
The Salient Features of Pay Equity Legislation 274
What Is Pay Equity? 274
The History of Pay Equity Legislation in Canada 275
Selected Provisions of Pay Equity Laws 275
The Pay Equity Plan 276
The Issue of Gender Bias in Job Analysis and Job Evaluation 278
Some Neglected Issues in Pay Equity Laws 281
Equity and Moral Rights 282
Equity Theory of Human Motivation and Pay Equity Laws 283
Effects of Pay Equity Laws 284
Conclusion 289
Summary 290
Key Terms 291
Review and Discussion Questions 291
Exercise: The Pay Equity Debate 292

CHAPTER 12: SALARY SURVEYS AND PAY STRUCTURE: EXTERNAL EQUITY 295

Chapter Synopsis 295
Learning Objectives 295
Introduction 296
The Sources or Bases of Pay Rates 296
The Relevant External Labour Market 298
Salary Surveys 299
What Is a Salary Survey? 299
Salary Survey Approaches and Methods 300
Techniques of Data Collection 303
A Critique of Salary Surveys 304
Analysis of Survey Data 304
Designing the Pay Structure 307
Pay Level Policy 307
Pricing the Job Structure 309
Constructing the Pay Structure: Pay Grades, Pay Ranges 311
Pay Structure and Salary Administration Policies 315
Summary 317
Key Terms 318
Review and Discussion Questions 318
Exercise: Constructing the Pay Structure 321

CHAPTER 13: EMPLOYEE BENEFITS PROGRAMMES 323

Chapter Synopsis 323
Learning Objectives 323
Employee Benefits Programmes 323
Income Protection Programmes 324
Reimbursed Time Off 330
Employee Services and Perquisites 331
The Flexible Benefits Approach 333
Guidelines in Designing the Benefits Programme 334
Summary 336
Key Terms 336
Review and Discussion Questions 336
Exercise: Evaluating a Benefits Programme 338

PART IV: MANAGING THE COMPENSATION SYSTEM 339

CHAPTER 14: MANAGING THE COMPENSATION SYSTEM 341

Chapter Synopsis 341
Learning Objectives 341
Introduction 342
The Salary Budget Process 342
The Top-Down Approach 343
The Bottom-Up Approach 345
Emerging Issues: Person-based Pay 346
Multi-Skilling 346
Knowledge-based Pay 348
Emerging Issues: Evaluating the Effectiveness of the Compensation System 350
An Action Programme 352
Illustration of the Action Programme 357
Summary 367
Key Terms 367
Review and Discussion Questions 368
Case: Getting the Motivational Bang from the Compensation Bucks 369

References 373
Index 381

Figures

1.1 The Reward System 7
1.2 Effective Reward Management: A Model 13
2.1 The Impact of the External and Internal Environments on the Compensation Programme 23
2.2 The Influence of the Sociocultural Environment on the Internal Work Culture 28
2.3 The Influence of the Sociocultural and Internal Environments on the Compensation Mix 34
4.1 The Expectancy Theory Model 69
5.1 Determinants of Pay Satisfaction 97
5.2 Consequences of Pay Dissatisfaction 104
6.1 The Effects of Employee Involvement in Decision Making 147
7.1 Expectancy Theory Model for Explaining Attendance Motivation 160
7.2 Expectancy Theory Model for Explaining Organizational Tenure 170
8.1 The Performance Appraisal Process and Its Essential Preconditions 204
14.1 Managerial Action Programme for Assessing and Designing a Reward System 353

Tables

1.1 A List of Work Rewards Offered by Organizations 6
3.1.1 Preferences for Pay and Other Job Outcomes 60
4.1.1 Expectancy Theory Worksheet 88
5.1 The Process of Job Redesign 115
6.1 Extracts from a Compensation Philosophy Statement Relating to Objectives, Market Position, and Performance-based Pay 132
10.1 The Six Major Divisions of the Position Analysis Questionnaire 244
10.2 Factor Evaluation System Factors, Weights, and Levels 251
10.3 Factor Comparison Method: Factor-based Ranking 256
10.4 Factor Comparison Method: Allocation of Pay to Each Factor and Pay-Allocation-based Ranking 258
10.5 Factor Comparison Method: Comparison of the Factor-based and Pay-Allocation-based Rankings 259
10.6 Factor Comparison Method: Job Evaluation Scale 260
10.1.1 Worksheet for Determining the Appropriateness of Job Analysis Methods 267
10.2.1 Job Descriptions — Job A and Job B 269
10.2.2 Job Evaluation Plan 270
11.1 A Summary of Selected Provisions of Pay Equity Laws in Canada 277
11.2 Data on the South Asian Visible Minority Group Relative to the Canadian Population on Selected Characteristics: Age, Education, Participation in Labour Force, and Professional Occupations 286
14.1 Multi-Skilling 347
14.2 Summary of Reward Costs, Organizational Priority for Targeted Behaviours, and Employee Perceptions of Rewards 358
14.3 A Comparison of the Intended and the Actual Effectiveness of Rewards 363
14.1.1 Summary of Organizational Priority for Targeted Behaviours and Employee Perceptions of Rewards 370

14.1.2 Employees' Responses to the Question Whether the Rewards Are Fairly or Not Fairly Administered 371
14.1.3 Employees' Responses to the Questions on Performance Appraisal Policies and Practices 371

CHAPTER 1
AN INTRODUCTION TO COMPENSATION

CHAPTER SYNOPSIS

This chapter introduces the subject of compensation and explores the components and objectives of the compensation system. The chapter develops the model of effective reward management, which provides an integrative and comprehensive framework for the concepts, techniques, and processes discussed in the various chapters. The model provides both a perspective of, and a structure for, the text.

LEARNING OBJECTIVES

- To understand the nature of compensation and how it affects individuals, organizations, and society at large.
- To identify the components of the compensation system and to understand the rationale for the classification of compensation.
- To become aware of the goals of the compensation system.
- To acquire a coherent perspective of compensation theories, techniques, and processes.

THE NATURE OF COMPENSATION

"Wine gladdens life, and money answers everything." (Ecclesiastes 10:19)
"The laborer deserves his wages." (Luke 10:7)

Conduct, patience, purity,
Manners, loving-kindness, birth,
After money disappears,
Cease to have the slightest worth.

Wisdom, sense and social charm,
Honest pride and self-esteem,
After money disappears,
All at once become a dream.

Money gets you anything,
Gets it in a flash;
Therefore let the prudent get
Cash, cash, cash.

(Panchatantra)

The idea of compensation is deeply rooted in every culture and society. Traditionally the term compensation has meant economic or monetary rewards in work contexts, but in this text the term will be used in its broadest sense to include all forms of rewards: monetary, payments in kind, and non-economic (for example, praise or recognition). In this broad sense, compensation is one of the most important aspects of human relationships. Relationships between two individuals are often perceived as exchange or reciprocity. People learn to say "Thank you" for any object, service, or compliment received. In some circumstances, the thank-you is an adequate recompense. In different circumstances, the thank-you needs to take on a substantial form, like a payment in kind or money. In work relationships, compensation takes the form of salary or wages, a variety of benefits, and non-economic rewards such as challenging assignments and praise from a supervisor.

This book focuses on compensation, both monetary and non-economic, in work relationships in an organizational context. It is nevertheless important to recognize that the need for adequate recompense is fundamental to human nature and the human condition. Other considerations further emphasize the critical nature of compensation for society, individuals, and organizations.

Because of its effects on justice, taxes, and the health of the economy, compensation in the form of monetary rewards has always been a societal concern. Different religions down the ages have ordained that the principles of justice should govern compensation. After the industrial revolution, the concept of a just wage was extended to include a living wage. Progressive gains in collective agreements brought unionized workers closer to the realization of these concepts. Minimum wage legislation provided some safeguards for non-unionized workers. All workers have benefited from social security legislation that provides for medicare, unemployment insurance, worker's compensation, and old age pensions.

Societal concerns today are also focused on the issue of pay equity for women. The Abella Royal Commission on Equality in Employment (1984) confirmed that in 1982 the wage rates of women were, on average, 64 per cent of the wage rates of men. To remedy this inequity and to move towards implementing "equal pay for work of equal value" (also known as "comparable worth"), the Federal Treasury Board Minister recently announced ad hoc increases of several hundred million dollars — about $5,000 per woman employee — to women in the federal civil service.

Societal concerns about economic compensation arise also because of the effects of compensation on taxes and the health of the economy. Compensation to government and municipal employees generally comes from tax revenues. Increases in compensation ordinarily lead to tax increases, which are usually disliked by members of society as a whole. Increases in compensation without corresponding increases in productivity can and do lead to inflationary pressures that could adversely affect the competitiveness of business and industry, with a consequence, for example, of unemployment.

Individuals are concerned about compensation. It is their source of income, a return on their investment in education and skills development, a return on their work contributions, and an important element of job satisfaction.

Individuals who work only for "love and fresh air" are a very rare breed. For the vast majority of people, monetary compensation is the primary, if not the only, source of the income that determines social status and standard of living. Compensation enables the individual to put food on the table, pay the rent, buy clothes, and send the children to school. The pay cheque is a crucial determinant of the individual's socio-economic well-being.

The pay cheque also represents a return on the individual's investment in education and skills training. The time spent in school or in a profession constitutes the individual's investment — often considerable, for example, for those in the professions — of time, effort, and expense. An organization will ordinarily benefit from such investments by its employees. Hence, it is not unreasonable for individuals to expect that their compensation will adequately reflect this investment.

Individuals also expect that their compensation will provide an adequate feedback on their work contributions. John and Jane joined the Montreal Trading Company on the same day as personnel officers, on salaries that adequately reflected their education, training, and experience. For their first year of service, the performance assessment report showed that Jane performed much better than John. Assuming that the performance assessment was conducted properly and equitably, Jane should receive a relatively higher merit pay than John. If this differentiation is not made, and both receive the same merit pay, then the organization does not provide the correct feedback on their work contributions.

The concerns and expectations of individuals about their monetary compensation are inextricably linked with job satisfaction. If Jane does not receive an equitable merit pay, she will experience considerable job dissatisfaction. While monetary compensation is only one component of job satisfaction (other components include satisfaction with co-workers and supervisors, working conditions, job security), satisfaction with financial compensation has been found to be a major contributor to job satisfaction.

From the point of view of organizations, financial compensation is also an obvious concern, since compensation is a major item of expenditure. In manufacturing organizations, the compensation package constitutes as much as 50 to 60 per cent of the total operating costs; in service organizations and in the government and its agencies the compensation package can go as high as 80 per cent of the total costs. But organizations that focus only on the high proportion of costs represented by compensation will earn the indictment that Oscar Wilde reserved for the cynic, "who knows the price of everything, and the value of nothing." The real concern of successful organizations, then, is to view the compensation package as an investment in people, their most valuable resource. Such a concern will lead organizations to develop compensation programmes that are consistent with, and that support, their business strategies. For example, organizations with a limited, stable product line and predictable markets tend to opt for a compensation strategy that emphasizes internal pay relationships, that is, maintaining the proper differentials between job values. Such a compensation strategy maximizes the perception of pay equity among job holders operating at different levels within the organization and thereby achieves maximum job satisfaction and minimum turnover of employees. On the other hand, organizations with a broad, changing product line and changing markets are successful with a compensation strategy that focuses on external pay relationships, which ensure that the organization can attract the talent, skills, and abilities needed to constantly meet the challenges of shifting market demands. In other words, the objectives of the organization provide the *raison d'être* of the compensation programme — the type and mix of the compensation elements.

Organizational concerns about a compensation package that includes both financial and non-financial elements are also expressed in terms of motivating potential. Can managers use a compensation package to effectively motivate their subordinates towards organizationally desired behaviours? What motivates an individual to choose an occupation, to select one particular organization over another? What motivates an employee to perform at varying levels? What motivates an employee to be absent from work? In Canada, the total costs to the economy due to absenteeism are estimated at between 3 to 7 billion dollars, or 10 to 11 times the costs resulting from strikes! What motivates an employee to want to grow on the job, to accept challenge, responsibility, and self-direction? And, finally, what motivates an employee to leave an organization? Lawler's (1971, 1981) seminal work on pay and organizational effectiveness has demonstrated that a properly designed compensation programme is an effective response to these questions and constitutes an important element of the strategies used to socialize and manage human resources.

Until recently, unions were the major source of organizational concerns about compensation issues. With the advent of pay equity legislation, organizations are now forced to look at compensation programmes not in paternalistic terms, as some were accustomed to, but in terms of fairness and equity.

The issue of compensation is fraught with conflict and tension among employees, between employees and their employer, between voters and civil servants, between legislators and employers, and among employers. It is beyond the scope of this text to address these issues. The focus in this text is primarily on compensation issues within an organization, with some consideration of those events and issues outside the organization that can help to better understand and resolve issues and concerns within the organization. The debate generated by the compensation issue of comparable worth is timely, and provides an opportunity and a challenge to bring a fresh, positive, and creative approach to the resolution of compensation issues.

CLASSIFICATION OF COMPENSATION: ECONOMIC AND NON-ECONOMIC REWARDS

Unlike small-scale business enterprises in traditional societies, which compensated their employees through basic wages, modern organizations offer a wide variety of rewards to employees in order to remain competitive. An extensive list of such rewards (Table 1.1) has been recently compiled by Kanungo and Hartwick (1987). The type and the number of reward items in a compensation package of an organization depend upon the organization's needs and its ingenuity in creating appropriate items to meet those needs. The list in Table 1.1 contains rewards that involve either direct or indirect cash payments and benefits. The list also contains reward items that do not involve any monetary payments or benefits, for example, personal challenge in assignments, feelings of worthwhile accomplishment, personal growth and development. Thus, the entirety of compensation or reward items can be classified into three basic categories: direct cash payments, benefits, and non-economic rewards (Figure 1.1).

The totality of compensation items is the *reward system*, with two major components: the economic compensation system, which includes cash payments and benefits; and the non-economic compensation system, which includes non-economic reward items. The reward system can be defined as constituting all the economic compensation and non-economic compensation items that an employee is entitled to earn and/or to receive by virtue of the employment contract or relationship.

TABLE 1.1
A LIST OF WORK REWARDS OFFERED BY ORGANIZATIONS
(IN ALPHABETICAL ORDER)

Accident and sickness insurance
Achieving the organization's goals
Authority
Awards for superior performance
Awards for long service
Cafeteria subsidies
Coffee breaks
Company-sponsored recreational activities
Company-sponsored life insurance
Company-sponsored professional services
Cost-of-living increase
Dental plan
Discounts on purchase of company products
Expense account
Extended lunch periods
Feelings of worthwhile accomplishment
Holiday bonus
Interesting work
Job security
Mortgage financing
Opportunity to make friends
Opportunity for creativity
Opportunity to use special abilities
Paid personal time off
Paid parking space
Paid absence for study
Participation in decision making
Pay
Personal growth and development
Personal challenge
Praise from supervisor
Praise from co-workers
Prestige
Pride in success of company
Pride in work
Profit-sharing plan
Promotion
Recognition
Responsibility
Retirement benefits
Sense of belonging
Sick leaves
Sick pay
Social status
Uniform/clothes allowance
Use of company car
Vacation
Variety of job

Figure 1.1
The Reward System

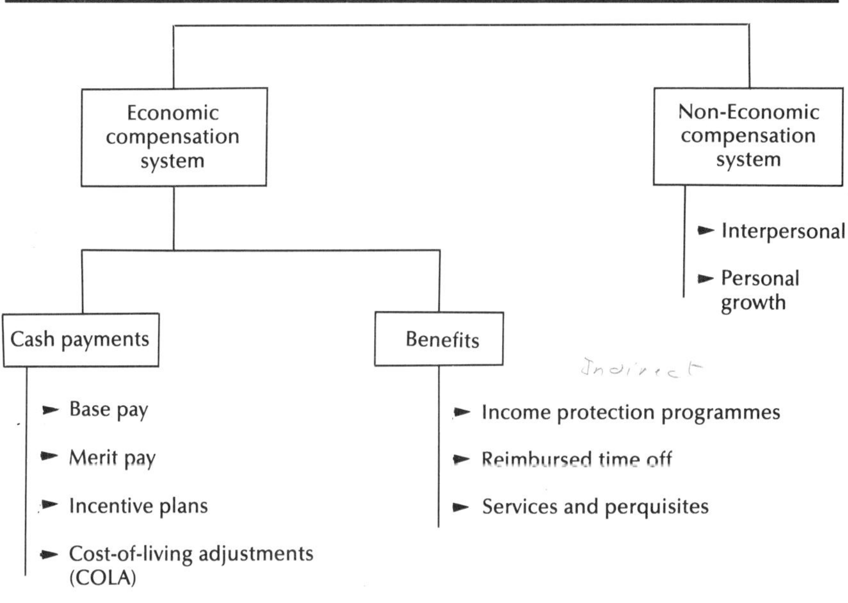

Source: Adapted from Milkovich and Newman (1990).

THE ECONOMIC COMPENSATION SYSTEM

Cash Payments

This category comprises: base pay, merit pay, incentive plans, and cost-of-living adjustments (COLA).

Base Pay

Base pay represents the basic exchange relationship of the employment contract. The employee expects the base pay to reflect the value of the inputs (education, skills, experience) that the employee brings to the job. The employer expects the base pay to reflect the value of the job's contribution to achieving the goals of the organization. Base pay represents a quid pro quo relationship between the employee (a return for services perceived to be rendered), and the employer (a payment for contribution perceived to be received). The type of job evaluation system used, its mechanics and process, and labour market conditions determine the base pay. The base pay of unionized employees is expressed in an hourly rate and is referred to as *wages*. The base pay of non-unionized employees is generally expressed and calculated on an annual basis and is referred to as *salary*. The culture of the organization can affect this distinction between wages and salary. Organizations that focus on high employee involvement and participation tend to eliminate status differentials, for example, by placing all employees on a salary basis.

Merit Pay

When employees put in a performance that exceeds the acceptable performance level, they expect a reward for it. This reward, related to the performance level, is called *merit pay*, and is paid in the form of a bonus or as an addition to base pay. Employees generally prefer the latter because such an increment becomes a part of base pay and continues to be received for the duration of employment, regardless of future performance levels. The bonus, on the other hand, is for a single time only and is not automatically received in subsequent years unless performance levels justify the bonus.

Incentive Plans

These are cash payments available to employees when they exceed predetermined job or organizational goals — usually the latter. Incentive plans serve as inducements to produce specific results desired by the organization, such as an increase in the volume of output, revenue, profits, or return on investment; or a reduction in costs or reject rate. The plans are designed to allow employees a share in the specific gains that result. Employee motivation and involvement are considerably enhanced when organizations give employees a "piece of the action." Incentive plans are based on the performance of individual employees, departmental units, or the organization as a whole. Often they are based on a combination of individual employee, departmental unit, and the organization. For example, if the total operating results of the organization on a specific measure exceed the predetermined standard, then the resulting gain is shared among the departmental units according to an established performance measure, and is distributed among the employees of that unit, also according to the individual measures of performance. As will be discussed in Chapter 9, incentive plans may be tied to short-term or long-term measures. The three most popular plans are the Scanlon Plan, the Rucker Plan, and the Improshare Plan.

Often a distinction is made between merit pay and incentive plans. The former is viewed as a reward for past performance and the latter as an incentive for future performance. In practice, the distinction gets blurred, especially when a merit pay programme is equitably designed and managed. In such a situation, employees are known to look forward to merit pay. Employee expectation of merit pay can, and does, serve as an inducement or incentive to future performance.

Cost-of-Living Adjustment

Also known as COLA, this cash payment is intended to compensate employees for the loss of the purchasing power of their compensation package usually resulting from inflation. Adjustments are made to the base pay when the cost of living increases as determined by the rise in the Consumer Price Index beyond a certain number of points. An interesting related issue is whether organizations should adjust the base pay to the full extent of the increase in the cost of living. If organizations do this without a corresponding increase in productivity, it is said that the present generation is passing on to future generations the full burden of inflation. The question is raised: Is it equitable that future generations bear the consequences of present economic decisions? This issue is often ignored because of the mistaken belief that the future will take care of itself. Eventually, society must face the issue and take drastic measures, as was the case in Canada when Parliament passed the Anti-Inflation Act in 1975 to control wages and prices.

BENEFITS

The multitude of employee benefits (and perquisites) programmes can be grouped into three categories: income protection programmes, reimbursed time off, and services and perquisites. These programmes, most of which were started during World War II, have increased both in variety and cost. For example, in 1950 these programmes cost organizations an average of $515 per year — less than 15 per cent of gross payroll costs. In 1986, they cost about $9,000 per year, or about 36.3 per cent of gross payroll costs (Peat Marwick Stevenson & Kellogg 1989). These costs continue to climb. Tax considerations (tax credit or allowable tax deduction) have often influenced the introduction of these programmes.

Income Protection Programmes

Unemployment insurance, worker's compensation, medical insurance, disability insurance, and pensions are examples of programmes designed to provide a continuation of income in a variety of circumstances and situations. Also included in this category are programmes that provide income continuation for the spouse and the family on the death of the employee. Some examples would be life insurance and pension plans whose features provide income for the family.

Reimbursed Time Off

Organizations pay for time not worked for a variety of reasons, for example, vacations, sick leave, maternity and paternity leave. Such reimbursed time off recognizes employees' needs to recreate and recuperate their health, and their obligations to attend to their family needs. Reimbursed time off is also given for jury duty, acknowledging that organizations, as good corporate citizens, should enable employees to fulfil their civic responsibilities.

Services and Perquisites

This miscellaneous category covers a wide range of services and perquisites that do not fall into the previous two categories, for example, dental plans, employee assistance plans (which provide for counselling relative to stress, burn-out, drug and alcohol addiction, etc.), use of a company automobile, discount on company products, and professional memberships.

THE NON-ECONOMIC COMPENSATION SYSTEM

The non-economic compensation system includes all non-monetary or non-pecuniary rewards. These rewards fall into two broad categories: interpersonal rewards, and personal growth rewards. The interpersonal rewards include items such as good interpersonal social relationships with co-workers and supervisors; social status in the workplace, which flows from the job position held and from on-the-job performance; social approval and social recognition for day-to-day job activities; and sense of belonging. Personal growth rewards include job variety, enhanced self-esteem for achieving organizational goals, personal sense of achievement, personal growth and development, pride in work, participation in decision making, and autonomy and control. These growth-related rewards are also referred to as intrinsic rewards in the sense that they are derived directly from job performance. It seems preferable, however, not to use the term intrinsic to describe this category of rewards because, as will be discussed in Chapter 3, the ambiguity that surrounds the term makes it unsuitable for the purpose of adequately identifying and managing rewards.

Henderson (1989) describes non-economic rewards under the seven dimensions of what he refers to as the non-compensation system. According to Henderson these dimensions include rewards that enhance dignity and satisfaction for work performed; enhance health, well-being, and emotional maturity; promote constructive social relationships with co-workers; design jobs requiring adequate attention and effort; allocate resources to perform work assignments; grant control over the job to meet personal demands; and offer supportive leadership and management.

Each of the above reward dimensions can be related to the twofold classification of non-economic rewards already suggested. The rewards in the non-economic compensation package do not involve monetary outlay, but they do demand that managers be sensitive to the needs and expectations of their subordinates. These rewards have a special appeal and are a powerful source of motivation to employees with high interpersonal and growth-need strength, provided that these employees have the knowledge and skill required by the job and are satisfied with the job context, that is, with pay, supervision, supervisors, job security, and working conditions.

Although the various reward elements described above suggest an extensive list of items in the overall total compensation package of an organization, very often the component features of a specific compensation package are determined by the classification of the employee for whom it is designed. The Canada Labour Code and its related regulations classify employees into those to whom the hours-of-work and overtime provisions apply (non-exempt employees) and those to whom these provisions do not apply (exempt employees such as managers and professionals). Employees are also often classified on the basis of unionization (unionized versus non-unionized), organizational hierarchy (senior versus junior levels; or top, middle, and first-line management levels), functions (administrators, professionals, technical, sales, secretarial and clerical, operatives), skill levels (skilled, semi-skilled, unskilled), employment contract (full-time, part-time), and so forth. Such classifications of employees determine the composition of specific compensation packages, that is, what reward elements should or should not be included in these packages.

OBJECTIVES OF THE REWARD SYSTEM

Rewards must be earned. The specific behaviours that employees must perform, and/or results they must achieve to earn the rewards, must be clearly stipulated and communicated to all employees. This behaviour-reward contingency, if it is to be meaningful and effective in producing the organizationally desired behaviours, must be spelt out for each reward item in specific terms. For example, it is not sufficient to say: "Employees will get merit pay if they perform well." The behaviours and/or results that constitute "perform well" — for example, sales of so many dollars, meeting report deadlines — must be stated.

An organization can choose from a variety of objectives for its reward system as a whole and for the reward items in particular. The appropriateness of the objectives, a critical consideration, can best be determined by this test: Do the compensation objectives support and direct the efforts and performance of employees towards the realization of the organization's business goals and objectives?

Organizations frequently choose from among the following major behavioural objectives:

- to attract individuals with the knowledge, ability, and talents demanded by specific organizational tasks;

- to retain valued and productive employees;
- to promote specific job behaviours conducive to higher levels of job performance;
- to promote attitudes conducive to loyalty and commitment to the organization, high job involvement, and job satisfaction;
- to stimulate employee growth that enables the employee to accept more challenging positions;
- to comply with the requirements of pay equity and related laws.

It is not uncommon to find "control of labour costs" or "efficiency" as a stated objective of the reward system. If the behavioural objectives listed above are addressed, the objective of labour costs control or efficiency will be a natural outcome.

EFFECTIVE REWARD MANAGEMENT: A COMPENSATION MODEL

This introductory chapter has discussed the nature of compensation or rewards, identified the components of the reward system, established a set of dimensions or classification categories to help make sense of the array of reward items, and explored the major objectives or goals of the reward system. The chapter has also been a preparation for probing the reward system in some depth, discovering the underlying principles and conditions that make the reward system effective in an organization, and suggesting a *modus operandi* for designing and managing the reward system. A good road map that shows clearly the highways and thruways, the major landmarks, and gas, food, and related facilities is essential not only to reach the destination, but also to make the trip enjoyable. This text, a road map that shows the different routes to designing and managing an organizational reward system, suggests specific routes, which are sometimes long and pass through rough terrain, but which, according to the predictions of sound and empirically proven theories, will ensure a greater and more enduring organizational effectiveness and employee satisfaction.

The model of effective reward management (Figure 1.2) provides a perspective of the text, and a comprehensive, logical, and coherent framework to graphically show the factors, concepts, processes, and techniques that impinge on the reward system. The model can be looked at in terms of the following four major questions a compensation specialist would need to address to ensure an effective reward system.

1. What are the various factors, events, and institutions that influence the composition and goals of the reward system?
2. On what does the effectiveness of the reward system depend? Or, can the effectiveness of the reward system be predicted?

Figure 1.2
Effective Reward Management: A Model

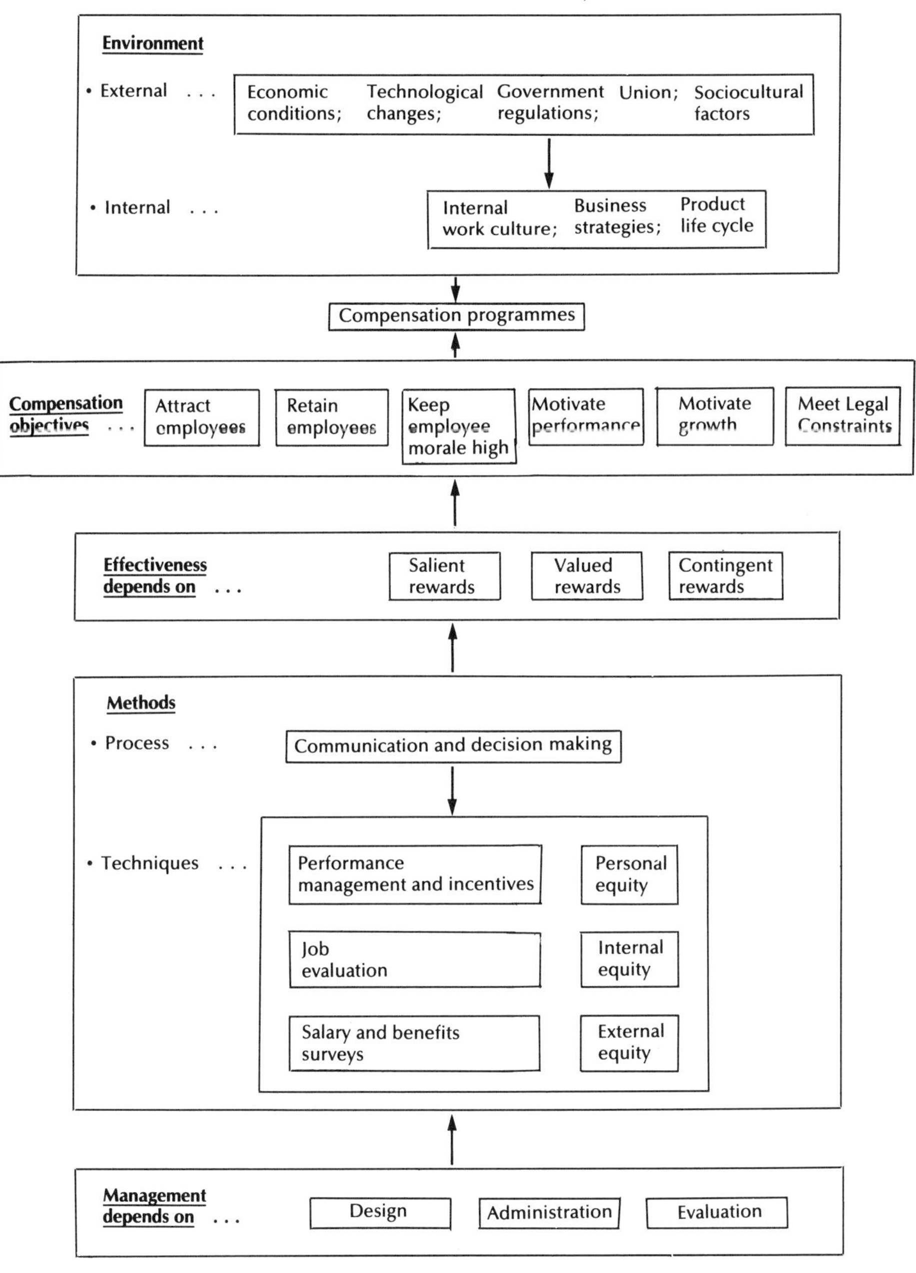

3. What are the critical methods — processes and techniques — that must be adopted in designing and implementing the reward system?
4. What are the key managerial issues and concerns in the design, administration, and evaluation of the reward system?

The responses to these questions constitute the four major parts of the book. Part I explores the strategic influence that the environment, external and internal, has on the composition and goals of the compensation programme. The important determinants of the external environment are economic conditions (e.g., state of the economy, the Canada-U.S. Free Trade Agreement, goods and services tax, product markets), technological changes (e.g., rapid advances in computerization), government regulations (e.g., pay equity laws), unions (the impact of collective agreements, the state of union-management relations), sociocultural factors (which shape the beliefs, attitudes, and action preferences of employees). The internal environment is the organization's business strategies, product life cycle, and work culture, which are developed or which evolve within the context of the external environment. Chapter 2 discusses these environmental factors, events, and issues, and their impact on the compensation programme.

Part II considers the various theoretical approaches put forward to guide policies and procedures of the compensation programme. Chapter 3 critically examines the content theories of work motivation. These theories have contributed much to current practices in compensation. However, the intrinsic-extrinsic reward classification, which has dominated the content theories, has been found to be inadequate in providing clear, practical guidelines for the effective design and administration of the reward system. Chapter 4 explores the process theories of work motivation, and presents a model that is conceptually sound, has strong empirical support, and is immensely practical in the design and evaluation of a compensation programme. This model, founded on the constructs of expectancy theory, is also consistent with the intuitively accepted view that a reward item is effective in motivating employees towards performing the desired behaviours only if the reward is salient (i.e., uppermost in the employee's mind), valued (i.e., perceived to satisfy important needs and to be equitable), and contingent (i.e., given only on performance of the organizationally desired behaviours). Satisfaction with pay and non-monetary outcomes has a considerable impact on employee motivation. Chapter 5 considers the determinants of pay satisfaction as well as the consequences of pay dissatisfaction. Job content factors, as determined by job design, are an important source of non-monetary outcomes, which also play a critical role in determining pay satisfaction and in moderating the consequences of pay dissatisfaction. Therefore, Chapter 5 will also consider the theory and process of job design and its implications for reward management.

Part III addresses the methods — process and techniques — that contribute to making the rewards salient, valued, and contingent. Chapter 6 considers the strategic and process issues that must be decided upon. These issues are related to and flow from the business objectives and the organizational culture. For example, if the business objectives include cost control, the appropriate compensation strategy would be either to lag behind or to be equal to the labour market in pricing the pay structure. Again, if the organizational culture is participative and favours high employee involvement, the appropriate communication process in compensation will be *open* rather than *secret*, and a *participative* rather than a *top-down* approach. The conceptual framework developed in Chapter 6 and in the previous chapters provides the fundamental rationale for the compensation programmes, techniques, and processes in the chapters that follow.

Chapter 7 develops reward programmes and practices that promote organizational membership behaviours such as regular attendance and punctuality, and retention. Chapter 8 explores performance-based pay issues and their relation to personal equity. This chapter shows how a properly developed performance-based pay programme enhances employee motivation by making rewards contingent on performance and by increasing reward valence (or importance) through an equitable performance appraisal programme. Chapter 9 explores issues in the design and development of incentive and gain-sharing plans. These are performance-based approaches, and, consequently, have a tremendous potential for motivating employee behaviours towards the attainment of organizational objectives. Employee involvement in the design and implementation of these plans will be considered because such involvement has been known to considerably enhance employee perceptions of reward saliency, valence, and contingency.

Chapter 10 examines the methods and techniques of job analysis and job evaluation. Job evaluation is critical to assessing the similarities and differences in job values. Since the pay structure reflects job values, the decisions made in this process have a considerable impact on equity, which in turn affects employees' perception of reward valence and their motivation. Of course, the mechanics of the methods alone do not determine equity. The process that is adopted is an equally important determinant of equity. Therefore, both mechanics and process issues will be considered. Chapter 11 examines pay equity legislation and the related jurisprudence with the objective of developing practical guidelines for the design and implementation of reward systems that comply with the provisions of the law.

Chapter 12 focuses on external equity, which also impacts on the valence or importance of rewards and eventually on employee motivation. Hence, it is important to examine the scope and process of salary surveys and the use of data in developing the organization's pay line. Also critical are the design of pay ranges and the formulation of a sound rationale for individual salary adjustments, which frequently become necessary after salary surveys.

Chapter 13 considers issues in the development of employee benefit programmes. Because it is not always possible to tie benefit programmes to the employee's performance, the contingency effect on employee motivation is limited. However, these programmes can still have an impact on employee motivation if they are perceived by employees to be salient and valuable. Employee involvement in the development of these programmes contributes to increasing saliency and valence.

Part IV (Chapter 14) examines managerial issues in the design, administration, and evaluation of the reward system. The greatest focus is on evaluation. Is the organization getting the intended motivational effects from its compensation expenditures? A managerial action plan is proposed to assess the effectiveness of each reward item and to introduce specific remedial interventions.

Each of the four parts of this model (in fact, each chapter in the book) can be studied as a topic separately and in isolation from the other parts. The perspective of this book, however, is to emphasize that if rewards are to contribute to organizational effectiveness, they must be viewed in a coherent manner. Both the techniques and the processes involved in the reward system and its subsystems are crucial. As shown in the model, they have an impact on reward effectiveness. The model also demonstrates that the compensation programme — its components, techniques, and processes — gains legitimacy only to the extent that it contributes to organizational effectiveness and employee satisfaction. The model thus provides coherence, logic, and conceptual support to the effective management of rewards.

SUMMARY

This chapter explored the nature of compensation or rewards from the point of view of society, individuals, and organizations. Each point of view has its own interests and concerns. However, the perspective of the text, as depicted in the model, is the effective management of rewards to contribute both to organizational effectiveness and to employee satisfaction. These two considerations should be kept in mind when compensation decisions are being made. These decisions may concern the components and goals of a compensation programme; the methods to be used in job analysis, job evaluation, salary surveys, and performance assessment; the development of salary ranges; adjustments to an employee's salary; or the type of incentives, benefits, and services. In the ultimate analysis, the *raison d'être* of a compensation programme is organizational effectiveness and employee satisfaction. To ensure this, the key managerial activity and concern will be the managerial action plan (Chapter 14), which appropriately appears as the foundation upon which the model rests.

KEY TERMS

compensation objectives
compensation processes
compensation techniques
compensation theories
economic compensation system
exempt employees
non-economic compensation system
non-exempt employees

REVIEW AND DISCUSSION QUESTIONS

1. "The issue of compensation is fraught with conflict and tension among employees, between employees and their employer, between voters and civil servants, between legislators and employees, and among employers." Do you agree with this statement? Cite specific examples from your personal experience and/or observation to support your position.
2. Using the classification system proposed in Figure 1.1, classify the reward items listed in Table 1.1.
3. Explore how the seven dimensions of Henderson's non-compensation system can be related to the twofold classification of non-economic rewards proposed in this chapter.
4. Refer to the six major behavioural objectives identified in the chapter, and give examples of reward items likely to attain these objectives. Try to think of different reward items for each behavioural objective.

CASE: THE TINKERMAN CORPORATION OF MONTREAL

Joe Tinkerman was always so forgetful and late that his friends called him "the dreamer" and coined a suitable epitaph for him: Here Lies the Late Joe Tinkerman. Little did they know that Joe was busy tinkering in his hobby workshop with any idea that occurred to him.

From that small beginning, Joe Tinkerman grew; he now presides over the Tinkerman Corporation of Montreal, which has become a force to be reckoned with in the world of high tech. The specialized know-how developed by the corporation earned for it a lucrative contract from Canada Aeronautics Ltd. His corporation now has a piece of the controversial F-18 contract awarded to Canada Aeronautics.

The Tinkerman Corporation believes in hiring competent, qualified people and has the usual mix of operating and support personnel. The F-18 contract has placed the corporation on the take-off stage as it expands from a small/medium-sized company to a large corporation. Joe Tinkerman has decided to take a hard look at all aspects of operations in preparation for the imminent expansion.

Discussion Questions

You are a member of the task force whose focus is the compensation programme of the company. Consider the following questions as you prepare to review the compensation programme of the company.

1. Are rewards important for the organization? Why? For the employee? Why?
2. Identify different types (categories) of rewards. Indicate the criteria used.
3. Is it necessary to differentiate between job categories in giving rewards? Why? How would one differentiate?
4. Is it necessary to differentiate between employees (in the same jobs) in giving rewards? Why? How would one differentiate?
5. Should Tinkerman pay more than other organizations? Why? How is this ensured?
6. When Tinkerman pay its employees, does it get what it pays for? How does the corporation know? Should the corporation get what it pays for? Why?

PART I
THE STRATEGIC INFLUENCE OF ENVIRONMENT

CHAPTER 2
THE EXTERNAL AND INTERNAL ENVIRONMENTS

CHAPTER SYNOPSIS

This chapter provides an overview of several important elements of the external and internal environments with which the organization must cope in order to function effectively. The influences of these elements in shaping the design and management of effective compensation systems are discussed.

LEARNING OBJECTIVES

- To identify the significant forces of the external environment within which an organization operates.
- To identify the significant forces of the internal environment of an organization that shape its policies and strategies in relation to people and products.
- To understand how internal and external environmental forces influence the compensation system.

THE ENVIRONMENT AND THE COMPENSATION SYSTEM

The compensation or reward system is neither designed nor managed in a vacuum. It operates in a vibrant, dynamic, and sometimes turbulent context that the organization either seeks by deliberately choosing specific business strategies, or finds itself thrust into by overwhelming environmental forces. A soundly managed organization is generally in the former category. Such an organization can, nevertheless, acutely feel the effect of environmental forces that bring unexpected benefits or burdens. For example, since approximately 75 per cent of Canada's exports go to the United States, the Canada-U.S. Free Trade Agreement will open a window of opportunity for some industries and sound a death knell for others. Because any event that affects the organization's capacity to operate successfully will have an impact on the design and management of the reward system, an overview of the external and internal environmental influences on organizations is necessary. The external sources of environmental influences to be explored are (1) economic conditions, (2) technological changes, (3) government regulations, (4) union expectations, and (5) the sociocultural climate. The internal sources of environmental influences to be considered are (1) the internal work culture of the organization, (2) the business strategies of the organization, and (3) the product life cycle. None of these influences operate in isolation, nor are they static. They continuously interact with one another to produce effects that often make conflicting demands on organizations. Figure 2.1 depicts the relationships of the external and internal environments as these combine to influence the compensation programme of an organization.

THE EXTERNAL ENVIRONMENT

ECONOMIC CONDITIONS

The economic conditions of any country are in a constant state of flux. Canada and its provinces are no exception. Out of a multitude of economic conditions whose impact can be considered, the focus will be on two, namely, the rate of inflation and the rate of productivity.

Inflation devastates corporate budgets and the purchasing power of the employee's pay cheque. Government measures to fight inflation, such as high interest rates, aggravate matters, at least in the short run. High interest rates have a depressing effect on home sales and discretionary purchases. As markets slacken, plans for plant expansion and increases in research and development activities are kept on hold. While inflationary pressures increased sharply in the first half of the 1980s, the rate of labour productivity increased by just 1.4 per cent in Canada compared with 2.4 per cent in West Germany and 6.3 per cent in Japan.

Both inflation and a sluggish growth in productivity have a direct impact on the competitivenes of organizations and drive them towards business strategies that enable them to cope with these conditions. For example, organizations prefer conservative investment programmes to high-risk ventures, and focus on the short run, where outcomes appear to be more controllable. Business strategies with a short-run perspective logically lead to compensation policies that emphasize short-term goals, often to the detriment of the economic health of the organization. Should business organizations be held responsible for "their excessive preoccupation with the short run?" Formbrun reviewed this argument and

FIGURE 2.1
THE IMPACT OF THE EXTERNAL AND INTERNAL ENVIRONMENTS ON THE COMPENSATION PROGRAMME

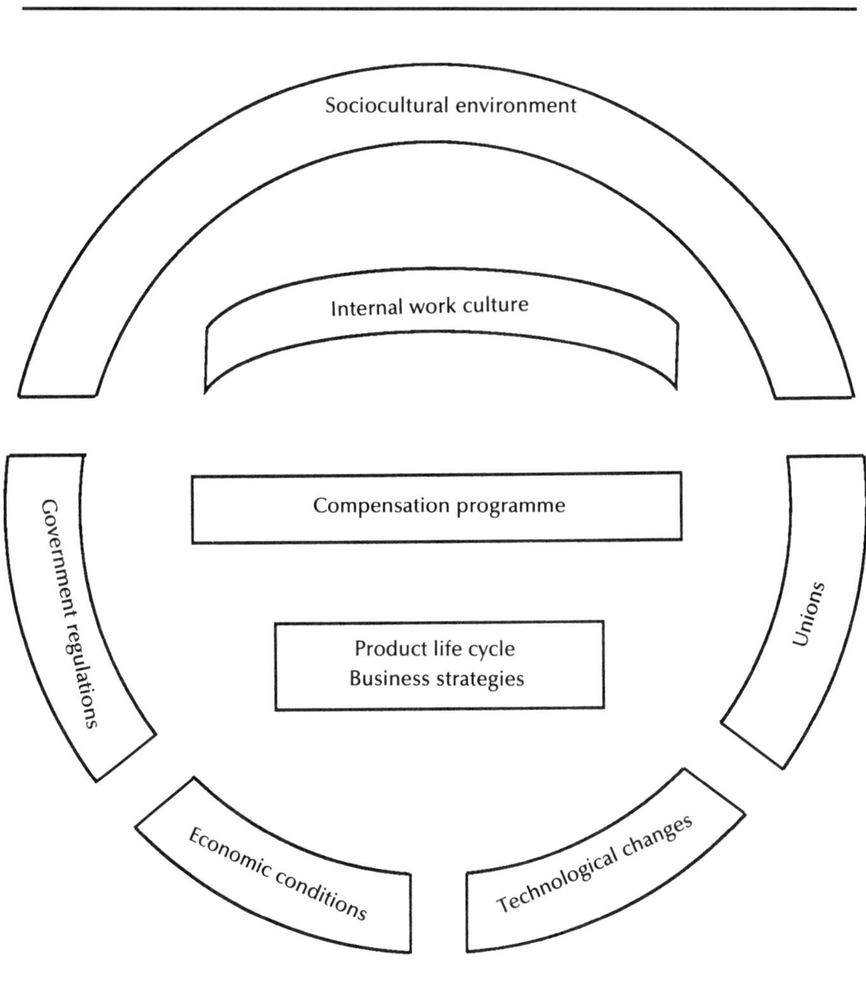

concluded that "corporations are as much the victims of economic events as the consumers, workers, and environmentalists who attack them" (1982, 65). For organizations with an international dimension, the ties between economic conditions and business strategies assume a greater complexity as the international economic order changes because of the momentous events in Eastern Europe and the proposed formation of a single European market in 1992.

TECHNOLOGICAL CHANGES

Rapid advances in computerization offer organizations the opportunity to step into the postindustrial age. In varying degrees, technology is becoming a critical vehicle for implementing an organization's business strategy, or a critical strategy in itself. In Canada, although the output from the manufacturing sector between 1967 and 1980 remained at 19 per cent of the Gross Domestic Product, this output was achieved with fewer workers because of the increasing use of new technologies. But technology alone is not sufficient. For example, in the course of developing the Saturn car project, General Motors (GM) learned that increasing employee involvement was equally critical to, if not more critical than, technology for both product quality and for the effective deployment of technology (Treece 1990). Nevertheless, incorporating technological innovations remains a critical strategic choice for organizations. That choice will, in turn, have an important bearing on the design and management of the reward system. For example, in the Saturn car project, GM formed a unique partnership with its employees not only through improved relations with the union but also through radical compensation practices such as the abolition of status differentials. For example, all employees are on salary and are eligible for productivity bonuses; furthermore, executive bonuses are similarly linked to the project's profits and not, as has been traditional, to the profits of GM's subsidiaries. Another example of the impact of technology on the reward system is that increased computerization facilitates decentralization, and decentralization enriches jobs, making them psychologically more rewarding. Computerization also makes the organization better able to generate performance measures that contribute to a more equitable administration of compensation programmes.

GOVERNMENT REGULATIONS

The impact of economic conditions and technological changes on compensation is primarily indirect, flowing from the organization's strategic decisions. The impact of government regulations is direct. The objective of regulations is to ensure social justice and to address societal concerns involved in the employer-employee relationship. Achieving such objectives cannot be left entirely to the discretion of organizations.

Legislation in this field traditionally regulated wages, overtime and vacation pay, and working conditions; and provided financial protection in the event of loss of employment, work accidents, and retirement. Some examples are the Minimum Wages Act, the Unemployment Insurance Act, the Workmen's Compensation Act, and the Canada (Quebec) Pension Plan. In the 1970s, Canada took a bold step in the field of pay equity, unprecedented among the western industrialized nations (except

Australia). It incorporated into law the concept of *comparable worth*, that is, equal pay for work of equal value. Pay equity law, not yet existing in all provinces, seeks to redress "systemic gender discrimination in compensation for work performed by employees in female job classes" without regard to the forces of demand and supply in the labour market, which traditionally were significant factors in determining the job rate.

The content and scope of government in regulations will be dealt with at length in Chapter 11. It is, however, necessary to be aware of the existence of a multitude of government regulations that make legal compliance an important and imperative objective for organizations developing compensation strategies, policies, and programmes.

Union Expectations

Like government regulations, although not to the same degree, unions have a direct impact on an organization's compensation policies and programmes. Unionized companies are compelled to follow the collective agreement, which spells out the compensation programme for non-exempt (unionized) employees. Non-unionized companies too are influenced by the wage and benefits settlements of the unionized firms in a region or industry. Moreover, labour-management cooperation appears to be a growing phenomenon. For example, both GM and the United Auto Workers (UAW) cooperated fully in the successful launching and operation of the Saturn car project (Treece 1990). At the Cardinal River Coal Mine near Hinton, Alberta, for 15 years, union-management relations were characterized by confrontation and hostility at every level of the organization. Since 1984, both the union and management have adopted a proactive approach to conflict resolution, which has since seen three collective agreements without a strike, an almost zero rate of grievances, and jointly sponsored financial planning for all employees. The Shell Canada Chemical Company in Sarnia, Ontario, has a collective agreement of barely six pages with the Energy and Chemical Workers Union. This agreement has made possible a successful Quality of Working Life programme with a person-based compensation system. More recently, April 1990, the union at GM's plant in Sainte Thérèse, Quebec, by a vote of 88 per cent, ratified major changes to its labour agreement that would make the company more competitive (*The Gazette*, 17 April 1990).

Unions, then, are a critical influence on organizations and their compensation programmes.

Sociocultural Environment

In the modern understanding, culture is viewed as a system of shared ideas, beliefs, values, and behaviour patterns. The sociocultural environment of a society plays a crucial role in influencing and shaping the beliefs, attitudes, and action preferences of its members. Employees bring to the workplace their cultural values and norms, which are instrumental in the formation of their expectations of, and responses to, reward systems. The sociocultural environment can thus profoundly influence the effectiveness of reward systems.

Hofstede's (1980a) empirical model differentiated the cultures of different countries on four dimensions:

1. Power distance, that is,

> the extent to which a society accepts the fact that power in institutions and organizations is distributed unequally. (1980b, 45)

2. Uncertainty avoidance, that is,

> the extent to which a society feels threatened by uncertain and ambiguous situations by providing career stability, establishing more formal rules, not tolerating deviant ideas and behaviors, and believing in absolute truths and the attainment of expertise. (1980b, 46)

3. Individualism, which

> implies a loosely knit social framework in which people are supposed to take care of themselves and their immediate families only, while collectivism is characterized by a tight social framework in which people distinguish between in-groups and out-groups; they expect their in-group (relatives, clan, organizations) to look after them, and in exchange for that they feel they owe absolute loyalty to it. (1980b, 45)

4. Masculinity, that is,

> the extent to which the dominant values in society are "masculine," that is, assertiveness, the acquisition of money and things, and not caring for others, the quality of life, or people. (1980b, 46)

In terms of these cultural dimensions, the sociocultural environment of developed countries like Canada can be characterized by high individualism and masculinity, and low power distance and uncertainty avoidance (Jaeger and Kanungo 1990). These characteristics manifest themselves in an organization in several ways. For example, high individualism suggests employee preferences for independence, self-reliance, and individual responsibility, and high masculinity denotes a performance rather than a people orientation; low power distance suggests that subordinates believe that they can participate with superiors in joint efforts to achieve organizational objectives, and low uncertainty avoidance implies a willingness to take risks and accept varied ways of achieving organizational objectives. Employees who are socialized in a sociocultural environment dominated by these characteristics will likely expect their reward system to focus primarily on material rewards that reflect individual rather than group performance, and are commensurate with the job risk and responsibilities and not merely the status of the job incumbent. In addition to the influence of the sociocultural environment, the content, structure, and direction of the reward system are shaped and directed by the internal work culture, the business strategies of the organization, and the product life cycle, all of which constitute the internal environment of the organization and are considered in the next section.

THE INTERNAL ENVIRONMENT

Internal Work Culture

An organization willingly or unwillingly develops its own unique work culture, which soon becomes the philosophical frame of reference for developing, understanding, and evaluating the company's mission objectives, policies, and programmes. All that is said and done in a company makes sense only by reference to its internal work culture. The compensation programme, an important vehicle of socialization in the organization's values and norms, is greatly affected by the internal work culture.

The internal work culture of an organization can be understood in terms of the three-level model proposed by Schein (1985). The first level consists of artifacts such as technology (e.g., degree of automation, mechanization), and of visible organizational structures and processes (e.g., authority hierarchy, top-down and lateral communication). The second level consists of values as expressed in strategies, goals, and philosophy, which explain and justify the behaviours, artifacts, and structures of the first level. The third level consists of the basic assumptions and premises held by managers and employees, which alone can explain the organization's activities, creations, and behaviours of the first and second levels. But these shared assumptions are often unstated; they are "preconscious" and taken-for-granted beliefs, habits of perception, thoughts, and feelings. Schein argues that one cannot understand an organization without an insight into these underlying assumptions. Sathe regards these assumptions as so critical that they become the sole content of his definition of culture: "Culture is the set of assumptions (often unstated) that members of a community share in common" (1985, 10).

The underlying assumptions of the internal work culture of an organization are largely the product of the conscious or unconscious efforts of the founder or top management, whose beliefs and ideas are also influenced by the prevailing sociocultural environment. What are these culture-determined assumptions? Elaborating upon Schein's (1988) notion of organizational culture, Jaeger and Kanungo (1990) have categorized culture-determined values and climate of beliefs and assumptions under two broad headings: (1) descriptive assumptions about human nature, and (2) prescriptive assumptions about the guiding principles of human conduct. The first category describes management's assumptions about human nature along the following dimensions: causality and control of outcomes (internal versus external locus of control), creative potential and malleability (unlimited versus fixed potential for growth), time perspective (past and present versus future orientation), and time units for action (short-term versus long-term). The second category spells out management's normative assumptions on whether or not to adopt a proactive or reactive stance in task performance, to judge success on a pragmatic or moral basis, to promote a collegial/participative or an authoritarian/paternalistic management style and orientation, to base one's behaviour on predetermined principles or on the exigencies of the situation. According to Jaeger and Kanungo (1990), there is a consistent pattern, in that one set of prescriptive assumptions about the guiding principles of human conduct flows logically from a set of management's descriptive assumptions about human nature. For example, managers may assume that employees have a high internal locus of control, an unlimited potential for growth, a future orientation, and a long-term perspective. Managers will then be expected to adopt a proactive stance in task performance, to judge success on a pragmatic basis, to be guided by predetermined principles and procedures, and to promote a collegial/participative management style or orientation. The sets of descriptive managerial assumptions about human nature and their corresponding assumptions about the guiding principles of human conduct are shown in Figure 2.2.

FIGURE 2.2
THE INFLUENCE OF THE SOCIOCULTURAL ENVIRONMENT ON THE INTERNAL WORK CULTURE

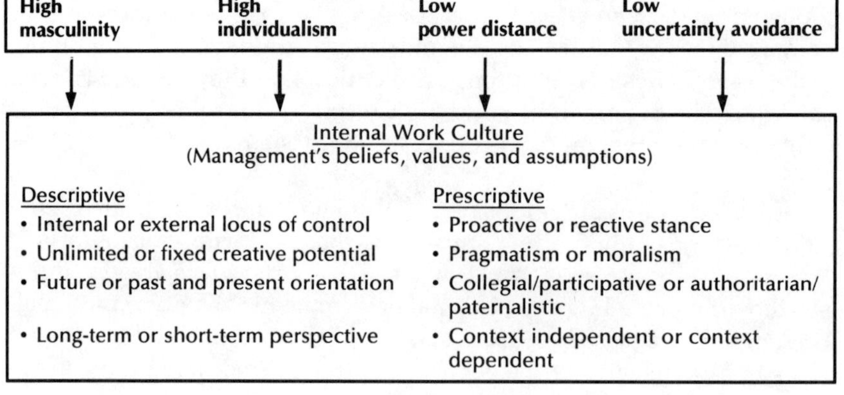

High masculinity
High individualism
Low power distance
Low uncertainty avoidance
Internal Work Culture
(Management's beliefs, values, and assumptions)
Descriptive
• Internal or external locus of control
• Unlimited or fixed creative potential
• Future or past and present orientation
• Long-term or short-term perspective
Prescriptive
• Proactive or reactive stance
• Pragmatism or moralism
• Collegial/participative or authoritarian/paternalistic
• Context independent or context dependent

What is the impact on the design and management of the organizational reward system under the descriptive and prescriptive assumptions that underlie the internal work culture? When management assumes that its employees have a high internal locus of control, high growth needs, a high potential for development, and are willing to defer immediate gratification for the returns that result from long-term career growth and development, then the reward system will likely reflect these assumptions. Thus, the reward system will place a greater emphasis on skill-based and performance-based pay, on fringe benefits that are the same for all levels, on non-economic rewards (such as participation in decision making, autonomy) that provide opportunities for growth and development, and on rewards (such as stock-ownership plans) that permit employees to participate in the future growth of the organization. All employees will generally be on an all-salary basis, and status symbols will be eliminated or restricted to jobs as necessitated by the external needs of the business. In such a reward system, managers will expect, value, and reward employees who are resourceful and innovative and who take, if necessary, personal risks in anticipating and meeting task challenges. In evaluating employee success, the key criterion will be the attainment of predetermined job targets without too much concern for how these are attained.

On the other hand, when management views employees as having an external locus of control, low growth needs, limited or fixed potential for development, and an interest only in the immediate gratification of physical, security, and social needs, then the reward system will emphasize economic and social rewards, status symbols, and fringe benefits that vary according to the level of the organization. In such a reward system, managers will be expected to adopt the authoritarian/paternalistic management style and orientation, and generally follow the Theory X model of management (McGregor 1960) — the carrot-and-stick approach to rewards design and management.

The preceding discussion described how the reward system flows from and reflects the internal work culture of the organization. The next section explores the direct impact of business strategies on the reward system.

Business Strategies

A strategy is "the pattern or plan that integrates an organization's major goals, policies, and action sequences into a cohesive whole" (Quinn 1988, 3). The reward system of an organization must be congruent with and supportive of the organization's business strategy. It does so principally in two ways: (1) it attracts and retains the people with the knowledge, abilities, skills, and willingness to support the business strategy; and (2) it motivates the employees to manifest behaviours (e.g., job performance and the acquisition of needed abilities and skills) that are conducive to the successful formulation and implementation of the business strategy. For example, organizations that operate in a highly entrepreneurial and/or innovative context need people who seek and enjoy challenging opportunities that involve considerable risk taking. Such people, in turn, expect rewards that truly reflect the risks and the challenges of the job. They will not be attracted by a fixed income, however stable that might be. They will want "a piece of the action" — a share in the gains generated by their performance. Consequently, the reward mix of organizations in the entrepreneurial context will emphasize variable rewards, with incentives forming a major component of the compensation package.

The need for compensation programmes to be linked to, and to support, the organization's business strategies is obvious and has always existed. Only recently, however, have organizations begun to acknowledge this linkage. In fact, it is part of the attention and status that North American corporations are now bestowing upon the human resource function. According to Miles and Snow (1984), this interest in human resource management has been triggered in part by the increasing realization that the "people" approach in Japanese organizations is one of the critical factors in giving them the competitive edge in today's global market. Also, the field of human resource management is gradually becoming a new speciality in its own right. In some organizations, the human resource specialists of today have developed a sophisticated, proactive posture in bringing to the organization's business-strategy-formulation process the essential contribution of the human resource management system. They have become adept at strategic human resources planning, which ensures that each subsystem of human resource management (i.e., staffing, training and development, compensation, labour relations) contributes to, reflects, and is driven by the business strategies.

How does the compensation subsystem of human resource management serve the business strategies of an organization? The research findings of Miles and Snow (1984) suggest that the variety of different business strategies can be grouped into three basic types, which they have designated as the Defender, the Prospector, and the Analyzer. This typology can be used to illustrate the compensation programme that is uniquely supportive of each type of strategy. Along with the business strategy, the stage in the product life cycle (i.e., start-up, growth, maturity, decline, renewal) in which the organization finds itself is also critical in determining the compensation mix and related strategies. The following discussion will therefore include a consideration of the impact of both business strategies and the product life cycle on the compensation programme.

According to Miles and Snow, the characteristics of the business strategy types are:

> The Defender strategy: a limited product line; single, capital-intensive technology; a functional structure; and skills in production efficiency, process engineering, and cost control. (1984, 37)
>
> The Prospector strategy: a diverse product line; multiple technologies; a product or divisionalized structure; and skills in product research and development, market research, and development engineering. (1984, 38)
>
> The Analyzer strategy: a limited basic product line; search for a small number of related product and/or market opportunities; cost-efficient technology for stable products and project technologies for new products; mixed (frequently matrix) structure; and skills in production efficiency, process engineering, and marketing. (1984, 38).

In the Defender-type organization, the products, markets, and technology are all relatively stable. This stability gives the tremendous advantage of accumulating expertise and know-how within the organization, which permits the organization to acquire human resources from outside at the entry level and then to develop them internally. The consequence for compensation management is that internal equity, rather than external equity, becomes the major preoccupation. The emphasis on efficiency and rigorous cost control requires a close monitoring of the performance-reward tie-up, with frequent performance evaluations using quantitative measures. It is quite common to use gain-sharing plans of the Scanlon type, whose requirement of stable performance conditions is more consistent with the Defender organization. The high degree of centralization in the control process also causes the compensation structure to reflect to a greater degree the organization's hierarchical levels and their relative differentials. The orientation towards the organizational hierarchy is also derived from the fact that the incentive for long-term personal development inevitable in the Defender-type organization is through internal promotion. These characteristics of the compensation system are found in the Lincoln Electric Company, which is regarded as a classic Defender.

The impact of the Prospector strategy on compensation is just the opposite of that of the Defender strategy. Performance-based compensation is the primary consideration. The Prospector-type organization needs to acquire human resources from outside the organization not just at the entry level but at all levels. The external labour market tends to heavily influence the compensation structure, which now needs to focus much more on external equity, and is often based on a pay level higher than that of the market. Furthermore, the innovative people required by the organization can only be attracted by a compensation programme that is performance based and allows creative individuals to share in the gains generated by their innovations. Hewlett-Packard and Texas Instruments are examples of firms that follow the Prospector strategy.

The Analyzer-type organization combines the features of the Defender and Prospector strategies. Although the Analyzer organization operates in both the stable and changing product-market domains, its operations are characterized by a balanced approach that seeks to minimize risk and at the same time to explore profitable opportunities. Consequently, the compensation philosophy programme of the Analyzer organization will also be characterized by a similar balance — between internal and external equity, between fixed and variable rewards, and between rewards that emphasize performance and those that reflect the position in the hierarchical levels and their relative differentials. Canadian Pacific is a good example of the Analyzer-type organization.

PRODUCT LIFE CYCLE

The preceding review underscores the fact that the compensation programme of the organization must be congruent with and supportive of the business strategies if the organization is to have success in achieving its objectives. The effectiveness of the business strategies, however, is also affected by the stage of the life cycle of its products. As Hofer (1975) observed, appropriate business strategies are required for the growth, maturity, and decline stages of the product life cycle. There is considerable empirical support for the fact that the environmental uncertainties that result from technological changes, product innovations, and product market conditions are significantly different in each stage of the product life cycle (Hofer 1975; Tilles 1966; Morrison 1966; Gupta and Govindarajan 1984). Any effort to cope with these differences demands the total mobilization of the organization's social and technical systems. It is therefore inevitable that the compensation system — particularly the mix of base pay, incentives, and benefits — should also be adapted to the business strategies and needs of each stage of the product life cycle.

What then is the appropriate pay mix for each stage of the product life cycle? What is the rationale for such a mix? To address these questions means to explore the conditions in which the organization finds itself in each stage of the product life cycle — start-up, growth, maturity, stability, decline, and renewal. In the start-up or introduction stage of a product, the organization's resources and efforts are devoted to entering the market. With high expenditures and low revenues, the organization's ability to generate cash flow is extremely limited, and so is its ability to include high base pay and benefits in its pay mix. The organization, nevertheless, needs to attract employees who will bring a high level of innovation and creative energy, and will expect a variable income plan. These expectations can be met by making incentives a major component of the pay mix, the other elements of the mix being low base pay and benefits. High incentives are also compatible with the organization's financial condition in this stage in the life cycle because incentives are paid only after the employees' efforts generate the predetermined financial resources.

The pay mix in the growth stage is competitive base pay, high incentives, and low benefits. The growth stage places the organization in a stronger financial position relative to the start-up stage, and the organization is then able to offer the competitive base pay that may be necessitated by shortages in the labour market. The major drawing card to attract and retain the "high flyers" (creative and innovative employees) continues to be high incentives, as was the case in the start-up stage. The organization still needs to invest its resources in activities that will provide a continuing impetus to growth. The mechanics of high incentives give the organization the flexibility it needs to channel its resources into growth and at the same time to meet the expectations of its high-performing employees.

In the maturity stage, the organization has carved out a relatively stable market niche for itself, and environmental uncertainty has been considerably reduced. Cash flow is now more predictable and generally reflects the higher revenues and earnings that result from economies of scale and a stable market share. The pay mix in this stage is competitive base pay, incentives, and benefits. The reduced emphasis on incentives reflects (*a*) the organization's capacity to pay a relatively higher base pay and benefits than before, and (*b*) the changing business environment of the organization, which now does not require that employees be motivated to be entrepreneurial and risk takers to the same extent as in the previous two stages.

The stability stage of the product life cycle is a natural sequel to the maturity stage. The old products, with some model changes and improvements, continue. But there is no heavy investment in research and development. The market share is maintained, and sometimes increased, by competitive pricing made possible by a greater emphasis on cost-efficient operations. The pay mix will be high base pay and benefits, for the same reasons as in the maturity stage. Although incentives form part of the mix, they play a relatively limited role. They are used mainly to improve productivity and ensure cost-efficient operations.

In the decline stage, the pay mix is really not one of the organization's choosing. To retain its present employees, the organization may be compelled to pay a high base pay and benefits. In a declining market, it would be anachronistic to offer incentives to improve productivity and output that the market is unable to absorb. Hence, incentives do not form part of the pay mix.

In the renewal stage, the organization adopts strategies and actions similar to those in the growth stage. Therefore, the pay mix at the renewal stage will be identical to that of the growth stage, that is, competitive base pay, high incentives, and low benefits, and for the same reasons.

FIGURE 2.3

THE INFLUENCE OF THE SOCIOCULTURAL AND INTERNAL ENVIRONMENTS ON THE COMPENSATION MIX

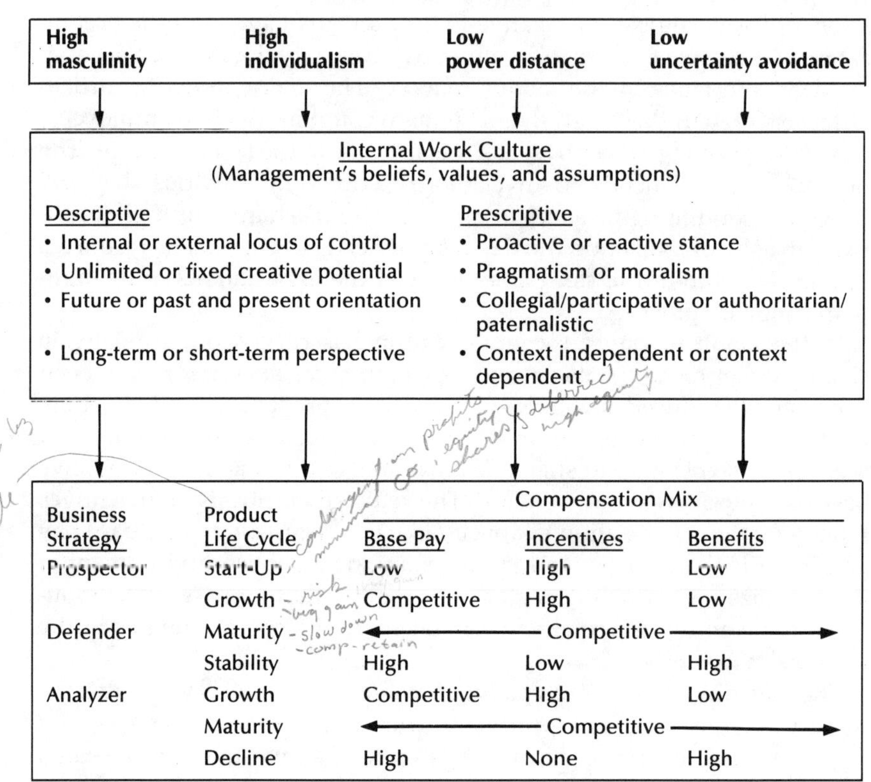

This discussion of the stages of the product life cycle and the pay mix associated with each stage, as summarized in Figure 2.3, suggests that the stage in the life cycle clearly has an impact on the organization's capacity to pay. It also demonstrates that the design of the pay mix can be strategically managed in the implementation of the overall strategies of the organization. Balkin and Gomez-Mejia (1987) have found that incentive pay forms a greater proportion of the total compensation package for firms at the growth stage than at the mature stage of the product life cycle. This finding was true for high-tech firms as well as for non-high-tech firms, except that in the high-tech firms, incentives formed a substantially larger component of the pay mix. Fixed income (base pay and benefits), on the other hand, constituted a greater proportion of the pay mix for firms at the mature stage than at the growth stage of the product life cycle. This finding was also true for both high-tech and non-high-tech firms. A notable difference, however, was that in the high-tech firms benefits were twice as large as salary, whereas in the non-high-tech firms the proportion of benefits and salary was about equal. Benefits cause a relatively lesser drain on cash and are, therefore, suitable for high-tech firms, which are usually cash short. An incentive-based compensation strategy was also found to be more effective as a recruitment and motivational tool for firms at the growth stage rather than at the mature stage of the product life cycle.

Balkin and Gomez-Mejia (1987) recognize that their findings may be skewed by the preponderance of high-tech firms in the sample. Hence it is necessary to recognize the limitations of the product-life-cycle approach to developing the pay mix. First, not all the products of an organization are at the same stage in the product life cycle. Second, the conditions of shortages and surpluses in the labour market can, and often do, compel the organization towards a pay mix different from that dictated solely by considerations of the stages in the product life cycle. Third, it is not too clear in which direction the life cycle stage-pay mix effect operates, that is, whether the stage in the product life cycle affects the pay mix or vice versa. Finally, because the issues of the organization's business strategy and product life cycle stages are macro-level issues, they are nebulous and do not easily lend themselves to empirical testing. One can therefore understand the difficulties involved in attempting to relate these issues to the design and management of a compensation system whose effectiveness can only be judged by the extent to which it succeeds in ensuring that the employees, who are the beneficiaries of the system, have performed in a manner that has helped the organization to achieve its objectives. The business strategies and the product life cycle stages are useful, and even necessary, starting points in reward design. They provide the compensation specialist with an overall sense of direction, information on the likely availability of resources, and a guide to the optimal allocation of these resources. The compensation analyst will incorporate these factors in the process of reward design and management. In the ultimate analysis, the effectiveness of a compensation system will be judged by the extent to which it has enabled the organization to be successful in three areas: (1) in attracting and retaining employees with the required knowledge, skills, and abilities; (2) in maintaining their morale, and motivating them to high performance and growth on the job; and (3) in complying with the legal provisions relative to compensation. To ensure that the organization is successful in these areas, the compensation specialist must focus on the micro-level issues that lead to a sound understanding of how the compensation package influences the motivational dynamics within employees and their consequent behaviour. Such a focus is the thrust of the remaining chapters of the book.

SUMMARY

The environmental forces that affect an organization's capacity to operate successfully have an impact on the design and the management of the compensation system. This chapter explored the impact of five external environmental forces: economic conditions, technological changes, government regulations, union expectations, and the sociocultural climate. In addition, the chapter outlined the impact of three factors internal to the organization: internal work culture, the business strategy, and the product life-cycle. The identification and understanding of the environmental forces described in this chapter provide the compensation specialist with an overall strategic sense of direction for the design and management of the reward system.

KEY TERMS

business strategies
compensation mix
external environment
internal environment
internal work culture
product life cycle
sociocultural environment

REVIEW AND DISCUSSION QUESTIONS

1. Discuss the impact of each of the following elements of the external environment on the compensation policies and programmes of an organization:
   - economic conditions
   - technological changes
   - government regulations
   - union expectations
   - sociocultural environment
2. Explain how the sociocultural environment affects the internal work culture of the organization.
3. Discuss the impact of the internal work culture on the design and management of the rewards system.
4. Explain why it is important to tailor the compensation system to support the business strategies of the organization.

5. Identify the appropriate compensation mix for each stage of the product life cycle, and explain the rationale for such a mix.
6. Discuss the limitations of the product life cycle approach to developing a compensation mix.

CASE: TANDOORI BURGERS LIMITED

Expo 67 was a memorable event in Canadian history. It also marked the beginning of young Jitender Singh's love affair with Canada. He was brought to Montreal from his native Ludhiana, in India, to work as a cook in an East Indian restaurant that specialized in tandoori cuisine, a rage with Montrealers that summer. Jitender recognized a tremendous business opportunity, and he was determined to bring the culinary delights of tandoori to all of Canada. In 1968, Jitender and his wife opened his first restaurant in Montreal, Jit's Tandoor. It was an instant success. By 1978, almost every major city in Quebec and Ontario had a Jit's Tandoor.

Although still popular, the restaurants were not profitable. The quality of management was poor, labour costs were high, and the food had deteriorated largely because most of the cooks were recruited locally and did not have the expertise of a tandoori chef. By 1985, with the exception of the Toronto restaurant, all of the Jit's Tandoors were experiencing severe losses. In 1986, Ray Prosper acquired a controlling interest in Jit's Tandoor. Ray's fascination with East Indian cuisine developed during his stay in India as a CUSO volunteer. His graduate work in business administration gave him the business and management skills to recognize a business opportunity as well as to assess realistically the challenges of making Jit's Tandoor succeed.

Ray shared in Jitender's vision of popularizing tandoori delicacies but decided on a different strategy — a fast-food operation. His winning formula would be a combination of flawless and speedy service, impeccable cleanliness, and quality food with the exotic tandoori flavour and taste. Recognizing the increasingly popular desire for nutritious foods that are tasty and low in cholesterol, Ray saw the skinless tandoori chicken as the perfect answer. He changed the name to Tandoori Burgers Limited (TBL) and decided to set up licensed franchises along with company-owned outlets. Each of the existing Jit's Tandoors was converted into a company-owned outlet of TBL. The TBL outlet, company-owned or franchised, is a fairly self-contained operation with a kitchen and a seating area. All the food is cooked in a tandoor, a specially designed clay oven.

Ray was aware of the problems usually associated with fast-food operations — shortages of crew labour and competent and trustworthy store managers, high turnover of staff, need for continuous training and motivation of employees, and rising labour costs. He also recognized that critical to the success of the operation were quality products, which in turn required specialist chefs. Such chefs are not home-grown in Canada. He considered training chefs, but eventually decided on hiring them directly from India.

The growth of franchises outpaced that of company-owned outlets, but by 1990, the number of company-owned outlets had increased dramatically and is expected to eventually constitute about 40 per cent of the total outlets by the end of the decade. Quality, cleanliness, and customer service are the main ingredients that translate into sales and profitability. Operating processes and equipment have been standardized and no changes are expected in this area. Ray is concerned, however, about some developments that may adversely affect TBL. First, the immigration department is reluctant to grant visas to chefs from India unless TBL can demonstrate that catering graduates from the community colleges are not suitable. Second, TBL's corporate office and warehouse, located in Ontario, is required to comply with Ontario's pay equity laws. Third, some attempts have been made to unionize TBL's workforce.

The success of the company-owned outlet depends to a considerable extent upon its manager, who has responsibility for operations, employee training, customer relations, and cost effectiveness. Last year, TBL experienced sales growth of 11 per cent, and expects the same rate this year. Cost effectiveness is particularly critical to TBL's success in the context of its major competitors — McDonald's, Burger King, Kentucky Fried Chicken, Harvey's, and similar fast-food operations. Ray is rather ambivalent in his attitude to the Free-Trade Agreement. He recognizes the potential for increased competition from Mexican-American fast-food outlets, as well as the opportunity for TBL to expand in the United States.

Discussion Questions

Using the concepts discussed in this chapter:

1. Identify the external environmental challenges faced by TBL.
2. Identify the internal environment of TBL, in particular, the business strategies and the internal work culture.
3. Recommend a compensation mix that will support TBL's business strategies and at the same time be consistent with TBL's internal work culture.

PART II
THEORETICAL APPROACHES TO COMPENSATION DESIGN AND MANAGEMENT

Chapter 3
Theoretical Foundations: Content Theories Approach

CHAPTER SYNOPSIS

This chapter examines content theories of work motivation in order to understand how the reward practices that flow from their concepts and processes can help in the design and management of an effective compensation system. The chapter begins with a distinction between *motives* and *motivation,* and then explores the scientific management movement and the human relations movement. These two major movements are not theories of work motivation, but their thinking on work motivation and their prescriptions for compensation practices have been dominated by *need satisfaction,* a basic characteristic of the content theories. The major concerns of the chapter, however, are Maslow's hierarchy of needs and Herzberg's two-factor theory, which gave rise to the distinction between intrinsic and extrinsic rewards. The impact of this distinction on compensation practices is discussed. More specifically, the chapter examines whether classifying rewards as intrinsic or extrinsic helps the manager better to design and manage a compensation system.

LEARNING OBJECTIVES

- To distinguish between motives and motivation as explanations for human behaviour.
- To distinguish between *content* and *process* theories of motivation.
- To explain the content approach to motivation.
- To understand how many current compensation practices have been influenced by the scientific management and human relations movements.
- To explain Herzberg's two-factor theory.

- To understand how Maslow's hierarchy of needs has influenced Herzberg's two-factor theory.
- To understand how Herzberg's two-factor theory worked its way into contemporary thinking on motivation and what impact the theory has had on reward classification.
- To evaluate critically the intrinsic-extrinsic dichotomy in rewards management.

INTRODUCTION

The discussion on the external and internal environments in the previous chapter concluded with the recognition that the real test of the effectiveness of a compensation system is whether it enables the organization to attract and retain employees, to motivate them to high performance in their present job, to induce them to want to prepare themselves to seek and accept additional responsibilities and challenges, and to promote commitment and loyalty to the organization. How does an organization design and reward a compensation system that will successfully meet this test? Before this critical question is addressed, it is essential to acquire a sound understanding of the motivational dynamics inherent in reward-behaviour relationships. Stated differently, it is necessary to have a clear idea of *why* and *how* a reward item motivates the recipient to manifest a certain desired behaviour. Employee motivation, then, is a critical consideration in the development of the compensation system.

This is not to deny the importance of the external and internal environments in developing the compensation system. The respective roles of both — environment and employee motivation — in the foundations of the compensation system can be best defined by saying that the environment provides the organization's underlying strengths, capabilities, and objectives in the foundational structure of the compensation system; employee motivation is the *raison d'être* of the compensation system and, accordingly, constitutes the core element of the foundational structure. It is necessary, then, to explore the concept and the process of motivation. This chapter and the next two chapters explore different approaches to work motivation in order to understand the practical implications of these approaches for the design and management of an effective compensation system. This chapter differentiates between *motives* and *motivation*, and considers the suitability of the *content* approach to motivation for compensation system design.

Chapter 4 considers the *process* approach to motivation and presents a motivation model together with the pertinent and relevant determinants and moderators of the motivational process. This model provides the essential characteristics that a reward item must possess if it is to be effective in motivating employees towards the desired work behaviours.

Chapter 5 draws further applications from the expectancy theory motivation model to address the phenomenon of satisfaction with pay and non-monetary outcomes. The chapter deals with the determinants of satisfaction and the consequences of dissatisfaction with pay and non-monetary outcomes.

MOTIVATION AND MOTIVES

The topic of motivation is of interest to any observer of human behaviour — especially to both the practising manager and the behavioural scientist. Most people have met individuals who are not particularly gifted, but who achieve a great deal by dint of sheer hard work, confirming Edison's observation: "Genius is one per cent inspiration and ninety-nine per cent perspiration." And most people have come across capable and talented individuals who are allergic to the very thought of work. What is it that causes some individuals to exert much more effort than others in what they do — their studies, jobs, or personal and social development? Consider, for instance, the case of Howard, the fudge sales manager's dream sales person. He is diligent, industrious, and persevering in his efforts to exceed the assigned sales targets. Why does Howard work so hard? To most people, the obvious explanation would be that he works hard to make money. This explanation supplies the motive for Howard's behaviour, but leaves several questions unanswered. Why does Howard not adopt some other behaviour to make money, for example, starting his own fudge business, buying a lottery ticket, or marrying a rich widow? Why does Howard prefer money to some other outcome such as the thrill of goal achievement or the exhilaration of overcoming challenges? Answers to these questions would explain not only the motive for the behaviour, but also the motivational process underlying the behaviour. A theory of motives provides a limited explanation for human behaviour. A theory of motivation explains "not only why goals are sought, but also the factors that influence how they are sought" (Lawler 1971, 80). A comprehensive theory of motivation, then, will seek to explain how behaviour is initiated and the different factors and influences that contribute to energizing, maintaining, and directing that behaviour. Such a definition of motivation goes beyond the question of motive, and establishes a set of behavioural characteristics manifested in the process of motivation.

THEORIES OF MOTIVATION

Motivation is a basic psychological process that has been subjected to considerable investigation in the domain of psychology — clinical, physiological, child, social, educational, industrial, organizational. The literature of psychology is filled with theories of motivation. This chapter will consider only those theories that help provide an understanding of how a compensation item can influence an individual to start and to persevere in a desired behaviour in the work context. Such an understanding will directly facilitate the effective design and management of the compensation system. The focus, therefore, will be on work motivation theories that have been traditionally categorized in the literature as the *content* and *process* models of work motivation. The content models explain human behaviour as an attempt to satisfy a need and therefore seek to identify *what* need prompts the behaviour. The process models explain human behaviour in terms of a cognitive process the individual goes through before and during the behaviour, and therefore seek to identify *how* an individual starts, directs, and stops a behaviour. The theories in each category will be discussed and their approaches to compensation system design will be evaluated.

CONTENT THEORIES OF WORK MOTIVATION

The content theorists postulate that when an individual's need is not met or satisfied, the individual experiences tension that motivates her or him towards a behaviour to satisfy that need, and thereby to reduce or relieve the tension. The content theorists, then, explain human behaviour as being started and sustained by a deprived need, and stopped when that need is satisfied. The content theories can be said to answer the *what* of the motivation process, that is, what needs, and in what order these needs initiate, energize, and sustain the individual's work behaviour. Of the several content theories, Maslow's hierarchy of needs and Herzberg's two-factor theory are of greater relevance in that they have spawned a variety of approaches to compensation design that are still current in North American organizations.

A discussion of the content category begins with the two major movements in the evolution of management thought, namely, the scientific management and the human relations movements. Although these are not theories of work motivation *per se*, the concept of need satisfaction has characterized their thinking on work motivation and their corresponding prescriptions for compensation practices. For example, the need for money was assumed by the scientific management movement to be the primary motivator of work behaviour, and the need for belonging and social recognition was assumed by the human relations movement to be the critical motivator of work behaviour. Luthans (1989) traces the content models to these two movements, and suggests that with Maslow and Herzberg the emphasis of the content theories shifted to higher-level or growth needs. Understanding these movements will also provide a historical perspective of developments in compensation practices. Such a discussion is essential to understanding the rationale underlying many of today's compensation practices.

The Scientific Management Movement

Around 1900, Frederick Taylor, known as the father of the scientific management movement, introduced the first systematized approach to compensation. Prior to Taylor, management established incentives systems with production standards and wage rates that were based on an inadequate knowledge of the reasonable and fair time necessary to complete a job. When workers met or exceeded these standards, management reduced the wage rates to keep costs down. Workers responded by restricting output. To resolve this continuing antagonism between labour and management, Taylor linked wage rates to work standards established rationally through time and motion study and related techniques. This rigorously scientific job analysis led to the development of the "one best way of doing a job." Consequently, much attention was devoted to the selection and placement of the worker appropriate to the predetermined best way of doing the job. Taylor's programme provided workers with an opportunity to earn high wages that depended on work standards that were rationally determined rather than on the caprice of management. At the same time, the employer was happy to see a reduction in labour costs resulting from increased productivity.

The scientific management movement operated on the "economic man" concept, which assumed that the worker's work behaviour is motivated primarily by a need for money. To ensure increased output, payments under the incentive system were contingent upon performance. Severe sanctions were imposed, ranging from loss of pay to dismissal if minimum standards were not met. This scientific management approach to compensation came to be known as the "carrot and stick" approach. Thus, the compensation system of an organization that subscribes to the beliefs, values, and assumptions of the scientific management movement emphasizes economic rewards that are conditional upon performance, with appropriate penalties for failure to meet minimum standards. Such a system focuses on providing adequate monetary compensation to satisfy the worker's need for money. However, the compensation is conditional on performance; that is, payment is based on results according to established job standards determined through job analysis, using time and motion studies and related techniques of industrial engineering. Implicit in the concept of contingent rewards is a performance appraisal process to ascertain if the predetermined job standards have been met.

The scientific management approach to motivation does not qualify as a "pure" content theory because it includes elements of both content and process theories. By assuming that the worker's need for money motivates work behaviour, it focuses on the *what* of the motivation process. But it also makes the satisfaction of the need for money dependent or contingent upon a certain work behaviour. By so doing, the scientific management movement, like the theories of motivation, also makes a statement on *how* behaviour can be started, energized, directed, and sustained.

THE HUMAN RELATIONS MOVEMENT

This movement, which began in the late 1920s, viewed the workplace as a social system with the potential for satisfying worker's social needs. The individual's work behaviour is motivated by a desire to satisfy his/her need for belonging and social recognition. The movement was sparked by the Hawthorne experiments, whose results, although inconclusive, led to other studies. The findings of these later studies reported that factors such as interpersonal and intergroup relationships and attitudes were important contributors to job satisfaction and productivity.

The human relations movement operated on the "social man" concept. The compensation system in an organization that subscribes to the beliefs, values, and assumptions of this movement emphasizes non-financial rewards in addition to reward items that satisfy physical and financial needs. Examples of non-financial rewards are opportunities to work in groups, social recognition, improved communication, pleasant supervisors and co-workers, company-sponsored recreational and social activities, and so forth. Unlike the scientific management movement, the human relations movement emphasized unconditional rewards, which meant that the worker's needs — physical, financial, social — had to be satisfied before the worker could be expected to perform the required job behaviours. The rationale underlying unconditional rewards is the implicit assumption that need satisfaction would cause the worker to develop a positive attitude, loyalty, and commitment to the organization. Unconditional need satisfaction was believed to strengthen the worker's membership affiliation to the organization, and this strengthened affiliation would lead to high performance. Stated differently, the human relations movement advocated the view that a happy worker would be a productive worker. The compensation system under the human relations movement is often described as the "carrot" approach, because of the apprehension among its proponents that the use of the "stick" would be too traumatic for employee morale and satisfaction and, as a result, would adversely affect performance.

Both the scientific management and human relations movements have had an enormous influence on the design and management of reward systems and practices. It is important to recognize the fundamental differences in their approach to compensation systems. As discussed in previous chapters, particularly in the introductory chapter, one of the objectives of the compensation system is to enable the organization to motivate its employees to manifest both membership and performance behaviours. Membership behaviour is attained through ensuring employee retention; performance behaviour, through the desired job behaviours. Through its emphasis on performance-contingent rewards, the scientific management movement focused on performance behaviour to the total exclusion of the social needs of workers. Such an overemphasis on productivity proved to be counter-productive, as was evident from employee dissatisfaction, sabotage of the production process, unionization, and resulting increases in the cost of production. The failure of the human relations movement, on the other hand, was its overemphasis on unconditional rewards that ensured membership behaviour to the total exclusion of performance behaviour. Organizations following this approach were successful in retaining their employees, keeping them happy, and even eliciting their loyalty and commitment. But membership and high employee morale and commitment do not by themselves lead to high job performance and productivity. In fact, many organizations were disillusioned with the human relations movement when they discovered that productivity had decreased, and that the adversarial role of the unions had intensified, probably because the unions saw in the paternalistic approach of the movement an attempt to alienate employees from their union affiliation.

Against this brief summary of the influence of the scientific management and human relation movements on compensation systems, the next content model — Herzberg's two-factor theory — can be discussed. This theory advocates the inclusion in the reward system of items that could satisfy physical, financial, social, and growth needs. In this way, the theory seeks to address not only the membership and performance behaviours, but also the growth behaviours, of the worker, with a major emphasis on the latter. Herzberg's theory also provides the background for the contemporary approach to rewards classification in terms of intrinsic and extrinsic rewards.

Herzberg's Two-Factor Theory of Reward Classification

In the early 1960s, Frederick Herzberg developed a content theory of motivation that postulated two categories of rewards or job factors to explain *what* it is that motivates work behaviour. Herzberg's approach was based on Maslow's hierarchy of needs and considerably influenced by its humanistic orientation, namely, that people do not work mainly for money but for ego-need gratification and self-fulfillment. Maslow's theory is a content model of human motivation in general, but not of work motivation *per se*. A brief exploration of Maslow's hierarchy of needs will help to place Herzberg's theory in its proper perspective.

According to Abraham Maslow (1954), an individual's behaviour can be explained as attempts to satisfy an unsatisifed need; a satisfied or satiated need is not a motivator of behaviour. Maslow grouped needs into five categories, which he arranged in a hierarchical order of prepotency or strength, from the most prepotent to the least prepotent, as follows: physiological and survival, safety and security, belongingness, ego-status, self-actualization. He postulated a specific sequence in which the individual will progress through the hierarchy. Thus, starting at the lowest level (the most prepotent), the individual will move to the next higher level only when the immediately preceding level need is largely satisfied. The first three lower level need categories — physiological and survival, safety and security, belongingness — are viewed as "deficiency needs," which means that when they are satisfied, the deficiency is removed and these will no longer operate to motivate behaviour. The self-actualization need level, and to a large extent the ego-status need level, function as higher level or "growth needs," which operate differently from the deficiency needs. As the growth needs are satisfied, their intensity may increase rather than decrease, particularly in the case of individuals with strong growth needs. This is so because the very process of self-actualization is both a challenging and gratifying experience, giving the individual a sense of accomplishment and achievement. Maslow did not develop his theory specifically to explain work motivation, but its influence is at the very core of Herzberg's two-factor theory.

Herzberg's two-factor theory is the typical and most popular of the content theories. It has direct implications for compensation design because it makes concrete and specific pronouncements and predictions on which reward items will motivate and which will not. According to this theory (Herzberg 1966), rewards affect work behaviour in substantially different ways depending on whether they are intrinsic rewards (the motivators) or extrinsic rewards (hygiene factors). Intrinsic rewards are those that are built into or are inherent in the job, for example, responsibility, autonomy, feelings of accomplishment. Employees gain these rewards directly as they perform the job tasks. Extrinsic rewards are those that are external to the job, for example, pay, benefits, praise, pleasant working conditions, job security.

Intrinsic rewards generate in employees a level of satisfaction with what they do on the job, and consequently these rewards induce a high level of performance. For this reason, intrinsic rewards are regarded as the real and only motivators. On the other hand, extrinsic rewards do not generate satisfaction with job activities and therefore do not motivate performance. However, if the extrinsic rewards surrounding one's job are not present up to a certain level, then such absence or deficiency causes dissatisfaction, which nullifies the positive effects of the intrinsic rewards. Extrinsic rewards are called hygiene factors, because just as hygienic conditions are necessary for, but do not by themselves cause, good health, so extrinsic rewards are necessary for, but do not motivate, performance. For example, an employee with autonomy and responsibility in a challenging job receives intrinsic rewards that generate a considerable degree of satisfaction; as a result, the employee will be motivated to put in a high level of performance. If at the same time this employee receives a low salary that is not commensurate with the job, the dissatisfaction caused by the low salary will prevent the employee from performing at the high level induced by the intrinsic rewards. Hence, Herzberg postulates that extrinsic rewards function as hygiene factors that must exist in the right amount and be of the right type before the intrinsic rewards, the motivators, can begin to operate.

The distinction between hygiene factors and motivators closely parallels the distinction between deficiency and growth needs in Maslow's hierarchy of needs. Just as deficiency needs when satisfied do not operate to motivate behaviour, so hygiene factors when provided do not operate to motivate job performance. On the other hand, just as growth needs continue to operate even when satisfied, so Herzberg's motivators continue to provide the impetus for improved job performance. In fact, a correspondence between hygiene factors and deficiency need levels can be established. For example, pay and working conditions correspond to the physiological and survival needs level; job security corresponds to the safety and security needs level; relations with co-workers correspond to the belongingness need level. Similarly, a correspondence can be established between the motivators and the growth needs levels. For example, recognition that results from job performance corresponds to the ego-status need level; and challenging assignments correspond to the self-actualization need level.

The Intrinsic-Extrinsic Reward Classification

The distinction between hygiene factors and motivators soon worked its way into contemporary thinking on motivation, with the result that the compensation system came to be looked at in terms of two categories: (1) extrinsic rewards that corresponded to hygiene factors: pay, working conditions, praise from supervisor, congenial co-workers and supervisors, and so forth; (2) intrinsic rewards that corresponded to motivators: challenging assignments, autonomy, participation in decision making, and so forth. The distinction between intrinsic and extrinsic rewards became popular among motivation theorists in explaining the contents of human motives. The impact of the intrinsic-extrinsic distinction on management practice was even more profound. It became an integral part of the manager's thought, vocabulary, and practice. The reason for this is easy to see. The intrinsic-extrinsic distinction provided a relatively direct, unambiguous answer to the practical question managers faced each work day: "What rewards do I give my employees to get them to be productive?" The programmed response was: Provide intrinsic rewards by job redesign to include more variety, more responsibility, more autonomy, and control.

Not only was the answer new, it was specific and its implementation seemed possible with relatively little expense and effort. It also seemed to provide a method to prevent or redress worker alienation, which Karl Marx had predicted would result when workers were denied control of and participation in matters relating to their jobs. This panacea for employees' motivational ills included an assortment of programmes: job rotation, job enrichment, flexible scheduling, semi-autonomous work groups, and quality circles.

Obsessed with the idea of intrinsic rewards as the only motivators of performance, academic researchers and practitioners alike relegated to the background the role of extrinsic rewards (Staw 1984). They were too preoccupied with job and work design to ask whether the organization was getting its money's worth from its expenditures on pay and benefits. Indeed, the manager would deny that this issue was germane to effective management if monetary rewards are least likely to induce productivity.

When a theory causes a results-oriented manager to be apathetic to such an enormous item of expenditure as pay and benefits, the inference is that a vital aspect of reality has been overlooked in the formulation of that theory. The fact is that the intrinsic-extrinsic dichotomy, which has dominated the compensation management literature for over three decades, is inadequate in providing clear, practical guidelines for the effective design and administration of the reward system. Much less does the concept lend itself to analytical investigations of whether the organization is maximizing the returns on its investment in the reward programme. The next section critically examines the meaning and the effectiveness of the intrinsic-extrinsic dichotomy approach to rewards management.

A Critique of the Intrinsic-Extrinsic Dichotomy in Rewards Management

Advocates of the intrinsic-extrinsic dichotomy approach claim that it is built on sound theory that provides the foundation for its techniques and practices. This section explores the myths surrounding this claim.

Myth 1

The intrinsic-extrinsic dichotomy assumes that people seek and need work that is meaningful and in which they are free to function on an independent basis. Implicit in this assumption is the belief that the work role is central to one's life and provides the best opportunity for the realization of the human potential for growth. This assumption is the fundamental rationale for giving intrinsic rewards a unique role. As McGregor observed: "Unless there are opportunities at work to satisfy these high level needs (esteem and self-actualization), people will be deprived, and their behaviour will reflect this deprivation" (McGregor 1966, 12–13). Intrinsic rewards, therefore, provide people with the opportunity to satisfy their need to find self-fulfillment in work.

Fact

The relevant research contradicts these motivational assumptions. A good example is Fein's study of blue-collar and white-collar motivation, which concluded that only about 15 to 20 per cent of the blue-collar workforce look for challenging jobs in order to satisfy their growth needs at work (Fein 1976). The studies of Dubin and others seriously question the importance attached to intrinsic growth needs and the centrality of work in one's life (Dubin 1956). They have found that for many people growth needs are not important and the work role is not their central life interest.

Myth 2

The concepts of intrinsic and extrinsic rewards provide a simple, straightforward, and unambiguous basis for rewards management.

Fact

The findings of a 1975 survey of industrial psychologists by Dyer and Parker tell the true story. In that survey, only 7 out of 21 rewards were classified as either intrinsic or extrinsic by more than 75 per cent of the respondents (Dyer and Parker 1976). This clearly suggests that even industrial psychologists have difficulty agreeing about whether a reward is intrinsic or extrinsic. In a 1985 study, Kanungo and Hartwick also found similar disagreement among Canadian managerial employees in classifying rewards as intrinsic or extrinsic (Kanungo and Hartwick 1987).

A persistent and fundamental problem relates to the criteria by which a reward is identified as intrinsic or extrinsic. Dyer and Parker's survey found that a wide range of conflicting criteria were being employed, the most popular being the *task* criterion and the *mediation of reward* criterion.

According to the task criterion, rewards that derive directly from or are inherently connected with job tasks are considered to be intrinsic rewards (Herzberg, Mausner, and Snyderman 1959). By this criterion, intrinsic rewards would typically include recognition, responsibility, achievement, autonomy. To receive intrinsic rewards, employees must be engaged in the task activities that define the job. They get these rewards directly as they perform the tasks in their jobs. In contrast, pay, praise from the supervisor, pleasant working conditions are all examples of extrinsic rewards because these rewards are external to or separate from the task. Employees will not automatically get extrinsic rewards immediately or directly upon performing the tasks involved. They must wait to receive them from the job environment or context rather than from the job content.

In the second criterion, the mediation of reward, the focus is on the persons who administer the reward (Deci 1972). These persons can be either the employees themselves or others. By this criterion, rewards that employees administer to themselves are called intrinsic rewards. Examples include pride in the job, interesting task, meaningful task, responsibility, autonomy. In all self-mediated rewards, the employees do not depend on others to receive the reward. Rewards that are not self-mediated but come from others are called extrinsic rewards. Examples include pay, promotion, recognition, praise from the supervisor, pleasant working conditions.

The definition of each criterion appears to be clear by itself. Now, if the two criteria, task and mediation of reward, refer to the same intrinsic-extrinsic dimension of reward classification, then a set of rewards classified as intrinsic or extrinsic using the task criterion should be similarly classified using the mediation of reward criterion.

In the Kanungo and Hartwick (1987) study referred to earlier, 13 out of the 48 rewards were differentially classified as intrinsic or extrinsic under the two criteria. For example, promotion, authority, participation, praise from supervisor and from co-worker, recognition, awards for superior performance were all classified as intrinsic rewards using the task criterion. These same rewards were also classified as extrinsic using the mediation of reward criterion. Another noteworthy finding from this study was that pride in the success of the company and opportunity to make friends were classified as extrinsic rewards using the task criterion. But when the mediation of reward criterion was used, these rewards were classified as intrinsic.

Thus, the concepts of intrinsic and extrinsic rewards do not provide managers with a clear, unambiguous basis for rewards identification and, consequently, for rewards management. Furthermore, the inability to classify rewards consistently as intrinsic or extrinsic, as reported by these studies, brings into question whether the intrinsic-extrinsic dichotomy has a similar meaning for all managers. The conclusion is that the intrinsic-extrinsic dichotomy is conceptually flawed. After reviewing four methods typically employed to dichotomize intrinsic and extrinsic rewards, Guzzo concluded: ". . .if a further understanding of work motivation is to be gained, it is imperative that characteristics of work rewards be conceived of in other than intrinsic-extrinsic terms. . ." (Guzzo 1979, 82).

Myth 3

Even if the intrinsic-extrinsic dichotomy is conceptually flawed, one must nevertheless accept the overall motivational value of designing jobs through job enrichment programmes that flow from the theories of motivation based on this dichotomy. It is assumed that job enrichment programmes provide motivators or intrinsic rewards to all employees and thereby enhance their job performance.

Fact

Job enrichment programmes have not fared any better than the theory from which they were derived. While some researchers have reported that these programmes are for the most part successful (David and Cherns 1975), others have questioned the data on which such conclusions are based (Fein 1974).

Even the proponents of job enrichment concede its limitations in respect of universal applicability and improved productivity. For instance, Luthans and Reif have shown that job enrichment programmes are applicable to only a narrow spectrum of jobs, that productivity gains from such programmes are, if any, minimal, and that workers frequently prefer jobs that are not enriched (Luthans and Reif 1973). Numerous studies have found that some workers actually prefer highly routine, repetitive jobs that are devoid of any challenge (Luthans and Reif 1972). For these workers, job security and the relative independence and the freedom to socialize at work are more important. Recognizing that not all workers want enriched jobs, labour leaders have taken the position that management should focus on providing extrinsic rewards such as good pay, working conditions, and job security (Winpisinger 1973).

Behavioural scientists have now recognized that workers will respond positively to enriched jobs only in the presence of certain conditions. A good example is Hackman and Oldhams' work redesign model, which, despite its emphasis on intrinsic need satisfaction, stipulates that its effectiveness depends upon the worker's knowledge and skill, growth need strength, and satisfaction with the work context, for example, pay, working conditions, supervisory practices, co-workers (Hackman and Oldham 1980).

Underlying the intrinsic-extrinsic approach to rewards management, although not expressly stated, is the belief that a reward has in itself a specific potency to generate specific effects. Somewhat in the manner of the medieval apothecary, the manager is advised to dispense different potions for different motivational ills. Thus, administer a concentrated dose of autonomy to activate the motivational adrenalin; administer pay to satisfy the appetite for things material.

It is not surprising that the experience with the intrinsic-extrinsic approach to rewards management has been disappointing. This approach looks at only one aspect of the behaviour-reward relationship, namely, the assumed inherent potency of the reward to produce the desired behaviour. It ignores the fact that a reward, whether intrinsic or extrinsic, will influence behaviour only when it is valued by the recipient and received as a consequence of that behaviour. Hence, any effective approach to rewards management must take into account the perceptions and expectations of the recipient. The process theories of work motivation discussed in the next chapter meet this requirement.

SUMMARY

Compensation plays a fundamental role in employee work motivation. Organizations use compensation programmes to attract and retain employees and to motivate them to perform behaviours that bring the organization closer to the attainment of its objectives. In order to use compensation programmes successfully, the compensation specialist needs to understand what it is about the reward item that prompts employees to start and maintain a desired behaviour, or to stop an undesired work behaviour.

This chapter explored the content models or approaches to work motivation that explain human behaviour as an attempt to satisfy a need. The chapter began with a discussion of the scientific management movement and the human relations movement, two major movements that viewed employees' work behaviour as a means to satisfy a need. The scientific management movement, which operated on the "economic man" concept and assumed that employees' work behaviour is motivated primarily by a need for money, emphasized economic rewards that were made contingent on performance.

The human relations movement, which operated on the "social man" concept and assumed that employees' work behaviour is motivated primarily by the desire to satisfy social needs, emphasized non-financial rewards in addition to reward items that satisfy physical and financial needs. The human relations movement emphasized unconditional rewards because of the belief that need satisfaction would promote loyalty and commitment and eventually lead to high performance. In reality, however, the reward system only contributed to retaining the employees and keeping them happy.

The compensation practices in each movement did not fully address the objectives of the compensation system. The scientific management movement focused on performance behaviours to the exclusion of the social needs of employees. The human relations movement focused on membership behaviours to the exclusion of performance behaviours.

Herzberg's two-factor theory, the typical and most popular of the content approaches to work motivation, was considered next. Based on Maslow's hierarchy of needs and influenced by its humanistic orientation, the two-factor theory included in the reward system items that could satisfy physical, financial, and social, as well as growth, needs. It addressed not only membership and performance behaviours, but also growth behaviours, which had been neglected by both the scientific management and human relations movements. However, it proposed that rewards affect work behaviour in substantially different ways, depending on whether they are intrinsic rewards (the motivators) or extrinsic rewards (hygiene factors). Herzberg claimed that intrinsic rewards — responsibility, autonomy, feelings of accomplishment, and so forth — are the real and only motivators of job performance. Extrinsic rewards — pay, benefits, praise, job security, and so forth — do not motivate employees to high job performance; their absence generates dissatisfaction. The extrinsic rewards, however, must be present before the intrinsic rewards, the motivators, can begin to operate.

Although the two-factor theory appears to have been popular with both practitioners and academic researchers, an examination of the intrinsic-extrinsic dichotomy reveals that (*a*) the empirical findings contradict its motivational assumptions; (*b*) it does not provide managers with a clear, unambiguous basis for rewards identification and management; (*c*) it is conceptually flawed; and (*d*) its approach to rewards management ignores the fact that a reward, whether it is intrinsic or extrinsic, will influence behaviour only when it is valued by the recipient and received as a consequence of that behaviour.

KEY TERMS

content theories
extrinsic rewards
hierarchy of needs
human relations movement
intrinsic rewards
motivation
motives
process theories
scientific management movement
two-factor theory

REVIEW AND DISCUSSION QUESTIONS

1. Explain why a theory of motives is not adequate to explain human behaviour.
2. Distinguish between the content and process theories of work motivation.
3. From the late nineteenth century till today, compensation practices have been profoundly influenced by the scientific management and human relations movements. Compare and contrast these movements with specific reference to:
   a) their assumptions about employee work motivation in so far as compensation is concerned;
   b) the reward items emphasized;
   c) the basis of giving rewards; and
   d) the types of behaviours promoted by the rewards.
4. How does Maslow's hierarchy of needs explain an individual's behaviour?
5. What are the salient features of Herzberg's two-factor theory? Explain in what way it has been influenced by Maslow's hierarchy of needs.
6. What are the reasons for the popularity of the intrinsic-extrinsic reward classification among motivation theorists and managers?
7. The advocates of the intrinsic-extrinsic dichotomy approach claim that it is built on sound theory that provides the foundation for its techniques and practices. Critically examine this claim with reference to:
   a) the assumptions underlying the intrinsic-extrinsic dichotomy;
   b) the validity of the constructs intrinsic, extrinsic;
   c) the effectiveness of job enrichment programmes derived from this approach; and
   d) the inherent potency of the reward implied in this approach.
8. What are the similarities between Maslow's hierarchy of needs and the scientific management movement, the human relations movement, and Herzberg's two-factor theory?

EXERCISE 3.1: PREFERENCES FOR PAY AND OTHER JOB OUTCOMES

Objective

This exercise will give you an opportunity to develop some insights into why different groups of employees prefer different job outcomes.

Procedure

1. After reading all the job outcomes listed in Table 3.1.1, decide which outcome you think is most preferred by factory workers; by managers/professionals.
2. In the blank column under Factory Workers, rank the outcomes in order from 1 to 15, using 1 for the most preferred outcome and 15 for the least preferred. Repeat for Managers/Professionals.
3. Share your individual decisions with your group. As a group, decide on the rankings. Make sure your spokesperson records the consensus of the group together with the rationale for the ranking decisions.
4. Each group reports its decisions.
5. Discussion will follow each presentation. The discussion could consider the following questions:
   - Using Maslow's hierarchy of needs, explain the outcome preferences of the two groups.
   - In view of your findings of differences in the outcome preferences of these employee groups, do you think that there might also be differences in the outcome preferences of:

     a) male and female employees?

     b) anglophone and francophone employees?

     Think of some reasons why this might be so.
   - What are the managerial implications of such outcome preferences for the design of the compensation system?

Table 3.1.1
Preferences for Pay and Other Job Outcomes

Job Outcomes (Things people look for in their jobs/careers)	Factory Workers	Managers/ Professionals
Security (Permanent job, steady work)		
Earnings (for a better standard of living)		
Merit pay (for high job performance)		
Benefits (vacations, bonus, pension, insurance, profit-sharing, medical benefits, disability, dental benefits, etc.)		
Working conditions (pleasant surroundings, good lighting, air-conditioning, adequate office space)		
Opportunity for future promotion		
Sound company policies and procedures (reasonable and non-discriminatory)		
Good peer relations (a job that gives you the opportunity to work with others whom you like)		
Considerate and sympathetic superior		
Technically competent superior		
Respect and recognition (from superiors and peers for your work)		
Interesting work (a job that you very much enjoy)		
Responsibility and independence (to work in your own way)		
Achievement (opportunity to achieve excellence in your work)		
Opportunity for growth (professionally; to become more skilled and competent on the job)		

EXERCISE 3.2: THE INTRINSIC-EXTRINSIC APPROACH TO REWARDS CLASSIFICATION

Objective

To understand the basis for classifying rewards.

Procedure

1. Refer to Table 1.1 in Chapter 1, and classify each item as either intrinsic or extrinsic.
2. Share your decision with your group. As a group, attempt to arrive at a consensus on each item. If the group is unable to reach a consensus on an item, make sure that your spokesperson records the reasons for the different points of view.
3. Each group reports its decisions and differences.
4. Discussion will follow each presentation. It may be instructive to consider the relevance of the Kanungo and Hartwick (1987) findings with regard to the ambiguity of the intrinsic-extrinsic basis of classifying rewards.

CHAPTER 4

THEORETICAL FOUNDATIONS: PROCESS THEORIES APPROACH

CHAPTER SYNOPSIS

Continuing the search for a suitable theoretical approach to guide the design and management of a compensation system, this chapter provides an extensive consideration of the process theories of work motivation. The chapter reviews equity theory, its elements and process, and then presents a comprehensive motivational model, the expectancy theory model for reward management. The model, founded on the basic framework and process of expectancy theory, incorporates the essence of equity theory and some of the more appropriate concepts of need theories. The chapter concludes with an examination of the empirical support for the model, and a discussion of the practical managerial implications of the model for the effective design, implementation, and evaluation of a compensation system.

LEARNING OBJECTIVES

- To understand how the *process* theories explain work motivation.
- To understand the elements and the process of equity theory and its explanation of the behaviour-reward relationship.
- To understand the elements and the process of the expectancy theory model for reward management.
- To identify and explain the determinants of each element of the expectancy theory model.
- To identify and explain the moderators of the process of the expectancy theory model.

- To explain the research findings that provide empirical support for the expectancy theory model.
- To understand the direct impact and the concrete, practical guidelines that the expectancy theory model offers with regard to the strategies, processes, and techniques used in the design and management of the compensation system.

PROCESS THEORIES OF WORK MOTIVATION

The previous chapter examined the approaches to reward design and management based on the content approach to motivation. Analysis showed that this approach is founded primarily on the theoretical constructs of the intrinsic-extrinsic dichotomy of work rewards, a dichotomy that has been questioned on both empirical and theoretical grounds. Furthermore, as was pointed out in the conclusion of the analysis, the content approach seems to ignore a fundamental fact of human motivation; namely, that a reward item will influence an individual's behaviour only when that individual values it *and* when it is received as a consequence of that behaviour — provided that the individual has the ability to perform that work behaviour. The process theories of work motivation recognize this fact and take into account both the perceptions and the expectations of the individual who receives the reward.

The process theories attempt to explain the *how* of an individual's work motivation, that is, how the individual's work behaviour is started, sustained, and stopped. These theories look at the cognitive processes involved in motivation, how an individual makes conscious choices that lead to a specific work behaviour. The process theories that have profound implications for the design, management, and administration of compensation programmes are expectancy theory and equity theory. The first formulations of expectancy theory are found in the works of psychologists Kurt Lewin (1935) and Edward Tolman (1932). Since then, several theorists have used the expectancy framework to develop their own theories on general human motivation. It was Victor Vroom, in his *Work and Motivation* (1964), who first applied expectancy theory to explain motivation in the work environment. His book received considerable theoretical and empirical attention, which led to several refinements of his model. This chapter will focus on Lawler's motivation model, which "draws on these developments to provide the best available model for understanding motivation in organizations" (1973, 49). This model also incorporates the important elements of equity theory that have direct relevance to and impact on the effectiveness of the compensation system.

EQUITY THEORY

This theory, formulated by J. Stacy Adams (1965), attempts to explain the process of how an individual comes to be satisfied or dissatisfied with a reward. In the event the individual is dissatisfied, equity theory predicts the behaviours to which the individual might have recourse in order to eliminate or to reduce the dissatisfaction. As its name explicitly declares, equity theory is based on the notion of the equity or fairness that individuals expect in the numerous exchanges of the work situation. An employee brings to the job what he/she perceives are his/her *inputs*, for example, knowledge, skills, abilities, experience, diligence, and industriousness. For these inputs the employee receives *outcomes*, for example, pay, praise from the supervisor, promotion, interesting assignments. According to equity theory, the employee will determine the equity or fairness of the outcomes by comparing the ratio of his/her outcomes to inputs with the ratio of the outcomes to inputs of a relevant other person. If such a comparison shows that the employee's perceived ratio of outcomes to inputs is equal to his/her perceived ratio of the other person's outcomes to inputs, then the employee will experience equity. If the employee perceives the two ratios to be unequal, then he/she will experience inequity.

The nature of the inequity could generate feelings of guilt or anger. If the employee perceives his/her ratio of outcomes to inputs to be greater than that of the relevant other, then the employee will perceive that he/she is overpaid and will likely experience feelings of guilt. If the employee perceives his/her ratio of outcomes to inputs to be less than that of the other, then the employee will perceive that he/she is underpaid and will likely experience feelings of anger. The feelings of guilt or anger resulting from the perceptions of inequity will motivate the employee to behaviours that the employee believes will restore equity or reduce inequity. The behaviours that the employee adopts can include increasing his/her own inputs (working harder) or outcomes (success in persuading the supervisor that a raise is justified); decreasing his/her own inputs (tardiness, absenteeism) or outcomes (if compensation is on a piece-rate basis, focusing on quality rather than on quantity); cognitively distorting his/her own or the other's inputs or outcomes (through re-evaluation of perceptions); acting on the other (sabotage, vandalism); changing the other (comparing self with a different worker); leaving the field (transfer or resignation).

These few examples of the behaviours resulting from inequity underscore the importance of equity theory for the compensation system. Three fundamental areas of the compensation infrastructure are highly vulnerable to the potentially damaging effects of inequity. First, the basic pay structure of the organization should reflect the value of the job, that is, jobs of equal value are paid the same and appropriate pay differentials recognize job dissimilarities. Compliance with this principle through an appropriate job evaluation system contributes to employee perceptions of equity — technically referred to as *internal equity*. Second, the compensation system should reflect market wage rates, in accordance with the organization's policy to lead, lag, or meet the market. Appropriate and correct decisions in this area, aided by periodic salary and benefit surveys, will ensure employee perceptions of another type of equity, which is referred to as *external equity*. Third, the compensation of employees should reflect their performance. Performance-based pay, determined through a fair performance appraisal system, will ensure employee perceptions of the third type of equity, referred to as either *personal equity* or *individual equity*. It cannot be emphasized enough that employee perceptions are at the very heart of feelings of equity or inequity. Therefore, the processes adopted to ensure internal, external, and personal equity are as important as, if not more important than, the mechanics, however sophisticated these might be.

Feelings of equity or inequity lead the employee to form judgements on the value (or valence) of a reward. When an employee perceives the reward item to be inequitable, either in its content or in the methods by which it is determined, the employee will not experience satisfaction with that reward item. The consequences of such dissatisfaction, in terms of employee behaviours to eliminate or reduce the dissatisfaction, will be fully discussed in Chapter 5. Such dissatisfaction will also result in the employee's not valuing the reward or not finding it to be attractive, and to that extent the reward will not be effective in motivating the employee towards the desired behaviour. By its explanation of reward satisfaction/dissatisfaction and its impact on work motivation, equity theory makes a substantial contribution to the behaviour-reward relationship. A fuller understanding of this relationship is provided by Lawler's expectancy motivation model.

EXPECTANCY THEORY

The underlying assumption of expectancy theory is that ". . .the choices made by a person among alternative courses of action are lawfully related to psychological events occurring contemporaneously with the behaviour" (Vroom 1964, 14–15). Expectancy theory is a cognitively oriented model of human behaviour. It recognizes that the individual's behaviours are the product of rational, conscious choices from alternative courses of action. These choices are based on the individual's perceptions and beliefs. Expectancy theory does not view individuals as automatons; neither are they assumed to be inherently motivated or unmotivated. In essence, it postulates that the motivational force to perform in a specified manner will depend on the individual's belief that he/she has the ability to perform the specified behaviours and that such performance will lead to the outcomes associated with the performance; and on the attractiveness of the outcomes to the individual. Expectancy theory, then, has three basic elements:

1. the effort-performance expectancy (E→P).
2. the performance-outcome expectancy (P→O).
3. the valence or attractiveness of the outcomes (V).

Lawler (1971) developed his motivation model on these basic elements, but incorporated into the model the determinants of each element to provide a more comprehensive explanation of both the what and how of the motivational process. The remainder of the chapter considers this model — its basic elements, the determinants of each element, the motivational process the model describes — and the implications of the model for the design and management of the compensation system.

The Elements of Expectancy Theory

There are three basic elements of expectancy theory.

1. The Effort-Performance Expectancy (E→P)

This is the individual's belief or probability estimate that in a given situation his/her expenditure of effort will lead to the intended level of performance. The probability can vary from 0, which is the certainty that the effort will not result in the required performance, to 1, which is the certainty that the effort will result in the required performance. For example, John, a machinist, is assigned to machine 500 widgets a week, an increase from 300 widgets a week. If John is certain that he can produce the 500 widgets as required, then his (E→P) expectancy will be 1. If John is certain that he cannot produce the 500 widgets as required, then his (E→P) expectancy will be 0. On the other hand, if John is uncertain of successful performance, then his (E→P) expectancy will be between 0 and 1, depending on his assessment of the chances of doing the assignment successfully. For example, the (E→P) expectancy will be .75 if John estimates that he has a 75 per cent chance of completing the assignment successfully. Later in the chapter, some of the factors that determine the (E→P) expectancy will be examined.

2. The Performance-Outcome Expectancy (P→O)

This expectancy represents the individual's belief, or estimate of probability, that a given performance level will result in a certain outcome. Since performance generally leads to several outcomes, the individual will develop probability estimates for each outcome. Consider again the case of John, the machinist. Suppose John perceives that the outcomes associated with producing the 500 widgets are a bonus, promotion, and lay-off. He estimates that the probability of each outcome following successful performance is .7 for the bonus, .3 for promotion, and .6 for lay-off. The (P ⟶ O) expectancy, then, must be viewed as a subjective probability estimate for each outcome associated with a performance level. This (P ⟶ O) expectancy can range from 0 (this performance level definitely would not lead to this outcome) through 1 (this performance level definitely would lead to this outcome). The determinants of (P ⟶ O) expectancy will be discussed in a later section.

3. Valence, or the Attractiveness of the Outcome (V)

Valence expresses the individual's preference for the outcome, or the value or importance of the outcome to the individual. It is the anticipated satisfaction (positive valence) or dissatisfaction (negative valence) that an individual associates with an outcome. Returning to the case of John, the machinist: his probability estimates of each outcome following successful performance were .7 for the bonus, .3 for promotion, and .6 for lay-off. How attractive are each of these outcomes to John? It is known that the attractiveness and the value of an outcome differ considerably from person to person. In fact, even for the same person, the value of an outcome will differ over time. John can value each outcome either positively or negatively. Thus, his valence for each outcome might be +.7 for the bonus, +.5 for the promotion, and −.8 for lay-off. The valence for an outcome can range from −1 (the outcome is extremely unattractive or undesirable) through 0 (the outcome is neither attractive nor unattractive), to +1 (the outcome is extremely attractive or desirable). The determinants of valence are discussed in the next section.

So far, each element of expectancy theory has been identified; and what each element means, as well as how it is expressed in the context of the theory, has been explored. Before these elements are put together to demonstrate the motivational process, it is worthwhile discussing the determinants of each element to understand how the expectancies come to be developed. Such a discussion will aid in a better understanding of the expectancy model; it will also provide the rationale for the managerial implications for effective reward management that flow from the model.

THE DETERMINANTS OF THE ELEMENTS OF EXPECTANCY THEORY

1. The (E ⟶ P) Expectancies

The determinants of (E ⟶ P) expectancies are the actual situation, communications from others, past experiences in similar situations, and self-esteem. These can be seen in the lefthand segment of Figure 4.1 as impacting on (E ⟶ P).

The Expectancy Theory Model

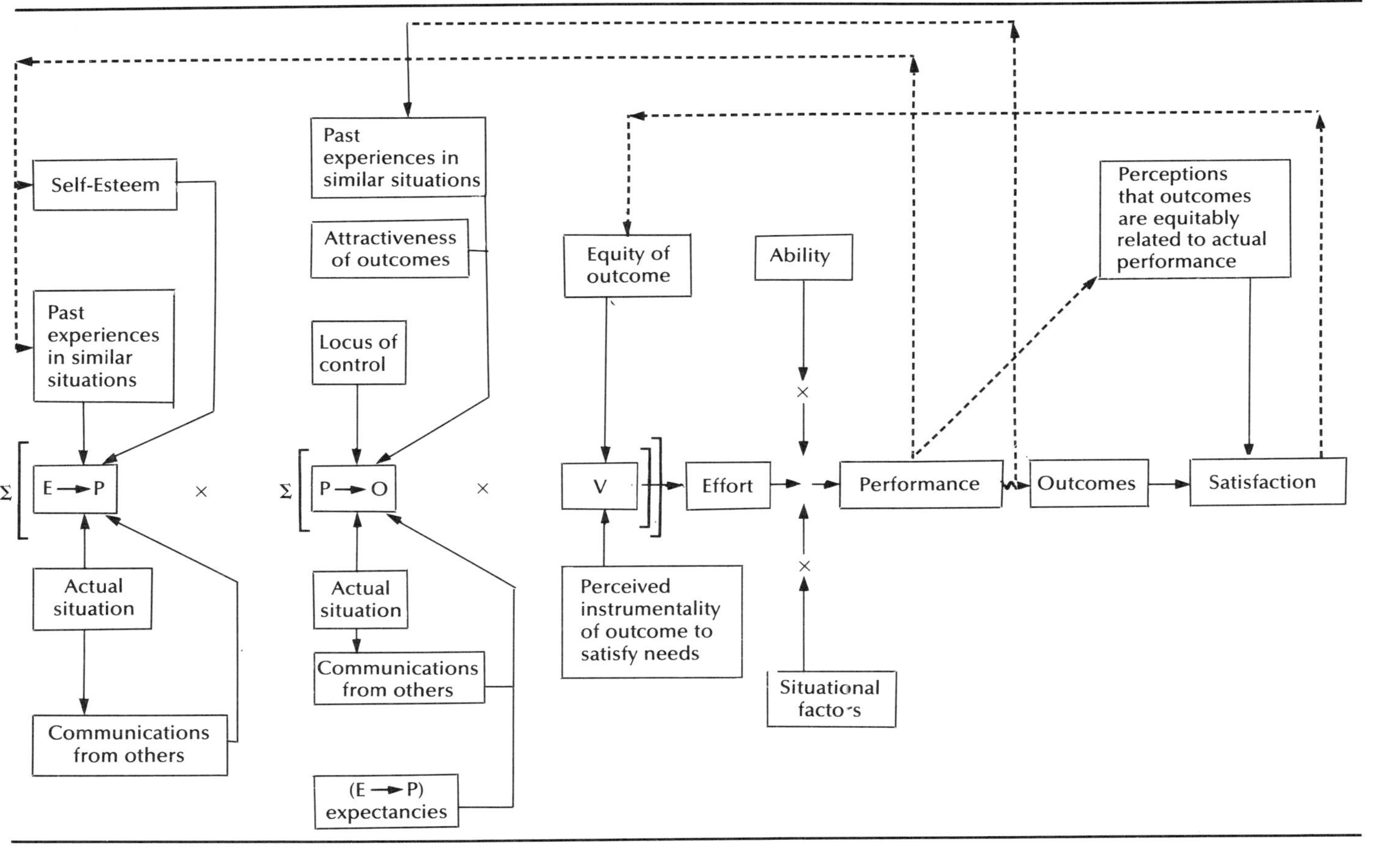

Source: Adapted from Lawler (1971, 1973).

The first determinant of (E→P) expectancies is the *actual situation*, which in the organizational context is the performance of job tasks at a required level. The individual's appraisal of the facts and circumstances of the actual situation leads him/her to assess the chances that his/her effort will lead to the required performance. Initially the individual can misread the situation and develop unrealistic expectancies that the effort expended may or may not lead to the required level of performance. In most organizations, however, these unrealistic expectancies are not held for an extensive period of time, because the employee gets direct feedback from the job and also from his/her peers and supervisor and adjusts his/her expectancies to a more realistic level.

The second determinant, *communications from others*, operates in two ways to influence (E→P) expectancies. The first way is the indirect impact on (E→P) expectancies discussed above, when a corrective is provided for the unrealistic assessment of the actual situation. The second way is the direct impact on (E→P) expectancies that happens, for example, when a peer and/or a supervisor provides direction and guidance. Such on-the-job training plays a crucial role in increasing the employee's belief that he/she has the ability to perform at the required level. Communications from others, particularly crucial to new employees, also include information relating to the availability of material, financial, and human resources needed for the required level of job performance.

The third determinant is *past experiences in similar situations*. What is learned from past experiences contributes immensely to (E→P) expectancies. If a person has had a series of failures at one or more job tasks, then the belief in his/her abilities to perform those tasks is considerably weakened, and to that extent the person's (E→P) expectancies will be quite low, if not 0. On the other hand, past successes at the same or similar job tasks will greatly increase (E→P) expectancies. The learning need not only be from personal past experiences. People can and do learn from their observations of others in similar situations. If I see Marie, who has training and experience similar to mine, perform a set of job tasks, then I will be inclined to conclude that I too can perform those tasks. Of course, this learning works in the opposite direction as well. If I see Marie failing at a set of tasks, then I will likely conclude that I too will fail at those tasks. Thus, past observations of relevant others in similar situations also have the potential to influence (E→P) expectancies.

The last determinant, *self-esteem*, comes from psychological research in personality. An individual's self-esteem constitutes a set of beliefs about his/her capabilities or competencies. The source of these beliefs is the individual's experience — successes and failures — in interacting with the environment. Individuals with a high self-esteem, that is, those who believe they have generally been successful in coping with their environment, tend to have realistic (E ⟶ P) expectancies. Individuals with a low self-esteem, that is, those who have a low concept of themselves and of their competence in dealing with the environment, tend to have low (E ⟶ P) expectancies. They generally appear to underestimate their abilities to perform successfully.

2. The (P ⟶ O) Expectancies

The determinants of (P ⟶ O) expectancies, as indicated in the second-from-left segment of Figure 4.1, are the actual situation, communications from others, (E ⟶ P) expectancies, belief in internal versus external locus of control, attractiveness of outcomes, and past experiences in similar situations.

The first-determinant is the *actual situation*, which refers to the individual's assessment of the outcomes following the performance, as in the case of the performance ⟶ pay relationship. For the new employee, the assessment is generally based on his/her acceptance of the information, including the documentation, given at the time of hiring.

This assessment is, however, considerably affected by the second determinant, *communications from others*, which is the host of interactions between peers, and between employee and supervisor, on questions of pay and a variety of outcomes, both positive and negative, for example, security, trust, congenial relationships, opportunity to use talents or skills, fatigue, harsh supervision, stress, lay-offs. The potency of communications from others, especially from one's peers, can be gauged from Whyte's study (1955) on incentive plans. This study reported that workers kept their productivity down because of information from their peers that if they were highly productive, management would reduce the pay rate. The workers believed their peers despite their own lack of personal knowledge, and despite management's statement that the pay rate would not be reduced. Whyte also reports that this peer communication led the workers to conclude that if they proceeded with high productivity there would be the additional outcome of being ostracized by other workers. When organizations keep their reward systems secret, they unwittingly foster speculative gossip that does not promote realistic (P ⟶ O) expectancies.

The third determinant is the (E ⟶ P) expectancies. This applies to the special case of individuals who have a high need for achievement, that is, those who are looking for achievement or successful task accomplishment as the outcome from their performance. A person with a high need for achievement (i.e., an n-ach person) is motivated to exert effort only if the probability of successful performance is .5, that is, (E ⟶ P) = .5, because it is only in a situation of moderate difficulty that the person will experience the achievement outcome. If (E ⟶ P) = 1, the task is too easy; if (E ⟶ P) = 0, the task is too difficult. When the task is either too easy or too difficult, the n-ach person will not experience a sense of achievement as a result of his/her performance. To an n-ach individual, then, when (E ⟶ P) = .5, performance will automatically lead to an outcome, that is, feelings of achievement. It can therefore be concluded that in the case of individuals who seek the feeling of achievement, when (E ⟶ P) = .5, the (P ⟶ O) expectancy will be 1.

Belief in internal versus external locus of control is the fourth determinant of (P ⟶ O) expectancies. An individual who is high on internal control generally believes that he/she personally can control or influence events and outcomes through his/her own ability and effort. Such a person is the type who "acts on the world." The internal control person does not wait for things to happen but acts to make them happen. Opposed to this personality type is the individual who is high on external control. Such a person feels that the outcomes are beyond his/her control and that external forces control his/her outcomes — "the world acts on me." A sense of fatalism pervades the thinking of the person with an external locus of control. As a result, the attitude of the external control person is to submit to the inevitability of events, as reflected by the expression "*Qué será, será*" (what will be, will be). The existence of these personality types and the degree to which, as well as the consistency with which, individuals differ on internal versus external control has been documented by Rotter (1966). The impact of this dimension on (P ⟶ O) expectancy is readily seen. High internal control persons will generally tend to believe that their performance will lead to the expected outcomes; external control persons will generally have a much lower belief that their performance will lead to the expected outcomes.

The fifth determinant is *attractiveness of outcomes*. According to Lawler (1973), the nature of outcomes influences (P ⟶ O) expectancies, since most people believe that positive outcomes are more likely to occur than negative outcomes, and that the extreme cases of very positive and very negative outcomes are unlikely to occur ("It's too good to be true!" or, "Surely, I can't receive *all* the back luck!") These tendencies to overplay the occurrence of positive outcomes and downplay the occurrence of extreme outcomes are likely to have an impact on the development of (P ⟶ O) expectancies in an organizational context.

The last determinant, *past experiences in similar situations*, refers to the experience in relation to outcomes. Suppose, for example, the organization introduces an incentive plan that is performance based. Suppose further that the organization also operates at the present time a merit pay plan with a cost-of-living adjustment that almost obliterates any differentials based on performance. Furthermore, the performance appraisal system is arbitrarily managed. With this experience, what is the likelihood of the employees' believing that the incentive plan will in practice be truly performance based? The past experience, that the merit plan is not truly based on performance, will influence employees' (P ⟶ O) expectancies for the proposed incentive plan.

3. Valence or the Attractiveness of Outcomes

There are basically two determinants of valence. These are the perceived instrumentality of the outcome to satisfy needs, and the perceived equity or fairness of the outcome (see Figure 4.1). First, an outcome that is *instrumental in satisfying an important need* would have greater valence. The needs that outcomes can satisfy are physiological and survival, safety and security, belongingness, ego-status, self-actualization. Which outcome will an individual use to satisfy which need? This depends on the way the individual has been socialized. Most people learn that money can satisfy physiological, security, and ego-status needs. The more of a need, or the more needs, it is believed, that an outcome will satisfy, the more positively that outcome will be valued. However, as mentioned earlier, for the outcome to be highly valued by an individual, the need satisfied by that outcome must itself be important to the individual. It will be recalled from the discussion of Maslow's hierarchy of needs that an individual whose physiological needs are not satisfied is unlikely to experience the need for self-actualization. Consequently, an outcome such as an enriched job high on autonomy and variety will not be valued by an individual if the pay and the benefits are extremely low, and if there is uncertainty with regard to job security.

With regard to the outcome of pay, the research evidence (Lawler 1971) suggests that pay is most instrumental for satisfying physiological, security, and ego-status needs, and not at all instrumental in satisfying social and self-actualization needs. These findings explain why pay is important to both low-paid and high-paid employees. To the former, pay is instrumental in satisfying their physiological and security needs; to the latter, pay becomes a symbol of recognition and is therefore instrumental in satisfying their ego-status needs. It is necessary to recognize that the valence or importance attributed to pay depends upon the salient needs of the individual and the extent to which other outcomes can satisfy those needs more effectively than pay. For example, it is not uncommon to find an individual turning down an attractive job offer for a job in another organization that pays less but offers opportunities for challenging and interesting work assignments. Likewise, certain people who are attracted to careers in government and hospitals tend to value pay less than people who are attracted to careers in business. This is so because people tend to work for the type of organization they believe will satisfy salient and important needs.

In addition, the role of cultural factors in determining the importance of outcomes cannot be ignored. For example, the outcome of promotion may not be valued by a French Canadian employee if the promotion necessitates a move away from the community in which the employee has established deep roots (Kanungo 1980).

To summarize, an individual will value an outcome when it serves to satisfy one or more important needs of the individual. The importance attributed to a need is the product of the person's socialization.

The *equity or fairness of the outcome* that is received is the second determinant of valence. It will be recalled that in order to determine equity or fairness, the individual will compare his/her outcome-input ratio with the outcome-input ratio of a relevant other. If the two ratios are perceived to be equal, then equity exists and the outcome's valence increases. If the two ratios are not perceived to be equal, then the outcome is inequitable, and to that extent there is a drop in valence.

To illustrate the effects of instrumentality to satisfy need and equity on the valence of outcomes, consider that Tom expects the outcome associated with his performance to be a merit bonus of $3,000. He values this outcome because it will meet his important need to pay his house tax bill. Therefore the valence of this outcome will be high. But Tom is also aware that the structure of the merit bonus system will not adequately reflect his performance *vis-à-vis* his colleague. This inequity will cause him to reduce the high valence of the $3,000. If Tom had perceived the merit bonus system to be fair, then the equity would have contributed towards an even greater increase in valence of the $3,000 bonus.

The discussion so far points out that the effective rewards for motivating employees to perform are those that are *valued* and *contingent on the desired behaviour*, or performance based. Underlying these two characteristics of an effective reward is a third characteristic, namely, *saliency*. A reward must be salient in the sense that the reward is uppermost in the minds of the employee. A reward may be valued and contingent, but if the employee is only vaguely aware of the existence of the reward and barely knows the conditions for earning it, then that reward is unlikely to influence his/her work behaviour. To make the reward salient to the employee, its existence and operative conditions must be properly and frequently communicated. The notion of saliency is implicit in the "communication from others" and "actual situation" determinants of the (P ⟶ O) expectancy. It is also implicitly in the "instrumentality" and "equity or fairness" determinants of valence. Unless one gets the proper information and feedback on the qualifying conditions, one is unable to make a judgement with regard to the instrumentality of the outcome to satisfy needs and to the fairness or otherwise of the reward.

THE PROCESS OF EXPECTANCY THEORY

The factors that influence each of the three elements have been identified and reviewed. The three elements can now be put together in the form of the following equation to see the motivational process (refer again to Figure 4.1) underlying expectancy theory: $(E \rightarrow P) \times [(P \rightarrow O) \times (V)]$ = Motivational Force to Exert Effort for achieving the desired performance. Apply this equation to the case of John, the machinist, used in the discussion of the three elements. Assume that John's $(E \rightarrow P) = 1$ for producing 500 widgets. The valence and the (P→O) probabilities for each of the three expected outcomes are bonus, promotion, and lay-off. The motivational forces in this example will be computed as follows:

{(E→P) × Σ [(P→O) × (V)]} = Motivational Force
(1.0) × (0.7) × (+.7) = 0.49 (due to bonus)
(1.0) × (0.3) × (+.5) = 0.15 (due to promotion)
(1.0) × (0.6) × (−.8) = −0.48 (due to lay-off)
Total Motivation Force = +0.16

The total motivational force is +.16. This shows that John is motivated to put in the effort to perform, but it is not a very strong force. The computation shows the depressing effect of a negative valence, without which John's motivational force would have been +.64. The higher, positive expectancy values of each term contribute eventually to a stronger motivational force.

The equation incorporates a multiplicative function rather than an additive function. There is no firm empirical basis for hypothesizing a multiplicative relationship between the three elements. However, in extreme situations, when either (E→P) or (P→O) is 0, or when (V) = −1, one can logically reason that the multiplicative function is most appropriate. For instance, if you believe that (E→P) = 0, namely, that your effort will not lead to successful performance, then you will not be motivated to put in the effort, even though you believe that the required performance would definitely lead to outcomes [i.e., (P→O) = 1], and you find the outcomes to be extremely desirable [i.e., (V) = +1]. Likewise, if you believe that (P→O) = 0, namely, that your performance will definitely not lead to the outcomes associated with the required performance level, then you will not be motivated to make the effort, even though you believe that you can perform at the required level [i.e., (E→P) = 1], and you find the outcomes associated with the required performance to be extremely desirable [i.e., (V) = +1]. Finally, if you expect that (V) = −1, namely, that the outcomes associated with the required performance are extremely undesirable, then you will not be motivated to make the effort, even though you believe that you can perform at the required level [i.e., (E→P) = 1], and that performance will lead to the associated outcomes [i.e., (P→O) = 1].

The assumption in the illustration is that John's (E→P) expectancy for 500 widgets was 1.0. In reality, an individual might consider several (E→P) expectancies for different performance levels, and for each performance level, a corresponding set of (P→O) expectancies and valence values. The motivational force to exert the effort to perform would then be computed for each alternative. The performance level with the strongest motivational force would be the likely decision of the individual.

This discussion could raise the question whether an individual does in fact explore all the possible alternative behaviours and compute the expectancies and valences of each before arriving at a decision. Theoretically, there is no limit to the number of alternatives that can be considered. The "economic man" view takes the approach that an individual has the capacity to consider, and in fact does consider, all possible alternatives, the corresponding outcomes of each alternative, and his/her preference for each outcome in order to arrive at an optimal decision that will optimize his/her satisfaction. Simon (1957) has argued against this "economic man" view, saying that an individual operates as more of a "satisfier" than as an "optimizer." In reality, when individuals decide on a course of action, they do not consider all the outcomes, but only those valued outcomes that are salient to them. Therefore, as Lawler observes: "In using the present model to predict an individual's behaviour, consideration must be limited to only those cognitions that the person is using as a basis for decision" (1973, 60).

The model, Figure 4.1, recognizes that although an individual is motivated to put in the effort to perform, the effort that is exerted will result in performance only if the two factors — ability and situational factors — that moderate the process are present. If the employee does not have the ability to perform the given tasks, then however eager and well-intentioned the employee is, the effort will not result in performance. Similarly, the effort will not result in the required performance level, despite the motivation and ability of the employee, if situational factors — the lack of essential material, technological, or financial resources — hinder performance. For example, the efforts of the most able and motivated truck driver to deliver the shipment on time could be frustrated if the driver has to cope with a poorly maintained vehicle.

In the model, performance is connected to outcomes by a wavy line to signify that the expected outcomes do not always result from performance. The employee's satisfaction with the outcomes depends upon his/her perceptions that the outcomes are, in fact, received and are equitably related to the actual level of performance.

The dynamic nature of the process can be seen in Figure 4.1 from the loops formed by the dotted lines that emanate from "performance," "performance $\rightarrow$ outcomes," and "satisfaction." The actual performance that results is a feedback that impacts on the individual's "self-esteem" and becomes part of his/her "past experiences in similar situations"; both factors will serve to confirm or revise the individual's (E $\rightarrow$ P) expectancies. Likewise, the actual outcomes that follow performance will revise the individual's (P $\rightarrow$ O) expectancy, inasmuch as this experience becomes a part of the individual's "past experience in similar situations." Finally, the satisfaction generated by the outcomes has the potential, through the individual's perceptions of the equity of each outcome, to modify his/her valences of the outcomes. The dynamic process underlying the model provides the rationale for varied managerial strategies in effective reward management to improve employee motivation and performance.

Empirical Support for the Expectancy Theory Model

Unlike the content theories, expectancy theory does not take a simplistic approach to human motivation. Expectancy theory is complex and intricate. It is therefore understandable that some practising managers feel intimidated by it. But managers who take a close, serious look at expectancy theory usually find that it recognizes the complexities of work motivation. Its logical and rigorous conceptual framework with strong empirical support enables the manager to better understand the components of motivation and, more importantly, how they relate to one another in the motivational process. The model provides a solid foundation upon which to erect an effective compensation structure. Before considering its practical implications, briefly recall the inferences from the model as far as the compensation system is concerned, and examine whether these inferences have empirical validity.

According to expectancy theory, employees will be motivated to perform at a given level if they believe that a series of conditions exists. These conditions seem so obvious that they tend to be taken for granted. First, employees believe that they have the necessary *skill* or *ability* to perform at the required level. If employees believe otherwise, then no reward will help. Instead, appropriate orientation and training may be the answer. Second, employees believe that the rewards are *contingent upon performance*. In other words, the rewards are directly linked to performance in such a way that a given level of performance is an absolute precondition for receiving the reward. Third, employees *value* the rewards. A valued reward or a reward with a high valence is a reward highly desired by employees, who see it as instrumental in satisfying one or more of their needs. The value of a reward is also affected by employees' perceptions of its equity or fairness, considering their overall efforts relative to the efforts and compensation of their peers. Finally, the reward must be *salient* in the sense that the reward is uppermost in the minds of employees. They must be fully aware of the existence of the reward and the conditions for earning it.

Thus, expectancy theory suggests that the critical attributes (properties) of organizational rewards are *contingency, valence,* and *saliency*. If the rewards are seen by employees in terms of these attributes, then expectancy theory postulates that the rewards will, to the extent of such perceptions, have a significant influence on work motivation. The crucial questions are: Do employees, in fact, see the rewards offered by their organization in terms of these attributes? What kind of influence does each of these attributes have on work motivation?

In an attempt to answer these questions, Kanungo and Hartwick (1987) investigated employees' perceptions of rewards typically offered by organizations. Their study used the following 10 attributes:

1. Is the reward intrinsic (i.e., related to or derived from the task) or extrinsic (i.e., not related to, or not derived from, the task) according to the task criterion?
2. Is the reward intrinsic (i.e., self-administered or self-mediated) or extrinsic (i.e., other-administered or mediated) according to the mediation criterion?
3. Saliency: is the reward salient?
4. Valence: is the reward valued?
5. Is the reward contingent on high performance?
6. Is the reward contingent on low performance?
7. Is the reward considered to be concrete or abstract?
8. The time of administration of the reward: how soon after one's performance is it administered or received (immediate or delayed)?
9. Is the reward given for the mere completion of task activities (desirable task behaviour) or for the successful outcomes of task activities (profit, productivity, etc.)?
10. The frequency of administration: how often is the reward typically used by organizations?

As Guzzo observed, "there is a tremendous variety in the properties of work rewards, and any one reward can be characterized by multiple attributes displayed in varying degrees" (1979, 82). These 10 particular attributes were chosen because both researchers and practitioners alike have used one or more of these attributes to study and manage rewards. An apparent rational basis exists for each of these attributes. Thus, the first 2 attributes correspond to the most popular criteria, task and mediation, for defining intrinsic and extrinsic rewards. The next 4 attributes correspond to the expectancy theory constructs of saliency, valence, and contingency. The next 3 attributes (concreteness, timing, and purpose of the compensation) were included because these have in the past been linked with the intrinsic-extrinsic dichotomy. The last attribute, frequency of administration, captures an important aspect of work rewards not found in the other attributes.

Kanungo and Hartwick (1987) found that rewards are perceived by employees in terms of three distinct dimensions (or clusters of attributes), or that there are three important meaningful ways in which rewards are perceived by employees.

The first and the most important dimension was described as the *high performance contingent, valued, and salient* reward dimension. On this dimension, rewards at one extreme are salient, frequently given to or received by high performers, and highly valued by them. Examples of rewards high on this dimension include pay, promotion, interesting work, and feelings of worthwhile accomplishment. Such rewards, according to expectancy theory, will definitely lead to a strong motivation to perform well at one's tasks. Rewards at the other end of the dimension are less salient, infrequently given to high performers, and less valued. Examples include a paid parking space, cafeteria subsidies, and discounts on the purchase of company products. Such rewards are unlikely to motivate task performance.

The second dimension represented an *intrinsic-extrinsic mediation* dimension. On this dimension, rewards at one extreme are self-administered, abstract, and received during or soon after the completion of the task. Examples include personal challenge, feelings of worthwhile accomplishment, pride in work, and personal growth and development. At the other end of the dimension are rewards that are administered by others for various performance outcomes, are concrete, and are received long after performance. Examples include profit-sharing, promotions, awards for long service, and retirement benefits.

A third dimension was described as *reward generality*. On this dimension, rewards at one extreme are given frequently by organizations regardless of performance, and have little connection with one's work activities. Examples include vacations, coffee breaks, accident and sickness insurance, sick pay, and retirement benefits. Such rewards, then, represent those items generally given to all organization members regardless of performance. Presumably, rewards of this type would tend to give the organization the image of a benefactor in the minds of its employees. At the other end of the dimension are rewards that are less frequently given and are more connected with one's work tasks. Examples include an expense account, use of a company car, and a uniform/clothes allowance. Such rewards are generally given only to those employees whose job functions or status demands it. These external trappings enhance the job status, making it more attractive.

The 10 attributes used in the Kanungo and Hartwick study provided the possibility of three ways to characterize compensation elements. These represent the ways in which employees do, in fact, perceive rewards. However, only one cluster of 3 attributes of rewards emerged to offer an incontrovertible explanation of the way in which employees are in fact motivated by rewards to perform in their jobs. It is significant that these attributes represent the expectancy theory constructs of contingency, saliency, and valence. Therefore, these findings provide a compelling reason to focus on the expectancy theory constructs in the management of employee compensation. Rewards can, of course, be classified in terms of the other two clusters of attributes — the intrinsic-extrinsic mediation dimension, and the reward generality dimension. But the findings show that these clusters ". . .seem to be unrelated to motivational effectiveness, and therefore have minimum practical utility" (Kanungo and Hartwick 1987, 765). From the practical perspective of compensation management, it is of very little consequence in the motivation of work behaviour whether a reward is mediated by oneself or by the other (the second dimension), or whether a reward is received frequently or infrequently (the third dimension). What is of consequence and is therefore critical to work motivation is that the reward be salient, valued, and contingent on a desired work behaviour.

IMPLICATIONS OF THE EXPECTANCY THEORY MODEL FOR REWARD MANAGEMENT

Under expectancy theory, the motivating power of rewards does not reside in the rewards themselves but in a process that reflects employee perceptions and expectations of these rewards, and the connection or tie-up of the rewards with performance. This process is crucial if the reward system is to be effective in motivating behaviour — job performance, organizational tenure or retention, job attendance, personal growth, or skill development. There are four fundamental elements of the process that management ought to initiate and manage. These elements have a direct impact on the compensation system, and offer concrete, practical guidelines for developing the strategies, process, and techniques of the compensation system.

The *first* element of the process is to ensure that employees have the ability to perform the desired behaviour at levels established by the organization. The obvious and logical action would be to select employees who have the knowledge, skills, and abilities for the job. Alternatively, appropriate training should be provided for potential job incumbents. The objective here is to increase the ($E \rightarrow P$) expectancy of the employees, an objective that can also be achieved through the performance management process to be discussed in Chapter 7. In this process supervisors clarify job responsibilities and procedures, provide necessary resources, and act as coaches and mentors to empower the subordinate, that is, to increase the employee's belief in his/her capabilities.

The *second* element of the process is to design and administer rewards that are highly valued by employees. Individuals value outcomes that help to satisfy their salient needs. But different people have different needs at different times. An outcome such as a promotion that is positively valued by one employee may have a negative valence for another if that promotion involves a transfer to another city. When managers recognize this fact, they will be more sensitive to employee needs and will provide, where possible, the most highly valued outcomes. Some companies have adopted a cafeteria-style approach to benefit plans to cater to the specific needs of employees.

However, perceptions of inequity either in the design or administration of a reward play a considerable role in the individual's valence of the reward. There are three types of inequities: individual (or personal), internal, and external. Individual inequity occurs when an employee perceives that his/her compensation does not adequately reflect his/her job performance. This usually happens when no distinction is made between mediocre and outstanding performers in the administration of rewards. Internal inequity arises when employees perceive that the company's pay rates for jobs do not reflect the relative internal value of each job. External inequity results when employees perceive that the company's pay rates do not correspond to those prevailing in the external job market. These inequities can be prevented by sound policies and procedures that are consistently and fairly administered. For example, proper performance appraisals accompanied by a fair merit increase system will ensure individual equity; a sound job evaluation programme with employee involvement in its mechanics as well as its process will contribute to internal equity; finally, salary surveys in the right job markets will help prevent external inequity.

The *third* element of the process is to ensure that the rewards are made contingent on the desired behaviour by directly linking the rewards to the specific behaviour, for example, commission on sales, performance-based pay increments, or promotions. The objective here is to increase the (P $\longrightarrow$ O) expectancy, which, like the increase in valence, can be achieved primarily through the reward system. The compensation philosophy (Chapter 6) and, in particular, performance-based pay (Chapter 8) and incentive system and gain-sharing plans (Chapter 9) are specific vehicles to make rewards contingent.

The *last*, but certainly not the least, important element of the process is to make the reward salient. For saliency to be achieved, the conditions for earning the reward, that is, the performance of specific behaviours, must be clearly spelt out and frequently communicated. A policy statement will help, but deeds speak louder than words. The things management does affect saliency as much as, if not more than, the things it says. For example, if the organization's merit pay policy states that it is to be performance based, but in practice no significant differentiation is made between poor and outstanding performers, saliency will not be ensured.

Expectancy theory is no longer "primarily a theory for the scholar and the scientist rather than for the practitioner . . . It is becoming increasingly evident, though, that applications are possible and that they might well prove very fruitful" (Miner 1980, 160–61). In fact, in addition to providing a basis for *reward design*, the elements of expectancy theory

— in particular, the saliency, valence, and contingency of outcomes — also provide management with the means of *evaluating the effectiveness* of each item of the compensation programme. For example, as discussed in Chapter 14, in one recent application, a diagnostic procedure incorporating expectancy theory constructs proved useful to a Canadian corporation in evaluating the motivational effectiveness of each item of its reward programme consistent with the human resource objectives (Kanungo and Mendonca 1988).

The process approach in the expectancy theory of motivation has the potential to provide sound guidelines for developing effective compensation programmes. This approach is at the very core of the effective reward management model presented in the first chapter. Therefore, every strategy, technique, practice, and process of the compensation system design and its evaluation that will be discussed in the text will flow from, and be judged in the light of, the principles and predictions of this model.

SUMMARY

The process theories provide a more comprehensive explanation of how an individual starts, sustains, directs, and stops work behaviour. The discussion in this chapter focused on equity theory and expectancy theory because of their direct relevance to understanding the role of compensation in the motivational process.

Equity theory explains motivation as an individual's attempt to restore equity or reduce the inequity the individual experiences in the numerous exchanges of the work situation. Individuals determine the equity or fairness of outcomes by comparing the ratio of their outcomes to inputs with the ratio of the outcomes to inputs of relevant other persons. If the ratios are perceived to be equal, then the individuals will experience equity; otherwise, they will experience inequity. The inequity generates feelings of guilt if individuals perceive that they are overpaid; and feelings of anger if they believe that they are underpaid. To restore equity or to reduce inequity, individuals can adopt a variety of strategies, for example, increasing or decreasing own inputs, increasing outcomes, cognitively distorting own or other's inputs or outcomes, changing the comparison other, or leaving the field.

In the area of compensation, equity plays a central role. Organizations strive for internal, external, and personal or individual equity. Internal equity is achieved when the basic pay structure reflects the value of the job. External equity is achieved when the compensation system reflects the wage rates of the relevant labour market. Personal or individual equity is achieved when the compensation reflects the individual's job performance. When individuals perceive inequity in any one or more of these areas, they will experience dissatisfaction with the compensation system. Such dissatisfaction will have an impact on the individual's work motivation.

Expectancy theory postulates that individuals will exert the effort to perform if they believe that their efforts will lead to the required level of performance [(E ⟶ P) expectancy], that the performance will result in outcomes [(P ⟶ O) expectancy], and that they positively value the outcomes [Valence of outcomes]. The expectancy theory model for reward management presented in this chapter incorporates the basic elements of expectancy theory as well as the determinants of each element, including equity theory's explanation of the satisfaction/dissatisfaction of outcomes. The model thus provides a more comprehensive explanation of both the what and the how of the motivational process.

The chapter examined the effort-performance, performance-outcomes, and valence expectancies; explored the dynamic process underlying the model and demonstrated how its different stages contribute to the individual's repertoire of expectancies and valence of outcomes; and showed the impact this contribution has on the individual's motivation to put in the effort to perform. The chapter also considered the moderators that either facilitate or hinder the effort resulting in performance. It was seen that the model is constructed on a sound conceptual foundation and has strong empirical support. But the model is not meant exclusively for research pursuits; its theoretical soundness makes it immensely practical. The conceptual framework of the model places at the manager's disposal a set of strategies that can confidently be adopted to enhance employee motivation and performance. The compensation specialist will find in the model a sure guide for effective compensation programmes, strategies, techniques, practices, and processes.

KEY TERMS

(E ⟶ P) expectancy
(P ⟶ O) expectancy
contingency
equity theory
expectancy theory
external equity
inputs-outcomes ratio
internal equity
personal or individual equity
relevant other person
saliency
valence

REVIEW AND DISCUSSION QUESTIONS

1. Carole Shaw was quite excited about her new job. After working for about a year, however, she discovered the following about her job and base pay:

    a) The base pay of her job is less than the base pay of the other jobs in the company that she has reason to believe are similar to hers.

    b) The base pay of her job is less than the base pay of the other jobs in the company that she has reason to believe are identical to hers.

    c) The base pay of her job is less than the base pay of the identical job in other companies.

    In which of these scenarios will Carole experience (i) the *most* dissatisfaction and (ii) the *least* dissatisfaction? Explain your responses with reference to the elements and the process of equity theory.

2. Recall a part-time or full-time job and answer the following questions with reference to that job:

    a) What motivated you to accept the job, that is, to put in the effort to perform on the job?
    Respond to this question by examining your (E ⟶ P), (P ⟶ O), and (V) expectancies while you were considering whether you should accept the job. Specifically, explore the determinant of each expectancy:

    - Was (E ⟶ P) high because of past experiences, actual situation, communications from others, self-esteem?
    - Was (P ⟶ O) high because of past experiences, actual situation, communications from others, and so forth?
    - Was (V) high because of a belief that outcomes will satisfy needs, and will be equitable?

    b) Assume you performed well on the job. What contributed to the high level of performance resulting from your effort? Respond to this question by exploring the moderators of ability and situational factors. Perhaps you had the ability, or the ability was enhanced by training; perhaps the situational factors were positive, that is, there were no obstacles to impede your performance.

    c) Assume that at the end of some period you received outcomes with which you were satisfied. What contributed to your satisfaction with the outcomes? Respond to this question by exploring the moderator of equity.

3. Refer to the experience you reflected upon in question 2. In the context of the implications of the expectancy theory model for reward management discussed in the chapter, think of specific actions the manager might have taken to increase your motivation to perform.
4. What are the key findings of the Kanungo and Hartwick (1987) study? Explain how these findings provide empirical support for the expectancy theory model.

EXERCISE: THE PRACTICAL IMPLICATIONS OF EXPECTANCY THEORY

Objective

To experience the process of expectancy theory. The exercise will enable you to determine how motivated you are to put in the effort to pursue a career (job) that is assigned to you.

Procedure

1. Divide the class into groups of about four or five participants.
2. Assign to each group one of the following jobs/careers:
   - high school teacher
   - assembly-line operator
   - travelling salesperson
   - computer programmer
   - truck driver
   - administrative assistant
   - human resource specialist/generalist
   - independent business entrepreneur
3. Keeping the assigned job/career in mind, each participant, working individually, responds to questions 1, 2, and 3 on the worksheet below and then completes the score-sheet to obtain his/her motivational force to put in the effort to pursue the assigned job/career.
4. Group discussion: The objective of the discussion is to understand the determinants of the expectancies of individuals in respect of the assigned job/career. The discussion could include

   a) the identification of similarities/differences in the motivational force score (MFS) of the group members.

   b) an exploration of the reasons for the similarities/differences. Consider the following issues:

   Re: question 1:
   Why do some more than others believe that they can do the assigned job/career? Is this because of
   —good grades in school?
   —success in past jobs? success in voluntary service projects?
   —specialized education and training?
   —role model in the family? in the community?
   —any other factor that enhanced the individual's self-efficacy belief?

Re: question 2:
Why do different individuals place different values on the listed outcomes? Is this because of
—a difference in needs?
—a difference in the sense or standard of equity or fairness?

Re: question 3:
Why do some more than others believe that if they perform the assigned job/career they will receive all or some of the listed outcomes? Is this because of
—past experiences? Did they always receive the expected outcomes/rewards?
—the assumption that such outcomes/rewards are naturally associated with the assigned job/career?
—the observed or narrated experiences of others? Did they see or were they told that such outcomes /rewards were associated with the assigned job/career? Did the knowledge of these experiences enhance their general belief that organizations honour their reward commitments to their employees?

5. Class discussion: Some areas to focus on include

- the determinants of the expectancies;
- the relationship between the MFS and actual performance. Assuming an individual has a high MFS, does this mean that the effort he/she puts in will, in fact, result in the expected level of performance? This question will uncover the role of the moderators in the expectancy theory model.
- Whether performance always lead to satisfaction with the outcomes received from that performance. Why or why not?
- Whether a person can have a high valence for a given outcome and a low feeling of equity for that outcome. Why?

Table 4.1.1
Expectancy Theory Worksheet

Question 1

Do you think that your hard work now as a student, your past jobs, life experiences, and so forth, will lead you to believe that you are likely to be successful in the assigned job/career? In other words, do you believe that if you put in the effort in the assigned job/career, that effort will likely lead to performance?

No chance at all					Possible					Absolutely certain
0	.1	.2	.3	.4	.5	.6	.7	.8	.9	1

Question 2

Below is a list of outcomes that may accompany or may be received in jobs/careers. How likely is it that each of these outcomes will be realized (received) in the assigned job/career? In other words, how likely is it that performance in the assigned job/career will lead to each outcome?

	No chance at all … Absolutely certain
a) Security (permanent job, steady work)	0 .1 .2 .3 .4 .5 .6 .7 .8 .9 1
b) Earnings (for a better standard of living)	0 .1 .2 .3 .4 .5 .6 .7 .8 .9 1
c) Merit pay (for high job performance)	0 .1 .2 .3 .4 .5 .6 .7 .8 .9 1
d) Benefits (vacations, pension, insurance, dental and medical benefits, etc.)	0 .1 .2 .3 .4 .5 .6 .7 .8 .9 1
e) Working conditions (pleasant surroundings, adequate and air-conditioned office space)	0 .1 .2 .3 .4 .5 .6 .7 .8 .9 1
f) Long working hours and frequent and extensive business trips, leaving no time for family/social life	0 .1 .2 .3 .4 .5 .6 .7 .8 .9 1
g) A high level of personal stress and/or financial risk	0 .1 .2 .3 .4 .5 .6 .7 .8 .9 1
h) Responsibility and independence (to work in your own way)	0 .1 .2 .3 .4 .5 .6 .7 .8 .9 1
i) Achievement (opportunity to achieve excellence in your work)	0 .1 .2 .3 .4 .5 .6 .7 .8 .9 1
j) Opportunity for growth (professionally; to become more skilled and competent on the job)	0 .1 .2 .3 .4 .5 .6 .7 .8 .9 1

Question 3

Below is a list of possible outcomes that can accompany or be received in jobs/careers. How favourable or unfavourable is each of the following outcomes to you personally? In other words, what kind of value do you place on each?

	Very unfavourable										Very favourable
a) Security (permanent job, steady work)	−1	−.8	−.6	−.4	−.2	0	.2	.4	.6	.8	1
b) Earnings (for a better standard of living)	−1	−.8	−.6	−.4	−.2	0	.2	.4	.6	.8	1
c) Merit pay (for high job performance)	−1	−.8	−.6	−.4	−.2	0	.2	.4	.6	.8	1
d) Benefits (vacations, pension, insurance, dental and medical benefits, etc.)	−1	−.8	−.6	−.4	−.2	0	.2	.4	.6	.8	1
e) Working conditions (pleasant surroundings, adequate and air-conditioned office space)	−1	−.8	−.6	−.4	−.2	0	.2	.4	.6	.8	1
f) Long working hours and frequent and extensive business trips, leaving no time for family/social life	−1	−.8	−.6	−.4	−.2	0	.2	.4	.6	.8	1
g) A high level of personal stress and/or financial risk	−1	−.8	−.6	−.4	−.2	0	.2	.4	.6	.8	1
h) Responsibility and independence (to work in your own way)	−1	−.8	−.6	−.4	−.2	0	.2	.4	.6	.8	1
i) Achievement (opportunity to achieve excellence in your work)	−1	−.8	−.6	−.4	−.2	0	.2	.4	.6	.8	1
j) Opportunity for growth (professionally; to become more skilled and competent on the job)	−1	−.8	−.6	−.4	−.2	0	.2	.4	.6	.8	1

Continued on next page

MOTIVATIONAL FORCE SCORE (MFS) SCORING INSTRUCTIONS AND SCORE-SHEET

To compute your motivational force score (MFS), proceed as follows:

Step 1: Refer to your response to question 1. Your response to this question provides an indication of your effort → performance expectancy for your assigned job. Suppose your response was .3. This measure is your belief that if you work at that job (i.e., put in the effort today), it is most unlikely that you will succeed in that job (i.e., reach the required performance level). Your response is a statement that says: "Yes, I think I can perform that job," or "No, I do not think I can perform that job," or any other belief level in between these two extremes.

Enter your response as the (E → P) score in the score-sheet.

Step 2: Refer to your response to question 2. Your response provides an indication of your performance → outcome expectancy for a given set of outcomes in the assigned job. The response for each outcome represents your belief that you will receive or not receive the outcome when you perform in the assigned job. In reality there may be more or a different set of outcomes to consider. Only a few have been chosen for this exercise.

Enter your response for each outcome (*a* to *j*) in the (P → O) column of the score-sheet.

Step 3: Refer to your responses to question 3. Your responses indicate the value you place on each outcome. It is your measure of the valence of each outcome. You could place a positive, neutral, or negative value for each outcome.

Enter your response for each outcome (*a* to *j*) in the Valence column of the score-sheet.

Step 4: According to expectancy theory, the motivational force score is obtained by the following formula:

$(E \rightarrow P) \times [(P \rightarrow O) \times (V)]$

You will multiply the (P → O) expectancy for each outcome by its corresponding valence. The sum of the products is then multiplied by the (E → P) expectancy. Complete the arithmetic in the manner laid out in the score-sheet to obtain the motivational force score. This score tells you how motivated you are *at this time* to put in the effort to pursue or accept the job assigned to you in the context of the outcomes spelt out for you. The value of the MFS is out of a possible value range of 0 to 10, with 0 = a low motivational force, and 10 = a high motivational force.

Score-Sheet

(E → P) expectancy, that is, score of Q. 1 ______________ (A)

(P → O) expectancy Q. 2 Scores		Valence Q. 3 Scores		Product of (P → O) (V)
a) ______________	×	______________	=	______________
b) ______________	×	______________	=	______________
c) ______________	×	______________	=	______________
d) ______________	×	______________	=	______________
e) ______________	×	______________	=	______________
f) ______________	×	______________	=	______________
g) ______________	×	______________	=	______________
h) ______________	×	______________	=	______________
i) ______________	×	______________	=	______________
j) ______________	×	______________	=	______________

Sum of products of [(P → O) (V)] = ______________ (B)

Motivational force score (MFS)	= {(E →	Σ [(P → O) (V)]}
	= (A)	× (B)
	= ________	× ________
	= ______________	

CHAPTER 5

SATISFACTION WITH PAY AND NON-ECONOMIC OUTCOMES

CHAPTER SYNOPSIS

An employee's satisfaction or dissatisfaction with a reward item can greatly enhance or impair the motivational effectiveness of that item. The comprehensive motivational model discussed in the previous chapter provides a conceptually sound but rather general explanation for an individual's satisfaction or dissatisfaction with outcomes, and the consequences for the individual's work motivation This chapter probes the satisfaction issue in some detail through a focus on pay, the major item of an organization's compensation system. Specifically, the chapter addresses three important questions: What factors contribute to or determine an employee's satisfaction with his/her pay? What are the consequences to the organization of the employee's dissatisfaction with his/her pay? What are some practical guidelines for enhancing pay satisfaction? The non-economic outcomes generated by the job content through the process of job design have been found to play a critical role not only in determining pay satisfaction, but also in moderating the consequences of pay dissatisfaction. The chapter will therefore examine the theory and the process of job design, which the organization can use to increase the non-economic outcomes component of the compensation system.

LEARNING OBJECTIVES

- To understand the meaning of *satisfaction*, which is derived from a combination of notions from equity theory and discrepancy theory.
- To understand the elements and the process of the determinants of the pay satisfaction model, with a special emphasis on the critical notion of social comparison.

- To identify the components of person-related, job-related, referent-other-related, and context-related factors, and to learn how these factors influence an individual's satisfaction with his/her pay.
- To understand the process of the consequences of pay dissatisfaction model.
- To identify the components of job context factors, job content factors, and external environmental factors, and to explain how these factors moderate the consequences of pay dissatisfaction.
- To learn how to use the practical guidelines for increasing pay satisfaction that flow from the determinants of pay satisfaction and the consequences of pay dissatisfaction models.
- To understand the nature, objective, and consequences of the classical approach to job design.
- To understand the nature and objective of the approach of the growth theories of Herzberg and Maslow to job design.
- To distinguish between the classical and growth theories approaches to job design.
- To understand the elements and the process of Hackman and Oldham's (1980) job characteristics model.
- To learn how the job characteristics model can be used to generate non-economic outcomes.

INTRODUCTION

From the discussion of expectancy theory, it can be seen that its basic elements — effort-to-performance expectancy, and the saliency, valence, and contingency of rewards — have a direct influence on employee motivation, and provide practical guidelines for rewards management. A compensation system that does not respect these guidelines is not effective in motivating employees towards the desired work behaviours. As a result, the organization is placed in triple jeopardy. First, the ability of the organization to function effectively through the high performance of its employees is seriously impaired. Second, to the extent that the compensation items are unsuccessful in promoting the desired work behaviours, the dollars expended on these items are a waste of scarce, valuable resources of the organization. Third, the employee dissatisfaction that results from such a reward system also produces consequences ranging from poor organizational performance to job dissatisfaction and turnover. An exploration of the issue of employee dissatisfaction with one or more of the reward items promotes awareness of the critical aspects that contribute to dissatisfaction, of the consequences that result from dissatisfaction, and of the factors that are likely to contribute to satisfaction or dissatisfaction with the compensation system.

At the present time the only systematic approaches to reward satisfaction and dissatisfaction that have some relevance for management practice are Lawler's (1971) models on the determinants of pay satisfaction and the consequences of pay dissatisfaction. These models focus exclusively on pay and do not consider the other compensation items. Nevertheless, these models are useful to compensation managers for two reasons. First, pay is the largest component of the reward system and constitutes from 50 to 75 per cent of the total operating costs of the organization. Second, the models illustrate the fact that satisfaction or dissatisfaction with a compensation item, and the resulting consequences, can be anticipated and incorporated in the design and administration of that compensation item. These models are discussed in the next section. In view of the dominant role of job content factors in moderating pay satisfaction, this chapter concludes with a discussion of the place of job design in the compensation system.

SATISFACTION WITH PAY

The psychological phenomenon of satisfaction has been dealt with by fulfilment theory, discrepancy theory, and equity theory. According to fulfilment theory, satisfaction results when one's needs are fulfilled. In the work context, fulfilment theory predicts that an employee who receives a greater amount of positively valued outcomes will fulfil his/her needs to a relatively greater extent and will therefore be more satisfied than an employee who receives a lesser quantity of the positively valued outcomes. It has frequently been found, however, that this proposition does not reflect the reality. For example, it is common to see an employee perfectly contented with an annual salary of $50,000 and another employee in the same organization totally dissatisfied with annual salary of $100,000. An insight into this anomaly is provided by a version of discrepancy theory that defines satisfaction as the perceived discrepancy between what one has received and what one believes one should receive. Thus, the employee with an annual salary of $50,000 is contented because that employee does not perceive any discrepancy between the amount received and the amount that should have been received. On the other hand, the employee with an annual salary of $100,000 might be dissatisfied because he/she perceives to be inequitable the discrepancy between the amount received and the amount to which he/she was entitled. But how does an individual determine what is fair and equitable? This question is addressed by equity theory.

According to equity theory, feelings of equity or inequity are generated by the individual's perceptions of his/her outcomes-inputs ratio and the outcomes-inputs ratio of the person with whom the comparison is being made. When these ratios are perceived to be equal, the individual regards the outcomes to be equitable and is satisfied with them. On the other hand, when these ratios are perceived to be unequal, the individual regards the outcomes to be inequitable or unfair and is therefore dissatisfied with them. Equity theory, then, leads to an understanding of the pay satisfaction of the employee earning the $50,000 and the pay dissatisfaction of the employee earning $100,000. The satisfied employee perceives his/her own and the relevant other's outcomes-inputs ratios to be equal; the dissatisfied employee perceives those ratios to be unequal. Unlike discrepancy theory, equity theory explains satisfaction through the use of *social comparison* and the individual's perceptions of the outcomes-inputs ratios. Discrepancy theory explains satisfaction through the *difference* in perceptions between what the outcome is and what it should be.

Combining the notion of social comparison (from equity theory) and the notion of difference in perceptions of what is and what should be (from discrepancy theory), Lawler (1971) concluded that an employee's satisfaction with pay is the difference between his/her perceptions of the *amount of pay received* and of the *amount of pay that should be received*. When the two perceptions are equal, the employee experiences pay satisfaction; when they are unequal, the employee experiences pay dissatisfaction. What then are the factors that influence the employee's perceptions of the amount of pay received and the amount of pay that should be received? In other words, what are the determinants of the employee perceptions that promote pay satisfaction? And what are the consequences of pay dissatisfaction? These questions are addressed in the next two sections.

DETERMINANTS OF PAY SATISFACTION

According to the model (Figure 5.1), the two sets of employee perceptions, the amount of pay received and the amount of pay that should be received, can be explained by a combination of four categories of variables: person-related, job-related, referent-other-related, and context-related. A proper understanding of the component elements of each category of variables and their impact on pay satisfaction is essential for the successful management of the several design and administrative issues in compensation.

Person-related Variables

This category can include a variety of inputs that an employee brings to the job, for example, knowledge, skills, and abilities; specialized training;

Figure 5.1
Determinants of Pay Satisfaction

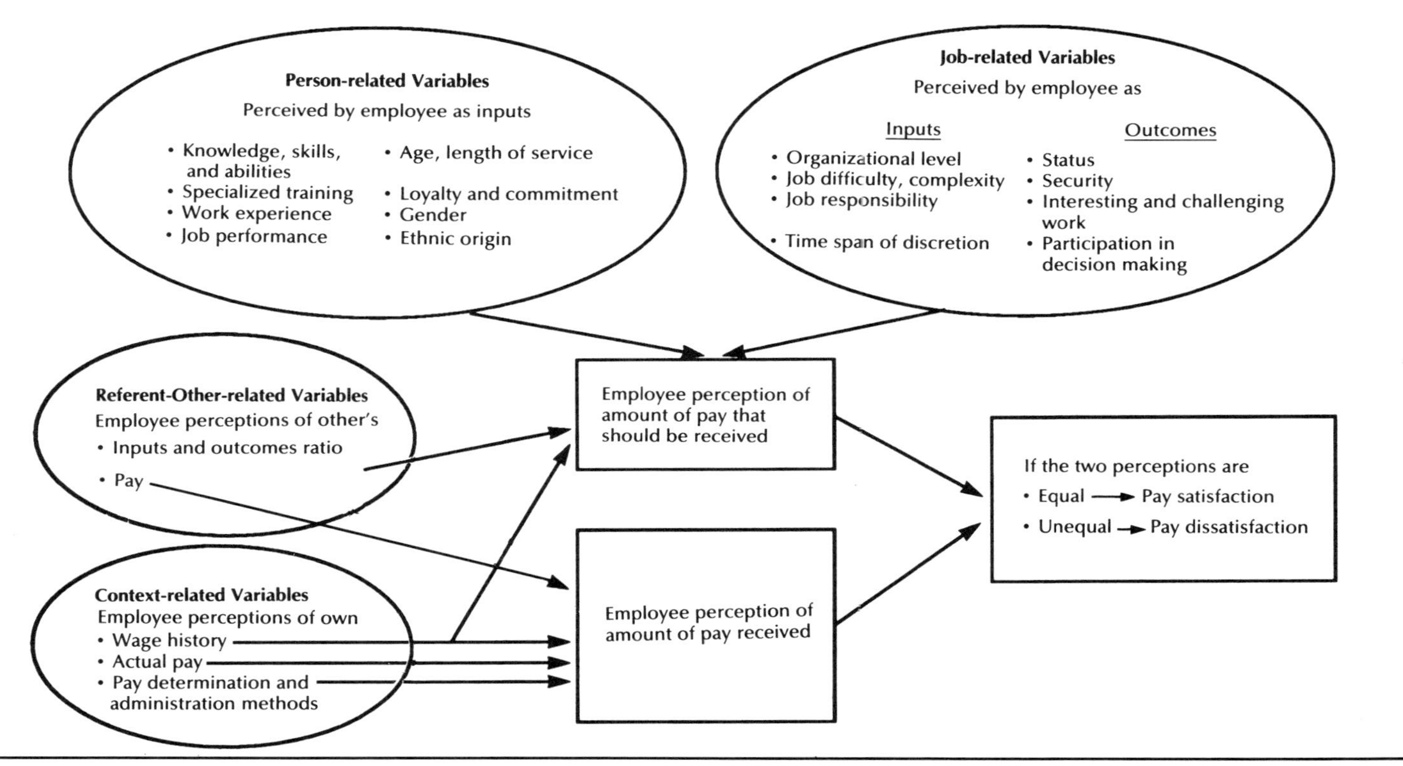

SOURCE: Adapted from Lawler (1971).

work experience; job performance; age, length of service; gender, ethnic origin; loyalty, commitment to the organization.

The research evidence reviewed by Lawler (1971) suggests that education, skills and abilities, and job performance are significant variables that must be recognized in the determination of the level of pay. It would seem logical and in accord with the norms of natural justice that employees would expect their pay to reflect these personal inputs. For example, an employee with a higher educational level or a recognized competence in a skill will expect to be paid more than another employee with a lower educational level or a lower level of competence in the required job skill. Similarly, employees who perceive that their job performance is superior to that of their peers will expect to be rewarded for this superior performance, that is, to receive a merit pay higher than that of mediocre or poor-performing employees. If pay does not reflect the qualitative and quantitative inputs that an employee brings to a job, then the employee will inevitably tend to experience greater pay dissatisfaction. Of course, it must be recognized that the actual pay dissatisfaction experienced by an employee will depend on the importance that the employee attributes to a particular input.

There is no conclusive evidence that age and length of service (i.e., seniority) are significant input variables, in the sense that they would cause employees to be dissatisfied with their pay if pay did not reflect these inputs. It must be recognized, however, that age and seniority may be culture-bound factors; that is, in certain cultures, age and seniority may be considered to be significant input variables. In such cultures, employees will be dissatisfied with their pay if it does not reflect age and seniority.

The employee's gender and ethnic origin are not inputs as such, but are employee characteristics that can moderate the influence of the variables known to determine pay satisfaction. For example, Kanungo (1975) found that women relative to men employees in Quebec were more satisfied with their pay; similarly, francophone relative to anglophone employees in Quebec were more satisfied with their pay. Perhaps both groups of employees, women and francophones, had lower expectations of pay. The experience of highly qualified new immigrants who are satisfied with their relatively lower level of pay could also be cited. Their euphoria at having been accepted in the country of their adoption tends to moderate on the lower side, initially at least, the pay level they expect for their high qualifications.

With regard to the other inputs, loyalty and commitment, no specific studies linking these factors to pay have been reported. However, it would not be unreasonable to speculate that an employee might perceive these inputs to be important enough to justify a higher pay, and might experience dissatisfaction if this expectation is unfulfilled.

Job-related Variables

This category includes factors perceived by the employee as inputs, and factors perceived by the employee as outcomes from the job. Examples of job-related inputs are characteristics of the job, for example, the job level in the organization's hierarchical structure; and the nature of the job in terms of the level of difficulty, complexity, responsibility, and time span of discretion (or degree of autonomy in making decisions on the job). Examples of job-related outcomes are job status and security, interesting and challenging work, opportunity for participation in decision making. These are commonly referred to as non-economic outcomes.

Employees in jobs at a higher level in the hierarchy will expect to be paid more than employees in jobs at a lower level of the organization's hierarchy. For example, senior managers expect to be paid more than middle managers, who in turn expect to be paid more than first-line supervisors. Likewise, employees in jobs that involve a relatively greater level of difficulty, complexity, or responsibility expect to be paid more than employees in jobs with a lower level of difficulty, complexity, or responsibility. A situation is *difficult* if the job incumbent is required to function with relatively less adequate or insufficient resources or support systems, or the job tasks themselves place relatively more stress on the job incumbent. By *complexity* is meant that the job demands the utilization of a variety of skills. For example, the job of a manager in a fast-food outlet is relatively more complex than the job of a cook. The manager's job calls for the exercise of conceptual, interpersonal, and leadership skills. Likewise an employee in a job with a longer time span of discretion expects to be paid more than an employee in a job with a relatively shorter time span of discretion. The *time span of discretion* is "that maximum period of time during which an employee can exercise responsibility, make decisions, and initiate activities on the basis of his own discretion without reporting to his supervisor for concurrence, approval, or review" (Dunn and Rachel 1971, 317). To summarize, employees in higher-level jobs, in jobs of greater difficulty, complexity, responsibility, or in jobs with a longer time span of discretion perceive that they contribute relatively more in terms of inputs and therefore expect in return relatively more pay. When the pay fails to reflect these inputs, the employee will experience pay dissatisfaction.

However, there are job-related variables that also function as *outcomes*. If, for example, the need for self-esteem is high in an employee, that employee will likely value any outcome — pay, status, or promotion — that satisfies that need. If the self-esteem need is met by a job perceived by the employee to be of high status, then to that extent the employee will not seek pay to satisfy this need. Consequently, the employee will likely not expect more pay. The underlying rationale is that pay is one of the many outcomes received by employees. When employees perceive other outcomes to be more instrumental than pay in satisfying a need, then employees will value the other outcomes more than pay. Such employees will not be dissatisfied with a lower pay when the other more valued outcomes are provided. For example, in periods of severe unemployment, employees tend to prefer the outcome of job security to that of higher pay. Likewise, it is not uncommon to find employees with high growth needs accepting jobs in an organization with relatively lower pay, because the jobs offer opportunities for challenging and interesting work, or greater participation in decision making. To summarize, when employees perceive that non-economic outcomes satisfy their important and salient needs better than pay, then to that extent employees will not be dissatisfied with pay. Their perceptions of the amount of pay that should be received will tend to be low. Other things being equal, the non-economic outcomes, when they are regarded as a substitute for pay, will promote pay satisfaction.

Referent-Other-related Variables

The term *referent-other* has the same meaning as, and is used synonymously with, the term *relevant other person* discussed under equity theory. This category includes employee perceptions of relevant other persons' inputs and outcomes, and employee perceptions of pay received by relevant other persons.

It will be recalled that in equity theory the employee's determination of equity or inequity is based on the comparison of the employee's perceptions of his/her own inputs-outcomes ratio with his/her perceptions of the inputs-outcomes ratio of the relevant other person. When equity theory is applied to pay, the employee's perception of the amount of pay that should be received will be influenced by his/her perceptions of the outcomes the relevant other person will likely receive relative to that person's inputs. For example, Elijah perceives that his colleague Melanie is likely to receive the following set of outcomes: a pay raise of $3,000, special recognition from the department head, and preferential treatment in the choice of assignments. Elijah recognizes that Melanie has specialized training, but that he has substantially more work experience and has put in a consistently superior job performance. Based on this assessment of Melanie's inputs-outcomes ratio relative to his own, Elijah develops an expectation of a pay raise of $4,500. It can thus be seen how an employee's perceptions of the relevant other person's inputs-outcomes ratio relative to his/her own will influence the amount of pay that should be received.

The other variable in this category, employee perceptions of the pay received by the relevant other person, has a direct impact on the employee's perception of the amount of pay received. Elijah believed that a pay raise of $4,500 would be equitable. Assume that Elijah receives the expected $4,500. Assume also that Elijah perceives that the actual pay raise received by Melanie is not the $4,000 that Elijah had earlier believed that Melanie would receive, but $4,200. *Before* Elijah formed any perceptions of Melanie's actual pay raise, Elijah had attributed a certain value to his actual pay raise of $4,500. As discussed in the previous paragraph, this value or valence resulted from, among other factors, a comparison of Elijah's perceptions of his inputs-outcomes ratio and his perception of Melanie's inputs-outcomes ratio. The valence was also based on what Elijah believed the $4,500 would fetch him in terms of the goods and services he needed. The reference here is to the instrumentality-of-the-outcome determinant of valence as postulated by expectancy theory. *After* Elijah perceives that Melanie's actual pay raise is $4,200, the value or valence he attributes to his $4,500 undergoes a change. The $4,500 will now have a relatively lower value or valence for Elijah. True, Elijah's $4,500 can and will still buy the same quantity of goods and services, regardless of what Melanie actually receives. In other words, the potential instrumentality of the $4,500 to satisfy certain needs is undiminished. What, then, is the reason for Elijah's lower valence of the $4,500? The answer is to be found in the expectancy theory model. As will be recalled from the model, valence is determined by both the instrumentality to satisfy needs *and* the equity of outcomes. The inequity of outcomes, which he perceives relative to Melanie, explains why Elijah now values the $4,500 much less than he did before his perceptions of Melanie's actual pay raise.

The discussion of the referent-other-related variables strongly underscores the significant and powerful effect of the notion of social comparison as a determinant of pay satisfaction, and the profound practical implications that flow from it.

Context-related Variables

These variables concern the outcomes the employee receives from the job context. The critical factors that affect pay satisfaction in this category are employee perceptions of the pay received in the past (wage history), the actual pay now received, and the methods of pay determination and administration.

The employee's perceptions of his/her wage history affect pay satisfaction by influencing employee perceptions of the amount of pay that should be received, and also of the amount of pay received. For example, employees who have had a record of high salaries and pay raises will generally expect their present pay to be consistent with that record of high salaries and pay raises. In other words, their high wage history leads to higher expectations, which influence their perceptions of the amount of pay that should be received. This phenomenon is similar to that of university students with a past record of a high cumulative grade point averages who develop higher expectations for their present course grades. The high wage history also affects employee perceptions of the amount of pay received. Employees who have had a high pay history tend to perceive their present pay as low. The magnitude of the dollars involved is viewed through the perspective of past pay history. Therefore, for the reasons discussed here, the higher the past pay level, the greater the pay dissatisfaction will be unless the amount of pay now received is also high, consistent with the expectations generated by the high wage history.

The actual pay received is, of course, the direct source of the employee's perception of the amount of pay received. The larger the amount of current pay, the greater is the pay satisfaction. The methods of pay determination and administration also affect pay satisfaction. For example, performance-based pay will be perceived as equitable if it is determined by a fair performance appraisal system, and administered by a process that is open rather than secret, and involves the employees concerned. In other words, pay ought to be determined and administered in a manner that permits the employee to see a linkage between pay and performance, that is, the (P ⟶ O) relationship of expectancy theory. When pay determination and administration methods enable employees to see clearly the performance-outcomes linkage, then employees are found to experience greater pay satisfaction (Lawler 1966).

To summarize, each of the four sets of variables determines pay satisfaction by its influence on employee perceptions of either the amount of pay that should be received or the amount of pay received or both. The person-related variables function as inputs. The more of these inputs the employee brings to the job, the greater the employee's expectations that he/she should receive more pay. Hence, the person-related variables are more likely to cause pay dissatisfaction. The job-related variables include some factors that function as inputs and other factors that function as outcomes. If the employee perceives his/her job to have more of the input factors, then he/she will have greater expectations that he/she should receive more pay. The input factors, therefore, are more likely to cause pay dissatisfaction. The outcome factors (e.g., job status, challenge) will, on the other hand, serve to generate satisfaction with the level of pay even if it is low, because the more of these non-economic factors are perceived by employees to exist in the job, the more tolerant they will be of lower levels of pay. These outcomes are often perceived as acceptable substitutes for pay.

The referent-other-related variables operate either to increase or to decrease pay satisfaction. When the employee compares his/her perceptions of the inputs-outcomes ratios (own and those of the relevant other person), such a comparison could lead to an expectation of more pay or less pay. Likewise, the employee's perceptions of the relevant other person's actual pay could lead to an increase or decrease in the value attributed to his/her pay. Therefore, both factors have the potential either to promote pay satisfaction or to cause pay dissatisfaction. The last set of variables, the context-related variables, operates in two ways. The employee's wage history functions as an input. A past record of high salaries and pay raises will lead the employee to expect more pay. A high-wage history, therefore, has the potential to generate pay dissatisfaction. Depending upon employee perceptions of the other factors, the actual pay, both in terms of its size and the methods by which it is determined and administered, has the potential to promote either pay satisfaction or pay dissatisfaction.

This section concludes with two observations that have already been mentioned but need to be reiterated. First, the elements of the model and its underlying process are essentially based on the perceptions of the employee. Second, the notion of social comparison is absolutely critical to the model. In a study by Shapiro and Wahba (1978), social comparison, actual pay, and wage history were the significant factors that explained the variance in pay satisfaction. From these observations flow several implications of practical interest to the compensation specialist and to managers. An in-depth treatment of these implications will be undertaken when the techniques, methods, and processes of the compensation system are considered. These observations do, however, reinforce the point that the effectiveness of the compensation system depends on the extent to which it takes into consideration and responds to the perceptions and expectations of the individual employee.

Consequences of Pay Dissatisfaction

What are the consequences of pay dissatisfaction? If this question were posed to ten managers, more than ten different answers might result, including low productivity; poor quality of products and service; high reject rates and wastage; unnecessary overtime; tighter supervisory controls; low morale and turned-off employees; strikes; attempts to unionize; high grievance rates; job dissatisfaction; pilferage and vandalism; tardiness, absenteeism, and turnover; psychological withdrawal and poor mental health. The answers of all ten managers would be right, because the managers would have witnessed such events when, for one reason or another, they could not satisfy an employee's desire or demand for more pay, or when an employee felt unfairly treated in the matter of a pay raise relative to the pay raise of a colleague. This question of pay dissatisfaction needs to be addressed because of the implication that huge expenditures on pay appear to be futile and fruitless. Besides, the consequences weaken the organization and sometimes threaten its very survival. It is an irony that expenditures such as pay, which are intended to motivate employee work behaviours towards organizational objectives, can themselves become the cause of work behaviours that frustrate, if not thwart, the objectives of the organization.

How is pay dissatisfaction related to the consequences attributed to it? Lawler (1971) proposed a model of the consequences of pay dissatisfaction (see box A and box B in Figure 5.2). According to this model, when employees experience pay dissatisfaction, the numerous consequences — including tardiness, absenteeism, and turnover — usually attributed to pay dissatisfaction do not automatically follow. Instead, the model posits that (1) employees experience a desire for more pay, or (2) employees find the job to be less attractive.

FIGURE 5.2
CONSEQUENCES OF PAY DISSATISFACTION

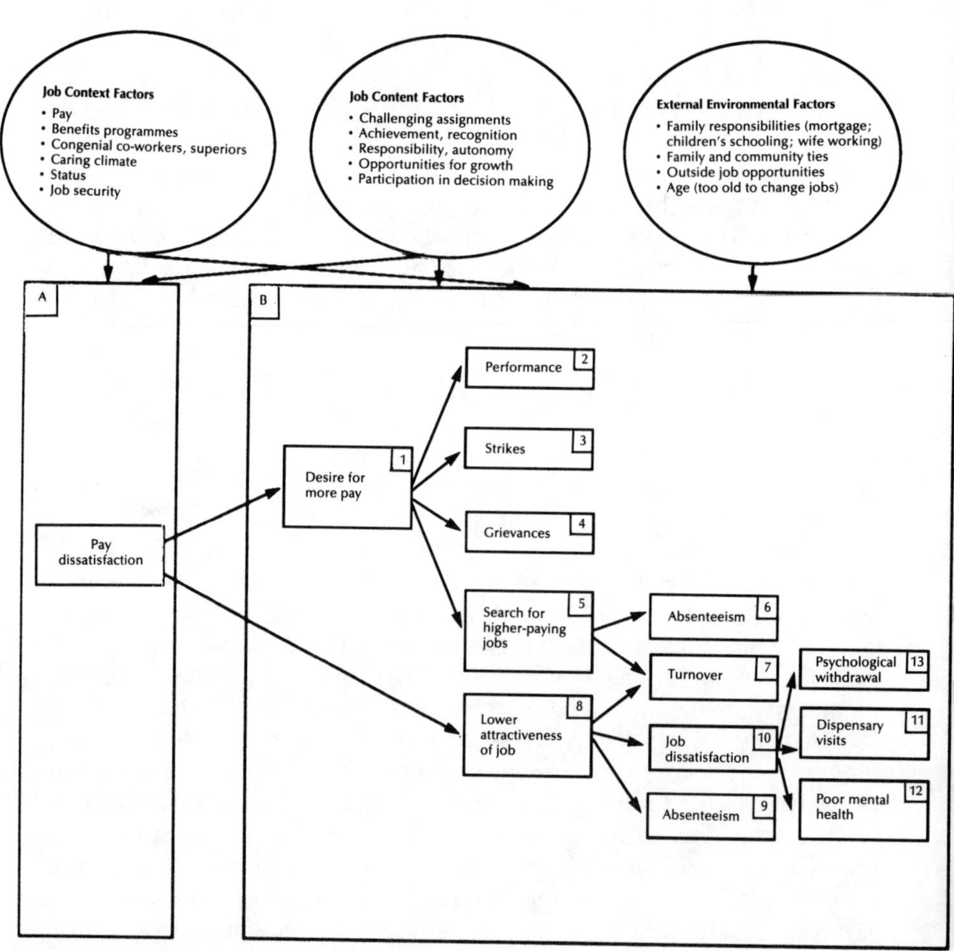

SOURCE: Adapted from Lawler (1971).

Let us pursue the first scenario: employees experience a desire for more pay (box 1). In this scenario, employees will be motivated to increase their performance, rather than lower it, *if* the compensation system is designed to pay for performance (box 2). If pay is not performance based, then employees will not be able to satisfy their desire for more pay by increasing or improving their performance. In such an event, employees will pursue other options to obtain more pay. Such options include union pressures on management, which if unsuccessful may eventually result in a strike (box 3); grievances filed by employees in an attempt to demonstrate their dissatisfaction (box 4); or a search for a higher-paying job (box 5). This last action would, acording to the model, lead to absenteeism (box 6) and possibly turnover (box 7). The reason for the absenteeism is that the employee must be absent as he/she explores job opportunities and attends interviews with placement agencies or prospective employers. If the search efforts prove successful, there will be turnover. Thus, in the first scenario, turnover would appear to be a measure of last resort.

In the second scenario, pay dissatisfaction is postulated to lead to a lower attractiveness of the job (box 8). The lower rewards attached to the job do not make it attractive any more. The employee's efforts in this situation are directed towards looking elsewhere for a job. The search efforts lead to absenteeism (box 9) and, if successful, to turnover (box 7). The employee could also use absenteeism as a strategy (i.e., reducing inputs) to restore equity, provided the absence does not result in a loss of pay. If the job search efforts are not successful, then the employee continues in the present job. At the same time, the employee's dissatisfaction with the job (box 10) also continues. If not addressed, this dissatisfaction will likely lead to illnesses (box 11), poor mental health (box 12), or psychological withdrawal (box 13).

Lawler's model identifies the psychological consequences of pay dissatisfaction — the desire for more pay, or the lower attractiveness of the job. However, the subsequent events posited by the model do not explicitly take into account a variety of other factors and considerations that may intervene. These factors can be categorized as job context factors, job content factors, and external environmental factors (see Figure 5.2). An examination of the role of these factors will give a more comprehensive understanding of pay dissatisfaction that will lead to developing appropriate remedial strategies.

Job context factors include, in addition to pay, items such as benefits programmes, job security, status, congenial co-workers and superiors, and a caring climate that reflects the company's concern for its employees. As was noted in an earlier discussion on the determinants of pay satisfaction, these factors can serve as substitutes for pay. For example, employees might tolerate a lower pay in exchange for job security or some benefit programme or even a congenial working environment. To the extent that job context factors compensate for a lower pay, these items will reduce pay dissatisfaction that might otherwise be experienced. In Figure 5.2, the arrow from the job context factors box to box A (Pay dissatisfaction) shows the moderating effect of job context factors.

Job content factors include items such as challenging assignments, achievement, recognition, responsibility, autonomy, opportunities for growth, participation in decision making. These factors can also be viewed by employees as substitutes for pay and, as a result, will likewise have the effect of moderating the pay dissatisfaction experienced by employees. For example, an employee, particularly one with high growth needs, might accept a job with a relatively lower salary if the job offers challenging assignments and opportunities for growth. The moderating effect of job content factors is depicted in Figure 5.2 by the arrow from the job content factors box to box A (Pay dissatisfaction). To summarize, employee satisfaction with job context and/or job content factors will tend to lower the employee's pay dissatisfaction.

It might well happen that job context and job content factors do not significantly weaken pay dissatisfaction. Will pay dissatisfaction lead inevitably to turnover and to the other consequences depicted in box B in Figure 5.2? One would expect that employees who are dissatisfied with their pay and do not receive alternate valued rewards to compensate for the lower pay will leave for higher-paying jobs elsewhere. But this consequence need not necessarily follow, primarily because of *external environmental* factors that often intervene in the decision to leave the organization. As shown in Figure 5.2, these factors include limited job opportunities, especially in times of high unemployment; family responsibilities such as a house mortgage and disruption of the children's schooling; the possible effects on the career of the spouse if the move requires a relocation; family and community ties; reluctance to change jobs because of age. One or more external environmental factors can operate to influence an employee against voluntary turnover.

The preceding discussion briefly illustrated how job context, job content, and external environmental factors moderate the extent of pay dissatisfaction and also its two major consequences, turnover and job dissatisfaction. The findings of Flowers and Hughes (1973) confirm the critical role of these factors, especially in explaining why one employee who is dissatisfied with his/her job might leave the organization, whereas another employee who is similarly dissatisfied might choose to remain with the organization despite the dissatisfaction. Employees who experience high job satisfaction are generally in enriched jobs, those that are high on job content factors. These employees stay with the organization solely because the enjoyment they experience with the work makes them "want to" stay. Pay satisfaction, as such, is not the motive for their remaining with the organization. Flowers and Hughes designate such employees the "turn-ons." But any drop in their job satisfaction, usually resulting from some problem or deficiency with job content factors, will tend to weaken their bonds with the organization and cause them to become "turnovers."

Employees who have high job satisfaction (because of enriched jobs) may also be attracted to the organization by job context factors (pay, benefits, or status, etc.), by external environmental factors (family responsibilities, family or community ties, etc.), or even by a combination of both job context and external environmental factors. Such employees can now be said to stay with the organization not only because they "want to" (the work attracts them), but also because they "have to" (pay and benefits attract them, and family responsibilities make it necessary for them to stay). Because their stay with the organization is doubly guaranteed, they are referred to as the "turn-ons-plus." Unlike the turn-ons, an irreversible and fairly permanent drop in their job satisfaction will not cause them to leave the organization. Job context factors will continue to attract them, and external environmental factors will make it necessary for them to stay. Unfortunately for the organization, however, such pressures to stay will prevent the dissatisfied employees from becoming turnovers; instead they will become "turn-offs." The turn-offs are likely to be the source of nuisance-value grievances, work slow-downs, strikes. The other manifestations of turning off could be psychological withdrawal, drug-abuse, and related mental illnesses.

Job context, job content, and external environmental factors give a much clearer perspective of the phenomenon of pay dissatisfaction and its consequences. This perspective provides the compensation specialist with the flexibility to draw upon the variety of factors in each category (job context, job content, external environmental) to devise strategies that fit the needs of employees. Some general guidelines in the development of such strategies are discussed in the next section, which deals with what organizations can do to ensure pay satisfaction.

Practical Guidelines for Enhancing Pay Satisfaction

There is no doubt that the consequences of pay dissatisfaction are debilitating both for the organization and for the employees. It is not surprising that organizations are concerned to ensure that their employees are satisfied with their pay. What concrete measures can an organization take to meet this concern? To begin with, it is important to recognize that any practical measure must be built upon a sound theoretical foundation. In the absence of a theory, the explanation or predictability of the measure takes on the characteristic of being merely a guess. A sound theory, on the other hand, provides a rational explanation of a phenomenon, situation, or event, and permits reasonable predictions.

As Kurt Lewin observed, there is nothing more practical than a sound theory.

On the basis primarily of the expectancy theory model (Figure 4.1) and its extensions, the determinants of pay satisfaction (Figure 5.1) and the consequences of pay dissatisfaction (Figure 5.2), some practical guidelines can be inferred to ensure pay satisfaction. These guidelines will be stated in general but concrete terms in this chapter and spelt out in detail in later chapters, when the specific compensation subsystem to which the guidelines relate will be considered. For example, one guideline would be that the organization should institute a fair and systematic job evaluation system in order to ensure internal equity, which contributes to pay satisfaction. The specific mechanics and the process of the job evaluation system will be treated in detail in Chapter 10.

The first guideline for ensuring high pay satisfaction would be to offer a high pay to all employees, resulting in a high average level of pay satisfaction. This, however, could be costly to the organization, and induce a feeling of inequity if no differentiation were made among the poor, mediocre, and superior performers. Hence, the pay level must take into account the organization's business strategies as well as the principles of internal, external, and individual equity. To ensure internal equity, the organization will need to institute and implement a job evaluation system that fairly reflects the job's value to the organization. External equity will be ensured by periodic salary surveys in the right labour markets. Individual equity calls for a performance appraisal system that enables the organization to properly differentiate between the performances of employees in the granting of merit raises.

The second guideline will be to monitor pay satisfaction levels through periodic surveys. If the level of pay satisfaction is found to be low, it does not automatically follow that pay should be increased. The organization must do an analysis of the benefits it will likely derive from increased pay and the costs of the consequences (absenteeism, turnover, etc.) of a low level of pay satisfaction. If, on the other hand, the pay satisfaction level is high and the organization still experiences high turnover, the remedy will not be to increase pay but rather to explore other job outcomes that the employees are likely not receiving. Pay satisfaction is moderated by job content factors and job context factors (other than pay). Managers can consider a mix of pay, benefits, and non-economic outcomes that are valued by the employees. The organization might also consider *cafeteria-style* plans, which enable employees to pick and choose items of pay and benefits that they value. Giving employees the choice will greatly enhance their pay satisfaction.

The third guideline relates to the important process issue of communication and employee involvement in pay determination and administration. Should the pay system be secret or open? Social comparison is a crucial determinant of pay satisfaction. When the pay system is secret, social comparison, based on rumour and speculation, inevitably produces distortions with detrimental effects to pay satisfaction. An open system, on the other hand, allows for a more realistic social comparison and to that extent enhances pay satisfaction — provided, however, that the employee perceives fairness and equity in pay decisions. Employee involvement in pay determination and administration contributes to the formation of relatively more accurate employee perceptions of one's own and the relevant other's inputs and outcomes. Employee involvement in pay determination and administration allows for a more realistic social comparison and generally promotes employee perceptions of fairness and equity, thus enhancing pay satisfaction.

The guidelines briefly outlined here ensure that pay is perceived by the employee to be a valued reward, contingent on the performance of the desired behaviours. The guidelines are consistent with the dictates of expectancy theory. Hence, one can be confident that the guidelines will lead not only to greater pay satisfaction but also to increased employee motivation to perform the organizationally desired behaviours — the real objective of any reward item.

SATISFACTION WITH NON-ECONOMIC OUTCOMES

The non-economic outcomes generated by all of the job content factors and some of the job context factors play a critical role in determining pay satisfaction, and also in moderating the consequences of pay dissatisfaction. This chapter has touched on the potential of the non-economic outcomes in the repertoire of the reward strategies that can be deployed by the compensation specialist to motivate employees in performing the desired work behaviours. The almost endless variety of non-economic outcomes includes items from the job context category, for example, job status, job security, congenial co-workers and supervisors, a caring organizational climate; and items from the job content category, for example, challenging assignments, exercise of autonomy and responsibility, participation in decision making, opportunities for growth. Of the two sets of factors, job context and job content, the non-monetary outcomes generated by job content factors, through the process of job design, have been found to be significantly effective in employee motivation.

Why does job design work in increasing employee motivation and improving job performance? How does the process of job design operate to produce non-economic outcomes? Answers to these questions provide the theoretical underpinnings of job design and explore the process of job design that enables the job holder to experience the internal rewards of an enriched job. This treatment of the theory and the process of job design will help the compensation specialist to integrate job design as an important element of the compensation system.

THEORETICAL APPROACHES TO JOB DESIGN

The potential of job design to improve performance was formally recognized by the scientific management movement, whose approach could be viewed as the classical approach to job design. This approach regarded division of labor, work simplification, and standardization as ethical imperatives for increased productivity. Through time and motion study and related industrial engineering techniques, job tasks were designed to eliminate unnecessary movements and exertion of effort. The resulting job content included a set of simplified, specialized tasks that were to be performed according to the predetermined "one best way" to attain the predetermined output. Management spelt out in great detail what was to be done in the job as well as how it was to be done. The job design did not allow for the exercise of any initiative or resourcefulness by job incumbents.

The classical approach to job design led to relatively simple jobs requiring unskilled workers who were easier to recruit and train. Simple jobs permitted considerable flexibility in meeting staffing needs. Like standardized machine spare parts, workers were easily interchangeable for different jobs, enabling management to overcome the adverse effects of absenteeism and turnover on production. Management control was also reinforced by the predetermined output for each job. The results were (1) low costs in terms of starting wage rates, recruitment, and training; (2) increased output; (3) greater management control over workers and the production process; (4) increased worker income from incentive plans. These advantages, however, were far outweighed by adverse consequences: (1) worker boredom and the monotony of a routinized job, which led to a demand for higher wages in the job; (2) employee dissatisfaction manifested by unusually high turnover and absenteeism, increased rate of grievances, and psychological withdrawal; (3) increased worker replacement and training costs; (4) low quality output. To summarize, the short-term output increase was soon followed by employee dissatisfaction and long-term productivity deficiencies.

In the theoretical scheme underlying the classical approach, job design was not intended to promote employee motivation. The sole objective of job design was to improve job performance through providing the worker with a clear description of the job, its tasks and output goals, supported by adequate training and the necessary tools and material resources. Employee motivation, it was believed, would be taken care of by the opportunity to earn relatively high incomes through fair incentive plans. The scientific management movement, it will be recalled, believed in the "economic man" concept — that the worker is primarily and solely motivated by monetary rewards contingent on performance. Job design was not therefore seen as a *work reward* that could motivate employees to improve performance.

The growth theories of Herzberg and Maslow provided a different perspective of the role of job design. As explained in Chapter 3, growth theories believed in the "self-actualizing man" concept. Every worker, claimed Herzberg (1968), is a living and growing organism, and can be motivated only by satisfying his/her growth needs. Job design is the sole vehicle that creates the conditions for growth needs satisfaction. Hence, job design is the only important motivational tool. Growth theories, for the first time, focused attention on job design as a work reward item, an item that constituted the intrinsic reward element of the compensation system. The outcomes from job content thus became the motivators that alone explained and therefore predicted the employee's high levels of work performance. In the process, the growth theorists, particularly Herzberg, de-emphasized the monetary and other outcomes from the job context as being significant to motivate employees. These outcomes constituted the extrinsic reward element of the compensation system.

The differences between the classical and the growth theories approaches to job design are reflected in the approaches to compensation design and practice shown by compensation theorists and practitioners on the one hand, and growth theorists and organizational development advocates on the other hand. Compensation theorists and practitioners, influenced by the classical approach, focused exclusively on pay as the dominant element of the compensation system. Since job design was not intended to be a motivational tool, they had difficulty in integrating it into the compensation system. Growth theorists (notably Herzberg) and organizational development advocates, on the other hand, saw pay and all forms of outcomes from the job context as of minimal importance in employee motivation. They focused exclusively on job design as the dominant element of the compensation system.

The true role of job design in the compensation system lies between these two extremes. Outcomes from both the job content and the job context constitute integral parts of the total compensation system. This perspective is derived from the contingency approach to job design, which is contained in expectancy theory and the job characteristics model of Hackman and Oldham (1980).

From the expectancy model discussed in Chapter 4, it is clear that any outcome, whether intrinsic or extrinsic to the job, has motivational potential so long as the outcome is *contingent* on the desired work behaviour and is *valued* by the employee. In job design — whether it is in the form of job enlargement, job rotation, or job enrichment — the contingency requirement is automatically fulfilled. The outcomes a worker experiences in performing a job — a sense of accomplishment, feeling good about one's performance — are the job's pleasant, non-economic outcomes. These outcomes are experienced by the individual only after he/she has performed. In other words, internal rewards, which flow from job design, are conditional upon performance.

However, not all employees might value these internal rewards; some might even find an enriched job to be threatening. If employees do not value the internal rewards of an enriched job, they will not be motivated by these non-economic outcomes. Furthermore, even if employees value internal rewards, they may not have the ability to perform well in an enriched job. When employees lack the ability to perform in a given task, they will fail to perform at the desired level. Such failure to perform will eventually lead to a low (E ⟶ P) expectancy, which will lower their motivation to put in the necessary effort to perform adequately on their job.

Hackman and Oldham's job characteristics model provides a specific and more comprehensive treatment of why job design works and how it can be used as a compensation strategy to provide effective non-economic outcomes to employees. According to Hackman and Oldham, a job can be structured in such a manner that its good performance gives employees a sense of accomplishment that makes them feel good about themselves and their work. Poor performance, on the other hand, produces the opposite effect — unhappy feelings about themselves and their work, which they regard as unpleasant outcomes. Employees will strive to perform well in order to experience good feelings and avoid unpleasant outcomes. Good performance becomes "an occasion for self-reward, which serves as an incentive for continuing to do well" (Hackman and Oldham 1980, 72). Hence, job design, through its potential for self-reward for good performance, is an effective vehicle for creating internal work motivation.

What characteristics must be incorporated in the job design to ensure high internal work motivation? According to the job characteristics model, the job should have five core characteristics: skill variety, task identity, task significance, autonomy, job feedback. Hackman and Oldham describe these characteristics as follows:

1. Skill variety: the degree to which a job requires a variety of different activities in carrying out the work, involving the use of a number of different skills and talents of the person. (1980, 78)
2. Task identity: the degree to which a job requires completion of a "whole" and identifiable piece of work, that is, doing a job from beginning to end with a visible outcome. (1980, 78)
3. Task significance: the degree to which the job has a substantial impact on the lives of other people, whether those people are in the immediate organization or in the world at large. (1980, 79)

4. Autonomy: the degree to which the job provides substantial freedom, independence, and discretion to the individual in scheduling the work and in determining the procedures to be used in carrying it out. (1980, 79)
5. Job feedback: the degree to which carrying out the work activities required by the job provides the individual with direct and clear information about the effectiveness of his or her performance. (1980, 80).

An individual performing a job that is high in the first three characteristics (skill variety, task identity, and task significance) will experience the work as meaningful. When the job is high in autonomy, the job holder will experience responsibility for the outcomes of the work, since these now flow from the exercise of his/her discretion and initiative. Finally, when the job is high in job feedback, the job holder will have direct knowledge of the results of his/her performance. The model postulates that when the job enables the employee to experience the work as meaningful, to feel responsible for the work outcomes, and to have knowledge of the work results, then the employee will have high internal work motivation.

It is necessary to recognize that an enriched job, that is, a job high in the core job characteristics, will not by that very fact produce high internal work motivation in the job holder. Rather, the enriched job only makes it possible for the individual who has performed well to experience the internal work rewards that will then motivate the individual to continue to perform well. In other words, merely placing the individual in an enriched job will not cause internal motivation; the individual must perform well in order to experience the internal rewards and thus be internally motivated. The question therefore arises: Will all employees perform well in an enriched job? This question requires that individual differences be taken into account. The job characteristics model recognizes individual differences in three areas: (1) knowledge and skill, (2) growth need strength, and (3) context satisfactions such as satisfaction with compensation, job security, co-workers, and superiors.

An individual who has neither the knowledge and skill nor the competence demanded by an enriched job will not be able to perform well. Likewise, an individual who does not have strong growth needs will not recognize or fully appreciate the opportunities for the exercise of autonomy and discretion, and for the growth or mastery of varied skills presented by an enriched job. In fact, such an individual might even feel threatened by the demands of such a job. On the other hand, suppose an individual has the knowledge and skill, and even high growth needs, but is dissatisfied with one or more aspects of the job context, for example, the pay of the enriched job or the lack of job security. This individual will be much too preoccupied with rectifying the perceived deficiencies in the job context to perform well on the job. Thus, the job-relevant knowledge and skill, growth need strength, and context satisfaction of an individual moderate his/her performance in an enriched job and, in turn, his/her internal work motivation. The more of these moderators (knowledge and skill, growth needs strength, context satisfaction) the individual has, the greater is the likelihood of high internal work motivation in an enriched job.

From this review of the theoretical approaches to job design, it can be seen that the job characteristics model provides a coherent and comprehensive approach to job design. It fully explains the process of how job design leads to the internal rewards that flow from good performance. It also identifies the conditions that must exist if the job holder is to experience the internal rewards of an enriched job. And the model goes further, by prescribing a set of specific, practical guidelines for job design, which will be treated in the next section.

THE PROCESS OF JOB DESIGN

The process of job design answers the question: How are the core characteristics of a job enhanced? In other words, how can skill variety, task identity, task significance, autonomy, and job feedback be increased? The job characteristics model proposes a set of five implementing principles: combining tasks, forming natural work units, establishing client relationships, vertically loading the job, and opening feedback channels. Each principle will be discussed, as well as how that principle contributes to improving one or more of the core characteristics of the job. A summary of the discussion as shown in Table 5.1.

Combining Tasks

This principle suggests the putting together of "existing, fractionalized, tasks to form new and larger modules of work" (Hackman and Oldham 1980, 135). This principle can be applied, for example, in the assembly-line operation for a small appliance. In such an operation, the entire task of assembling the appliance is broken down into several smaller operations, which are performed as the appliance moves from one point of the assembly line to the next. When the combining-tasks principle is implemented, the entire assembling operation is done by one person. (If the combined task is too large for one worker, it can be done by a team of workers who are responsible for the finished product.) Restructuring the work in this manner enables the individual to identify with the complete appliance. Hence, task identity is improved. As the individual now has to perform many more tasks and activities than before, more of his/her skills, abilities, and talents are being used, and skill variety is increased. Thus, redesigning the job by combining tasks enhances the core job characteristics of task identity and skill variety.

Forming Natural Work Units

According to this implementing principle, the items of work are "arranged into logical or inherently meaningful groups" (Hackman and

TABLE 5.1
THE PROCESS OF JOB REDESIGN
(BASED ON THE JOB CHARACTERISTICS MODEL)

To increase the job characteristic of	Managerial Action
SKILL VARIETY	*Combine Tasks*: As the employee performs many more tasks than before, more of the employee's skills and abilities will be used.
	Establish Client Relationships: This additional set of tasks will call for a greater use of the employee's interpersonal and communication skills.
TASK IDENTITY	*Combine Tasks*: Employees are now able to see themselves contributing to more of the finished product.
	Forming Natural Work Units: Employees develop a sense of ownership as they identify with a customer group.
TASK SIGNIFICANCE	*Forming Natural Work Units*: Employees' close association with their customer group enables them to see the impact of their work.
AUTONOMY	*Vertically Loading the Job*: Control in areas such as developing work schedule, methods, procedures, etc., enables employees to experience autonomy and responsibility for their work.
	Establish Client Relationships: The exercise of discretion and decision making in managing client relationships inevitably increases autonomy.
JOB FEEDBACK	*Opening Feedback Channels*: When employees are given responsibility for quality control checks, for example, they are able to see fairly immediately the results of their work.
	Establish Client Relationships: Direct client contact allows employees to receive information on the quality of the goods/services they provide.

Oldham 1980, 136). The staff of a travel agency might be randomly assigned to the customers, or the staff might be assigned to particular groups of customers, for example, government, business, or individual accounts. The redesign to form natural work units allows the staff to develop a sense of ownership as they identify with a customer group, thereby increasing task identity. The close association of the staff with their customer group will also enable them to see for themselves the impact of their work on their customers, thus contributing to task significance. The task identify and the task significance characteristics of the job are greatly enhanced when the job is redesigned to form natural work units.

Establishing Client Relationships

This principle prescribes that, as far as possible, the employee deal directly with the clients and be responsible for managing client relationships. This prescription also involves the establishment of the criteria that the client will use in providing feedback to the employee. Suppose that the job of the travel agency staff in the previous example is redesigned to form natural work units. This redesign could be taken a step further by allowing the employees to establish relationships with their clients and to manage these relationships. Such a redesign will increase the job's core characteristics of skill variety, autonomy, and job feedback. The increase in skill variety comes about because client relationships call for a greater use of interpersonal and communication skills. The exercise of discretion and decision making in the management of client relationships will increase the degree of autonomy in the job. The increase in feedback comes from the fact that dealing directly with the clients places the staff in a position to receive information on the quality of service they provide.

Vertically Loading the Job

This principle gives workers "increased control over the work by 'pushing down' responsibility and authority that were formerly reserved for higher levels of management" (Hackman and Oldham 1980, 138). This control could be in a variety of areas, for example, developing the work schedule, methods, and procedures; decision making (even if it is limited) in budget and financial matters related to the job; involvement in planning. Redesigning the job by vertical loading will increase the core job characteristic of autonomy.

Opening Feedback Channels

This principle prescribes that job redesign enable employees to receive feedback directly from the job, preferably immediately upon performance rather than later from the supervisor. Establishing client relationships is one way of feedback from the job. Other ways are giving workers responsibility for quality control checks; and performance records such as production data and budget reports that are sent to both the employee and the supervisor. With computerization, direct feedback from job performance tends to be more feasible. Opening feedback channels increases the job feedback characteristics of a job.

To summarize, the implementing principles or concepts proposed by the job characteristics model provide practical prescriptions for job enrichment. These prescriptions operate to specifically increase the core job characteristics of skill variety, task identity, task significance, autonomy, and job feedback. As discussed in the previous section, the greater the degree of these characteristics in a job, the more the job holder who performs well will experience internal work rewards. The process is, however, moderated by the individual's job-relevant knowledge and skill, growth needs strength, and satisfaction with the context — all of which will considerably influence his/her job performance.

Implications for Reward Management

The job diagnostics survey developed by Hackman and Oldham (1980) provides a job profile that identifies the core characteristics needing improvement. The implementing concepts can then be applied to improve these job characteristics. The job characteristics model is a sound, empirically proven approach to job design, which now makes it possible for job design to be integrated into the compensation system as a realistic and practical compensation strategy for providing non-economic outcomes. Thus, as was discussed earlier, the expectancy model establishes the rationale for including job design as an important component of the total compensation system, and the job characteristics model provides a theory-based technology to put job design into pratice.

SUMMARY

The issue of satisfaction with a compensation item is critical to the effectiveness of a compensation system. Combining notions from equity and discrepancy theories, this chapter has discussed satisfaction in terms of the difference between an individual's perceptions of what should be received and what is received. In dealing with the issue of satisfaction with pay, the determinants of pay satisfaction model identified four factors — person-related, job-related, referent-other-related, and context-related — that contribute to the employee's perceptions of the amount that should be received and the amount that is received. The difference between these perceptions causes employees to be satisfied or dissatisfied with their pay. These factors represent the employee's inputs, which tend to increase the perception of pay that should be received; the job outcomes, which are perceived as acceptable substitutes for pay and therefore tend to decrease the perception of pay that should be received; the significant and powerful effect of social comparison, which can serve to increase or decrease both sets of perceptions — amount of pay that should be received and amount of pay that is received.

The two major consequences of pay dissatisfaction, according to the consequences of pay dissatisfaction model, are the desire for more pay, and the reduced attractiveness of the job. Each consequence has its own set of employee reactions. The desire for more pay leads to a higher level of job performance if pay is performance-based; otherwise, the non-fulfilment of this desire leads to a variety of employee reactions ranging from absenteeism and turnover to the filing of grievances and union pressures, which might even include a strike. Employees reactions to the reduced attractiveness of the job have been found to vary from absenteeism and turnover to job dissatisfaction, which might result in poor mental health or psychological withdrawal. It is, however, necessary to recognize that the very fact of employees' pay dissatisfaction, whether it will occur and what its nature will be as well as employees' reactions to it, are moderated not only by the content and the context of the job but also by the external environmental factors in which employees find themselves.

Both models, the determinants of pay satisfaction and the consequences of pay dissatisfaction, provide a firm conceptual basis on which to develop a repertoire of strategies for ensuring pay satisfaction and for coping with the consequences of pay dissatisfaction. One such strategy is the use of job design to generate non-economic outcomes. Of the several approaches to job design, the job characteristics model offers an empirically proven technology that allows an organization to adopt job design as a practical compensation strategy to provide non-economic outcomes for its employees.

KEY TERMS

classical approaches to job design
core job characteristics
discrepancy theory
growth theories approaches to job design
implementing principles of job design
job characteristics model
job content factors
job context factors
job design
satisfaction

REVIEW AND DISCUSSION QUESTIONS

1. Consider the following cases of dissatisfaction with pay:

   Case 1

   Robert is not satisfied with his pay as a bank teller, because it does not enable him to maintain the standard of living he was accustomed to before he married a widow with three children. He concedes that the pay fairly reflects the job's value relative to the other jobs in the bank. He also concedes that the pay reflects his performance.

Case 2

Richelle is not satisfied with her pay as a bank teller, because she believes that, although her job title is the same as Robert's, her job has additional responsibilities. These responsibilities require her to work extra hours for which she is not paid. She also believes that the pay does not adequately reward her superior performance. Richelle is single and lives with her parents. Her only dependents are her pets, a cat named Fluffy and a dog named Fido.

Which case corresponds with the notion of dissatisfaction in equity theory? Why?

2. Identify and explain the factors that influence an individual's satisfaction with his/her pay.
3. It is not uncommon to find that individuals who are dissatisfied with their pay still

   a) stay on with the organization;

   b) maintain a high level of performance.

   How would you explain these situations, which seem to be inconsistent with the predictions of the consequences of pay dissatisfaction model?
4. Discuss some practice guidelines for increasing pay satisfaction.
5. Distinguish between the classical and growth theories approaches to job design.
6. Using examples, discuss the potential of Hackman and Oldham's job characteristics model as an effective compensation tool.

CASE: STAR WARS

When Ted Sharp joined the Space Age Technology Company (SATCO) as a design engineer, he brought to the job an exceptionally strong academic record and three years of related work experience. SATCO was a relatively small and unknown company in suburban Montreal, but its association with Star Wars technology offered Ted an unusual opportunity for professional growth.

Ted was pleased with his decision to join SATCO. It had certainly come up to his expectations: challenging assignments and opportunities for creativity and innovation as well as professional growth and development; and signals from top management that he was being considered for a management position. Of course, Ted's career progress had had its costs — hard work, long hours, and frequent travels. The last two were especially hard on his wife and their teenage daughter. A tragic automobile accident had rendered his wife a paraplegic requiring constant attention. The daughter had had to assume the responsibility of attending to the mother, in addition to the household chores and school work. However, Ted's career received strong encouragement from his wife and daughter. They loved Montreal and had become very attached to their neighbours, who were very friendly and provided them with support and assistance.

As Ted looked out of his office window, the bright sunshine, unusual for Montreal in February, seemed to reflect his optimism about his future in SATCO. He had just finished talking to his boss, Jeremy Harper, and was delighted to learn of his merit raise, the largest in the design engineering department. Recognition was not new to Ted; he had received prizes and honours in school and university, and in his previous job he had received above-average raises. The fact that he had been awarded the highest raise for each of the last five years he had been at SATCO made him look forward to a satisfying and productive association with the company.

His cheery, upbeat mood was cut short when George burst into his office with a printout of the salaries and merit raises of the department. George was a competent engineer but in his weaker moments he regressed to being a computer hacker, a bad habit he had picked up as an undergraduate. In one of these moments he had come across the salary information that Ted was staring at in disbelief. It confirmed that he had the highest merit raise, but he was totally flabbergasted to see the almost negligible difference between his salary and that of Ron Brown. When Ron Brown was hired two years back, there was considerable opposition for two reasons. First, he was hired in preference to several other applicants who were better qualified. The major consideration seemed to be that he was the nephew of a senior vice-president of SATCO. Second, his starting salary was about $2,500 more than the salary of most engineers who were equally, if not more, qualified and had been with SATCO for over two years.

At that time, Ted had with difficulty reconciled himself to receiving almost the same salary as Ron because he was hopeful that his merit raises would eventually remedy the situation. To his utter disappointment, he now found that his merit raises had not put him very much ahead of Ron. At the first opportunity, he met Jeremy Harper and demanded an explanation, saying: "I'm tired of working for just the joys of engineering. My salary should fairly reflect my competence and contribution to SATCO." Jeremy tried to explain the merit system: "Our performance rating system consists of three categories: outstanding, acceptable, unacceptable. Each year your performance was assessed as outstanding, which entitled you to 6.5 per cent increase. Ron's performance was assessed as acceptable, which entitled him to a 5.5 per cent increase. You must not forget that the merit increase includes a COLA of 5 per cent for everyone." Expressing his disappointment that SATCO did not think very highly of him, Ted stormed out of the office.

Discussion Questions

1. What are the reasons for the inequity that Ted experienced?
2. Explore all the possible actions that Ted can take. Which of these actions do you think Ted might actually take? Why?
3. As a compensation specialist, what are your recommendations for resolving this situation?
4. Assume that instead of Ron Brown, the person who was hired belonged to one of the "protected groups" (i.e., women, visible minorities, aboriginal peoples, persons with disabilities) and had qualifications identical with Ron Brown's. Assume further that this person was hired as part of SATCO's affirmative action programme. In this scenario, explore the possible impact of the programme on the employees' perceptions of equity, and the strategy that SATCO might adopt to address such an impact.

PART III

PROCESSES AND TECHNIQUES IN DESIGNING THE COMPENSATION SYSTEM

CHAPTER 6
THE STRATEGIC AND PROCESS ISSUES IN COMPENSATION

CHAPTER SYNOPSIS

When an organization begins the process of designing a total compensation system, it must first make some important decisions on the strategic and process issues that are essential to the development and implementation of an effective compensation system. This chapter identifies and examines the nature and the contents of the strategic and process issues in compensation, and the ciritical options that are contained in each issue. The chapter also considers the criteria for the organization's choice of the options as it seeks a compensation system that is supportive of its business objectives and congruent with its internal work culture.

LEARNING OBJECTIVES

- To identify the major strategic and process issues, and explain why they are critical in designing a total compensation system.
- To distinguish between the strategic and process issues.
- To identify and explain the criteria for the choice of the critical alternative options contained in the strategic and process issues.
- To understand the strategic and process issues and, for each issue, to discuss the conditions under which its alternative options would be most appropriate.
- To explain how the decisions on the strategic and process issues can enhance or impair the effectiveness of the compensation system.

INTRODUCTION

So far, the nature of compensation and the foundations of a compensation system have been explored. When the foundations were discussed, the external and internal environments of the organization that affect the compensation system were considered. Also discussed were the various theoretical models and approaches, from which were derived a set of broad but coherent guidelines for the characteristics a reward item must exhibit if it is to be effective in motivating employees to perform desired work behaviours. Finally, a projection was made of the likely consequences when a reward item of pay does not show these characteristics.

Upon these foundations the compensation system will be constructed. In designing the total compensation system of any organization, however, the compensation specialist is faced with a bewildering variety of issues that concern both the strategies for, or the direction of, compensation programmes and the process of designing and administering such programmes. The following scenario conveys the cardinal importance of some of the strategic and process issues in compensation.

THE CASE OF THE BEWILDERED COMPENSATION SPECIALIST

On his flight back to his division from a visit to the corporate office, Ed Fairpay, a compensation specialist, found himself sitting next to Ann Dumont, a friend from university days who now operated her own consulting firm in human resource management. After the usual social chatter, Ed poured out his woes. At his company, despite an elaborate pay structure based on a complex and mathematically precise job evaluation programme, there was considerable dissatisfaction with the compensation programme, resulting in the loss of good people. The conversation went as follows:

Ann: You're not alone, Ed. Compensation activity has caused many a human resource person to nurse an ulcer. Let's begin at the beginning. Do you have a compensation philosophy in your organization?

Ed: Sure, we do. Our company is known to pay well.

Ann: Do your employees know of your philosophy?

Ed: That's what the theorists say. Our employees are interested in money, and we have a first-rate job evaluation programme that guarantees our employees are paid the right salary. Our expertise in this respect is the envy of the competition. Isn't this more important?

Ann: It depends upon whether you want to base the total compensation on the job or on the person. The former produces one set of consequences; the latter, quite a different set.

Ed: There you go again — theorizing!

Ann: Ed, do you see your compensation system as an end in itself or as a means to an end?

Ed: I forgot your forte in college was the Socratic method. But, really, Ann, means and ends are okay for an academic discussion. I don't see the relevance. As I told you already, my concern is why we're losing people like Leo when his compensation was determined fairly *vis-à-vis* the other jobs in the company.

Ann: Your concern raises another question: Are you striving for internal equity?

Ed: You bet we are. We have to be fair and equitable.

Ann: At the risk of external inequity?

Ed: Every time I mention the need for salary surveys, the treasurer screams "costs"!

Ann: Poor Ed, you seem caught between the devil and the deep blue sea.

Ed: You'd better believe it. Although our division is a profit centre, major compensation decisions are made in the corporate office. I'm now carrying back one of those decisions.

Ann: Perhaps I can address your concern from a different angle. What role does your organization assign to performance in determining the compensation of an individual?

Ed: Isn't it obvious that pay should be related to performance? Don't all organizations relate pay to performance?

Ann: It depends. Some organizations focus on seniority rather than performance, just as they vary widely on the compensation mix.

Ed: Why should organizations differ on the compensation mix?

Ann: *Touché*! You sure pick up the Socratic method fast.

Ed: Thanks. Let me move to a really academic issue. What do you think of the practice of secrecy in compensation?

Ann: How can a discussion about a practice be academic?

Ed: Because one Dr. Lawler wrote about secrecy in compensation while sitting in his academic ivory tower.

Ann: Dr. Lawler's work on pay secrecy is based on empirical research. So is his work on employee participation in pay decision making.

Ed: Openness in pay is bad enough. Employee participation in pay decisions? Why, that's downright terrorism. . .

From this conversation, it can be seen that a compensation system is more than a mere collection of compensation practices and techniques hastily put together in an attempt to ward off crises as they occur. Instead, the component elements of compensation programmes and processes, methods and techniques, are blended into a meaningful pattern to serve the interests of both employees and the organization. To craft such a coherent and purposeful compensation system requires that management carefully think through the strategic and process issues listed below — issues that Lawler (1981) has identified as being critical in the design of a total compensation system. It would be more appropriate to describe them as cardinal (i.e., on which something hinges) issues because the effectiveness of the component elements of the compensation system and of the system itself depends upon the decisions on these issues.

The strategic issues are

1. Whether or not to have a compensation philosophy;
2. What the balance should be between the mechanistic and process issues in compensation;
3. Whether compensation should be based on a job-content-based evaluation system or on a person-based evaluation system;
4. Whether the compensation system will be an end in itself or a means to an end;
5. Whether the compensation system will emphasize internal or external equity;
6. What the choice will be of external labour markets for salary surveys;
7. Whether the design and the administration of the compensation system will be centralized or decentralized;
8. Whether compensation will be based on performance or on other considerations such as seniority;
9. What the choice will be of the compensation mix — cash and benefits.

The process issues are

1. What aspects of the compensation system should be communicated and what aspects should be kept secret;
2. Whether employees should be involved in decision making in the design and the administration of the compensation system.

Before each of these issues is considered, it is necessary to define the overall nature of the strategic and process issues in compensation and the criteria that must be considered when decisions are made on these issues. The strategic issues call for a set of mutually exclusive approaches. Decisions on these issues will provide the direction for the compensation system for an extended period of time. The organization cannot adopt a neutral position on the choice of the direction, because there is a right direction and a wrong direction. The right direction will result in an effective use of the compensation dollar; the wrong direction will lead to an ineffective deployment of organizational resources. It is more than a question of just the compensation dollars. Employee dissatisfaction with compensation can and does have adverse consequences for the organization's effectiveness. The process issues also call for a set of mutually exclusive approaches that determine *how* the decisions on the strategic issues are implemented. The mode of implementation is just as crucial to the effectiveness of the compensation system as the strategies chosen, and may be more crucial, because the beneficial effects of a right choice on a strategic issue may be completely eliminated by a wrong choice on a process issue.

What are the criteria by which to decide on the strategic and process issues? The specific criteria will be discussed when each issue is considered. The overall criterion, however, is the business strategy of the organization. It will be recalled from Chapter 2 that the reward system of an organization must be congruent with and supportive of the organization's business strategy. If the choice of the compensation strategy is consistent with and supports the business strategy, then the compensation system will contribute to the accomplishment of the organization's mission. It was also shown in Chapter 2 that since the effectiveness of business strategies is affected by the product life cycle, the compensation system should be adapted to the specific needs of each stage of the product life cycle. Chapter 2 provided illustrations of the compensation strategies that would be suitable for different types of business strategies. Illustrations were also provided of the appropriate compensation strategy relative to the compensation mix for the each stage of the product life cycle. In this chapter each of the strategic and process issues will be examined in terms of its contents, alternative approaches, and the conditions that favour one approach over another.

THE STRATEGIC ISSUES

1. Compensation Philosophy

In addressing this issue, four considerations are paramount. First, compensation is a major item of expenditure to the organization. Second, compensation is a major motivational tool. Third, the compensation system must be congruent with and supportive of the organization's business strategy. Fourth, compensation is also extremely important to the employees. These considerations will prompt the organization to think seriously and systematically about its compensation system in an attempt to answer such questions as: What are the objectives of the compensation system? Does the compensation system support the business strategies? Is it compatible with the work culture of the organization? How is the compensation mix determined? How can the organization ensure that the compensation mix is fair and equitable? Should employees be involved in the design and the administration of the compensation system? Answers to these and related questions will crystallize the organization's thinking on compensation and enable the organization to develop a coherent compensation philosophy.

A well-thought-out compensation philosophy will state in clear and unambiguous terms the objectives of the compensation system, which serve as a guide for managerial decisions in compensation. The organization may also usefully state that the compensation system is a means to an end, which is to attract and retain qualified employees and to motivate them to perform work behaviours that help attain the organizational objectives. Therefore, the system will be suitably modified when necessary to serve these needs of the organization. When all managers in an organization use the same guide or frame of reference for their compensation decisions, there is a greater likelihood of consistency and equity, and the credibility of the compensation system is increased. Credibility in the compensation system is also increased through the stability of the system. A compensation philosophy promotes stability when it spells out the circumstances under which compensation changes will occur. Consequently, unless the stipulated circumstances come about, employees will not expect changes in compensation, regardless of how much they may desire a change. For example, if the compensation philosophy stipulates that pay will be performance based, employees will not be disappointed or dissatisfied if the mere fact of seniority is not rewarded by a pay increase.

The effects of consistency, equity, and credibility contribute to increasing employees' valence of the compensation items, and hence to improved employee motivation. Employee motivation is also improved when the clearly articulated contents of the compensation philosophy communicate the performance-outcomes linkage, which increases the employee's (P ⟶ O) expectancy.

What are the specific contents of a compensation philosophy? There is no one exhaustive list of contents. The organization's philosophy on compensation should simply reflect the situation and the needs of that organization. Lawler (1981) recommends that the compensation philosophy include the organization's decisions on the following items:

- Objectives of the compensation system: What specific benefits (returns) does the organization expect from its enormous compensation expenditures? When these objectives are spelt out in behavioural terms, preferably for each reward item, then the effectiveness of the reward item can be evaluated in terms of these objectives. The methodology for such an evaluation is discussed in Chapter 14.
- Communication policy: The degree of secrecy and openness of the compensation system.
- Decision-making approach: The degree of top-down or participative decision making regarding the compensation system.
- Market position: Does the organization intend to meet, lead, or lag the market in determining its package of pay and benefits?

- Centralization or decentralization: This issue applies largely to organizations in more than one location or in more than one business. Will the design and the administration of the compensation system be centralized or decentralized?
- Compensation mix: Cash and benefits, fixed pay and variable pay, and so forth.
- Roles of performance-based and seniority-based compensation.
- Performance appraisal: The nature of the performance appraisal system and its relation to compensation.
- Compensation-system fit with the internal work culture of the organization. Will the compensation system emphasize skill-based or performance-based pay and non-economic rewards, or only flat-rate monetary pay, benefits, and social rewards? The former emphasis reflects a work culture that believes its employees to have high growth needs and a high potential for development. The latter emphasis reflects a work culture that believes its employees to have low growth needs and to be interested only in the immediate gratification of physical, security, and social needs.

These items ought to be carefully considered because they can make a significant difference to the effective design and administration of the compensation system. A fuller discussion of these items will take place after the related strategic and process issues have been considered. Some of the contents of the compensation philosophy statement of a major Canadian corporation in the transportation industry are illustrated in Figure 6.1

2. Balancing the Mechanistic and Process Issues

By *mechanistic* is meant the mechanics of the techniques used in compensation. For example, for the purpose of fixing wage rates, jobs are often evaluated using a technique called the point factor method of job evaluation. A purely mechanistic approach to job evaluation presupposes that the point factor method has the capacity to come up with job values that are valid, that is, that accurately reflect job differentials in the organization. Using the point factor method to rate a job, however, still involves considerable subjectivity. Besides, each employee has his/her own perception of a fair and equitable job value, which will frequently differ from that determined by the job evaluation technique, however sophisticated it might be. In the final analysis, it is the employee's perception that determines whether the job value is equitable or not. Therefore, a sole reliance on the mechanics of a job evaluation technique does not produce an equitable result. And this has been found to be the

Table 6.1

Extracts from a Compensation Philosophy Statement Relating to Objectives, Market Position, and Performance-based Pay

Objectives

The Cash Compensation Program's primary objectives are:

- to attract and retain qualified employees;
- to reward effective performance;
- to provide incentives to further improve performance; and
- to accomplish the above objectives in a manner that will ensure fair and equitable treatment of all employees.

Market Position

We pay particular attention to the salary practices of large national organizations representative of major and primarily unionized employers in Canada.

The market surveys we use allow us to:

- look at specific types of jobs throughout many companies;
- select industries;
- select companies within those industries;
- select companies by geographic location;
- select specific jobs by numerical value; or
- combinations of the above.

Performance-based Pay

The objectives are:

- to improve on the job performance;
- to provide linkages to other plans through
  —identification of individual potential and
  —support for career development;
- to increase the overall effectiveness of the organization.

Based on your assessed performance your superiors will establish an appropriate salary level within your salary range. Progress towards the salary range maximum will be dependent upon your performance level.

An employee should progress through the salary range based on achievement of objectives and continued performance improvement. Once the employee has reached the fully competent level, that employee should normally be paid the full value of the job.

Any reward beyond the fully competent level is for superior performance and is provided for by our Performance Incentive Plan.

These are the features of the Performance Incentive Plan:

- recognizes superior performance;
- provides reward beyond the salary range maximum;
- is delivered in an annual lump sum payment;
- must be earned annually.

It is important to remember that awards made under the Performance Incentive Plan, as well as salary increases, are based on the performance rating given in the last Assessment of Performance.

An individual may receive compensation for superior performance in one of three forms:

- all salary
- part salary and part incentive
- all incentive.

case with almost every other technique of salary design and administration — salary surveys, performance appraisals, incentive and gainsharing plans, salary structure, and so forth.

A total reliance on the most complex and elaborate set of techniques will not change the fact that ". . . there is no such thing as an objectively right pay that will be accepted by everyone . . . what is perceived to be right by one individual often is not perceived to be right by others . . . pay determination involves differing perceptions, values, and conflict" (Lawler 1981, 33). The issue of differing perceptions can only be addressed by greater attention to the process issues. By *process* is meant how the techniques are implemented. The process consideration in implementing the point factor method of job evaluation would be to involve employees (through their representatives on the job evaluation committee) in the various stages of the evaluation process. Such an involvement would increase two-way communication and employee participation and hence contribute to a better understanding of the technique. Involving employees in design and implementation also leads to a greater sense of "ownership." In terms of the expectancy theory model, taking care of the process issues will clarify the effort-performance and the performance-outcomes relationships in the case of techniques where these relationships are relevant, for example, in the technique of performance appraisal used in performance-based pay programmes. A clarification of these relationships will greatly increase employees' (E $\rightarrow$ P) and (P $\rightarrow$ O) expectancies. Furthermore, employee involvement will contribute to a more realistic perception of the equity of outcomes, and this perception will have a significant positive impact on the employees' valence of the outcomes. It can be concluded that a proper attention to the process issues will improve the motivational efficacy of the technique.

The point of raising the issue of balance between mechanics and process in compensation is to draw attention to an overemphasis on techniques and technology. This overemphasis on techniques can be traced to the assumptions and practices of the scientific management movement, which assumed that workers would produce only if they received economic rewards. Hence, compensation design efforts were concentrated on developing techniques to tie pay with performance. The process issues in pay effectiveness were completely neglected. Organizations need to become aware of this legacy of the scientific management movement. They should recognize that an effective compensation system should include a judicious balance of the mechanics and process issues; in other words, organizations should ensure that techniques are implemented with the appropriate degree of communication and employee involvement.

3. THE CHOICE OF A JOB-CONTENT-BASED OR A PERSON-BASED EVALUATION SYSTEM

A job-content-based evaluation system is a mechanism to determine the pay grade. Traditionally, it has achieved this objective by developing a job structure (hierarchy) that reflects the differential in the job's value or worth to the organization. This differentiation also achieves internal equity if the pay reflects the relative value of various jobs within the organization. The focus of the evaluation effort is on the value (or contribution) of the *job alone* to the organization. The qualifications of the individual are disregarded in determining the job's worth and the corresponding pay grade attached to it.

How does this sytem develop its sources of job value? This depends on the method used. As will be discussed in Chapter 10, some methods (ranking, for example) are entirely subjective and use vague criteria for job evaluation; others (point factor and factor comparison methods, for example) evaluate jobs on the basis of compensable factors. *Compensable factors* are judgements about the specific aspects of jobs that the organization values to the extent that it is willing to pay for them. Examples of compensable factors are skills, effort, responsibility, work conditions. It must be noted, though, that the factors (skills, for example) are not the skills possessed by the job incumbent but rather the skills required by the job. If the job incumbent possesses more skills than those required by the job, the job will not be worth more; it will still be valued on the basis of the skills that are judged to be necessary for the job. The focus of the system is on the job content, not the person holding the job.

The job-content-based evaluation system has often been subjected to severe criticism (Lawler 1986), which will be reviewed in Chapter 14. For now, it is sufficient to note some of its unintended adverse effects. For example, a heavy weight is usually assigned to the factor of responsibility; jobs high on this factor will fetch a higher dollar value. Most managerial jobs rate high on this factor. Consequently, employees will seek these jobs in order to earn a higher salary. The problem with this is that employees who have neither the competence nor the inclination for managerial jobs may, and often do, get those jobs. For example, in a school the only way for a teacher to earn a higher salary is to move into a principal's position. Many a school superintendent has ruefully witnessed the dysfunctional consequences of such a move. Often, the classroom loses an exceptionally gifted teacher, and the school gains an inept, incompetent principal. Brilliant scientists are often promoted as managers without much attention paid to their managerial skills; the primary consideration for the promotion is the reward of more pay.

The other dysfunctional effects identified by Lawler (1981) are empire building and resistance to reorganization plans. When compensable factors include responsibility for people and budgets, managers may be tempted needlessly to increase the size of their staff and budgets in order that their job may qualify for a higher job value, and a higher salary. The job-content-based evaluation system is also known to have become an obstacle to a company's reorganization plans. When a job is redefined in a reorganization, its position in the hierarchy, as established by the evaluation system, is threatened. To preserve such vested interests, efforts are soon initiated to discard the reorganization plans.

The person-based job evaluation system is often proposed as an alternative to the job-content-based evaluation system. Under the person-based approach, the base pay is designed to reflect the knowledge and the skills of the job holder, even though the individual's job might require the use of only some of the knowledge and skills. For example, in the Montreal Catholic School Commission, teachers are paid on the basis of their *scolarité*, that is, their number of years of university schooling. A teacher with an M.A. in history and a teacher with a B.A. in history may be assigned to teach Canadian history in Grade 9. Both teachers are responsible for teaching the same curriculum, both have classes of identical size, and both prepare students for the identical provincial examinations. Yet the teacher with the M.A. earns a higher base pay. In the Shell Canada Chemical Company plant in Sarnia, the person-based approach takes the form of multi-skilling. The base pay is computed according to the number of skill modules in which the worker is proficient. The greater the number of skill modules in which the worker has acquired proficiency, the greater is the base pay — even though the assigned job may not require the worker to use all the acquired skills.

There are several advantages to a person-based evaluation system. It encourages the employees to acquire additional skills and expertise, which makes for a more flexible and capable workforce. It permits the development of "career ladders," which enable employees to earn higher salaries as they acquire professional or technical expertise; these employees need not now seek managerial jobs in order to earn higher pay. The person-based approach eliminates the dysfunctional effects of the job-content-based approach. The motivational effectiveness of the person-based approach is also greater because of the impact on the employees' (E → P) expectancy and the valence of outcomes. The acquisition of knowledge and skills also increases the (E → P) expectancy. The visible, direct linkage between knowledge and skills acquisition and pay improves the perceptions of equity and thus increases the valence of pay.

However, the person-based approach is not widely used, and as will be discussed in Chapter 14, it requires a fairly drastic reorientation of the internal work culture for successful implementation. Nevertheless, the person-based approach is suitable where technical expertise is critical, and in organizations that operate employee involvement programmes and autonomous work teams. Job-content-based evaluation is more suitable where responsibility for human, financial, and material resources is the critical compensable factor.

4. THE COMPENSATION SYSTEM AS AN END OR AS A MEANS TO AN END

The compensation system is a means to an end. Compensable programmes are designed to serve the needs of the organization, that is, to attract and retain qualified employees, and to motivate them to perform work behaviours that help to attain organizational objectives. If compensation programmes fail to attract and retain qualified employees, or are unsuccessful in motivating employees to perform the desired work behaviours, they must be modified.

The reality, however, is often very different. Traditionally, the most important consideration in developing a compensation system has been an overwhelming concern for internal equity. To ensure internal equity, organizations have taken great care to create a hierarchy of jobs that adequately reflects the differential in job values to the organization. This objective is worthwhile as long as job and salary structures serve organizational needs and objectives.

The problem arises when this structure is treated as if it were immutable. Most organizations today operate not in a stable but in a turbulent environment. For example, a Canadian crown corporation that once operated in a regulated industry now finds itself privatized, in a deregulated industry, and in a fiercely competitive free trade market. To cope with the new environment and to respond to its changing dynamics, the corporation might need to reorganize, with inevitable changes in the compensation system, for example, redefined jobs that necessitate a shift to external equity to attract qualified employees, decentralization, and performance-based programmes rather than the automatic seniority-based pay increase. A compensation system that cannot readily respond to the required changes has become an end in itself.

In companies that have been in existence for a long time, systems and practices, if not regularly reviewed, tend to become rigid and resistant to change. Longevity itself becomes an argument for continuing with the status quo. This is acceptable as long as the organization's needs are well served. In today's changing business environment, however, an organization is better served if it takes specific steps that will allow it to modify the compensation system. The most important step is to incorporate the organization's intentions in the compensation philosophy. An explicit statement that compensation is a means to meet the needs of the organization will serve as a clear message to all employees to expect changes if the organization's conditions so require. In terms of the expectancy theory model, such a statement will give employees a better understanding of the performance-outcomes relationship and will help towards a more realistic (P→O) expectancy. It will also prevent an adverse effect on employees' valence of outcomes should business conditions necessitate modifications to the compensation system — assuming that such modifications are done in an equitable manner and that such process issues as communication and employee involvement are prudently managed. If the modifications are managed properly, employee motivation should not suffer.

5. The Choice of Internal or External Equity

This strategic issue, along with the next four strategic issues, directly influences both organizational effectiveness in terms of labour costs and turnover and the job satisfaction of employees.

Internal equity means that the pay rates of jobs in an organization reflect the relative value of those jobs, or their relative contribution to organizational objectives. External equity means that the pay rates of jobs in an organization correspond to the rates of those jobs in the external labour market. Consider the following data about five jobs in the ABC Company. Since the internal pay rates of these jobs reflect their job value as indicated by their job evaluation points, it can be concluded that internal equity exists in the organization. There is external equity for all jobs except for job 3, which is underpaid relative to the external labour market.

Job	Job Evaluation Points	Organization's Pay/Year $	Pay Rate/ Year in External Labour Market $	Option A Maintain Internal Equity $	Option B Maintain External Equity $
1	1,100	77,000	77,000	88,000	77,000
2	1,000	70,000	70,000	80,000	70,000
3	800	56,000	64,000	64,000	64,000
4	500	35,000	35,000	40,000	35,000
5	300	21,000	21,000	24,000	21,000

The ABC Company has three basic options: option A, to maintain both internal and external equity; option B, to maintain external equity only; and option C, to maintain internal equity only. If the company chooses option A, job 3 must be paid the market rate of $64,000 to ensure external equity. The pay of the other jobs would have to be increased proportionately to maintain the differentials of job value in order to ensure internal equity. The costs of this option are prohibitive. If the company chooses option B, job 3 is paid the market rate of $64,000 to ensure external equity. No other changes are made, because this option does not seek to maintain internal equity. If the company chooses option C, to maintain internal equity alone, it decides in favor of the status quo.

What are the consequences of these options? The consequence of maintaining the status quo is — other things being equal — a relatively higher rate of turnover among employees in job 3. Most likely a shortage in the external labour market of the skills of job 3 is driving up the pay rates. The consequence of option A is the costs, which can only be justified if the organizational needs can be better served by maintaining both internal and external equity. An organization whose business strategies call for a policy of leading in the external market might choose option A. The consequences of option B are controlled costs, the elimination of pay as a cause of turnover among employees in job 3, but dissatisfaction among employees in the other jobs, because these employees will now experience internal inequity. The last consequence of option B need not arise if ABC Company's compensation philosophy has explicitly provided for such a situation, by stating, for example, that although the compensation system strives to pursue the objective of internal equity, yet if the exigencies of business and the conditions of the external labour market make it necessary, then external equity will apply in determining the pay rates of jobs that are in short supply. As discussed in the means-ends issue, such a statement will contribute to a more realistic ($P \rightarrow O$) expectancy and prevent any adverse impact on the employees' valence of outcomes. Therefore, the preferred option will be option B — external equity alone — if there is a shortage in the external labour market of people with job 3 knowledge, skills, and abilities.

6. The Choice of External Labour Markets for Salary Surveys

Almost every organization collects data on wages and salaries. The issues, methods, and techniques for salary surveys are fully discussed in Chapter 12. This section explores some basic strategic and policy questions that provide direction to the compensation system and therefore need to be addressed at the design stage of the compensation system. Lawler (1981) has identified these questions: What are the right market data? Is one survey for all jobs in the organization adequate? Should employees be involved?

What are the right market data? Organizations generally collect data from comparable companies in the same industry. This guideline for determining the data source overlooks the fact that many jobs in an organization also exist outside the industry. Clerical jobs, for example, exist across all industries. A more relevant guideline would be to survey those organizations at the local, regional, national, or international level to which employees are likely to move. Employees in clerical and low-level skilled jobs are more likely to move to organizations in the local area. Employees in managerial, professional, and high-tech jobs are more mobile and therefore more likely to seek jobs nationwide and sometimes worldwide.

Is one survey for all jobs in the organization adequate? In view of what has just been said, the organization needs more than one survey, each survey to cover a set of jobs that have the same labour market. Should employees be involved? The entire process should be "demystified and made subject to participation, due process, and open communication" (Lawler 1981, 38). The organization should allow employees to contribute any data they might have and also make it possible for them or their representatives to review the data collected by the surveys. Employee involvement increases trust in the process, and often provides convincing proof that the grass on the other side of the street is really not that green after all. Such involvement improves employees' perceptions of external equity, and these perceptions will contribute to increasing the valence and satisfaction of pay. Besides gaining the advantages of improved employee motivation, the organization benefits from the surveys because the data enable it to develop a more rational approach to managing payroll costs.

7. Centralization versus Decentralization

In a centralized compensation system, all decisions relating to the pay and benefits structure and the policies, procedures, and methods used in the design and administration of the system are made by one unit, usually in the corporate office, for the entire organization. In a decentralized compensation system, the different divisions of the organization have the autonomy to design and administer the system to suit the specific needs of their business operations in accord with the conditions of the labour market in which they operate.

A centralized compensation system ensures internal equity throughout the organization, facilitates the movements of people across the organization, and ensures the uniform and consistent treatment of compensation issues. Centralization also allows the organization to control compensation costs effectively. There are, however, disadvantages to centralization. Centralization does not allow the organizational units that are substantially different to design a system that better suits their local needs and conditions. For example, a unit might find that it has to raise the company's pay rates in order to compete with the local labour market to attract and retain a qualified workforce. A centralized compensation system will not give the required autonomy to the unit for reasons of internal equity and cost control. When a compensation system permits different pay structures, policies, and procedures for different organizational units, the system loses the advantages of internal equity. The compensation system could retain internal equity by revising upward the pay rates in the entire organization, but this is resisted usually because it is seen to be costly. However, it can be argued that this is a myopic view of costs, because the failure of an organizational unit to attract and retain a qualified workforce could seriously undermine the organization's capacity to be effective and would therefore eventually prove to be more costly. The absence of autonomy in a centralized system also prevents the different parts of the organization from experiencing the motivational benefits that come from employee participation and involvement in the compensation system.

A centralized compensation system is more suitable for a small organization, where it is feasible to get a clear understanding of the needs of all the parts of the organization and to reflect these needs in the compensation system. A large organization that operates a single business and is located in one place can similarly get a clear understanding of the needs of the business and the conditions of the one local labour market. If the organization also pays attention to employee involvement issues, it should succeed in operating a centralized compensation system.

Large organizations with multiple businesses and operating in multiple locations are better served by a decentralized compensation system that adequately addresses the often conflicting needs of the different businesses and locations. The divisional, or local, autonomy made possible in a decentralized system is conducive to employee involvement and participation in the design and administration of the system.

8. Performance versus Seniority

Compensation can be based on performance, on membership, on seniority, or on the whims of the supervisor. When compensation is based on performance, there is a clear distinction in pay outcomes between outstanding and mediocre performers, with the former receiving higher pay than the latter. Such a distinction promotes employee perceptions of individual or personal equity, which is the recognition of the individual's performance inputs. Compensation based on performance has a powerful impact on employee motivation because it is fair and equitable and therefore increases the employee's valence of pay and contributes to satisfaction. It also reinforces the performance-outcomes relationship, and thus increases the employee's (P ⟶ O) expectancy.

If compensation is not based on performance, outstanding performers will experience inequity. This experience of inequity will lower their valence of pay and contribute to dissatisfaction, with such consequences as absenteeism and turnover. It will also weaken the performance-outcome relationship and thus decrease employees' (P ⟶ O) expectancy. For these reasons, pay will not be effective in motivating the good performers to continue performing well; nor will it be effective in retaining them in the organization. They will likely become turnovers. The organization will also experience difficulty in attracting good, innovative employees who expect that their performance will be rewarded.

Poor performers will not be motivated by pay, because a reward item is effective only when it is contingent on performance. When pay is not contingent on performance, it is contingent on some other behaviour or consideration such as membership behaviour, length of service, or the supervisor's caprices. Pay that is not contingent on performance will promote behaviours that are not conducive to making the organization effective. Nor will the poor performers become turnovers; they will become turn-offs — a source of innumerable problems to the organization.

The critical nature and the strategic importance of performance-based pay cannot be overemphasized. Decisions on this issue strike at the very core of managing human resources in a manner that contributes both to organizational effectiveness and to employee satisfaction.

9. The Choice of the Compensation Mix

For a long time, the compensation package in industry consisted mainly of cash — base pay, incentives, merit pay. The benefits component became significant during World War II when wage and price controls to support the war effort placed a freeze on wages and salaries. Conscription to the army, navy, and air force produced acute shortages of available workers for business and industry, compelling organizations to take extraordinary measures to retain their workforce and compete for a smaller labour pool. Prevented from offering higher wages, organizations offered deferred benefits such as life insurance, which the government permitted because these did not involve an immediate large cash outlay. After the war, favourable tax treatment for employers and employees, along with the demands of the labour unions, led to the introduction of a plethora of benefits. In Canada today, benefits packages — those voluntarily offered by organizations and those mandated by law — constitute as much as 35 per cent of the gross annual payroll (Peat Marwick Stevenson & Kellogg 1986).

What is an ideal mix of cash and benefits in a compensation package? The answer depends on the organization's business strategies and the stage of the life cycle of its products. As was discussed in Chapter 2, the different stages of the product life cycle make possible differing mixes of cash (pay and incentives) and benefits. The other determinants are employee preferences, union demands, legal obligations, and preferential tax treatment as applicable both to employers and employees. Chapter 13 considers at length the critical issues in the development and implementation of a benefits programme. At this stage, it is important to note two aspects of the role of benefits in employee motivation. First, performance-based benefits programmes are difficult to develop. For example, a dental plan stipulating that the entitlement of cavity fillings or root canal work depended upon an employee's performance appraisal — unrestricted fillings or root canals for an outstanding rating, two fillings and one root canal for a superior rating, and so on — would not be practical. Therefore, it is difficult to assess the potential of some benefits to motivate performance behaviours. Benefits programmes can, however, be developed to motivate membership behaviours. For example, providing transportation can reduce tardiness and absenteeism. Second, benefits cater to individual need satisfaction and thus contribute to maximizing the total satisfaction of the individual.

THE PROCESS ISSUES

1. COMMUNICATING THE COMPENSATION SYSTEM

This issue can also be framed as secrecy versus openness with regard to pay information. There has been a long-standing practice in the area of compensation administration that pay information is personal and confidential and secrecy should prevail. Is this practice sanctioned by cultural norms? In other words, do organizations keep pay information secret in deference to the wishes of their employees? Or is it in the interest of the organization to keep pay information secret?

Many managers choose to hide behind the veil of pay secrecy lest they be called upon to explain or defend their pay decisions. If an organization's pay administration practices are indefensible, then openness in that organization will have disastrous consequences for employee pay satisfaction as the inequities are disclosed. Do employees wish to keep their pay secret? Studies suggest that employees generally favor secrecy about the individual's salary, but favor disclosure of pay ranges and pay administration policies; employees do not mind openness once it has been introduced, provided the pay is fairly and equitably administered (Lawler 1981). In the management category, the manager who is paid the lowest in each management level has been found to resist openness, probably out of fear that such disclosure would reveal his/her identity (Lawler 1972). The pay scales and related information of unionized employees have always been made public.

What are the effects of secrecy? This question can be discussed in the light of the research findings of Lawler (1972, 1981). Secrecy has two major effects: (1) a lowering of the pay satisfaction of the employee, and (2) a reduction of the employee's motivation to perform.

A strong argument usually advanced for pay secrecy is that it protects low-paid employees from being dissatisfied with their pay. According to this argument, when low-paid employees do not know that others are being paid more, they will not make unfavourable comparisons and will not be dissatisfied with their pay. This argument does not seem to recognize the reality: employees compare their pay with that of others all the time. In the absence of the actual pay information, employees base their comparisons on speculation and on information generated by the grapevine. As one manager observed: "I don't like to do it, but I can't help but look at other managers' houses, cars, and things and wonder if they are making more money than I do" (Lawler 1972, 461). It was shown in Chapter 5 that social comparison is one of the key determinants of pay satisfaction. When employees make comparisons based on inadequate, inaccurate, or grossly exaggerated information, they tend to overestimate the pay of their peers and subordinates and underestimate the pay of their superiors.

The same erroneous perceptions have been found where the size and the frequency of merit raises have been kept secret. On the basis of speculation and rumours, employees overestimated the merit raises of their peers and subordinates and underestimated the merit raises of their superiors. The consequence of the misperceptions stemming from secrecy is the employee's belief that his/her pay or merit raise relative to that of his/her peers (the relevant other persons) is unfair and inequitable, a belief that causes him/her to be dissatisfied with the pay or merit raise. In actuality, the employee's pay or merit raise might have been more than that of his/her peers. But in a secret system employees have no way of making the comparison except by speculation and rumour.

Secrecy reduces the employee's motivation to perform in three ways: (1) by failing to engender trust, (2) by causing misperceptions of the performance-outcome linkage, and (3) by causing misperceptions of feedback.

In terms of the expectancy theory model, the motivation to perform is generated by the employee's beliefs about the performance-outcomes relationship — the (P → O) expectancy — and the equity of outcomes (valence). Beliefs are based on trust. But secrecy cannot engender trust. Therefore, the employee will not have the basis on which to develop the expectancies of (P → O) and valence. Without these expectancies, the employee will not be motivated to perform.

Secrecy causes misperceptions of the performance-outcomes linkage. The merit raise, which is a sign or a score that provides feedback on performance, depends for its effectiveness on employee perceptions that merit raises do differentiate between employees according to their performance. In an open system, employee pay perceptions are formed by direct knowledge of the actual situation. If the open pay system is fairly and equitably administered, employees will have access to the reality and will be able to conclude for themselves that the merit raises are equitably administered. Suppose, however, that the pay system is equitably administered, but there is secrecy in the system. The only source of information, then, is speculation that leads to an overestimation of the size and the frequency of the merit raises of one's peers. When an employee so overestimates, his/her own merit raise appears low relative to that of his/her peers. This perception of a low merit raise causes the employee to feel that he/she has been inequitably rewarded for his/her performance. The reality, however, is that the merit raise equitably reflects his/her performance. Only the misperceptions brought about by secrecy create the feeling of inequity and obliterate the motivational effects of a fairly administered merit pay plan.

A study (Lawler 1972) of the merit plan of managers in one organization illustrates this phenomenon. The average merit raise, 6 per cent, was not disclosed to the managers because of a pay secrecy policy. Most managers, overestimating their peers' pay raises, speculated that the average merit raise was 8 per cent. Any manager who received an 8 per cent raise concluded that it was merely average. Such a conclusion demotivated the manager, who believed that his/her performance was above average and deserved an above-average raise. Only the secrecy policy prevented the manager from experiencing the motivational force of the merit raise, which was more than the average, recognizing an above-average performance, and therefore equitable and fair.

Secrecy also causes misperceptions of feedback on performance. The job characteristics model discussed in Chapter 5 demonstrates how feedback contributes to the job holder's experiencing internal work motivation. Job performance feedback has a significant impact on the employee's ($E \rightarrow P$) and ($P \rightarrow O$) expectancies, as well as on the employee's valence of outcomes. Among the many forms of feedback an employee receives in the course of performance, pay is direct, visible, and concrete. When an individual receives high pay relative to his/her peers, that pay is a positive feedback to signify that his/her performance is outstanding or superior relative to that of his/her peers. A low pay relative to one's peers is a negative feedback, indicating that the performance relative to one's peers is unsatisfactory. An open pay system allows individuals to make realistic and factual pay comparisons that give individuals accurate feedback, either positive or negative. A secret pay system, on the other hand, prevents factual pay comparisons. The overestimation of a peer's pay relative to one's own pay causes the individual to perceive his/her pay to be low and automatically provides negative feedback. Such negative feedback reduces the motivational effects of pay. Furthermore, such feedback is a message to the individual that his/her performance needs to be improved — a perplexing message, because the individual is performing well. Pay secrecy has the insidious effect of providing negative feedback not warranted by the actual situation.

Pay secrecy seriously inhibits the motivational effects of pay, causing employees to be dissatisfied with pay and reducing their motivation to perform. Should all organizations make their pay system public? An organization whose pay history is riddled with inequitable pay practices should first strive to make improvements in this area before going public. When an organization is ready to make pay public, it is usually advised to disclose the pay range gradually, revealing the minimum, the midpoint, and the maximum of the different pay grades. The organization should also involve employees in implementing compensation techniques such as performance appraisals, job evaluations, and salary surveys. Specific proposals in this regard are discussed in later chapters. A good practice is to involve employees in the design of the merit pay programme. As employees develop confidence that the programme is operating in a fair manner, information on the size, the frequency, and the recipients of merit raises can be made public. The pay level of individuals is the last information to be made public.

Lawler's experience with organizations on this issue is to the point: "Clearly not every organization is ready for, or should have, public individual pay rates . . . most can tolerate and gain by making pay ranges and other salary administration information public . . . after an initial flurry of interest it becomes an accepted fact of organizational life which, in many cases, increases people's feelings about the fairness of the pay system" (Lawler 1981, 49).

2. Involving Employees in Decision Making

In discussing the need for a balance between the mechanistic and process issues, it was noted that however sophisticated the compensation technique might be, it does not produce the intended results. For instance, management might design an elaborate and mathematically complex job evaluation technique with the sole objective of ensuring fairness and equity in the resulting job and pay structure; employees might view the complex design as a deliberate management attempt to manipulate the results in order to pay lower salaries. The same could be said of other compensation techniques such as performance appraisals and gain-sharing plans designed to increase both the performance-outcomes linkage as well as equity. If employees do not perceive these techniques to enhance the performance-outcomes linkage and equity, the motivational effects of the techniques will not be achieved. What can management do to ensure that compensation techniques are understood and accepted by employees? The answer is to pay close attention to the process issues of communication, and employee involvement in decision making in the design and the administration of the compensation system. The previous section dealt with communication. This section considers employee involvement in decision making.

There are two aspects to employee involvement in decision making: (1) involvement in the design of the compensation system, and (2) involvement in the administration of the compensation system. A complete discussion of these two aspects should include a consideration of *why* employees should be involved and *how* employees should be involved in decision making. In later chapters devoted to specific techniques, practical strategies are developed for involving employees in decision making.

Employee involvement in decision making means that management does not unilaterally impose a particular compensation programme or technique but actively seeks and genuinely considers the employees' views and concerns about making the programme fair and equitable. Why should employees be involved in decision making? In general, employee involvement leads to increased organizational effectiveness and employee satisfaction. In this section the question of why employees should be involved in decision making is addressed with regard to employee involvement in the design of a compensation system, that is, in the design of programmes and in decisions on the use of appropriate techniques. Examples of such programmes and techniques are performance-based pay and performance appraisals, incentive systems and gain-sharing plans, job evaluation techniques, development of job and salary structures, salary surveys, benefits programmes (box A of Figure 6.2).

As shown in Figure 6.2, when employees are involved in designing programmes and techniques, they receive information from the other participants in the design effort. In addition, as equal partners, they feel inclined to provide their own insights and to raise the questions and concerns of the constituency they represent, thus increasing the information pool about the programme or technique (box 1). The unrestricted flow of information and participation produces two effects. First, it gives employees a better and fuller understanding of the programme or technique. Second, it makes them experience the feeling of ownership of the programme, which they no longer view as just another management programme; rather, they feel that they share the responsibility for its development (box 2).

The expertise they have now acquired makes them confident that they control the programme. Responsibility and control are critical elements of ownership. When employees feel they control a programme, they are more open to change and to new ideas because they have the responsibility and the competence to propose appropriate modifications that will achieve fairness and equity. Ownership of a programme naturally leads to commitment to it. Involvement and participation in programme design thus increase the employees' understanding of, and competence in dealing with, the relevant issues of the programme and also make employees responsible and committed to it (box 2). In other words, the programme is theirs. Not surprisingly, employees trust the system (box 3). They can gain a proper understanding of the programme and because they are an integral part of the structure and process, they have the capability and the mandate to exercise whatever controls are necessary to ensure that the programme contributes to fairness and equity.

Figure 6.1
The Effects of Employee Involvement in Decision Making

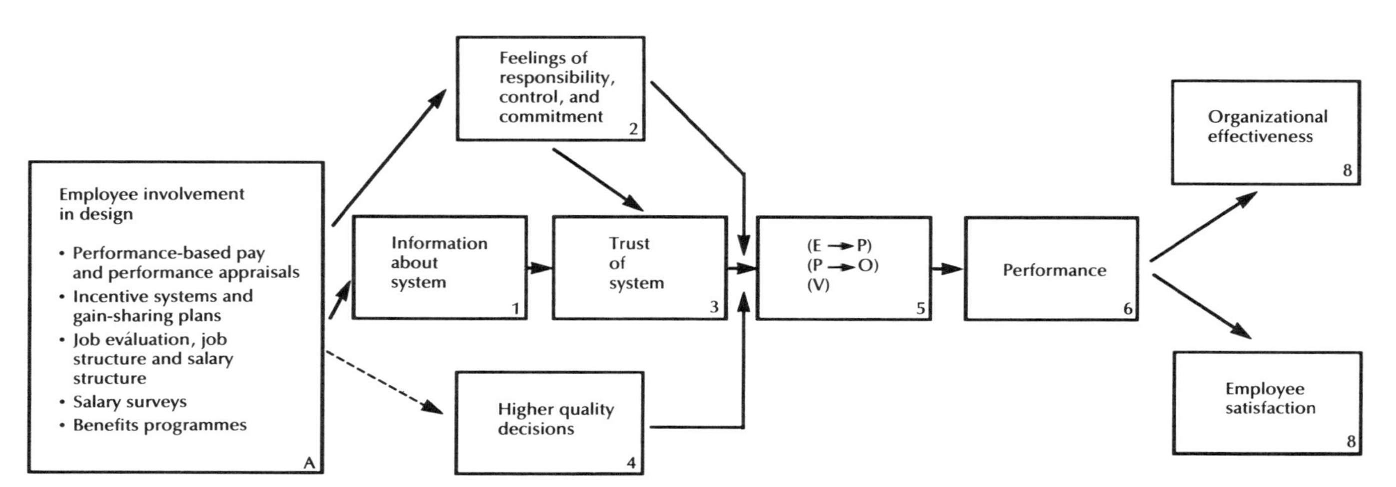

Source: Adapted from Lawler (1981).

Do employee involvement and participation contribute to decisions of a higher quality? Some believe that they so contribute only when employees are knowledgeable and can bring some special expertise to the process. But they do not always contribute. This view is reflected by the broken line from the Employee involvement in design (box A) to Higher quality decisions (box 4). However, if a higher quality decision is one that improves employee perceptions of the fairness and equity of a programme, then employee participation should always lead to higher quality decisions. The process shown in Figure 6.2 reveals that employee ownership and commitment, trust, and higher quality decisions all contribute to enhancing employees' expectancies relating to ($E \rightarrow P$), ($P \rightarrow O$), and the valence of outcomes (box 5). As predicted by the expectancy theory model, the increase in expectancies will increase the motivation to perform (box 6), resulting in organizational effectiveness and employee satisfaction (box 8).

Such results are well illustrated by the Lawler and Jenkins (1976) study of a small manufacturing plant that used a committee of workers and managers to develop a job and pay structure. The new structure resulted in increased salary costs, which would have been inevitable without employee participation. The real pay-off for the organization came within six months, when the organization's turnover rate improved dramatically. A survey of employee attitudes revealed that job satisfaction had increased from 44.4 per cent to 72.2 per cent, pay satisfaction had increased from 7.1 per cent to 37.5 per cent, and satisfaction with pay administration had also improved, from 12.7 per cent to 54.5 per cent.

Similar effects have also been found when employees participate in the administration of the compensation system by making decisions that set their own pay or that of their peers. Employee decisions on the pay of one's peers are quite common in organizations that have adopted the practice of multi-skilling or skill-based pay, and have structured the work into autonomous work teams. For example, in the Shell Canada Chemical Company plant in Sarnia, Ontario, members of the work team evaluate each other's performance and make decisions on the merit pay of their peers. In other organizations with similar Quality of Working Life programmes, employees also decide whether their peers have acquired the needed proficiency level in a skill. These decisions determine whether employees will move to the next higher pay level. The experience of organizations that let employees set their peers' pay is that the employees can be trusted to make responsible decisions. Furthermore, the pay satisfaction of these employees is quite high (Lawler and Jenkins 1976; Lawler 1977).

Not as widespread as the practice of allowing employees to set the pay of their peers is the practice of allowing employees to set their own pay, possibly because organizations have difficulty trusting their employees to make responsible decisions in this area. Where employees have set their own pay, the results have been positive. For example, in one organization employees who had a free hand in deciding their own pay restricted it to 8 per cent, a raise that corresponded to the 50th percentile of market wages (Lawler and Jenkins 1976). Other studies have reported similar responsible behaviour in pay decisions. For example, Lawler and Hackman (1969) cite the case of janitors who, left to themselves to decide on a bonus, opted for a relatively small one. In another case, employees in a small workshop had the autonomy to determine what price for a job lot would be to be quoted to a customer. In computing the price, the workers factored in their wage rates at a level that would ensure the workshop got the order (Gillespie 1948).

Lawler (1981, 55) cites a dramatic case of employees' responsibility in setting their own wages, reported in the *Washington Post* (23 Feb. 1975) under the headline: "Arthur Friedman's Outrage: Employees Decide Their Own Pay." Arthur Friedman left his employees completely free to decide on their pay, working hours, and vacations. Employees who wanted more pay simply had to walk to the payroll clerk and state the amount desired. They would get it, no questions asked. The first demand came from Friedman's wife, who felt she deserved an extra $1 per hour. The other requests ranged from $50 to $60 a week more. The behaviour of two employees reveals some of the potential benefits to be gained in allowing employees to set their own pay. The first employee, a truck driver who was lazy, tardy, and inefficient, demanded a raise of $100 a week, which he got. Almost immediately he changed into a model worker whose performance provided value to the organization far exceeding the cost of the raise. The second employee, a serviceman who did not ask to be paid the same as his co-workers, said, "I don't want to work that hard."

Allowing employees to set their own pay works best under certain conditions. First, the organization should be small and the relationship between management and employees characterized by openness and trust. Second, employees should know and understand the nature and the economics of the business. Third, the pay decision should be made public. Because the company is small, employees can see and evaluate one another's contributions to the attainment of the company's objectives, and can ascertain that pay raises reflect performance. An understanding of the nature and the economics of the business gives employees a better appreciation of the impact of their pay decisions on the costs and margins of the business. The realization that pay is made public operates as a restraining mechanism on employees who might be tempted to set salaries that adversely affect the continued operations of the business.

Employee involvement in decision making undoubtedly contributes to the effectiveness of the compensation system by improving employee perceptions of the performance-outcomes linkage and of the equity of outcomes — perceptions that enhance employee motivation, and pay and job satisfaction. The use of participation, however, is restricted to pay design rather than pay administration. Pay design lends itself to employee involvement and participation because there is a fairly universal acceptance among management and employees of the principles underlying pay design. For instance, there is general agreement that pay ought to reflect the job structure that is developed in accordance with a job-based or person-based job evaluation system. There is also general agreement that pay rates in the labour market should be considered in developing the pay structure. Barring some differences in emphasis, most organizations accept that seniority and performance should also be reflected in the pay of an individual.

Employee participation in pay administration, on the other hand, is feasible only in small organizations that can create the necessary conditions described earlier. In large organizations these conditions do not generally exist, and employees have difficulty recognizing that their interests are closely linked with the interests of the organization. In the absence of such a recognition, an employee's pay decision in setting his/her own pay might be guided only by self-interest to the detriment of the interest of the organization. Employee participation in deciding the merit raises of one's peers is more feasible provided an appropriate procedure exists to ensure that these decisions are made in groups. Group decisions are fair and equitable when based on predetermined performance standards that are developed by the group itself (Lawler 1981). This procedure leads to an effective pay decision, engenders trust, promotes autonomy and responsibility, and generally provides opportunities for employee growth and development.

THE ROLE OF THE STRATEGIC AND PROCESS ISSUES IN COMPENSATION DESIGN AND ADMINISTRATION

The strategic and process issues that have been discussed represent a set of critical options available to an organization as it designs and administers a compensation system. The organization's choice of the options will provide the direction for its compensation system. The compensation philosophy of the organization will guide the choice of the options, which will then become the means to ensure that compensation decisions are consistent with the philosophy.

The issues can be categorized into three groups: (1) the strategic macro-level issues, (2) the strategic micro-level issues, and (3) the process issues. In the first group are the issues of compensation philosophy, process versus mechanics, job-based versus person-based job evaluation, and compensation system as a means or an end. This category provides the overall thinking and framework for the compensation system, giving it its rationale, purpose, and direction. In the light of this framework, the choices of the micro-level issues, the second group, derive their meaning.

The second group contains the issues of internal versus external equity, choice of labour markets for compensation surveys, centralization versus decentralization, performance versus seniority, and choice of the compensation mix. These issues directly affect the individual employee. Through the choice of programme, method, and technique, and through the work behaviour objective, decisions on these issues influence the individual's expectancies relating to (E → P), (P → O), and the valence of outcomes. As a result, these issues have a significant impact on employee motivation, pay satisfaction, and job satisfaction.

The third group are the process issues — communciation, and employee participation in decision making in the design and administration of compensation systems. The choices in these issues determine the effectiveness of the strategic issues, particularly the implementation of management decisions with regard to the micro-level issues.

The choices in the three groups of issues are interlinked and together they contribute to the effective design and administration of the total compensation system. It cannot be overemphasized that the test for a correct choice of the options involved is to determine whether, as a result of the choice, the reward item is perceived by employees to be salient, valued, and contingent on the desired work behaviours.

SUMMARY

This chapter has discussed the strategic and process issues in compensation. These issues provide a set of critical alternative options that an organization must choose when it designs a total compensation system. Decisions on these issues will provide the direction for, and determine the effectiveness of, the compensation system. In general, the organization's business strategies and internal work culture are the criteria for decisions on the alternative options contained in these issues.

The compensation philosophy, together with the other macro-level strategic issues (process vs. mechanics, job-based vs. person-based job evaluation, and means vs. end), provides the rationale, purpose, and direction for the compensation system. Decisions on the micro-level strategic issues (internal vs. external equity, choice of labour markets and market position, performance vs. seniority, and compensation mix) have an impact on employee motivation. Choices in the process issues (communication and employee participation in decision making) influence the effectiveness of the strategic decisions, particularly in regard to the micro-level strategic issues. Thus, the strategic and process issues taken together play a pivotal role in the effective design and administration of the total compensation system.

KEY TERMS

centralized compensation system
compensation philosophy
decentralized compensation system
job-content-based evaluation system
pay secrecy
person-based evaluation system
process issues in compensation
strategic issues in compensation

REVIEW AND DISCUSSION QUESTIONS

1. What are the major strategic and process issues? Explain why these issues are critical in compensation system design.
2. Distinguish between the strategic and process issues.
3. Identify and explain the criteria that must be borne in mind when deciding on the options inherent in the strategic and process issues.
4. What useful purpose does a compensation philosophy serve in an organization? What are some of the items that should be included in a compensation philosophy?
5. "An effective compensation system should include a judicious balance of the mechanics and process issues." Why?
6. Distinguished between the job-content-based and the person-based job evaluation system. What are the dysfunctional effects of the job-content-based job evaluation system?
7. How can an organization ensure that its compensation system does not become an end in itself?
8. An organization has three basic options: to maintain both internal and external equity; to maintain internal equity only; to maintain external equity only. Discuss the consequences of each option.
9. With regard to salary surveys, what are the right market data? Is one survey for all jobs in the organization adequate? Should employees be involved?

10. Explain the conditions under which
    - a centralized compensation system is more appropriate.
    - a decentralized compensation system is more appropriate.
11. Discuss the consequences of using seniority rather than performance as a basis for compensation decisions.
12. What are some of the conditions that determine the mix of cash and benefits in a compensation package?
13. Discuss the effects of pay secrecy. What are the advantages and risks in an open policy as opposed to a secret pay policy?
14. Employee involvement in decision making has been found to contribute to both organizational effectiveness and employee satisfaction. Discuss why this is so.

EXERCISE: DECIDING ON STRATEGIC AND PROCESS ISSUES IN COMPENSATION SYSTEM DESIGN

Objective

To identify and make decisions on the strategic and process issues that contribute to the effectiveness of the organization's compensation sytem.

Procedure

Note: The case analysis of Tandoori Burgers of Chapter 2 is a prerequisite for this exercise. First, do activities 1 to 4 individually. Then discuss your decisions in your work group, and arrive at a group consensus, keeping note of the major differences.

1. Refer to the case Tandoori Burgers Limited (TBL) in Chapter 2.
2. Identify the strategic and process issues that should be considered in designing a total compensation system for TBL.
3. Examine the alternative options under each strategy and each process issue you have identified, and decide on the option that will enable TBL to craft a coherent and purposeful compensation system.
4. Write up a compensation philosophy for TBL.
5. Each group reports its decisions to the class. The class discussion could include a consideration of the reasons for the recommendations. Specifically:
   - Do the choices on the strategic and process issues support the business strategies of TBL that were identified when you analysed the case in Chapter 2?
   - Are the choices consistent with the internal work culture of TBL as it was identified when you analysed the case in Chapter 2?

CHAPTER 7
PROMOTING ORGANIZATIONAL MEMBERSHIP BEHAVIOURS

CHAPTER SYNOPSIS

Previous chapters have established the conceptual framework that provides the rationale for and outlines the conditions under which compensation programmes, techniques, and processes promote equity and are effective in motivating desired work behaviours. This chapter uses the conceptual framework to design reward programmes and practices that promote organizational membership behaviours such as regular attendance, punctuality, and staying with the organization.

LEARNING OBJECTIVES

- To identify some of the effects of employee absenteeism on the Canadian economy and organizations.
- To recognize the personal and job factors related to absenteeism.
- To explain the reasons for absenteeism, using the expectancy theory model of motivation.
- To develop practical proposals for controlling absenteeism and tardiness, with an emphasis on the use of positive rewards to motivate regular attendance.
- To explain the reasons for employee turnover, using the expectancy theory model of motivation.
- To develop practical proposals for controlling turnover, with an emphasis on the role of the equity of the compensation system.

INTRODUCTION

No organization is satisfied with merely attracting qualified and competent individuals. It also endeavours to retain them and wants them to report to work regularly and punctually. Stated differently, the organization's major preoccupation with its workforce is often to reduce absenteeism, tardiness, and turnover. The questions this chapter addresses are: How can rewards be used to reduce absenteeism and tardiness? How can rewards be used to reduce turnover? The responses to these questions will explore the variety of factors that are related to these questions, and propose practical strategies whose effectiveness is predicted by the conceptual framework discussed in the previous chapters.

HOW CAN REWARDS BE USED TO REDUCE ABSENTEEISM?

This issue will be examined by considering the problem and the effects of absenteeism, the personal and job factors related to absenteeism, the reasons for absenteeism, and the methods of controlling absenteeism, with an emphasis on the role of the compensation programme in the control effort.

PROBLEM AND EFFECTS OF ABSENTEEISM

Since 1957, absenteeism in Canada has been increasing at an average annual rate of 2.8 per cent. A 1980 study (*The Gazette* 1980) reported that

- absenteeism cost Canada an estimated $7.7 billion a year, which, relative to the size of the Canadian workforce, is substantially higher than the estimated $26.4 billion it cost in the U.S.;
- 400,000 employees are absent each working day in Canada; 350,000 call in sick, and another 50,000 are absent for other reasons;
- the cost due to absenteeism is 10 times the cost of time lost through strikes;
- the cost to the Canadian economy has been estimated at 100 million working days each year.

These statistics become even more of a concern when it is shown that 84 per cent of Canadian companies do not have an adequate system for monitoring and diagramming absence patterns (Johns 1980).

This picture of absenteeism, although bleak, does not portray the detrimental effects to organizations in terms of idle machinery and unused plant capacity, lower productivity, disrupted work schedules, increased cost in finding and substituting untrained labour, increased spoilage, poor product quality, increased overtime costs of carrying a higher inventory to offset production foul-ups brought about by absenteeism, and the inability to maintain contracted delivery schedules.

FACTORS RELATED TO ABSENTEEISM

An awareness of the factors related to absenteeism will provide the manager with the understanding needed to address this problem. These factors can be categorized into personal and job factors.

Personal Factors

Personal factors are age, sex, family, skill level, education. There is conflicting evidence with regard to age. Some studies suggest that absenteeism is higher among younger than older employees; other studies report that absenteeism increases with age. This conflict may be reconciled if the duration of the absences is considered. Younger employees have the highest rate of short-term absences: older employees, who may be more prone to illness, have the highest rate of week-long absences (Chadwick-Jones, Brown, and Nicholson 1973) relative to younger employees.

Sex and family have been found to be positively related to absenteeism (Chadwick-Jones, Brown, and Nicholson 1973). Married women who are newly hired and are in low-skilled, low-paid occupations show greater absenteeism — probably reflecting the traditional expectation that women should attend to family responsibilities. Furthermore, in the case of unpaid absences, it might make economic sense for women in low-paid occupations to be absent because they will suffer less of a financial loss relative to the husband — assuming that the husband is in a higher-paid job. Single or divorced women have a better attendance record. On the other hand, unmarried men with low skills show a greater incidence of absenteeism.

Employees with only a high school education are more likely to be absent than employees who have graduated from college. Likewise, employees with a relatively low skill level are more likely to be absent than employees who are relatively highly skilled. That employees with low education and low skills are likely to be in low-skill, unstimulating, low-paid jobs may explain the higher absenteeism.

Job Factors

Included in this category are job content and job context factors, for example, the nature of the work, the size of the work group, income, working conditions, the nature of supervision, sick leave policies, time of absence, and organizational commitment. The nature of the work is the most critical determinant of absenteeism. As was discussed in Chapter 5, employees with high growth needs who are placed in jobs that do not provide challenge and opportunities for personal accomplishment will not experience internal work motivation and their overall job satisfaction will be low. For these employees, absenteeism is one way of coping with an unsatisfying job. For similar reasons, monotonous, repetitive jobs tend to cause more absenteeism. Employees in a smaller work group are less likely to be absent than employees in a larger work group. A small group is conducive to cohesive and intimate social relations that permit group pressure if absenteeism is inconsistent with the group norms. In a small group, supervision is also more employee centred and less formal; employees can get time off with relative ease when they genuinely need it. Because high-income-group employees are likely to be in jobs with a higher motivating potential, they tend to be relatively less absent than low-income-group employees. The perceived fairness of income is also related to absenteeism. Employees who perceive that income is fairly determined will be less likely to be absent than those who do not perceive it to be fairly determined, because the latter will then use absenteeism as a means of restoring equity.

Hazardous working conditions and monotonous, repetitive jobs contribute to a higher rate of absenteeism. The high incidence of absenteeism in the auto industry has been attributed to monotonous, repetitive jobs. Shift workers have a better attendance record than regular day workers. Perhaps this is because traffic at the time of shift changes is generally not heavy.

The nature of supervision also has an impact on absenteeism. When employees experience satisfaction with supervision, they are more likely to have a better attendance record. Employees will experience greater job satisfaction, and hence have a better attendance record, with a democratic supervision style rather than an autocratic supervision style. If managers and supervisors are indifferent to absenteeism, absenteeism will increase.

Vacation and sick leave policies often have the unintended effect of promoting absenteeism. Some of the design features in sick leave policies for promoting a better attendance record are (*a*) establishing the exact sick leave entitlement in terms of paid days; (*b*) allowing employees to accumulate all or the unused portion of their sick leave entitlement; and (*c*) not paying for the first day of absence (Ng 1989).

The time preference for remaining absent also provides useful insights for understanding absenteeism. Absences are more likely to occur on the first and the last day of the work week, on the day following payday, and on the days immediately preceding and following holidays. Employees may want to avoid an uninteresting job and will do so as soon as their personal cash-flow position permits.

Employees with a strong sense of loyalty and commitment to the organization are more likely to have a better attendance record (Clegg 1983). Being present on the job is a good way of demonstrating loyalty and commitment.

REASONS FOR ABSENTEEISM

The phenomenon of absenteeism is a rupture of the bonds that tie the employee to the organization and motivate him/her to attend. Understanding absenteeism means understanding an employee's attendance motivation. The expectancy theory model provides a useful conceptual framework for explaining attendance motivation.

As can be seen in Figure 7.1, employees will be motivated to put in the effort to attend work if (*a*) they believe that they can attend, (*b*) they believe that when they attend they will receive outcomes, and (*c*) they value these outcomes. In other words, their attendance motivation is a function of their effort ——► attendance and attendance ——► outcomes expectancies, and the valence of the outcomes. The terms are added and multiplied, as discussed in the expectancy theory model in Chapter 4. This section considers the determinants of the expectancies and how they influence the attendance motivation process.

The Effort ——► Attendance Expectancy

Employees' effort ——► attendance expectancy is determined primarily by their perceptions of the *actual situation*. Several factors or circumstances in the actual situation can prevent or make attendance difficult. These are employees' health, family obligations, and the availability of transportation.

Employee illness and accidents are a frequent cause of absenteeism, particularly as the employee advances in age. Most illnesses are the result of natural causes but can sometimes be the result of drug and alcohol abuse. If such abuse is related to the monotonous and repetitive nature of the work or the stressful conditions under which the work is done, the illness becomes the special concern and responsibility of the organization. Illnesses and accidents that render an employee unable to attend work can be categorized as involuntary absence. Not included as illness is the voluntary absence that masquerades as illness. Some years ago a newsletter, the *Morgan Guaranty Survey* (n.d.), reported that a company experienced a 43 per cent rise in absence due to sickness within a five-year period. A close examination revealed that a substantial improvement in sick leave benefits during that period had apparently provided malingering employees with positive incentives. This form of absence will be discussed further in considering the impact of sick leave and benefits.

Family obligations often work as an impediment to regular attendance at work. This appears to be so, more in the case of married women who, regardless of the job held, are traditionally expected to attend to the care of their sick children. With husbands now increasingly involved in the raising of their children through such benefits as paternity leave, the absenteeism of married females will likely decrease. Absenteeism due to family obligations can be classified as involuntary or unavoidable absence. Availability of transportation can also make attending work — or attending work on time — difficult. This is especially true when

Figure 7.1
Expectancy Theory Model for Explaining Attendance Motivation

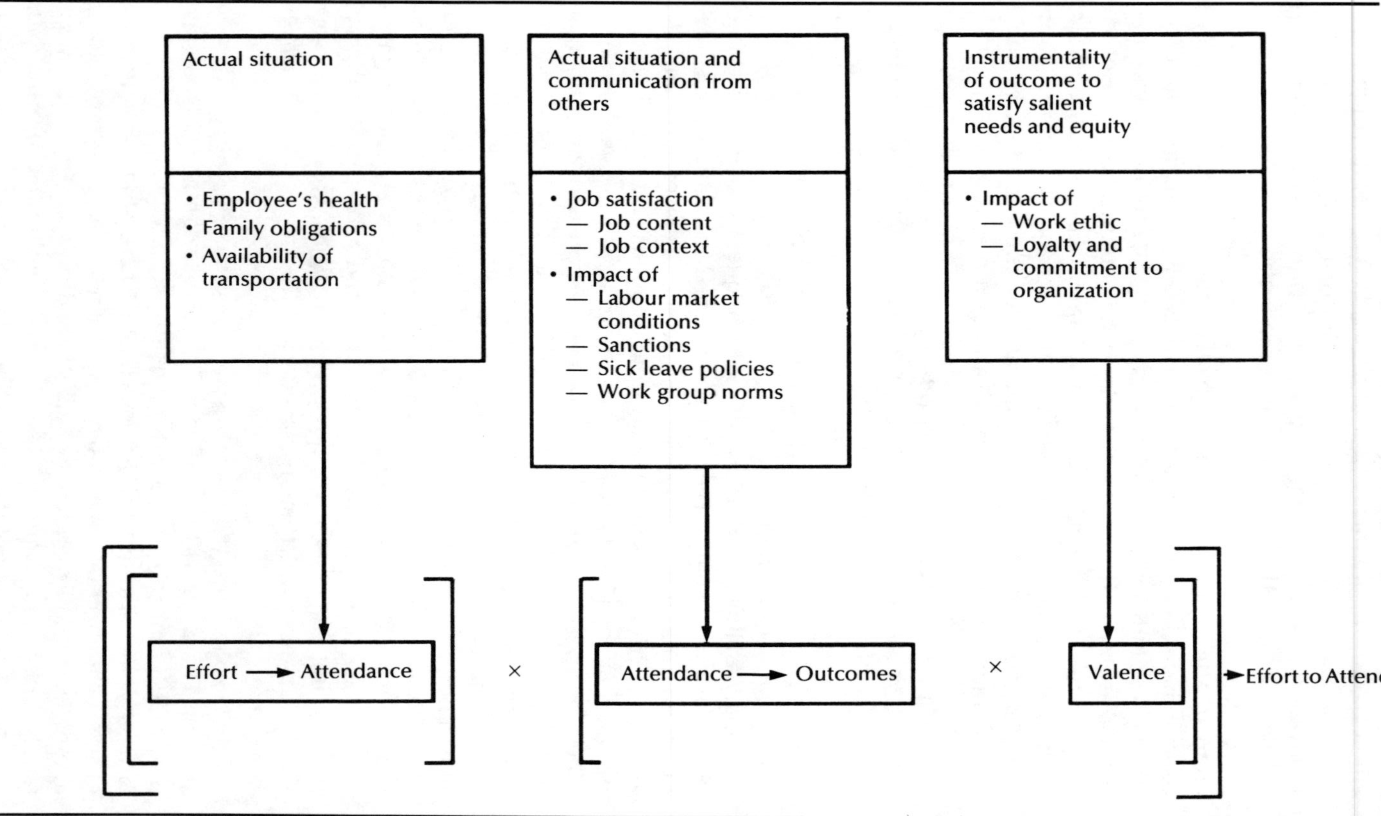

transport services are disrupted by bad weather or by the strikes of public transportation employees. Absence from work because of transportation problems is often unavoidable and involuntary.

The Attendance ⟶ Outcomes Expectancy

The critical determinants of this expectancy are the *actual situation* (i.e., the prospects of satisfaction with the job content and the job context resulting from work attendance; and the impact of labour market conditions, sanctions for non-attendance, and sick leave policies), and *communication from others* (i.e., work group norms).

As was shown in Chapter 5, the job content greatly influences an individual's internal work motivation, including the motivation to attend work. Employees with high growth needs and the requisite knowledge and skill will be motivated by an enriched job. Such a job makes employees want to go to work, because it provides them with an opportunity to experience challenge, feelings of accomplishment, and feelings of being needed in the job. If the core characteristics of an enriched job are missing, however, the employee's attendance motivation will be severely affected, and the likelihood of voluntary absence will greatly increase. If dissatisfaction from the unfulfilling job is intolerable, the individual may engage in a job search that will cause absence from work.

Dissatisfaction with the job context — working conditions, pay, co-workers, supervisors — also weakens the employee's motivation to attend work. Absenteeism under these conditions can also be considered voluntary, and is generally a device to redress the inequity experienced by the employee, particularly pay inequity. Voluntary absenteeism and job dissatisfaction are closely associated. When employees are satisfied with both the content and context of the job, regular work attendance becomes an occasion for experiencing outcomes that are attractive and desirable. But when attendance becomes an occasion for experiencing dissatisfaction, as is usually the case when employees are not satisfied with the job content or the job context, absenteeism is usually the result. Other factors in the actual situation can operate to alleviate or worsen the absenteeism that results from job dissatisfaction. For instance, when unemployment is high, job search activities will be reduced and the rate of absenteeism will be lower; on the other hand, low unemployment could increase absenteeism. Sanctions for non-attendance (e.g., the docking of pay, undesirable assignments, the refusal of opportunities to earn overtime pay) can also serve to reduce voluntary absences. Sick leave policies sometimes control absenteeism and sometimes contribute to its increase. The experience of one Montreal organization provides a graphic illustration of how a sick leave policy can have the unintended effect of increasing absenteeism. The policy granted employees 15 paid sick days per year, but the unused days could be accumulated and cashed on retirement. Despite this incentive, the average rate of absenteeism did not decrease and cost the organization $11 million (Johns 1980). Younger employees preferred to use the sick days at the time for casual absences rather than benefit from them later, at retirement.

Work group norms are a powerful factor in determining the attendance-outcomes expectancy, but they are two-edged. If the norms of a highly cohesive work group are supportive of regular attendance, employee absence in that group will be low. But if group norms operate to socially ostracize members who attend regularly, absenteeism will be high.

The Valence of Outcomes

Before the valence of outcomes is discussed, it is important to recognize that the attendance-outcomes linkage and the absence-outcomes linkage are really two sides of the same phenomenon. The valence of outcomes, whether the outcomes are from attendance or from absenteeism, is determined by the instrumentality of outcomes to satisfy needs and the equity of outcomes. When employees with high growth needs attend work, they anticipate that they will be working in an enriched job that will be instrumental in satisfying their growth needs. But if these same employees are required to attend work on a monotonous, repetitive job that is low on the core job characteristics, they will find their growth needs frustrated, and are likely to resort to absence from work in order to indulge in more autonomous activities such as golfing and fishing, which they enjoy. Absenteeism in such cases becomes instrumental in providing outcomes that they value. By remaining absent from work, they are also able to avoid outcomes that they find unattractive, and do not value.

There are many occasions when, despite the negative valence of outcomes from attending work (unsatisfactory job content or job context), employees might not resort to absenteeism. Their work ethic, a compelling belief in the goodness of work itself, might induce in them a moral compulsion to attend work. Also, employees' loyalty and commitment to the organization's objectives might compel them to attend work even if they find the actual job tasks to be repulsive and unpleasant. Attending work for reasons of the work ethic or organizational commitment generates outcomes that are valued because they are instrumental in satisfying salient needs born of the individual's personal value system. These positive valences far outweigh the negative valence of the outcomes of an unsatisfactory job content or job context. Employees also resort to absenteeism in order to reduce the inequities they might experience in the job context, particularly in the area of compensation. This point was discussed at some length in considering the determinants of pay satisfaction and the consequences of pay dissatisfaction.

Methods of Controlling Absenteeism

The preceding analysis of the reasons for absenteeism provides a useful framework for developing practical proposals for controlling absenteeism. The discussion of the effort ⟶ attendance expectancy highlights the need to differentiate between involuntary and voluntary absences. The former are unavoidable, the latter are avoidable. Absences caused by illness and accidents, by the necessity to attend to family obligations, or by the unavailability of transportation are involuntary, unavoidable absences. Nevertheless, some organizational interventions in this area might help. For instance, drug or alcohol abuse and the resulting illnesses or accidents might be related to the nature of the work — its design, its stresses, and so forth. An employee counselling or related programme, such as the now commonly used employee assistance programme (EAP), would be an appropriate way to address this kind of situation. Along with the EAP, efforts should be made to identify and eliminate the work-related sources of the problem.

Controlling absenteeism, particularly where there is a high incidence of voluntary or avoidable absences, needs approaches that are specifically designed to address the cause of the absence. The approach that is adopted must be specific both to the organization and to the employee. A considerable burden is placed on the ingenuity of managers to develop strategies that are appropriate for their employees. The strategies that will be discussed in this section are flex time, shorter work week; transportation facilities; job design; job context satisfaction; sick leave policies; the use of sanctions; and the use of positive rewards.

Flex Time, Shorter Work Week

Absences caused by the need to meet family obligations have been reduced to some extent by day-care centres situated in the workplace. Some organizations have introduced flex time and a four-day, 40-hour work week. Flex time gives employees the flexibility to attend to some of their family obligations. Flex time also eliminates the employee tendency to covert tardiness into a full day's absence. Sometimes, attending to personal matters will cause an employee to be late for work by an hour or so. If the organization's attendance policy requires that employees' pay be docked for the period they are late, an employee might decide to be absent for the whole day, since the additional loss of pay will not appear to be especially painful. With a shorter work week, the organization still receives 40 hours of work, but the employee gets an additional day off for attending to personal and family obligations. Organizations must consider the possibility of fatigue that the extended work day might cause, and its effects on absenteeism or productivity.

Transportation Facilities

Attendance problems created by transportation difficulties are sometimes addressed by a company-organized shuttle bus, especially where the plant is not adequately served by public transportation. Some organizations encourage their employees to organize car pools and as an incentive provide special parking facilities to these employees. These measures, where feasible, should alleviate the problems of absenteeism and tardiness.

Job Design

A well-designed job contributes greatly to attendance. Hence, job redesign is appropriate when a job diagnostic survey reveals a job profile that is low on the core job characteristics. Special attention should also be paid to increasing employees' commitment to the organization. Such commitment has a beneficial effect on attendance. The rationale and the implementing procedures for job redesign have been discussed in Chapter 5. Employee training and career development programmes should also be considered for promoting job satisfaction.

Job Context Satisfaction

Dissatisfaction with the job context requires several interventions, depending upon the aspect of the context that causes the dissatisfaction. The most frequent cause is pay — more specifically, the perceived inequities of the compensation system, which could be in the area of personal, internal, or external equity. Specific recommendations to address such inequities will be discussed when compensation programmes and techniques of performance-based pay (for personal equity), job evaluation (for internal equity), and salary and benefit surveys (for external equity) are considered. Organizational stressors such as an oppressive supervision style can have detrimental effects on employee attendance. Efforts to remove these stressors, possibly through appropriate training for supervisors and managers, will help to reduce absenteeism. Furthermore, employees are generally not satisfied with autocratic supervision. In an autocratic environment, control of absenteeism is obtained through incentive plans to promote attendance. In a democratic environment, employees experience relatively greater job satisfaction. Control of absenteeism can be accomplished through plans that involve the satisfaction of the higher-level needs. This point will be considered again when the use of positive rewards to promote attendance is discussed.

Improving the physical working environment (e.g., by illumination, by building design) contributes to reducing absenteeism. Closely related to the work environment are work group norms, which can facilitate or punish regular attendance. An organizational culture should promote the development of work norms that support regular attendance. Autonomous work teams created by Quality of Working Life and related employee involvement programmes are usually successful in developing work norms that bring pressure on members to attend work regularly. Although the work team is given the freedom and resources to achieve its objectives, it is also held accountable for them. Any behaviour by a member that hinders the group's effectiveness is subjected to sanctions whose efficacy is ensured by the remarkably high degree of cohesiveness in the group. Another aspect of the work context that affects work attendance is employee perceptions of job security. Open and honest communication on matters that threaten job security will tend to reduce the uncertainty that often causes employees to search for alternative job opportunities. The elimination of the need for job search will contribute to reducing absenteeism.

Sick Leave Policies

An organization's sick leave policies need to be carefully reviewed. A useful set of guidelines would be to (*a*) clearly specify the exact entitlement of the paid sick leave (e.g., 7, 10, or 12 paid sick days per year); (*b*) allow employees to accumulate or carry forward unused sick days; (*c*) pay only from the second day of absence (Ng 1989). When the entitlement is clearly specified, there is a greater likelihood that decisions on this issue will be consistent, and hence fair and equitable. Also, a clearly specified entitlement can be monitored better. Employees who are allowed to accumulate unused sick days are encouraged to utilize them for genuine illnesses, either now or in the future. An organization that does not permit such accumulation fosters an irresponsible use of sick days, for example, for casual absences, particularly towards the end of the year when the entitlement lapses. The rationale for not paying for the first day of absence is to discourage the use of sick days for casual absences. A casual absence is expensive, particularly if employees are on a four-day, 40-hour week. The organization also sends a message that sick days are for genuine illness and not for occasional indispositions. An organization might consider more generous long-term illness or disability benefits that employees can use when necessary in place of the fixed, annual entitlement of sick days, which tend to be used for casual absences.

Use of Sanctions

Many organizations use sanctions to control absenteeism. The objective of sanctions is primarily to control casual absences of a short duration. A programme of sanctions requires that a detailed record of attendance be kept, and every absence is checked to ensure that the employee has complied with reporting procedures and produced the medical documentation required. Failure to comply with stringent reporting procedures exposes the employee to a host of measures ranging from docking of pay to disciplinary measures that in cases of chronic absenteeism might even lead to termination. Are sanctions effective? A programme that is well publicized, consistently and uniformly applied, and based on a rigorous monitoring of absences tends to be effective. Such a programme, however, controls only casual absences, because ingenious employees soon find creative ways around the system, such as staying absent for longer periods that fall outside the scope of the sanctions programme. Thus, sanctions reduce the frequency of absences, but the fewer absences are of a longer duration. There are two basic problems with sanctions: (1) the measurement problem; and (2) the side-effects, which are inevitable in any programme based on punitive measures.

The Measurement Problem

The following can be used to measure absenteeism: the percentage time-lost index, the frequency index, the blue Monday index, and the worst-day index.

The percentage time-lost index is a measure of the absence level expressed as a percentage of time lost from the total available working time. The time lost includes both voluntary and involuntary absences and therefore covers long-term sicknesses as well as casual absences. The percentage time-lost index, which is weighted heavily in favor of long-term unavoidable absences, does not provide a realistic picture of voluntary absences, which are usually the target of the sanctions programme. Nevertheless, the percentage time-lost is a good indicator of the total economic cost to the organization.

The frequency index is a count of the number of times an absence of a given length has occurred per employee. The length of absence could be one day, two days, three days, and so forth. For example, Victor has had 5 two-day absences in the last 12 months. The frequency index gives greater weight to shorter absences, which are more likely to be the target of the sanctions programme. Note that the organization must question which is preferable — 10 one-day absences or 3 three-day absences.

The blue Monday index keeps track of absences that occur on Mondays and Fridays. Because this index emphasizes casual absences on predetermined weekdays, but ignores absences on the other days of the week, it does not provide a complete picture of all casual absences. Nevertheless, if the index serves to highlight a historical pattern in the organization, it might be worthwhile. For example, assembly-line workers in the auto industry have been known to have a high blue Monday index.

The worst-day index attempts to document which days of the week have the best and worst record of absences.

Which measures are appropriate for a sanctions programme? No one answer is universally applicable to all organizations. Each organization must keep detailed absence records, from which absence patterns will emerge. An analysis of the emergent patterns relative to their economic and non-economic costs should help the organization to identify one or more absence patterns that need to be subjected to the control processes of the sanctions programme.

The Side-Effects of Sanctions

The punitive measures involved (docking of pay, stringent administrative controls) are effective in reducing absenteeism, but they also produce a variety of side-effects, for example, an increase in grievance rates, vandalism, the sabotage of operations, and stress on the managers and supervisors who are required to implement the programme. The poor climate produced by sanctions could lead to an increase in turnover. In any event, sanctions do not reduce the average rate of absenteeism; they only reduce the frequency of absences. For these reasons, the use of positive rewards is preferred to the use of sanctions.

Use of Positive Rewards

In this approach, employees who put in the desired attendance at work receive rewards that reinforce the attendance behaviour. This reinforcement will be achieved only if the reward is designed in such a manner that it is directly linked to the desired level of attendance that is within the reach of the employees. In other words, the required attendance level to earn the reward must be capable of being achieved. For example, suppose the reward is set for perfect attendance for a 12-month period. If an employee happens to miss work in the first couple of months, he/she will not be eligible for the reward, and the reward will cease to be an incentive for this employee to strive for perfect attendance for the remainder of the year. The qualifying attendance period needs to be short. "The best documented successful cases have used time periods of 13 weeks or less — usually much less, ranging down to a week" (Johns 1980, 56).

The reward must be valued by the employees. Some employees prefer time off credited to their vacation; others prefer cash. Furthermore, employees should be involved in the design of the rewards. Such employees have a much better attendance record than employees who are not given the opportunity to participate (Lawler and Hackman 1969).

Rewards for perfect attendance can also take the form of lotteries. Employees who have perfect attendance for a predetermined period qualify to have their names drawn for a lottery prize. The qualifying attendance period should be short, for reasons discussed earlier. Recognition of perfect attendance by one's peers and supervisors is also effective in promoting attendance. The overtime policy of the organization should be carefully reviewed, since it has the potential to promote either absenteeism or perfect attendance. For example, a policy that allows employees who have had a paid casual absence to catch up with their work on overtime at the premium rate of pay encourages employees to be absent. If the opportunity to work overtime and to earn the premium pay is given only to perfect attenders, the overtime policy rewards attendance. However, overtime should not be an imposition on an employee who attends regularly if for some reason that employee is unwilling to work overtime. Special assignments that are perceived by employees to be particularly attractive and therefore desired by all should be given to the perfect attenders.

HOW CAN REWARDS BE USED TO REDUCE TARDINESS?

How can positive rewards be designed to control tardiness and the practice of leaving work before the scheduled time? A clock-in and clock-out procedure with pay computed on the basis of the time clocked is a common practice in many organizations. Often, tardiness and early departures receive strong disapprovals from the supervisor and one's peers, particularly if one is a member of an autonomous work team. Both the loss of pay and the disapproval of the supervisor or of peers are sanctions that have the potential to create undesirable consequences. A more positive approach would be to adopt practices that reward punctuality both for starting and ending the work day. Some organizations use lotteries that give employees who are punctual an opportunity to win reasonably handsome prizes. Other organizations provide for ego-need satisfaction, which is done on an individual as well as on a group basis. For example, the names of employees who have never been late for a predetermined period of time can be publicized through the organization's communication media — house magazine, bulletin boards, letters from the appropriate unit supervisor. Employees should also receive direct, straightforward feedback on their tardiness, given on an individual basis as part of coaching and mentoring efforts.

As in the case of absenteeism control, the opportunity to work overtime with premium pay should first be made available to punctual employees. Similarly, specially prized work assignments should be given to punctual employees. In both cases, the element of compulsion should be avoided. Neither overtime nor the special assignment should be imposed on the punctual employee who might be reluctant to accept it.

A variety of proposals for controlling absenteeism and tardiness have been reviewed. The effectiveness of the proposals is enhanced when superior-subordinate trust is high, and when workers' initial experiences with the measures have been positive. In controlling absenteeism and tardiness, the fundamental first step that managers should take is to recognize the severity of the problem and accept their responsibility for confronting and controlling it. Managers should be evaluated on their initiatives and efforts in controlling absenteeism and tardiness.

HOW CAN REWARDS BE USED TO REDUCE TURNOVER?

Employee turnover usually hurts the organization. The costs of turnover range from the cost of replacing the employee (costs of recruitment, selection, training) to the costs resulting from loss of revenue or the inefficiency and ineffectiveness of operating an understaffed organization. Of course, not all turnover is undesirable. The departure of poor performers is a blessing, as is the departure of employees who can, without detriment to the organization's effectiveness, be replaced by low-paid employees. In practice, this last scenario is rare, and highly improbable in a well-managed organization, where high pay is commensurate with the employee's contribution to attaining the organization's objectives. Most organizations strive to minimize the turnover rate because they cannot afford the luxury of an unstable and inexperienced workforce.

Although many factors contribute to employee turnover, dissatisfaction with the compensation system is an important determinant. Therefore, the compensation system, properly designed and administered, becomes a critical strategy that organizations use to retain their employees. What factors influence the employee's decision to stay with the organization? How — and more importantly, why — do the elements of the compensation system play such a key role in the employee's decision to stay or leave the organization? The sections that follow address these questions, and suggest how managers can effectively use the compensation system to control employee turnover.

WHY EMPLOYEES STAY WITH OR LEAVE AN ORGANIZATION

A frequent response to this question is job dissatisfaction. But some dissatisfied employees leave the organization and some stay. With what aspect of the job must an employee be dissatisfied before leaving the organization? As discussed in Chapter 5, pay dissatisfaction, an important element of job dissatisfaction, does not necessarily lead to turnover; on the contrary, it could lead to a desire for higher pay and in turn to higher performance if pay is performance based. Therefore, a more complete and satisfactory treatment of the issue of turnover must consider related factors, for example, job content, job context, and external environmental factors. These factors were dealt with in Chapter 5 in the context of the issue of the consequences of pay dissatisfaction. These factors will be examined again within the conceptual framework of the expectancy theory model of motivation to provide a better understanding of the phenomenon of turnover and some preparation for developing specific and practical guidelines for controlling turnover.

As can be seen in Figure 7.2, employees will be motivated to put in the

Figure 7.2
Expectancy Theory Model for Explaining Organizational Tenure

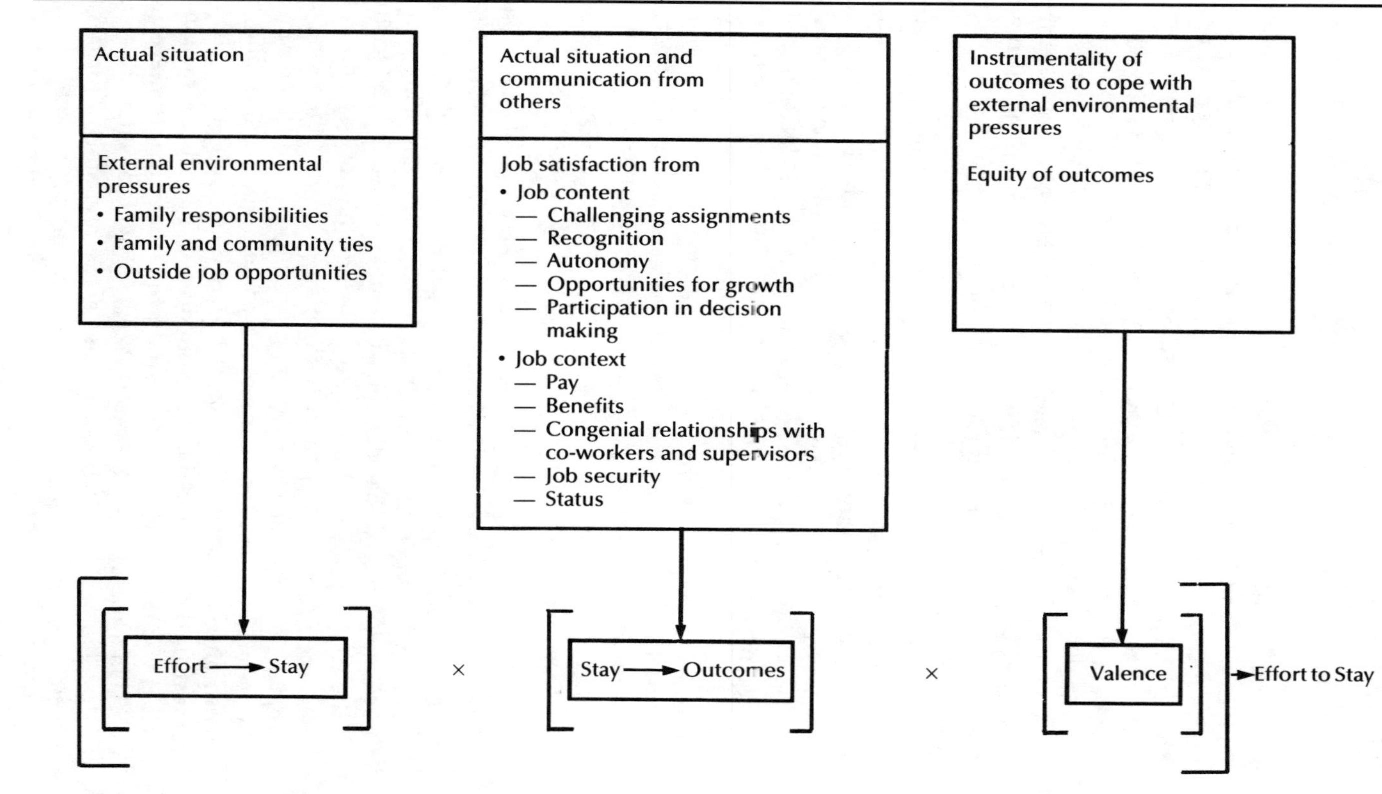

effort to stay with an organization if (*a*) they believe that they can stay, (*b*) they believe that when they stay they will receive a set of outcomes, and (*c*) they value these outcomes. In other words, their motivation to stay is a function of their effort → stay and stay → outcomes expectancies, and the valence of the outcomes. The terms are added and multiplied, as discussed in the expectancy theory model in Chapter 4. The next sections consider the determinants of the expectancies and how they influence the individual's motivation to stay.

The Effort → Stay Expectancy

Employees' effort → stay expectancy is determined primarily by their perceptions of the *actual situation*. The factors or circumstances of the actual situation are the external environmental pressures experienced by employees, for example, family responsibilities, family and community ties, and available outside job opportunities. The effort → stay expectancy is complementary to the effort → leave expectancy; the effort-stay and the effort-leave linkages are really two sides of the same phenomenon. Hence, external environmental pressures can be viewed as influencing the employees either to stay with or to leave the organization.

A variety of family responsibilities can determine employees' effort → stay expectancy. Employees who have financial obligations such as a home mortgage or the cost of their children's university education are less able to bear the risks involved in a move to another organization, unless the move enables them to cope better with these obligations. If the move involves relocation to another city and the spouse is also pursuing a career, whether the move will adversely affect the spouse's career must be considered. If the move will be detrimental to the spouse, the employee is compelled to stay on in the organization. Strong family and community ties, including the undesirability of disrupting children's schooling, will increase the pressures to stay. The third critical factor in the actual situation, the availability of outside job opportunities, can also increase the pressure to stay. This is especially true in times of high unemployment when job opportunities are few or when the individual perceives that he/she has few marketable skills. Environmental pressures can thus operate to increase or decrease the employee's belief that he/she must stay with the organization or can leave the organization.

The Stay → Outcomes Expectancy

The critical determinants of this expectancy are the *actual situation*, and *communication from others*. The outcomes in Figure 7.2 are derived primarily from the job content and the job context. As was seen in Chapter 5, the job content greatly influences employees' internal work motivation. Employees with high growth needs and the requisite knowledge and skill will experience the non-economic outcomes that flow from challenging assignments, achievement, recognition, responsibility, and opportunities for growth, and these outcomes will influence employees to stay with the organization because they want to stay. On the other hand, if the core characteristics of the job are missing, the job content will not be a significant factor in employees' motivation to stay with the organization.

Outcomes from the job context also play a role in motivating employees to stay with the organization. As shown in Figure 7.2, outcomes from the job context are pay, benefits, job security, status, congenial co-workers, satisfactory supervision, and a generally good working environment in the workplace. These outcomes serve as pressures from within the organization (internal environmental pressures) that make it attractive for employees to stay with the organization. When employees' expectancy of these outcomes is low, either in respect of the job content or the job context, then employees will be less inclined to stay with the organization and will be more inclined to leave the organization — provided the effort ⟶ stay expectancy is also low.

The Valence of Outcomes

Consistent with the expectancy theory model, the determinants of the valence of outcomes are equity and the instrumentality of outcomes to satisfy needs. The greater the employee perceptions of the equity of outcomes, the greater the valence of these outcomes. Generally, outcomes from the job content are within the employee's control because these are received or experienced by the employee as he/she performs the job. On the other hand, outcomes from the job context are administered by the organization. They are therefore more susceptible to being perceived by employees to be inequitable, either because of the size of the outcomes or because of inequity in the modality used to determine the outcomes.

Outcomes from the job content are the means of satisfying employees' growth needs. Employees with high growth needs will regard these as essential to their satisfaction with the job and to their willingness to stay with the organization. Outcomes from the job context contribute to satisfying many of the employee's salient needs, which are significant factors in the employee's decision to stay with the organization. For example, the outcome of pay, which enables the employee to meet his/her financial obligations, may be the major reason why the employee stays with the organization. Similarly, a congenial working environment may be the factor that makes the organization attractive to the employee.

The preceding analysis, based on the expectancy theory model, predicts that the employee's decision to stay with or leave the organization will be determined by environmental pressures and by the employee's reaction to the nature of the job, that is, the job content. Environmental pressure takes two forms — the external pressure and the job context, which is the source of the internal pressure to say with the organization. It follows that the external environmental pressure, the job content, and the job context provide the basis for effective strategies to control turnover.

Methods of Controlling Turnover

A systematic approach to controlling turnover must begin with efforts to assess the organization's annual turnover rate. The annual turnover rate is usually computed as a percentage, which is derived by dividing the total new hires in a one-year period by the average workforce in that same period. For example, the ABC Company hired 100 new employees in one year, and its average workforce in that same period was 1,000 employees. The annual turnover rate of the ABC Company is 10 per cent, that is, 100/1,000. Although the annual turnover rate is frequently computed for the entire organization, it is more usefully assessed for each work unit in order to identify the problem areas.

From the analysis in the preceding section it can be seen that the optimal situation for the organization will be to have its employees stay because they are satisfied with both the job content and the job context, and because pressures from the external environment compel them to stay. In other words, employees will stay because they "want to" (the work attracts them) and also because they "have to" (pay and benefits are attractive, and family responsibilities or family ties make it necessary for them to stay). An organization cannot control external environmental pressures, but it can closely monitor the job content and the job context. The practical guidelines discussed in Chapter 5 for managing the job content and pay (which is a major item of the job context) are also relevant and effective in controlling turnover.

In addition, the organization should pay particular attention to the issue of the equity of the compensation system, namely, personal, internal, and external equity. Turnover is one of the means that employees adopt to remedy inequity. Employees expect personal or individual equity, which is achieved when pay is based on performance. When merit pay does not significantly differentiate between mediocre and superior performers, superior performers are demotivated and may leave the organization. Specific action plans for addressing personal equity are discussed in Chapters 8 and 9.

Employees also expect that internal equity exists when their base pay is determined. Through internal equity, the organization recognizes the knowledge, skills, and abilities required for the job, as well as the level of difficulty and complexity of the job. Internal equity is achieved through job evaluation systems. Chapter 10 examines the policies, techniques, and processes that make for effective job evaluation programmes. Turnover is often a warning signal that there are external equity problems in the organization's compensation system. External equity is achieved when the organization's pay and benefits level is comparable to that of the external labour market. Chapter 12 discusses the techniques of pay and benefit surveys and related processes that an organization can use in order to ensure that its compensation system is consistent with the conditions of the external labour market.

The policies, techniques, and processes used to achieve equity in the compensation system are some of the principal strategies used to combat turnover. In addition, however, the organization needs to be vigilant in detecting the signs of turnover. Many organizations maintain employee turnover statistics on a regular basis and analyse them periodically to identify significant variations that might portend a high incidence of turnover. Exit interviews, systematically conducted, can also be useful in uncovering reasons for turnover. Finally, the diagnostic procedure discussed in Chapter 14 can be used in the turnover-control programme. The procedure evaluates the effectiveness of each compensation item and identifies equity problem areas.

SUMMARY

This chapter explored the phenomena of employee absenteeism, tardiness, and turnover, and developed practical proposals for controlling them. Employees' basic motivation to attend and to be punctual is affected by several personal and job-related factors. Health and family obligations, particularly in the case of married women employees, are critical determinants of absenteeism and tardiness. In certain circumstances, the lack of availability of regular transportation is also a contributory factor. Employees' motivation to attend is also affected by the content and the context of the job. Employees with high growth needs are frequently found to remain absent to avoid a monotonous and repetitive job. Dissatisfaction with the job context — pay, co-workers, or supervisors — also weakens employees' motivation to attend work. Absenteeism may also serve as a means of reducing the inequities that the employee perceives in the job context.

A wide variety of strategies exist to control absenteeism and tardiness. These range from flex time and a shorter work week to transportation facilities. In many cases, job design and career development programmes are effective in motivating attendance. So are the several measures that improve satisfaction with the job context, for example, equitable compensation, removal of organizational stressors, and improvements in the physical environment of the workplace. Although sanctions are useful and have a role in the control of absenteeism and tardiness, positive rewards that are valued by the employees have been found to be more effective. The organization's sick leave policies need to be carefully reviewed to determine that these do not produce the unintended effect of promoting absenteeism.

Programmes to control employee turnover should recognize the impact of the job content and context factors as well as of external environmental factors. Although dissatisfaction with the outcomes from the job content or job context might cause employees to consider leaving the organization, the ultimate determinants of employees' decision to leave are external environmental pressures from family responsibilities, family or community ties, or outside job opportunities. A programme to control turnover should include the practical guidelines discussed in Chapter 5 for managing job content and pay, the major item of job context. The other principal strategies in turnover control are the policies, techniques, and processes used to achieve personal equity (Chapters 8 and 9), internal equity (Chapters 10 and 11), and external equity (Chapter 12). The diagnostic procedure (Chapter 14) is also an invaluable tool for identifying equity problem areas in the compensation system.

KEY TERMS

blue Monday index
employee assistance programme
flex time
frequency index
organizational stressors
percentage time-lost index
worst-day index

REVIEW AND DISCUSSION QUESTIONS

1. Why are some personal and job factors more related to absenteeism than others?

2. "The expectancy theory model provides a useful conceptual framework for explaining attendance motivation." In the light of this model discuss the reasons for absenteeism.

3. Discuss some methods of controlling absenteeism. (Be sure to consider the conditions that contribute to their effectiveness.)

4. Lisa, an undergraduate student in business management, makes the following comments about her part-time sales job in a relatively fashionable, moderately priced retail clothing store in downtown Montreal:

"It's a great place . . . friendly co-workers and customers . . . terrific discounts on clothes. The company is very successful but its human resource policies aren't! The wages of salespersons are individually negotiated with wide variations for no rhyme or reason; and all employees are asked not to discuss their pay rates. The supervisors run the store as feudal lords . . ."

Lisa and her co-workers are dissatisfied. Why then do they still continue to work there? Using the expectancy theory model, explore the conditions and circumstances that cause an employee to stay or leave the organization.

5. Discuss how compensation strategies can be used to control turnover.

CASE: INTEXPRO INC. MEETS ABSENTEEISM HEAD-ON

Intexpro Inc., a relatively small manufacturer of industrial textile products, was plagued by the problem of absenteeism and decided to do something about it. Intexpro introduced an attendance bonus plan (ABP); its salient features were as follows:

- Rule 1: A bonus of $75 if the employee's total absence in one quarter was less than three hours.
- Rule 2: An additional bonus of $75 if the employee earned the attendance bonus stipulated in rule 1 in *each* of the four quarters.

Intexpro had a workforce of 213; about 90 per cent were women and 10 per cent were men. The average age was about 50 years and the average tenure in the company was about 12.4 years. The nature of the job tasks was moderately skilled. The cash compensation, made up of base rate and piece-work bonus, amounted to an average of $60 per day. The company was not unionized.

SOURCE: Based on Schneller and Kopelman (1983).

Discussion Questions

1. Do you think the attendance bonus plan was successful in reducing absenteeism? Why or why not?
2. Do you think that the plan would provide the low-pay employee group with a relatively stronger incentive to attend compared to the high-pay employee group? Why or why not?
3. Do you think the marital status of the employees would have an impact on the effectiveness of the plan? In other words, would the plan provide the unmarried employee group with a relatively stronger incentive to attend compared to the married employee group? Why or why not?
4. Would the prior absence rate (i.e., absence rate prior to the introduction of the plan) moderate the effectiveness of the plan? To consider this question, think in terms of the following employee groups:
   - low prior absence rate group
   - moderate prior absence rate group
   - high prior absence rate group

   Which group(s) would likely respond most favorably to the plan? Why?
5. What are some of the changes you would make to the plan? Why?

CHAPTER 8

PERFORMANCE-BASED PAY: PERSONAL EQUITY I

CHAPTER SYNOPSIS

This chapter, which continues the task of compensation system design, deals with performance-based rewards. These are the indispensable elements of a compensation system that seeks to achieve individual or personal equity. The chapter explores the concept of performance-based rewards, with a focus on performance-based pay, and considers the strategic and process issues in the design of a performance-based compensation system. In view of the critical role of performance appraisal in the effective administration of performance-based pay, the chapter concludes with a discussion of the performance appraisal process and practical guidelines for the successful conduct of the major activities in each step of the process.

LEARNING OBJECTIVES

- To define *job performance,* and to distinguish it from *effort* and *productivity.*
- To explain the objectives of performance-based rewards.
- To understand the conditions that must exist before pay can motivate employees to higher job performance.
- To understand the content of the strategic and process issues in performance-based pay.
- To develop appropriate criteria for strategic decisions that are critical to an effective performance-based pay plan.
- To describe the performance appraisal process.
- To develop practical guidelines for the major steps of the performance appraisal process in order to make it effective in the administration of performance-based pay.
- To understand the essential preconditions for an effective performance appraisal programme.

INTRODUCTION

An organization hires and retains employees for just one purpose, which is to enable the organization to achieve its objectives through their job performance. It follows that the organization's compensation system should be designed to reward only those job behaviours that contribute to achieving the organization's objectives. In principle, no reasonable employee would quarrel with this proposition. In practice, however, employees often, and justifiably, have difficulty accepting it. Their objection is not to the concept of performance-based rewards *per se*, but rather to the inequity or unfairness of the methods and the processes through which the concept is implemented. So, in exploring this very important topic on which the organization's effectiveness hinges, this chapter addresses some fundamental questions relating to the concept of performance-based rewards, and the methods and processes of its implementation. These questions are: What are job performance behaviours? What are the objectives of performance-based rewards? What are the conditions under which rewards increase or improve job performance? What are the strategic and process issues that must be considered in designing an effective performance-based compensation system? What is the role of performance appraisal in the administration of performance-based rewards?

JOB PERFORMANCE BEHAVIOURS

What are job performance behaviours? This is a simple but crucial question in the design and administration of performance-based rewards. If a manager intends to reward performance behaviours, then both the manager and the subordinate must be of one mind about what constitutes performance behaviours. To arrive at this agreement, they must be able to distinguish between effort, performance, and productivity. Consider the job of Sandra LaPierre, a salesperson, who is hired on a commission basis. She is assigned a sales target of $100,000 per month. By the third week of the month, she succeeds in closing a sale of $300,000, with the usual delivery period of two weeks. But a strike at her plant prevents adherence to the scheduled delivery date, and the customer cancels the order. Has Sandra performed? Should she be rewarded? From the point of view of Sandra, she has performed the required job behaviours that resulted in the sale. From the point of view of the organization, the end result has not been achieved. But can Sandra be held responsible for this end result? These questions arise because the reward system has focused on the end result or productivity, rather than on performance.

Performance refers to an employee's actual manifest behaviour at work. It is the set of the behaviours that are organizationally required. These behaviours are usually spelt out as tasks or behaviours in the official description of the job for which the employee is being paid or compensated. Performance depends on the employee's knowledge, skills, ability, and motivation. All these factors can be considered to be within the employee's control. Therefore, an employee can be held accountable for performance that is defined in this manner. When a performance appraisal is done, the evaluation of the individual's performance will be a check to see if these behaviours were performed, and how well they were performed.

Productivity, on the other hand, is the result, in terms of output, of performance, that is, of the organizationally required behaviours. For productivity (i.e., output) to occur, the employee's performance must interact with the inputs of the socio-technical system and the environment of the organization. In addition to the employee's own inputs, the other inputs of the social system are from co-workers, supervisors, and subordinates. The inputs of the technical system are materials, tools, machines, and the transforming or production process that is used. The environmental inputs are from the market, the economy, the union, and government regulations. Now, performance depends on the employee's inputs, which are under the employee's control. But productivity depends upon the employee's performance and the inputs of the socio-technical system and the environment. These latter inputs are *not* under the control of the employee. Sandra LaPierre's performance made the sale, but the sale did not materialize in terms of output or end result (i.e., productivity) because of an environmental factor that was not under her control. Sandra will not be rewarded, because the reward is based on productivity (i.e., end result) and not on Sandra's performance. Sandra and other employees who operate under such a reward system will be demotivated — and with good reason.

This discussion is not intended to suggest that rewards should not be tied to productivity. Rather, the point is that rewards should be tied to a performance or an end result that is clearly and unmistakably under the control of the employee. In fact, if both the performance and the end result are under the employee's control, then the rewards should be tied to both. For example, Sandra's job as salesperson includes the responsibility of deciding on her customers' credit applications, and her terms of compensation stipulate commission on sales that is subject to a charge back if the customer defaults on the payments. In this situation, Sandra's performance (her credit decisions) and sales (end result) are under her control. Therefore, the charge back is perfectly reasonable because it flows directly from Sandra's credit decision, which was under her control.

How does effort differ from performance? Effort can be defined as the expenditure of time and energy incurred in preparation for performance. Of course, time and energy (i.e., effort) are also expended when one performs. In the context of this text, effort is viewed as a set of behaviours that are not organizationally required, but that the individual must engage in, in order to better perform the required job behaviours. Sandra's job requires her to make credit decisions in respect of her customers. These decisions constitute her performance. Prior to making these decisions, she researches the customer's background and related matters, and this work involves effort. This effort, however, is not performance, but behaviours preparatory to making the decision that is the performance. An organization would ordinarily not pay for effort, but only for performance or end results (productivity), or both. Rewards should not be based on effort as defined here.

If a compensation system rewards employees for productivity only, it risks demotivating employees if the expected end results are not within the employees' control. Such rewards will be ineffective. A compensation system designed to reward employees for their efforts will likely not motivate them to put in the desired performance behaviours. Organizations with such a compensation system should not be surprised if some of their employees expect to be rewarded only for the effort, for example, the mere effort of attending work. A common stereotype of the work performance of government employees suggests that they appear to be paid primarily for coming to work, that is, for membership behaviours only. A close probe might reveal that this type of compensation design also exists in private-sector organizations. It is a question of degree and not of kind. Hence, the distinction between effort, performance, and productivity behaviours needs to be kept in mind in designing effective performance-based reward programmes.

OBJECTIVES OF PERFORMANCE-BASED REWARDS

The use of performance-based rewards is an excellent strategy available to an organization to achieve a variety of objectives in the management of its human resources. First, performance-based rewards have a significant influence on the type of personnel attracted to the organization. Employees who are achievement-oriented — the high-flyers and innovative employees — prefer and seek an organization in which their work contributions will be recognized and suitably rewarded. Organizations that do not differentiate between mediocre and outstanding performers but simply treat them alike will not be able to attract qualified, high-performing individuals. Second, even if an organization succeeds in hiring the high performers, it will not be successful in retaining them. At selection time, either because of an unrealistic job preview, inadequate research, or lack of employment opportunities, these candidates might join an organization that does not believe in or implement performance-based rewards. Such high performers soon realize the total lack of fit between their concept of rewards and the company's. Employees socialized in North America's highly individualistic culture naturally expect a work culture in which they are held accountable for their performance and are correspondingly rewarded. If these expectations are not met, it is unlikely that the organization will be able to retain the employees for long. Performance-based rewards, then, serve to retain high-performing employees.

The third objective of performance-based rewards is to motivate employees to attain organizational objectives. When employees perceive that their performance goes unrewarded, their perception of the performance-outcomes linkage is considerably weakened and their (P→O) expectancy is eventually lowered. Consequently, employees will not be motivated to perform, and job objectives will not be achieved. Fourth, performance-based rewards also increase employee satisfaction. As has already been seen, the equity or fairness of a reward determines satisfaction. Rewards administered by a rational process that adequately reflects employees' inputs will increase employees' perception of the fairness of the rewards. Performance-based rewards, supported by such a process, contribute to employee perceptions of equity, which in turn increase satisfaction. The resulting increase in satisfaction also contributes to reducing absenteeism and turnover. It can thus been seen that performance-based rewards provide effective support to the organization's efforts to attract, retain, and motivate its employees to attain the goals and objectives of the organization.

THE ROLE OF PAY IN INCREASING JOB PERFORMANCE

One of the critical objectives of performance-based rewards is to increase job performance. The experience of many organizations is that the mere introduction of these rewards does not lead to increased performance. There are, however, underlying conditions that facilitate the effectiveness of these rewards. Without these conditions, performance-based rewards often prove to be dysfunctional. Sometimes these rewards do not motivate the desired job behaviours, in which case the efforts at implementation prove futile. At other times the rewards produce dissatisfaction, with all its adverse consequences. Hence it is important to explore the conditions that make performance-based rewards effective. The discussion in this section focuses on one type of performance-based rewards, namely, pay. Other forms of monetary rewards, such as incentives and gain-sharing plans, will be discussed in Chapter 9. Performance-based pay has been selected because it is the largest reward item in an organization, both in absolute and relative terms, and because it lends itself relatively easily to being tied to performance. In fact, most organizations intend and hope that pay will motivate employees to attain organizational goals and objectives. Besides, historically, pay has invariably been based on performance, hence the expression: No work, no pay.

Under what conditions, then, does pay increase job performance? To begin with, money must be valued by employees. As the expectancy theory model shows, money is valued when it is instrumental in satisfying the salient needs of the employee *and* when it is perceived by employees to be fair and equitable. Hence, the amount of pay that rewards performance should be sufficiently large. Once the employee's salient needs have been satisfied, the amount of money that was required is no longer necessary. To that extent, pay tends to decrease in importance. Of course, pay also functions to satisfy esteem needs. If the self-esteem needs of the employee are salient, then pay will continue to be instrumental in satisfying these needs and will therefore continue to be valued by the employee. Employee perceptions of the fairness of the process by which the amount of merit pay is arrived at also influence the degree to which the merit pay will be valued.

The second condition is that employees have an accurate perception of the performance-pay linkage, so that their (P → O) expectancy will be increased. The performance-pay linkage should be made visible through effective communication and the proper implementation of the performance-based pay policy. Such communication and implementation will promote the performance behaviours necessary to support the organization's objectives. In a situation where the organization's objectives require employee cooperation, it is important that the pay be linked to the performance of cooperative behaviours. A good example is the reward system for players in the National Hockey League, where the success of a team depends upon the teamwork of its players. In order to foster and encourage teamwork, the reward system recognizes not only the scorers of the goals but also the other players who have contributed through assists. Such recognition extends to the efforts of the defencemen and the goalie. The defencemen are rewarded for clearing the puck from their end as well as for offensive play. The goalie's contribution is recognized on the basis of both shut-outs and shots saved relative to shots on goal.

It can happen that good performance results in negative consequences for employees. For example, a performance-based pay programme becomes effective in increasing the organization's productivity, and increased productivity eventually leads to lay-offs. The fear of such negative consequences could seriously jeopardize the effectiveness of performance-based pay. The third condition for ensuring that pay increases performance is that performance-based pay be designed and administered in such a way as to minimize the negative consequences of performing well.

The fourth condition under which pay increases job performance relates to the administration of the performance-based pay programme. The process of design and administration should not only minimize the negative consequences of performing well but should also produce positive consequences, for example, feedback on the specific aspect of performance that needs to be improved and how that improvement can be made, empowerment of employees leading to an increase in their self-efficacy beliefs, and removal of organizational obstacles to good performance.

The relationship between managers and subordinates must be characterized by trust and openness. The previous four conditions would inevitably lead to such a relationship, but management must make a special effort to see that such a relationship precedes the design and installation of a performance-based pay programme. Hence, the establishment of trust and confidence in manager-subordinate relations is the fifth condition under which pay increases performance.

These conditions under which pay increases performance suggest the criteria that a performance-based pay plan must meet in order for it to be effective. The plan should ensure that employees value money; should tie pay to performance; should minimize negative side effects; should promote positive consequences; should encourage cooperation; and should generally enhance the acceptance of performance-based rewards.

ISSUES IN PERFORMANCE-BASED PAY

The discussion so far, particularly the consideration of the conditions under which pay increases performance, provides the conceptual backdrop for the development of a performance-based pay plan. The actual structure and mechanics of such a plan for an organization require decisions on several other issues. Lawler (1981) has identified these issues as the level of aggregation, the number of performance-based pay plans, the mode of payment, the size of the payment, the measurement of performance, the frequency of the payment, and the process through which these issues are decided upon and the related techniques and procedures are implemented. Stated differently, the organization must decide on several critical options when it installs a performance-based pay plan. These options could be formulated in terms of the following questions:

1. Rewarding employees on the basis of individual, group, or organizational performance.

2. The number of performance-based pay plans.
3. Merit pay as a salary increase or a one-time bonus payment.
4. The appropriate amount of merit pay.
5. Subjective versus objective measures of performance.
6. The length of the payout periods.
7. Employee involvement in designing and administering merit pay.

The choices made are largely dependent on the specific circumstances of the organization — the nature of its business, its organizational structure and culture, and the preferences of its employees. Nevertheless, the choices must also be consistent with the basic characteristics of an effective reward as defined by the expectancy theory model and discussed in the previous section. The discussion in this section, based on Lawler's (1981) work, examines the choices involved in each question and explores the organizational and environmental factors that affect the choices. How a given set of choices will impact on the effectiveness of the merit pay programme is also considered.

1. Rewarding Employees on the Basis of Individual, Group, or Organizational Performance

The issue underlying this option is that of the *level of aggregation*, which is the basis for measuring and rewarding performance. In an organization, performance can be measured and rewarded at the level of the individual, of a predetermined work group or department, of the organization as a whole, or of a combination of one or more of these levels. Should the employee be rewarded for his/her outstanding performance even though the work group of which he/she is a member does not meet its objectives? Likewise, should the members of a work group be rewarded for their excellent performance even though the organization as a whole has not achieved its objectives? Each case raises the fundamental questions of performance-outcomes linkage, and of equity. When an individual's meritorious performance goes unrewarded because of factors beyond the individual's control, such as the poor performance of the other group members or of the organization, the individual's perceptions of the performance-outcomes linkage is weakened, if not completely ruptured. As a result, the individual's (P ⟶ O) expectancy is lowered and his/her motivation to perform is decreased. In addition, the individual will experience inequity, which will lower his/her valence of the outcomes. The drop in valence will also contribute to decreasing the motivation to perform. Furthermore, if the policy of secrecy prevails, the employee will likely receive inadequate and inaccurate feedback on performance. Such feedback has been found to lower the individual's (E ⟶ P) expectancy, thus adversely affecting the individual's performance motivation.

In addition to having a motivational impact, the level of aggregation permits the organization to promote both cooperation and competition among its employees, depending upon which is beneficial for the organization. For example, if the organizational needs are better served by autonomous work teams, then the level of aggregation will be the work team. By measuring and rewarding team performance, the organization will promote team cohesiveness and motivate team members to work cooperatively. This intrateam cohesiveness and cooperation might produce interteam competition, which will benefit the organization so long as the teams are not dependent on one another. If the teams are interdependent, then the organization will need to opt for a higher aggregation level that promotes cooperation rather than competition. This point will be reviewed in considering the factors that influence the level of aggregation.

By adjusting the level of aggregation of the performance-based pay programme, the organization can obtain more objective measures of performance. For example, the performance of certain individuals or smaller work groups in the organization may not lend itself to objective measures. In this case, a higher level of aggregation — a division or a plant, for example — will produce more objective measures of performance. Profit, for instance, is generally a more reliable indicator of the performance of a division rather than of a work group or even of a department. Likewise, the total number of finished products is a more objective measure of the performance of the plant as a whole than of a work unit.

Because the level of aggregation is a critical decision in the design of a performance-based pay system, is useful to identify the factors that an organization must consider in deciding on a level of aggregation that will enable its performance-based pay system to be effective. These factors are technology, information system, size, trust, and union status (Lawler 1981). The rest of this section will consider the separate impact of each factor on the determination of the level of aggregation and will then explore how the factors, as they exist in an organization, can be utilized to combine the different aggregation levels to develop a performance-based pay plan that suits the specific conditions in an organization.

Technology

The technological characteristics that are relevant to the level of aggregation are complexity and interdependence. In a job whose tasks require a relatively simple technology, the individual's job output or job performance behaviours can be easily identified and attributed to the individual's performance. The individual can be held accountable and rewarded for his/her performance. Where the job tasks require a complex technology, the output of the job, or the individual's performance behaviours in that job, are likely to be influenced by the performance of other employees. That being so, it may be unfair to attribute success or failure in meeting the job's objectives *entirely* to the individual's performance. A more complete measure of the individual's performance will be obtained if the contribution of the other employees is adequately considered. Therefore, the performance of all the employees involved will need to be measured and rewarded.

To sum up, where jobs involve a less complex technology, the aggregation level will likely be the individual; where jobs involve a highly complex technology, the aggregation level will likely be the group, the department, or a segment of the plant. A similar logic applies where the technology necessitates a job design with independent or interdependent tasks. The independent tasks of a job will support the individual level of aggregation. The interdependent tasks of a job will need a group or some other higher level of aggregation.

Information System

The process of evaluating employee performance is usually a combination of the measure of the job output and the supervisor's judgments of the performance of the job tasks. The measures of the job output (e.g., units produced, customers served, reports completed, sales closed) are the objective criteria; the supervisor's judgements (how well the required job behaviours were performed) are the subjective criteria. Generally, objective measures of performance are more acceptable to employees than subjective measures. Therefore, the preferred level of aggregation will be one that provides objective measures of performance. If the performance of the job tasks results in output that is capable of objective measurement, then the preferred aggregation level will be the individual. On the other hand, if the evaluation of the individual's performance involves a preponderance of subjective judgements, then an aggregation level higher than that of the individual should be used. The specific aggregation level will be one that permits the development of reasonably objective measures of performance; such a level might be the work group, a departmental unit, the plant, or the organization itself.

Size

The influence of organization size on the aggregation level is derived from the fact that the effectiveness of the performance-based pay system is dependent on employee perceptions that the predetermined performance measures (goals, targets, objectives) are under his/her control. If these measures are under the employee's control, then the appropriate aggregation level will be the individual. If not, then the appropriate aggregation level will be the work group, or some larger entity whose members feel reasonably confident that they have the resources and the necessary organizational support to attain the established goals. How does the size of the organization affect employee perceptions of influence and control of the measures of performance? In a large organization, individual employees will generally not be able to see any significant connection between their performance and the overall net results of the organization measured in terms of profit, return on investment, market share, and so forth. That being the case, establishing performance-based pay at the organizational level will be inappropriate. Performance-based pay will need to be established at the individual level and related to the individual's job objectives. This conclusion imposes a challenge and a responsibility on supervisors to come up with performance measures that truly reflect their employees' job tasks and objectives.

In a small organization, on the other hand, individual employees are in a relatively better position to see that their performance contributes to the realization of organizational objectives. Performance-based pay in a smaller organization can be established in terms of the overall results of the organization. It might happen that individuals are unable to see how their performance influences overall organizational objectives. Even so, in a smaller organization, individuals are more likely to see the influence of their performance on their work group or department. Thus, performance-based pay can be established at an aggregation level higher than that of the individual.

Trust

The element of trust is an important determinant of the aggregation level, because trust is at the very heart of employee perceptions of equity or fairness. This is especially so in the case of the performance-based pay system, which relies for its effectiveness on the employee's perceptions that the system is designed to measure and reward performance fairly and equitably. The evaluation of employees' performance is rarely an exercise in complete objectivity. Consider a performance-based pay system in which the performance target is 1,000 units per month. Such a measure could reasonably be considered as objective. However, one could always argue, for example, that a supervisor's subjectivity might be involved in determining which units are acceptable, that is, which conform to the organization's quality standards. In the vast majority of jobs in an organization, the evaluation of performance has a large component of subjectivity. Therefore, a climate of trust is an absolute imperative. The greater the trust of the employees, the greater their perceptions of the equity of the decisions, even in situations where the element of a supervisor's subjectivity in performance evaluation is high. On the other hand, where the trust is low, employees will likely be less inclined to accept a supervisor's subjective judgment of their performance.

There are two aspects of this trust: the employee's trust of the supervisor, and the employee's trust of the work group, department, or organization. Suppose the supervisor has developed good relations with his/her employees, engendering in them a high trust for their supervisor. This situation will be conducive to establishing performance-based pay at the individual level because the employee's perceptions of the equity of the supervisor's decisions of his/her performance will be high. On the other hand, suppose that employee trust of the supervisor is low, but the culture of the department has been supportive of an open communication policy, which has clearly spelt out the department's objectives and the expected standards of performance. In this situation, employees will develop considerable trust in the department, which will become the appropriate aggregation level. Thus, where employee's trust of the supervisor is high, rewarding employees on the basis of their individual performance is likely to be more effective. However, when employees' trust of an organizational unit or of the organization itself is high, then this higher aggregation level is more conducive to an effective performance-based pay.

Union Status

Unions generally shy away from individual performance-based pay systems, because these systems provide management with the mechanisms to compensate employees on a differential basis. Unions have traditionally been reluctant to repose much confidence, not so much in the ability of managers, but in managers' willingness and inclination to administer performance-based pay programmes in a fair and equitable manner. Individual performance-based pay programmes do not lend themselves to influence and control by the unions. In fact, unions often suspect that these programmes are utilized to reward employees who are opposed to unionization. Hence, the programmes are viewed by unions as a threat to their security. Unions are more inclined to accept performance-based pay programmes where the level of aggregation is the organization.

The preceding discussion of the determinants of the level of aggregation suggests that the choice before an organization is either of an individual level or of a higher level such as the work group, the department, or the entire organization. The characteristics of a situation that is most conducive to an individual aggregation level are a technology that is less complex and permits work design in which the job tasks are relatively independent; an information system that provides objective measures of the individual employee's performance; a relatively large organization in which the individual is unable to influence or control to any significant degree the overall net results of the organization's operations; high employee trust of the supervisor's judgment of their performance; and a non-unionized organization. The characteristics of a situation that is most conducive to a higher aggregation level are a complex technology which necessitates that the job tasks are interdependent; an information system that provides objective performance measures only at the work group or a higher aggregation level; a small organization whose structure and operations allow the individual to influence or control the overall net results of the organization's activities; on the part of employees, an understanding of the work unit's objectives, an acceptance of the performance standards, and trust of the organization; and union support or cooperation in implementing the performance-based pay plan.

For many organizations, the choice of the aggregation level will most likely not be either one of the two extremes, the individual or the group, but will probably involve a combination of the aggregation levels. An illustration of one such combination is the case of a large, non-unionized corporation whose internal work culture has successfully fostered a climate of trust and has encouraged its supervisors to function as coach and mentor to their subordinates. The positive response of employees is demonstrated by their effort and commitment to the specific, measurable job objectives set jointly by the supervisor and the subordinate. The job tasks are interdependent, and it is strategically important for the company's operations to be cost-efficient. The company has therefore decided on a merit pay programme linked to an objective measure of its overall performance, which is available from the company's information system. What would be the appropriate aggregation level for this corporation? The interdependent tasks and the availability of objective performance measures clearly suggests that the aggregation level be the total organization. However, the employees' trust of their supervisors, the availability of good measures of individual job performance (i.e., measurable job objectives), the large size of the organization, and the non-union status all favour an individual level of aggregation.

This apparent conflict can be resolved by a combination of the aggregation levels. Thus, the measures of organizational performance can be used to develop a fund for merit pay. The individual's merit pay, drawn from this fund, will be decided on his/her performance, that is, the meeting of the established job objectives. Because the combination plan is usually fraught with administrative difficulties, the critical factors in its success are the trust and the good supervisor-subordinate relations engendered by the internal work culture of the organization.

2. The Number of Performance-based Pay Plans

Organizations often choose to have more than one performance-based pay plan. Sometimes, it may be that organizational conditions necessitate different aggregation levels, and a plan to combine these levels is not feasible. At other times, conditions such as the nature of business operations, industry practices, and strategic considerations will induce the organization to explore the feasibility of installing more than one performance-based pay plan. What are the conditions under which an organization can effectively operate more than one plan? It will be recalled that the effectiveness of any plan depends on the employee's perception of the performance-outcomes linkage, and the equity of the plan.

Now, suppose that the organization decides to have three different plans for three different work units of the organization. Each plan will be effective if the employees covered by it believe that the predetermined performance measures truly reflect their performance. Furthermore, the employees should also believe that the results of their performance, on which the reward is based, are within their control. For instance, if the job tasks of the employees in one plan are dependent on the job tasks of the employees in the other plan(s), then this element of influence or control suffers. Having more than one plan when such interdependence exists is certain to prove dysfunctional and counterproductive, because the several plans will more likely promote competition rather than the cooperation that is appropriate for the situation.

As long as these conditions are met, organizations can quite successfully operate more than one performance-based pay plan. Some of the bases for establishing multiple plans in an organization are (*a*) a plan for each level of the organization, (*b*) a plan for each department or function in the organization, (*c*) a plan for each time span of performance (Lawler 1981).

A plan on the basis of the organizational level views the organization as a set of independent entities that exist horizontally in the organization, for example, senior-management, middle-management, first-line-management, professional, clerical, operations, and maintenance employees. Each of these horizontal levels has a separate plan to recognize the performance of the entity. Is such an approach, which virtually follows the organizational hierarchy, effective? Because of the homogeneous nature of the job tasks, it would be relatively easy to develop performance measures that are controllable by the employees. This approach, however, tends to assume that the horizontal levels are independent of each other. If, in fact, the interdependence of these levels and the need for cooperation among them is high, then the separate plans may prove to be dysfunctional.

Another basis for multiple plans takes a vertical approach to organizations. Thus, the entire organization is viewed as a set of departments, functions, or projects. Each of these entities encompasses all of the employees, management as well as non-management, and the plan's intent is to recognize the performance of each entity. This approach is at the heart of the profit centre concept. Is this approach effective? The heterogeneity of the job tasks — management, professional, clerical, operations, and maintenance employees — in one entity will make it difficult to develop measures that adequately reflect the contribution of each employee category to achieving the targets established for the entity. This situation also makes it difficult for the individual employee to perceive that he/she can influence or control the net results of the entity on which the rewards are based. The positive aspect of this plan is that it recognizes the interdependence that usually exists within a department or function. To that extent, the plan promotes cooperation within the entity. However, the plan might not recognize the interdependence that may exist between and among departments or functions. Hence, the plan design should ensure that the plan facilitates the cooperation that is needed among the interdependent entities.

An organization can have multiple plans to recognize the time span of performance. In some jobs, the employees, left to themselves, can focus either on the short-term or long-term objectives of the organization. The multiple-plans design is an excellent means through which the organization can send the right signals to these employees. For example, one plan might focus on the short-term objectives, another on the long-term objectives. This point will be reviewed in the discussion of the length of payout periods. The time span of performance basis is usually incorporated into plans that use horizontal or vertical approaches. Its effectiveness can therefore be enhanced by the positive features of the horizontal or vertical approach; its effectiveness can also be hindered by the negative features of these approaches. Nevertheless, the time span of performance emphasizes the temporal dimension of organizational objectives that often tends to be neglected in the design of performance-based rewards.

3. Merit Pay as a Salary Increase or a One-Time Bonus Payment

In addressing this issue, the chief consideration is: Which form strengthens employee perceptions of the performance-pay linkage? Traditionally, a salary increase has come to symbolize good performance. However, few organizations appear to administer a "salary decrease" when performance is below the expected standard. Consequently, an employee whose performance merits a salary increase in one year will continue to receive this increase in perpetuity even though his/her performance drops significantly in subsequent years. Furthermore, in order to maintain external equity, organizations often use the salary increase as a device to adjust their pay level following changes in the cost of living and/or market pay levels.

This practice of combining the merit increase with salary adjustments has the unintended consequence of weakening the employee's perception of the performance-pay linkage in two ways. First, all employees receive the salary adjustment increase, which frequently is a substantial component of the individual's total salary increase. As a result, the total salary increase conceals the differentiation that might be made between superior and mediocre performers. The effects of such concealment are aggravated in a secret merit pay system. Some organizations attempt to minimize the effect of concealment by clearly spelling out the merit-increase component of the total salary increase. Second, the merit component of the total salary increase would need to be substantial in order to create the desired motivational impact. But cost considerations might not make this feasible, especially when salary adjustments are necessitated by a spiralling increase in the cost of living, such as was experienced in the 1970s. The next section returns to other aspects relating to the issue of the size of the merit increase.

Merit pay in the form of a one-time bonus is a better alternative to salary increase because it enables employees to perceive much more clearly the performance-pay linkage. The individual's performance is followed by a bonus according to a predetermined schedule. Unlike the salary increase, the bonus does not become part of the salary and therefore does not constitute a perennial payment. A bonus is not paid when performance falls below the established standards. The bonus, moreover, is not suitable for adjustments to reflect changes in the cost of living and market pay levels. Some organizations adopt both forms of payment. The salary increase, which compensates for changes in the cost of living and in market pay levels, is granted to all employees; such adjustments promote external equity. The one-time bonus, awarded entirely on performance, seeks to achieve individual or personal equity.

4. THE APPROPRIATE AMOUNT OF MERIT PAY

This issue is the size of the merit pay that will motivate employees to perform effectively on the job. In terms of the expectancy model, it is essentially the issue of the employee's valence of merit pay, which is crucial in employee motivation. An employee will value merit pay when it is instrumental in satisfying his/her salient needs. But if a sizeable merit raise leads to the satisfaction of the salient needs, the result can be a lower valence of merit pay. However, as a recognition of performance, merit pay will be most instrumental in satisfying the employee's self-esteem needs. One can expect that the self-esteem needs of an individual with a high income will be better satisfied with a relatively larger amount of merit pay. As discussed previously, equity or fairness in determining the size of the merit pay should also be considered because it influences the employee's valence of merit pay.

Are there specific, quantitative guidelines for the size of merit pay? "A good rule of thumb here is that at least a 3 per cent change is needed in order for the individual to *notice a difference*" (Lawler 1981, 89). The suggested figure is 3 per cent of base salary and represents the average merit pay. This figure will obviously have to be revised upward during periods of inflation. Another factor that will influence the size of the merit pay is the extent of openness of the merit pay system. The greater the openness of the system, the greater is the motivational impact of a relatively smaller size of the merit pay. As was noted in the discussion of the effects of secrecy in Chapter 6, the motivational impact of even an above-average merit raise is completely dissipated by the perceptions of inequity that are generated by social comparison based on speculation and rumour. The size of the merit pay also has a motivational impact in a vicarious sense. Suppose an employee does not receive a merit raise because of poor performance, but is aware of the sizeable merit raises awarded to superior performers. The fact that the organization rewards superior performance by sizeable merit raises can in itself be a significant factor in motivating poor performers to improve their performance.

5. Subjective versus Objective Measures of Performance

A valid, accurate measure of performance is a crucial element of the performance-based pay system. If the organization intends to reward performance, then the performance has to be properly assessed and measured. Such assessment and measurement cannot be a unilateral activity, the judgement of the supervisor alone. The employee's assessment too is critical. If the employee feels that the supervisor's assessment does not adequately reflect the performance, then the employee will not perceive the outcomes to be equitable. As a result, the employee's valence of the merit raise will drop, and so will the motivational impact of the merit pay system.

Hence, it is imperative that the supervisor and the subordinate agree on the assessment of the performance. In reality, however, this prescription is difficult to follow, primarily because of the nature of the criteria used in measuring performance. Performance can be measured in terms of objective and subjective criteria. Objective criteria lend themselves to some form of quantitative measure such as output, sales, profits, or scrap rate. These measures have a high degree of validity and are therefore more credible and acceptable to both the supervisor and the subordinates. Of course, even for objective measures, the employee's trust of the supervisor is necessary, particularly in the choice and interpretation of the measures. But because these measures are verifiable, the degree of trust need not be high.

The subjective measures are the supervisor's judgements of the employee's performance. By their very nature, these measures are not verifiable. Therefore, their acceptance by employees is determined to a large degree by the trustworthiness of the supervisor. Once this credibility has been established, the subjective measures contribute to providing a more complete picture of performance, because it is virtually impossible to develop objective quantifiable measures for *all* the behaviours necessary to fulfil the job objectives. Supervisors often tend to treat objective measures as sacred cows, with results that are counterproductive and dysfunctional to the organization. For example, it is not uncommon for salespersons to achieve sales targets by neglecting customer service; or for a supervisor to achieve the short-term objectives of a department without the proper attention to employees' satisfaction with job content or job context that is necessary for the long-term effectiveness of the department.

Subjective measures allow the supervisor to focus on employee behaviours that are critical to attaining the job objectives. Besides, these measures do not require sophisticated and costly reporting systems. They do, however, need competent managers who are willing to "manage" their subordinates, not as mere administrators, but as coaches and mentors deeply committed to providing employees with the guidance, development, and resources they need for effective performance. It is, therefore, not a question of a choice between objective and subjective criteria. Rather, it is a question of choosing a set of measures, objective and subjective, that adequately capture the job behaviours needed to attain organizational objectives. The performance management process discussed later in this chapter spells out in greater detail the specific activities and requirements that are involved in this process.

6. The Length of the Payout Periods

This issue requires decisions on the frequency of merit payments. In principle, the frequency should be such as to strengthen employee perceptions of the performance-outcomes linkage, and to increase the saliency of merit pay. Ideally, the reward should immediately follow the performance of the desired behaviour, thus allowing the employee to see the performance-outcomes linkage. Such immediacy also increases the saliency of the reward and enhances its motivational value. Moreover, in terms of the behaviour modification approach, the greater frequency of the payout would generally contribute to reinforcing the desired behaviours. There is, however, the concern that the increased frequency might cause employees to focus on the short-term objectives of the job to the detriment of the long-term objectives. This legitimate concern can be addressed by a reward system that makes rewards contingent upon both the short-term and long-term objectives of the job.

The National Hockey League reward system illustrates the recognition of short-term and long-term objectives. To win the Stanley Cup is a relatively long-term objective of every team. But the team's chances of reaching that objective get better only when the team does well in the short-term, that is, in each game. It has already been shown how the reward system promotes performance behaviours that help the team win each game. When the team is in the Stanley Cup play-offs, the need for teamwork is even more crucial, because any player's attempt to perform like a prima donna can ruin the team's chances of success. For the promotion of teamwork, the rewards for winning the Stanley Cup are distributed equally among the team members.

An important consideration in the decision on payout frequency is the time delay in the availability of performance measures. If the nature of the job is such that there is a time lag before pertinent performance information becomes available, then the merit payout will be delayed. This is often the case in managerial jobs where the effectiveness of decisions can be realistically and fairly assessed only at relatively longer intervals. For such jobs the frequency of merit payments will be low. Will the low frequency adversely affect the performance motivation of these employees? Some argue that it will not, because such job incumbents are accustomed to delayed rewards. The determining factor in performance motivation, however, is employee perceptions of *when* the performance-outcomes linkage can reasonably be made. So long as employees perceive that the payout intervals are fairly consistent with the time lag in the availability of performance information, the low frequency of merit payments will not affect their performance motivation.

The decision on the frequency of merit payments thus requires a careful consideration of the nature of the job objectives, short-term and long-term, and the inherent time delay in the availability of performance information.

7. Employee Involvement in Designing and Administering Merit Pay

This option addresses the process issues of secrecy versus openness of the merit pay system, and the advantages of employee participation in the design and administration of the merit pay system. Openness in the compensation system contributes to employee motivation in three ways: it engenders employee trust in the system, it promotes employee perceptions of the performance-outcomes linkage, and it provides adequate feedback on performance. These effects of openness in the compensation system are all the more crucial for a performance-based pay system. The preceding discussion of the strategic issues relating to performance-based pay has repeatedly argued the need for trust between supervisor and subordinates, the need for strengthening employee perceptions of the performance-outcomes linkage, and the need for adequate feedback to ensure equity and employee development.

The performance-based reward system should be clearly communicated. Employees should know and understand what constitutes job performance, what are the expected performance standards, and how and when the performance will be rewarded. In an open system, employees do not have to rely on speculation and the grapevine to evaluate whether the merit pay system is functioning as intended. In a well-designed and properly implemented performance-based reward system, employees see that the predetermined or agreed performance levels are equitably rewarded. They also receive feedback on their performance deficiencies with specific suggestions and assistance relating to training and development that may be necessary.

There are, of course, disadvantages to an open system. When employees see that the performance-based system is not equitably administered, they lose trust in the system and it ceases to have the desired motivational value. The previous chapter examined the arguments against openness in the compensation system and concluded that, on balance, openness was preferred to secrecy. The argument against openness becomes even weaker in the case of performance-based pay. The very notion of rewarding performance implies that employees need to be satisfied that their rewards are equitable relative to their performance and the performance of their peers. For reasons discussed in the previous chapter, employees can obtain this satisfaction only under conditions of a more open system.

The previous chapter also discussed the beneficial effects of employee involvement in compensation design and administration, and the reasons why these effects are produced. The same effects and reasons apply with a much greater force to performance-based pay because of the direct contingencies involved between performance and rewards. Thus, employee involvement in the design and administration of merit pay will have the effect of strengthening employee perceptions of the performance-outcomes linkage and equity of outcomes, and hence the employee will experience a greater satisfaction with the job.

THE ROLE OF PERFORMANCE APPRAISAL IN THE ADMINISTRATION OF PERFORMANCE-BASED REWARDS

If rewards are to be based on performance, there is a need to evaluate or assess that performance in order to determine the rewards that it deserves. Performance appraisal is an essential part of a performance-based rewards programme. A well-designed performance appraisal system will assure equity and fairness in determining rewards. It will also assure that only those performance behaviours that achieve the organization's objectives are rewarded. Consequently, the performance appraisal system plays an indispensable role in performance-based pay. In view of its importance, the discussion of the performance appraisal system will include not only a description of the major steps of the performance appraisal process but also practical guidelines for the successful conduct of the activities involved in each step and a consideration of some of the essential preconditions that make performance appraisal effective.

THE PERFORMANCE APPRAISAL PROCESS

The performance appraisal system is not a once-a-year ritual that managers plough through reluctantly; it is essentially the on-going, cyclical process of managing employee performance. It begins with the definition of the subordinate's job, unless the job is so simple that there is no doubt about what is the expected job behaviour. In this first step, the manager must *identify* all the important aspects of the job and *clarify* how the job is related to the goals of the organization. One way of identifying job objectives that are concrete and appropriate to organizational goals is to view the recipient of the jobs' products as the "customer" of that job. In this approach, managers assist their employees to identify the customers of their output. For example, the sales analyst who prepares monthly sales statistics that are routed to the sales manager, the marketing manager, and senior managers sees each recipient as a customer and becomes conscious of the job's responsibility to satisfy the specific needs of the customers. The customer approach enables employees to experience the significance of their tasks and promotes, in varying degrees, identification with the organization's goals. These outcomes are ensured only if the process of job definition is a joint effort of the manager and the employees that leads to an agreed understanding of, and commitment to, the appropriate job behaviours.

The second step of the cycle is the *setting of expectations*. The first step spelt out what needs to be done. The second step specifies how well the tasks must be done; it sets the standards by which the job performance will be appraised. Goal-setting theory (Locke and Bryan 1968), abundantly supported by empirical evidence (Locke et al. 1981), stipulates that employee performance is greatly enhanced when the assigned goals are difficult, but attainable; and specific, but appropriate to the goals of the organization. This step also establishes the performance period, usually six months to a year for non-managerial jobs and two years and more for managerial jobs, the rationale being that it takes longer for performance results to become visible in the latter case than in the former.

The process of performance appraisal, despite the most sophisticated attempts to introduce objective procedures, will always remain a subjective process, highly vulnerable to fallible judgements, even with all the goodwill in the world. Hence, the participation of employees in the establishment of standards and measures of performance is crucial. The knowledge and expertise of both the supervisor and the employees contributes to performance standards and measures that are reasonable, realistic, and appropriate. This is not to suggest that subordinates, left to themselves, would set unrealistically low standards. In fact, there is considerable evidence that subordinates tend to set unrealistically high goals (Lawler 1977). The mutual-influence process would, in addition to injecting realism, ensure manager-subordinate agreement and give the subordinates ownership and control, which go a long way to generating the trust, acceptance, and commitment so necessary to this highly subjective system (Locke and Latham 1984).

As an illustration of these two steps, which constitute the foundation of the appraisal system, consider the job of a salesperson. On the basis of his/her own knowledge and experience and that of his/her salesforce, the sales manager lists all the job behaviours that result in successful sales performance, for example, developing a prospects list, setting up appointments with customers, demonstrating products, customer follow-up, responding to customer complaints/enquiries, communications with the sales manager, developing budgets, sales reports, training juniors, initiating new sales approaches. These behaviours are then arranged according to how critical they are to increasing sales. Specific measures such as 5 customer demonstrations per week, 10 new appointments every month, or a sales report by the first of each month are assigned to each behaviour, and become the standards and measures of performance.

The deliberations of the manager and the employee at this stage of the cycle have the potential for generating mistrust and conflict. Preoccupied with productivity, the manager sets the performance goals (expectations) in terms of some measure of productivity. The employee, intent on reaching these goals, performs all the required behaviours only to find his/her efforts thwarted by environmental or other constraints entirely beyond his/her control. Both the manager and the employee will be spared this needless frustration if they recognize the fundamental difference (discussed earlier in this chapter) between performance and productivity. Then, in addition to establishing job objectives and measures of performance, the manager will also identify and remove environmental constraints that might interfere with the employee's job performance. If these constraints cannot be removed, the performance standards must be adjusted, because these constraints are beyond the control of the employee.

The third step of the performance management cycle is *monitoring the performance*. During this phase, the manager provides informal ongoing feedback, which is to be viewed not as of fault-finding but rather as on-the-job coaching. When managers function as coaches, they seek to help employees grow and reach desired performance levels. Coaching involves knowing how well employees are performing relative to performance standards in terms of specific, measurable behaviours, and discussing areas for improvement. The coach gives praise for work well done and offers constructive criticism when appropriate. In the latter case, the manager cites specific behaviours, with specific suggestions on how to correct the performance problems. Performance standards can never be etched in stone; their validity always assumes a relatively stable environment. The manager who functions like a coach will be sensitive to changing environmental factors, and will make suitable adjustments to performance standards. Perhaps the shortfall in performance is due to a deficiency in the employee in certain skills. The coaching approach will cause the manager to be immediately aware of such deficiencies and provide remedial measures, for example, training. In their coaching stance, managers are careful to create an open, relaxed atmosphere that encourages employees to seek guidance in sorting out priorities or in resolving problems.

The fourth step is the *formal appraisal review*, at the end of the predetermined performance period. During this review managers record their assessment of the individual's performance. This phase usually poses the greatest problem for managers as it demands that they play two apparently conflicting roles, that of coach and that of judge. The most frequently recommended approach to this phase is termed the problem-solving approach because its focus is on the removal of such obstacles to good performance as inappropriate or obsolete work procedures, lack of resources and certain skills, and lack of a clear understanding of the job role and requirements. This approach also encourages a joint discussion between the manager and the subordinate. The mutual exchange of information provides a clearer picture of the individual's job performance and the context in which the job was carried out. As a result, subordinates' trust in the fairness of the process increases because they are now certain that the manager does indeed have all the information needed for a reasonable assessment. Furthermore, the exchange provides an opportunity for discussing the short-term and long-term career objectives of subordinates, as well as their training and development needs. The problem-solving approach creates a climate of mutual trust, is non-threatening, and makes the appraisal review the ideal event for discussing and setting goals for the next performance period. In this approach, managers function as both coach and judge, but the emphasis is on their mentoring role as they seek to nurture subordinates' strengths and minimize the negative effects of their weaknesses, if these cannot be completely eliminated.

Managers can choose from a wide variety of techniques to rate employees' performance; some organizations combine techniques or use different techniques to rate different categories of employees. The criterion for the choice of technique must be the capacity of the technique to capture employee performance in terms of the predetermined job behaviours. The use of personal traits to appraise performance should be avoided unless these are critical to the performance of the job, in which case the traits should form part of the performance standards. For example, a good salesperson or an employee who is a member of a work team needs to be high on the personal trait of ability to work with others. A bench scientist who works alone may not need that personal trait.

If personal traits are critical to the job, the rating format should encourage the manager not merely to record observations in terms of the presence or absence of the traits, but to illustrate the traits specifically with examples of the job behaviours observed. For instance, if a manager rates a supervisor low on resourcefulness, the supervisor will be helped to improve his/her performance if the manager records an example of a behaviour that reflected a lack of initiative and the consequence of the behaviour for the organization, for example, "Your attention to the high rate of equipment failure would have impelled you to alert the maintenance department in time to prevent a needless shutdown for three days."

The rating instrument is not an end in itself but a means of bringing together in one medium information that supports the problem-solving method. Any displacement of the means-end relationship that results in according to the mechanics of the instrument a more important role than to the process that it is designed to support will not contribute to the effective management of performance.

If the performance review is to aid in performance management, the assessment recorded should provide information that facilitates equitable compensation decisions and identifies training and development needs. When managers ensure equity in compensation decisions, they unleash the tremendous motivational power of the compensation programme, with two positive consequences among the many that follow. First, the correct and desirable performance behaviours are reinforced, with a resultant increase in the probability that such behaviours will be repeated in the future. The employees get a clear, direct, and unambiguous message about the type and level of performance behaviours expected from them. Second, the satisfaction that follows equitable compensation increases the value employees place on the rewards they receive from the organization. The empirical evidence is overwhelmingly conclusive that employee motivation is high when rewards are contingent upon performance behaviour and are valued by the employees (Kanungo and Mendonca 1988).

Identifying training and development needs is the necessary, but not sufficient, first step to improving performance. It must be followed through with appropriate programmes that remedy specific performance deficiencies or provide opportunities for the acquisition or enhancement of certain skills and abilities. This activity is especially critical to organizations that compete in highly dynamic and rapidly growing industries.

ESSENTIAL PRECONDITIONS FOR EFFECTIVE PERFORMANCE APPRAISAL

The four steps of the performance appraisal programme described constitute a process that is essential to an equitable and effective performance-based pay system. However, the success of this process is largely dependent on the organizational climate and the internal work culture. In an extensive study of performance appraisal practices in nine very different companies of the General Electric conglomerate and covering 700 manager-subordinate pairs from all levels of management, Lawler, Mohrman, and Resnick (1984) found that organizational climate had a significant impact on how well the performance appraisal process went. "When the climate was one of high trust, support, and openness," appraisers and subordinates both reported "greater participation and contribution by the subordinate, and a higher degree of trust, openness, and constructiveness during the appraisal interview" (p. 31).

The assumptions that managers make about their subordinates are at the core of an organizational culture that is conducive to an effective performance appraisal programme. Managers must be convinced that their employees are a vital resource and that most employees welcome an opportunity to use their talents and abilities for the mutual benefit of themselves and the organization. How does an organization promote the idea that employees are its most important resource? Such an idea begins at the top and forms an integral part of the organization's culture, its core beliefs and values. The strong commitment of top management to this view should be unequivocally communicated throughout the organization. A practical approach that works if it is consistently followed is to reward managers for developing their subordinates. Managers do respond to rewards and punishments. Frequently, however, managers are not only not rewarded for employee development but are in fact penalized. For example, when managers take seriously their responsibilities to coach and develop their employees, they often find a high turnover of these well-trained employees through transfer to better positions in other departments. The managers are still held responsible for meeting departmental goals, although they now have to function with new, inexperienced employees. It is unlikely that these managers will continue to invest the needed time and effort in employee development. Implicit in the approach of rewarding managers for employee development is the concomitant condition that managers be trained with the necessary skills for implementing the performance appraisal programme.

Figure 8.1 summarizes the performance appraisal process and its essential preconditions.

SUMMARY

Performance-based rewards are an indispensable element of an organization's compensation system. Through these rewards, the organization can attract and retain achievement-oriented employees, and motivate them towards the desired job performance behaviours. These rewards

Figure 8.1
The Performance Appraisal Process and Its Essential Preconditions

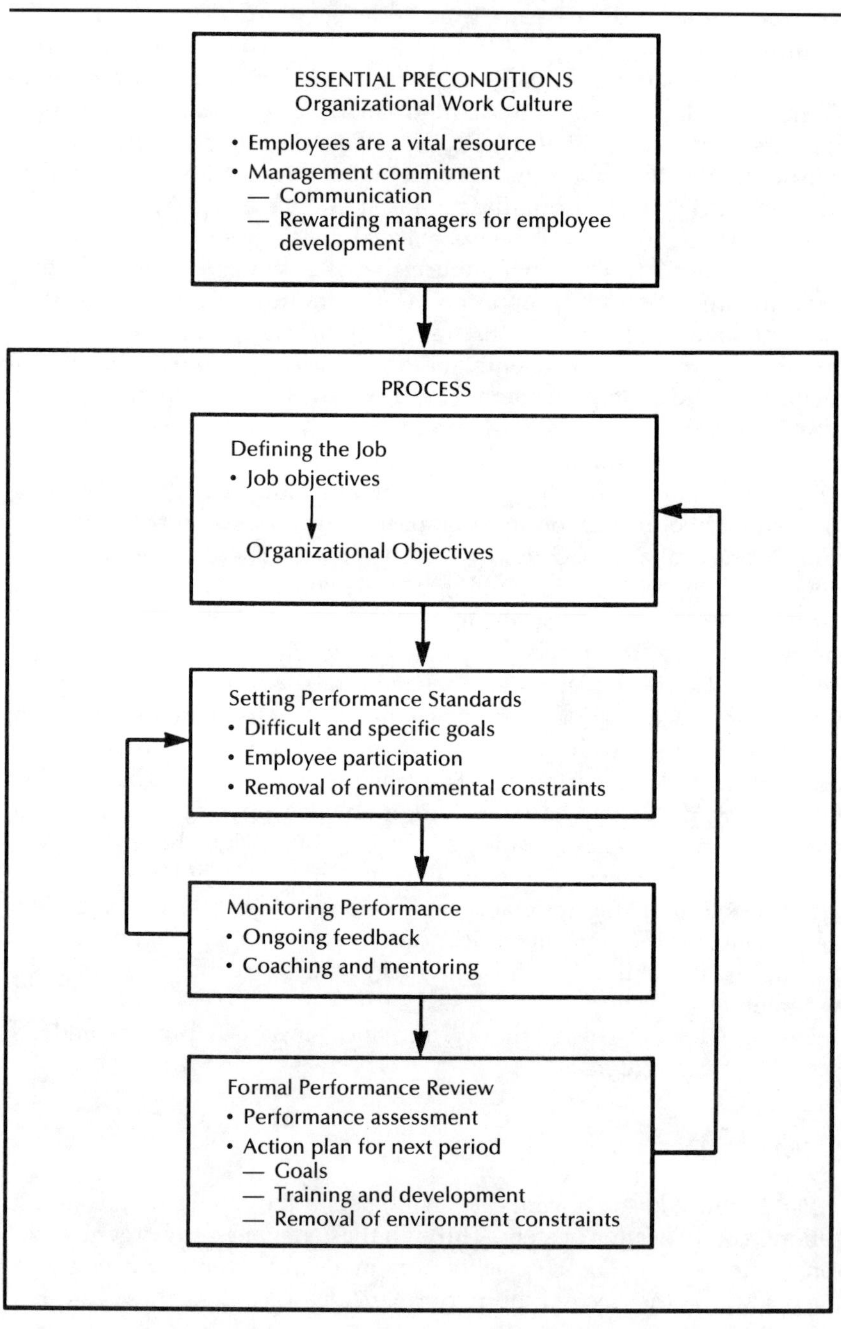

also contribute to employee satisfaction by increasing employee perceptions of personal or individual equity.

This chapter explored the concept of performance-based rewards in general and performance-based pay in particular. A well-designed performance-based pay plan ties pay to performance, minimizes the negative side-effects of high performance, promotes positive consequences, encourages cooperation, and generally enhances the acceptance of performance-based rewards. In addition, employees must value money. In order to develop such a plan, the organization must decide on the strategic issues, which are the level of aggregation, individual or group; the number of plans; the mode of payment; the size of the payment; the measurement of performance; the frequency of payment; and the process issues of communication of the plan and employee involvement in the design and administration of the plan. On these critical decisions will depend employee perceptions of the performance-outcomes linkage and the fairness or equity of the plan.

The effectiveness of a performance-based pay plan also depends on how well it is managed. The performance appraisal process plays an important role in the management of performance-based pay. It not only assures equity and fairness in determining the rewards, but it also provides a mechanism for rewarding only those behaviours that contribute to the attainment of the organization's objectives.

KEY TERMS

effort
job performance
level of aggregation
objective measures of performance
payout frequency
performance appraisal process
performance-based rewards
productivity
subjective measures of performance

REVIEW AND DISCUSSION QUESTIONS

1. Define job performance. How is job performance different from effort and productivity?
2. "Performance-based rewards enable an organization to achieve a

variety of objectives in the management of its human resources." Do you agree? Why or why not?

3. "Our performance-based rewards not only do absolutely nothing to increase performance, but they have also proved to promote dysfunctional behaviours." Discuss this comment in the light of the conditions that facilitate the effectiveness of performance-based rewards.

4. What factors should you consider in deciding whether a performance-based pay plan should be on an individual or a group (i.e., work unit, department, entire organization) basis? Explain your reasons for your choice of these factors.

5. Most organizations prefer that merit pay be in the form of a one-time bonus, whereas most employees prefer it to be in the form of a salary increase. Which form of payment is likely to be more effective? Why?

6. In measuring performance, some advocate a strictly objective measure. Others claim that all measures are ultimately subjective. Still others believe that both objective and subjective measures are needed. Which position do you take? Why?

7. It has been argued that for a merit pay programme to be effective, employees must be involved not only in its design but also in its administration. Do you subscribe to this argument? Why? If you agree only partially, state your position and defend it.

8. Refer to the case Star Wars in Chapter 5. From the little information given, explore what you think might be deficient in SATCO's merit system. What changes would you recommend? Why?

9. Review the major steps and the essential preconditions of the performance appraisal process described in the chapter. Do you think any one step is more important or critical to an effective performance appraisal than the others? Why or why not?

CASE: CARPENTER CREATIONS LIMITED

Carpenter Creations is a manufacturer of furniture. Started in 1983 by Brian Carpenter, a master cabinet-maker, as a custom-furniture operation, Carpenter Creations has since added an assembly-line operation for certain items. The organizational structure of Carpenter Creations is as follows:

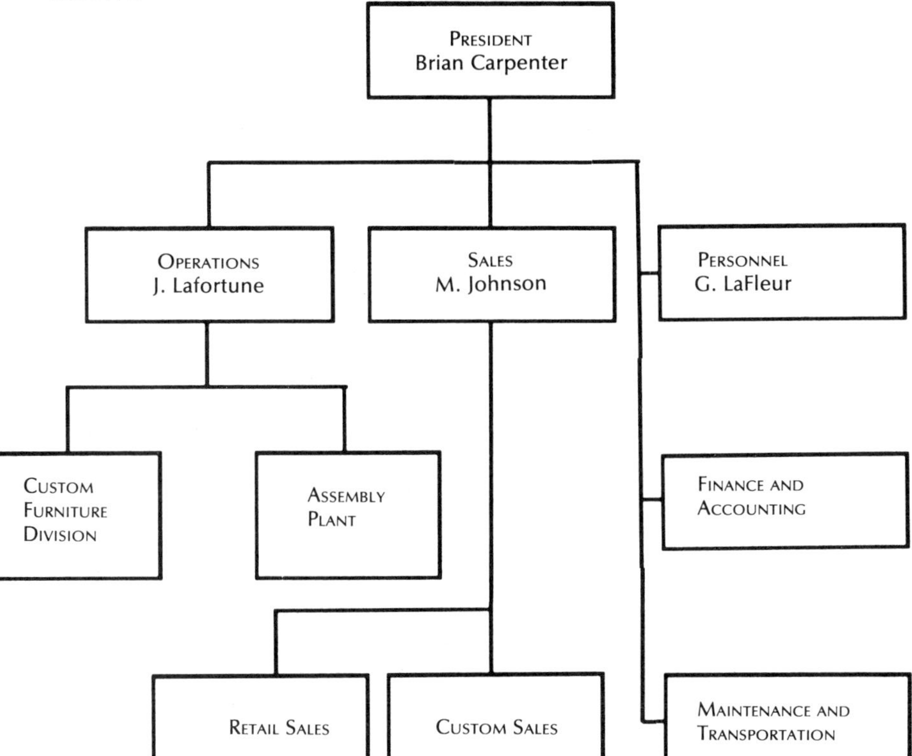

In addition to his technical expertise, Brian brought a strong entrepreneurial ability to the business. He is also a perfectionist, and this characteristic, along with his emphasis on creativity, has attracted some of the best cabinet-makers and carpenters to the custom furniture division, which enjoys a reputation for excellence in the industry. A demanding employer, Brian believes in rewarding outstanding performance. Accordingly, he has operated a performance-based pay system from the inception of the company.

For the past two years, Brian has been concerned that profits have declined despite an increase in sales. Discussions with department managers have uncovered the additional problem of employee dissatisfaction, particularly in the assembly plant. Brian is furious. He can't understand; Carpenter Creations has been the only firm in the industry to operate such a generous reward system.

LaFleur, the new personnel manager, who has been with the company for just two months, suspects that the performance-based system is the cause of the trouble. He has succeeded in persuading Brian to subject the system to a comprehensive review.

On the basis of his review of the documentation and discussions with managers and some employees, LaFleur has come up with the following facts and observations relating to the performance-based pay system.

1. At the start of the company, the system was communicated by Brian to the cabinet-makers, each of whom worked independently on the custom-furniture jobs assigned to them. The mutual respect that existed between the cabinet-makers and Brian resulted in a free exchange of ideas on the system, and any suitable modifications, where necessary, were agreed upon.

2. In the assembly plant, information on the system was supposed to have been communicated by the department manager and the group supervisors. The assembly employees were unionized; the union was indifferent to the system. As is typical of an assembly operation, the measurement of any individual's contribution to the end product was difficult. In administering the system, the supervisor exercised his judgement in rewarding performance. Good performers have been socially ostracized; production slowed down during peak periods. Employee complaints resulting in grievance actions unrelated to the system have been unusually high. Supervisors have responded with tighter controls.

3. A salesperson operates relatively independently in his/her territory with responsibility for both custom sales and retail sales. In the sales department, the system pays a commission that is related to the dollar value of sales. Custom sales is a high-ticket item with a low profit margin; retail sales is low-priced but has a high profit margin.

4. In the other departments (personnel, finance and accounting, maintenance and transportation), the system rewards performance on the basis of a subjective evaluation by the supervisor. There are no complaints against the system, but the employees are not particularly enthusiastic about it.

5. The budget for the system is developed as follows:
For the operating divisions — as a percentage of total production
For the sales department — as a percentage of sales dollars
For the other departments — as a percentage of the net profit of the company
Management, employees, and even the union, agree that the

formula for developing the budget is satisfactory. However, only the president and the department managers know the amount of the budget. There is also secrecy with respect to the amount paid to each individual.

Before LaFleur prepares his report to the President, he seeks your advice on

1. the strengths and weaknesses of the performance-based pay system in relation to
   - the design of the system
   - the implementation of the system;
2. the questions and issues he should explore that will help him to clarify what is critical to an effective performance-based pay system;
3. specific recommendations for improving the system.

CHAPTER 9

INCENTIVE SYSTEMS AND GAIN-SHARING PLANS: PERSONAL EQUITY II

CHAPTER SYNOPSIS

This chapter examines individual and group incentives, which are a form of performance-based rewards, with a primary focus on the attainment of a predetermined end result. The individual incentive plans discussed are piece-rate or piece-work plans, standard-hour plans, and sales commissions and bonuses. The group incentive plans described are the Scanlon, Rucker, and Improshare plans. The chapter also discusses in some detail the strategic and process issues and the preconditions that contribute to the effectiveness of individual and group incentive plans.

LEARNING OBJECTIVES

- To understand the rationale underlying the piece-rate, standard-hour, and sales commissions and bonuses plans.
- To identify and explain the conditions that favour individual incentive plans.
- To identify and explain the content of the strategic and process issues that must be addressed in the design and management of gain-sharing plans.
- To understand and describe the Scanlon Plan, the Rucker Plan, and the Improshare Plan.
- To identify and explain the conditions that favour gain-sharing plans.

INTRODUCTION

The previous chapter discussed the role of merit pay in motivating employees to increase their job performance. Merit pay is essentially a form of results-oriented compensation. It recognizes the superior job performance of individuals because of the belief that such performance has made a valuable contribution to the organization's effectiveness. The recognition also enhances the individual's perceptions of personal or individual equity. Other forms of results-oriented compensation are incentive plans established on an individual or a group basis. In an incentive plan, monetary rewards are designed to vary with some predetermined measure of performance. In addition to increasing output, incentive plans are used to enhance performance, for example, by improving quality, by reducing the reject rate, by reducing costs, by increasing the market share, by reducing customer complaints, and by controlling absenteeism. Successful incentive plans enable the organization to motivate its employees to make the incremental effort to produce more, better, and efficiently.

Incentive systems are the focus of this chapter. The chapter considers individual and group incentive plans, and gain-sharing plans, which is the name given to incentive plans based on the effort and results of the entire organization. The chapter also explores the nature of incentive plans (individual, group, organization-wide), the conditions under which such plans are effective, and the major issues involved in their design and implementation. The chapter concludes with a brief description of the more popular organization-wide gain-sharing plans.

INDIVIDUAL INCENTIVE PLANS

A variety of incentive plans have been developed on the basis of the effort or output (results) of an individual's performance. The basic characteristic of these plans is that the worker has control over the operation or the process involved in the job. In some plans, the worker receives the entire incremental gains that result from the increased worker productivity. In other plans, the incremental gains are shared between the worker and the organization. The rationale for this sharing is that the organization has contributed to the gains through the additional resources it has provided. The incentive plans to be explored here are (1) piece-work or piece-rate incentives, (2) standard-hour plans, and (3) sales commissions and bonuses.

PIECE-RATE PLAN

These incentives, still in use today, can be traced back to the practices that prevailed among craftsmen in ancient times. Craftsmen were paid for a product that conformed to the desired specifications. Today, the piece-rate is determined by taking into account the external market rate for the job as well as a careful analysis of the job, supported by engineered time studies. For example, suppose the market rate (or the union-negotiated rate) for an assembler of components is $12/hour, and the job analysis reveals that an average employee can assemble six units of acceptable quality per hour. The assumption underlying "average" employee is that the employee possesses the average knowledge, skills, and ability required by the job, and works at a normal pace using the specified method. The computation also makes allowances for fatigue and delay factors. The piece-rate for the job will be calculated thus:

$$\frac{\text{Market Rate/hour}}{\text{Estimated Average Output/hour}} = \frac{\$12}{6} = \$2\text{/unit or piece}$$

An employee's income per day will be: Units (or pieces) produced × $2/unit.

It is clear that the more the employee produces in a day, the greater will be his/her earnings.

There are several variations in the design of the piece-rate plan. Two of these variations, the Taylor Plan and the Merrick Plan, will be briefly described. The Taylor Plan, also known as the differential piece-rate plan, truly incorporates the contingent-rewards concept. This plan sets a relatively high, but fair and equitable, task or production standard. The piece-rate for output at or above the established standard is higher than the piece-rate for output below the established standard. The differential can vary between 20 per cent and 30 per cent.

The Merrick Plan, also known as the multiple piece-rate plan, has three piece-rates. The highest piece-rate is for output above the production standard, which is usually set at a high but equitable level. The next highest piece-rate is for output between 83 per cent and 100 per cent of the production standard. The lowest piece-rate is for output below 83 per cent of the production standard (Schwinger 1975). Both the Taylor and Merrick plans are designed to provide powerful incentives for employees to produce at or above the production standard. The additional merit of the Merrick Plan is that its second piece-rate is designed to accommodate new employees who need encouragement as they settle into their jobs.

STANDARD-HOUR PLAN

Under this plan, workers qualify for an incentive payment when performance exceeds "a standard expressed as a 'percentage' or an index of the actual time worked in relation to standard time" (Dunn and Rachel 1971, 247). Consider again the piece-rate example of the assembler. Since the average assembler can produce 6 units/hour, the weekly standard output will be 240 units (i.e., 6 units/hour × 8 hours × 5 days). For this output, the regular (or standard) pay will be $480 week (i.e., $12/hour × 40 hours). Assume that an assembler produces 300 units in a week, that is, 60 units over the weekly standard. The 60 units represent 10 standard hours, indicating that the assembler has done 50 hours of work in a 40-hour week — an efficiency of 125 per cent. Consequently, according to the standard hour plan, the assembler would qualify for an incentive of 25 per cent over and above the base or standard pay. The incentive computation will be

Base or standard pay	=	$480/week
25% efficiency incentive	=	$120
Total earnings	=	$600

The efficiency of 25 per cent can also be viewed as a saving of 10 hours of production time; that is, an output that would have taken 50 *standard hours* has been produced in 40 hours. The savings of 10 hours qualifies for an incentive payment of 10 hours × $12/hour = $120.

Some of the variations of the standard-hour plan are the Halsey 50-50 Method, the Rowan Plan, and the Gantt Plan. All three plans are similar in that they reward workers for performing their tasks in less time than the standard time established for their tasks. They differ in the mode of computing the bonus and on the question of whether the resulting efficiencies should be shared between workers and management.

Under the Halsey 50-50 Method, workers receive a guaranteed hourly wage and a bonus that is based on the time saved. Workers are required, however, to share this bonus with management, usually on a 50-50 basis; hence, the name of the method. For example, suppose the worker completes a task in 6 hours as against the standard time of 8 hours — a saving of 2 hours. The worker will receive payment for only 1 hour, because the other 1 hour is shared with management. The Rowan Plan operates in a similar fashion. The major difference lies in the manner in which the time saving is shared. In the Rowan Plan, unlike the Halsey Plan, the worker's share is directly determined by the extent of the saving in relation to the standard time. Suppose the worker completes in 6 hours a task that has a standard time of 8 hours. The worker will receive a bonus of 25 per cent, that is, [(8 − 6)/8)] of his/her hourly wage. If the time saving is 4 hours, then the bonus increases to 50 per cent. Thus, under the Rowan Plan, the worker's bonus increases with the increases in the time saved.

The Gantt Plan sets a high standard time, and workers who complete the task in less than or equal to the standard time receive earnings equal to 120 per cent of the time saved. Unlike the Halsey and Rowan plans, the time saved is not shared between workers and management. Further, workers who do not meet the standard receive a guaranteed base wage.

Sales Commissions and Bonuses

This is a variation of the piece-rate plan designed exclusively for sales people. In its simplest form, the employee is paid a percentage of the sales (defined as gross or net sales). Generally, the commission plan structure will provide a minimum base earnings, and vary the commission percentages, at an increasing rate, for higher sales levels. The plan will also take into account the nature of the products and the sales territories in determining the standards for each commission level. As will be discussed later, careful thought must be given to incorporating in the plan the desirable behaviours that the organization intends to promote as well as the specific objectives it seeks to achieve, for example, market share, developing new accounts, gross profit, expense control, employee development.

There are basically two approaches to incentive programmes in this category: a piece-rate system, and a task-and-bonus system. Under the piece-rate system, every sale is rewarded with a commission, even though the predetermined sales quota has not been reached. Under the task-and-bonus approach, the reward (bonus) is paid only when the employee meets or exceeds the predetermined quota. This is the issue of the threshold at which the salesperson becomes eligible for the incentive. The piece-rate system works best with difficult sales targets. This reward-as-you-achieve approach induces employees to strive for the entire goal because they know that if they fail, their efforts will not go unrewarded. In other words, they will be rewarded for whatever they have achieved. The task-and-bonus approach is not appropriate for difficult goals. The all-or-nothing concept underlying the task-and-bonus approach does not induce employees to strive for a difficult goal, because they know that should they fail, their efforts will go completely uncompensated. The task-and-bonus approach seems to be appropriate for relatively easy goals. The ease of attaining the goal tends to increase their confidence of earning the bonus and as a result serves as an inducement to strive for the goal. The design of incentive plans usually combines elements of these two approaches in order to suit the particular needs of the organization. As Freedman (1986) observes: "Whatever threshold will make 85% to 90% of the sales force active players in the sales compensation game is the proper threshold to use. If a threshold is set so high that it excludes most of the sales force, it will not motivate the overall sales effort effectively. After all, an incremental dollar of sales is worth the same profit increment whether it comes from an average achiever or a superior one; if the sales incentive plan inspires only superior achievers, it may well be counter-productive" (p. 46).

CONDITIONS THAT FAVOUR THE EFFECTIVENESS OF INDIVIDUAL INCENTIVE PLANS

The preceding discussion identified the salient features and the mechanics involved in the implementation of individual incentive plans. Mechanics alone, however, despite their mathematical sophistication, do not ensure a plan's effectiveness. The plan must satisfy certain criteria that are critical prerequisites for its success. The theoretical models presented in this text clearly spell out the criteria that a compensation item must meet in order to produce the desired motivational effect in the recipient. The criteria are these: The employee is capable of performing the desired behaviour; and the employee perceives that the reward is valued and contingent on performance. An incentive plan programme must be thoroughly proved to ensure its compliance with these criteria. An organization can be falsely complacent in thinking that a plan meets these criteria, because incentive plans are especially designed to be rewards that are contingent, that are performance-based. In the process, adequate attention may not be paid to the other criteria, that is, the employee's ability and his/her valence of rewards. Even in respect of the criterion of contingency, the plan may actually promote dysfunctional and counter-productive behaviours. Hence, it is useful to consider the conditions that enable individual incentive plans to meet these criteria, and thereby ensure their effectiveness.

First, an incentive plan programme must ensure that the performance behaviours which it seeks to promote and influence do indeed lead to attaining the objectives of the job and of the organization. Incentive plans are intended to increase output and profits with practically no increase in fixed costs. However, not uncommonly, increases in output (whether of a product or a service) are achieved at the expense of quality. Not infrequently, the high output is achieved at the cost of the inefficient use of physical and financial resources. Often, the plan will focus on competition between departments that are interdependent. Second, the employee's (E ⟶ P) expectancy in respect of the performance targets must be high; otherwise, the employee's motivational force to put in the effort to perform will be low. An awareness of this criterion will enable the organization to identify training needs and institute appropriate actions such as empowerment (Conger and Kanungo 1988) to enhance the self-efficacy beliefs of the employee.

Third, the performance-outcomes linkage must be clearly spelt out and communicated, with special care taken to see that the terms, computation formulae, and mode of administration are clearly understood and accepted by employees. This is especially true with regard to the *time standard* that is at the core of incentive plans. The time standard has been defined as the ". . . time required by a typical worker, working at a normal pace, to complete a specific task, using a defined method, with adequate allowance for personal, fatigue, and delay times" (Aft 1985, 217). This definition highlights the several elements that must be considered and interpreted. Decisions in this area are a potential source of dispute with regard to the equity of the plan. At this stage, the desirability of involving employees in the design of the programme must be emphasized. As was discussed in Chapter 6, employee involvement produces many positive effects. It increases information about the plan. Workers have an opportunity to understand the plan, its standards and computations, and propose changes that are accepted if they are found to have merit. Workers soon realize that plan administrators are genuinely open to employee involvement and participation, and such openness generates in employees feelings of responsibility, control, and commitment. The net effect of this process is increased trust in the plan, and both workers and management function as co-partners in its design and administration.

In unionized organizations, it is imperative to involve the union and obtain its commitment as well. Many plans have foundered on the rocks of adversarial union-management relations. When the union is involved, both the union and management have an opportunity to jointly address their mutual concerns right from the beginning. The involvement also promotes trust between the union and management, and paves the way for the development of the harmonious relationship that is essential for the success of incentive plans. As a labour leader once observed: ". . . practically any sound system of wage payment can be made to work when a harmonious relationship prevails between labour and management" (Neibel 1976, 633).

The plan design should include a mechanism for modifying it in the event that changed circumstances make such modification necessary. Often a change is necessitated because of the improper development of standards in the first place, or because changes in production or operating processes render the plan inappropriate. When modifications become necessary, employees must fully understand the need for the changes. Otherwise, employees may conclude these changes are arbitrary on the part of management and undertaken to cut rates or increase standards. Employee involvement in the process from the design stage will ensure that the needed changes are implemented with the collaboration of employees.

Open communication is essential before and during the implementation of a plan. Decisions about the establishment of work standards involve a variety of interpretations relating to definitions of typical worker, normal work pace, and defined work method; and interpretations relating, for example, to adequate allowances for personal, fatigue, and delay factors. There can be honest differences of opinion on these issues not only between workers and management but also between workers themselves. Any attempt at secrecy or even a reluctance to disclose information will create doubts that can undermine the high level of employee trust indispensable for the plan's success.

Fourth, implicit in incentive plans is the concept that the worker's extra effort should lead to extra earnings. Hence, the plan's design should ensure that workers in all jobs covered by the plan have the opportunity to earn incentive pay in direct proportion to their increased productivity. Ceilings on incentive pay will be viewed by employees as unjust and inequitable so long as the high earnings correspond with the increases in production. Incentive plans often include a guaranteed minimum wage in order to provide for differences in employee abilities. To ensure the motivational effect of the standard rate, however, a considerable spread should be maintained between the minimum and the standard rate.

Fifth, the performance objectives are measurable and, equally important, are within the control of the employee. When the employee's earnings are related to job performance, the measures of performance should be clear, unambiguous, and capable of measurement. Vagueness in measurement will seriously affect the (P → O) linkage, and also give rise to employee perceptions of inequity or unfairness. Individual incentive plans are effective when earnings are computed regularly — preferably on a daily basis, although the payment is on a weekly basis. Such regular, periodic computation and payments cannot allow for ambiguity or vagueness in the measurements. Hence, the need for sound work-measurement procedures.

In individual incentive plans, the rewards should be based solely on the performance of the individual. It is unreasonable and unacceptable for the employee to suffer a loss or reduction of earnings because of situations beyond his/her control. For example, an employee's output might suffer because of the failure of another department or employee to properly maintain the machines or to supply materials of the required specifications. In other situations, the job might be machine-paced, and delay an employee's completion of a task. The development of the standards of incentive plans should allow for such exigencies, which are beyond the employee's control. When performance objectives are not under the employee's control, the performance-outcomes linkage is either weak or non-existent, and the resulting inequity will cause the employee not to value the outcomes. For both reasons (lack of employee control over the performance objective and vagueness in the measurement of the performance objective), the incentive programme will not produce the desired motivational effect on the employee.

The sixth condition for ensuring an effective individual incentive plan is that the participants value money. Money is valued for its instrumentality to satisfy needs, among other reasons. As the needs are satisfied, the importance of money, and hence its value, decreases — unless money begins to serve as a source of recognition and thus satifies self-esteem needs. Unless workers value money, for whatever reason, incentive plans will not work. Also, incentive plans affect individuals differently, depending upon whether they are intrinsically or extrinsically oriented. Employees who have a high need for achievement — the n-ach types — will strive to produce more if they believe they are likely to be successful. The n-ach individual is motivated by the satisfaction derived from performance — the feelings of personal accomplishment. An n-ach individual will not strive for a higher level of performance, even though it carries a far greater reward, if the individual believes that he/she does not have a reasonably moderate chance of success. For the n-ach individual, the increase in performance is not motivated by the incentive plan as such. On the other hand, for low n-ach types, incentive plans can contribute to an increase in performance, and also to satisfaction from receiving incentive payments.

The seventh condition for ensuring an effective individual incentive plan is keeping in mind the nature of the tasks involved. Incentive plans increase employee performance where the job tasks are relatively simple. When the job tasks are relatively complex, however, performance is often adversely affected. The opportunity for increased earnings provided by incentive plans can become a preoccupation and a distraction and thus can interfere with the attention and concentration demanded by complex tasks. An awareness of this condition will help organizations to design incentive plans in such a way that they reward the behaviours required for complex tasks.

This section concludes with some observations about the side-effects of individual incentive plans, for example, restriction of output, encouragement of competition, and higher accident rates. Output restriction generally results when there is considerable mistrust between employees and management. Such mistrust fosters the belief that high productivity will lead to rate changes, an increase in standards (quotas), or lay-offs resulting from a high inventory and the inability of the company's marketing efforts to absorb the extra high production. Employees respond to the likely occurrence of these negative outcomes by restricting production. Their efforts in this direction are assisted by social pressures among their peers that operate to socially ostracize the high performers. Individual incentives have the potential to promote dysfunctional behaviours. By their very nature, individual incentive plans encourage the individual to focus on his/her self-interest. This is a recipe for disaster when jobs are interdependent and call for the norm of cooperation to take precedence over the norm of competition. It is also not uncommon to see higher accident rates in situations where individual incentive plans operate, especially when the task standard is set too high. The desire to increase earnings often causes employees to cut corners, ignore safety regulations, and expose themselves to a higher level of risk. In addition, there are severe adverse effects on workers' health, morale, and efficiency. For these consequences to be avoided, incentive systems should have a guaranteed minimum wage. As mentioned earlier, there should be a sufficient spread between the guaranteed minimum rate and the standard rate.

GROUP INCENTIVE PLANS

The basic objective of group incentive plans is similar to that of individual plans — namely, to increase production (or some other desirable organizational objective) by providing employees with the opportunity to increase their earnings when they contribute to organizational objectives. The group approach is necessitated by a variety of factors. To begin with, the nature of the production process is such that the individual is unable to see a strong link between his/her efforts and the output. Furthermore, the process requires the cooperative effort of all the employees because of the interdependence of the work operations. In such a situation, the group plan will reward such behaviours as teamwork and cooperation. The group plan is also useful when individual performance measures are not available or when individual performances are difficult to measure with the required degree of objectivity. Employees in a group incentive plan also have the opportunity to experience non-financial rewards, such as the satisfaction of their social needs. Finally, group plans can minimize the negative side-effects of individual incentive plans. Because group norms play a crucial role in the successful implementation of these plans, employee involvement in design and implementation is highly recommended. Such employee involvement is also helpful when the plan attempts to recognize and reward the performance both of the group and of the individual. Some plans use the performance of the group to come up with the total earnings for which the group qualifies. The group is then entrusted with the responsibility of distributing this amount to individual members through a system of peer evaluation.

The conditions that favour the effectiveness of a group plan are generally similar to those that favour individual incentive plans. A group plan should enable members to see that they have the expertise and the capability to perform the tasks, and that they have control of the job tasks, events, and measures that form the basis of the plan. And, equally important, the plan design and implementation should enhance members' perceptions that the plan is fairly and equitably administered.

CRITICAL ISSUES IN ORGANIZATION-WIDE GAIN-SHARING PLANS

Incentive plans are designed to motivate employees to improved performance by offering them an opportunity to benefit either entirely or in part from the gains that result from improved performance. Such plans can be designed on an individual or a group basis. Some organizations have designed and established group plans on the basis of the entire organization. The approach has its roots in the management philosophy that all employees play a vital role in the success of the organization. As Max De Pree, C.E.O., Herman Miller, Inc., observed: "Participative ownership offers Herman Miller a competitive edge" (1989). This philosophy recognizes that every single employee can contribute to the overall effectiveness and continued survival of the organization. The work is structured in such a manner that employees are encouraged to fully utilize their talents, skills, and abilities on the job. Employee involvement and participation are naturally rewarded by a share in the gains that result — for example, from improvements in cost reduction, quality, profits, market share, customer service. The experience of Donelly Mirrors, Herman Miller, Lincoln Electric, Nucor Corporation — to name just a few corporations that have successfully used gain-sharing plans — suggests that gain-sharing plans are more than a mere device to increase productivity; they represent a way of life.

The design and installation of gain-sharing plans requires considerable thought, care, expertise, commitment, and involvement. Besides the issues of the formula of computation, and of distribution in a fair and equitable manner, other critical issues must be addressed. This chapter considers these issues and the conditions that contribute to the success of gain-sharing plans, then briefly describes three popular gain-sharing plans — Scanlon, Rucker, and Improshare.

According to Lawler (1981), the critical issues are the process of design, the determination of the bonus, the development of a standard, the costs to be covered, the sharing of gains, the frequency of bonus payments, the process to manage change/modifications, and the participative system inherent in the plan. Each of these will now be considered.

WHAT PROCESS WILL BE USED IN SETTING UP THE PLAN?

The options here are top-down, participative, and third-party involvement. In the top-down approach, employees are not involved. This approach is not appropriate. Because of the high level of aggregation, employees will not see the performance-outcomes linkage, nor will they have a basis on which to decide whether rewards are determined in a fair and equitable manner. Employees will not be motivated, and the employee involvement that is sought as one of the principal objectives of an organization-wide plan will not be achieved. The participative approach has been found to be more appropriate. The increased input, trust, and understanding that result from employee involvement and participation will lead to a greater acceptance of the plan and to the increased cooperation that is necessary for its successful implementation. Involvement by a third party (an outside consultant) can be helpful in advising on the technical aspects of the plan, so long as the final decisions are made within the organization with the full participation of the employees.

WHAT ARE THE ISSUES CONCERNING THE NATURE OF THE BONUS FORMULA?

In determining the bonus, an organization can use the standard of costs or profits. Any improvement over the standard will be shared. To establish a standard, the organization must consider whether to use historical data, or engineered or estimated data. When historical data are used, an average of the previous five or so years is generally considered. The difficulty with historical data is the implied assumption that the past is an accurate indicator of the future. This assumption does not appear to be realistic for organizations operating in turbulent environments, where technology, markets, and so forth are changing. Also, historical data are not feasible for a new company. Engineered or estimated data work fine if a high level of trust exists between employees and management, and if the expertise of the estimator is credible.

IF COSTS ARE TO BE THE STANDARD, WHICH COSTS ARE TO BE USED?

The most popular plan, the Scanlon Plan, uses labour costs as a proportion of sales. Thus, any improvement in the labour-costs-to-sales ratio is distributed as a bonus. A focus on labour costs has the advantage that these costs are directly under the control of employees. Besides, the formula can be kept simple and easy for all to understand. Both considerations strengthen the performance-outcomes linkage and increase the valence of outcomes. However, such a focus on labour costs tends to be unrealistic in that it ignores other costs, for example, material and utilities. Although the addition of these costs makes the plan more realistic, it still suffers from two major difficulties. First, employees may not be in a position to control these costs. Second, as more costs are included, the plan grows more complex and difficult to understand and hence less acceptable to employees as being fair and equitable.

HOW ARE GAINS TO BE SHARED?

The response to this question involves decisions on such matters as the following:

- the proportion according to which the gains are shared between the company and the employees;
- the proportion according to which the employees' share is distributed among the various categories, for example, office versus factory employees, management versus non-management employees;
- how the share is distributed to each employee: on the basis of salary? on the basis of the employee's performance as assessed by a performance appraisal?

The plans described later in the chapter illustrate these decisions.

What Will the Frequency of Payment Be?

Will the payout be monthly, quarterly, or annually? Most plans pay out monthly, but the entire amount is not distributed. A portion is kept in a reserve fund to provide for unforeseen exigencies; the fund is held in trust for the employees. The plans of some companies that operate on a seasonal basis pay out at the end of the season to better reflect the performance in that season. The more frequent the payment is, the more visible is the connection between employee efforts and rewards and, therefore, the more effective the reward is.

Should There Be a Mechanism for Managing Plan Modifications?

This issue is critical, particularly for organizations that operate in a changing environment. Major changes in the fields of technology, product mix, markets, products, and so forth will affect the plan standards and formula either adversely or favourably, for either the employees or the company. The plan should provide for a mechanism and a process that will identify and initiate changes to the plan.

How Will the Participative Process Be Maintained?

The participative process is critical to the successful operation of the plan. Some organizations have adopted a parallel structure, a steering committee that includes representatives of employees and management from all levels and functions as well as representatives of the union. Other organizations have used the suggestion system, with special awards for suggestions that have proved to be effective.

TYPES OF GAIN-SHARING PLANS

This section describes three of the more popular organization-wide gain-sharing plans — the Scanlon Plan, the Rucker Plan, and the Improshare Plan. The description focuses on how these plans address the critical issues of the design and implementation process, the bonus formula and distribution scheme, and change management. The discussion also includes a brief assessment of the plans.

SCANLON PLAN

Purpose

In the mid-1930s Joseph Scanlon of the United Steelworkers of America developed the Scanlon plan to promote labour-management cooperation because he was convinced that the efficiency of organizations depended upon such cooperation. Scanlon believed that both employees and the organization would benefit if employees' suggestions for efficient operations were implemented and rewarded. Today, the Scanlon Plan is promoted as a "total system" that seeks to achieve, through a participative and cooperative process, both organizational effectiveness and employee development. The plan covers all employees.

Design and Implementation Process

From its inception, the plan introduced a participative process. Each department has a production committee comprising representatives of workers and management. The committee seeks ways and means to improve productivity, quality, and methods of operations. In addition, the plan provides for an organization-wide screening committee composed of top management and worker representatives. The screening committee administers the plan, decides on employee suggestions, and is generally the forum for reviewing the impact of major business trends on the organization. The basic objective of the committee is to share the maximum information about the company and its operations with the employees, and to genuinely seek their ideas and efforts to make the organization effective.

Bonus Formula and Distribution Scheme

The bonus formula attempts to assess improvements in productivity through the ratio of total payroll to the sales value of production. This relationship tends to be fairly stable in many organizations. The sales value of production is obtained by adjusting net sales for inventory and goods-in-process. The data relating to labour costs and the sales value of production are analyzed, and a base period is selected, so that the formula provides a ratio that truly reflects the relationship of these variables in the organization. Projected labour costs are determined by applying the ratio to the current sales value of production. Current (actual) labour costs are then compared with projected labour costs; the excess of projected labour costs over actual labour costs represents an improvement in productivity, and constitutes the bonus pool.

The bonus pool, usually calculated on a monthly basis, is distributed as follows:

- The first 25 per cent is set aside as a reserve fund for situations when actual labour costs exceed projected labour costs.
- The balance (75 per cent) in the bonus pool is shared between the employees and the company, 75 per cent of the balance to the employees and 25 per cent to the company.
- At the end of the year, the balance in the reserve fund is also shared by the employees and the company on the same 75 per cent - 25 per cent basis.

Each employee's share is proportionate to that employee's share of the total payroll.

Example

The computation and distribution of the bonus are illustrated in the folllowing example. The ABC Company determined that the data of the previous two years reflected with reasonable accuracy the relationship of its payroll costs to its sales value of production. It used the averages of the previous two years to compute the base or standard ratio:

$$\frac{\text{Average Payroll Costs of Previous Two Years}}{\text{Average Sales Value of Production of Previous Two Years}}$$

$$= \frac{\$\ 5{,}000{,}000}{\$12{,}000{,}000} = 41.7\%$$

Suppose for the first month of the plan period the actual payroll was $300,000 and the sales value of production was $900,000. According to the standard ratio, projected payroll costs for the current sales value of production will be

$$(\$900{,}000 \times .417) = \$375{,}300$$

The savings for the month, which constitute the bonus pool, will be

$$(\text{Projected Payroll Costs} - \text{Actual Payroll Costs}) = \text{Bonus Pool}$$

$$(\$375{,}000 - \$300{,}000) = \$75{,}000$$

This bonus pool will be distributed as follows:

$$\text{Reserve Fund: } (25\% \times 75{,}000) = \$18{,}750$$

Bonus Pool Balance (available for distribution):

(75,000 − 18,750) = $56,250

Company Share of Bonus Pool Balance:

(25% × 56,250) = $14,062.50

Employees' Share of Bonus Pool Balance:

(75% × 56,250) = $42,187.50

If Emilia Donato's monthly salary is .007 of ABC Company's payroll, her share of the bonus for the first month will be

(42,187.50 × .007) = $295.31

Managing Change

Gain-sharing plans need a structure and a process for modifying the plan in response to changes in such factors as product mix, technology, market, economic environment. Such changes can affect the validity of the ratio as a measure of improvements in productivity. In the Scanlon Plan, the committees closely monitor the standard ratio and introduce the necessary changes. Such changes are particularly needed during inflationary spirals like those of the mid-1970s. The Scanlon Plans in most organizations responded to these changes without too much difficulty (Henderson 1989). The Plan's adaptability is also well-illustrated by the 30 years' experience of Herman Miller, Inc., which changed the plan to suit its changing conditions (Frost, Greenwood and Associates 1982).

An Assessment of the Scanlon Plan

The Scanlon Plan has produced positive results: cost-saving suggestions; a committed and cooperative workforce with a much greater focus on the economics, goals, and operations of the business; improved labour-management relations; and high levels of employee satisfaction. Critical to the success of the plan is the precondition of trust between labour and management. This is particularly important in times of standard ratio adjustments that could result in a reduction of earnings. Another factor that can create difficulty for the plan is the attitude of middle managers who see employee involvement as a threat to their traditional authority and decision-making role.

The Scanlon Plan, which has been found to be successful in small manufacturing companies, has in recent years been used by many large companies as well (Lawler 1986a).

Rucker Plan

Purpose

The Rucker Plan was developed by Allan Rucker of Eddy-Rucker-Nickels, a firm of consultants. Like the Scanlon Plan, the Rucker Plan is an organization-wide gain-sharing plan with the underlying mission of promoting harmonious employee-management relations. Unlike the Scanlon Plan, it has been adopted mostly by non-unionized companies.

Design and Implementation Process

The Rucker Plan also has a structure of committees composed of employee and management representatives. These committees evaluate employee suggestions for improving productivity. The committees also coordinate the various processes relating to the plan.

Bonus Formula and Distribution Scheme

Productivity improvements in the Rucker Plan are assessed by a ratio that indicates the production value added for each dollar of labour costs in relation to the sales value of production. It is claimed that a reasonably stable relationship exists between total labour costs and the sales value of production (Lawler 1986a). The production value added for each dollar of labour costs is computed by subtracting from the sales value of production the cost of raw materials, supplies, and items related to the services used up in the production and delivery of the product. Data from accounting and production records for a base period are used to determine the percentage of the sales dollar that can be attributed to labour. That percentage is then used to compute the standard productivity ratio. The productivity ratio is applied to the current total labour costs to project the standard production value for this level of labour costs, which is also referred to as the projected (or expected) sales value of production. The excess of the current (actual) sales value of production over the projected sales value of production represents an improvement in productivity, and constitutes the bonus pool.

The bonus pool is distributed to employees on the basis of labour's contribution to production value; the remainder goes to the company. Usually, about 25 per cent of labour's share is withheld in a reserve fund to cover situations when the current value of production is less than the projected (or standard) sales value of production. However, at the end of the year, any balance in the reserve fund is paid out to the employees. The bonus computation and distribution are illustrated in the following example.

Example

The ABC Company determined that the data of the previous two years were typical of its operations. It therefore decided to use the averages of these years to compute the productivity ratio. On the basis of these data, the company estimates that the cost of raw materials, supplies, and items related to the services used up in the production and delivery of the product constitutes 60 per cent of the sales dollar; therefore, 40 per cent of the sales dollar is attributable to labour.

The Productivity Ratio will be

$$\frac{100}{\text{Value Added Attributed to Labour}}$$

$$= \frac{100}{40} = 2.5$$

Suppose the actual payroll for the first month of the plan period was \$300,000, and the sales value of production was \$900,000. According to the standard productivity ratio, the projected sales value of production will be

$$\$300,000 \times 2.5 = \$750,000$$

The savings for the month, which constitute the bonus pool, will be

$$\left(\begin{array}{ccc} \text{Actual Sales Value of Production} & - & \text{Projected Sales Value of Production} \\ = (\$900,000 & - & \$750,000) \\ = \$150,000 & & \end{array}\right)$$

The bonus pool will be distributed as follows:

Company Share: (60% × 150,000) = \$90,000

Employees' Share: (40% × 150,000) = \$60,000

Reserve Fund (25% of Employees' Share): (25% × 60,000) = \$15,000

Immediate Payout to Employees: (60,000 − 15,000) × \$45,000

If Emilia Donato's monthly salary constitutes .007 of ABC's total payroll, her share of the bonus for the first month will be

$$(45,000 \times .007) = \$315$$

Managing Change

The committee structure attends to the study and modification of the standard productivity ratio as necessitated by significant changes in such factors as technology and work methods.

An Assessment of the Rucker Plan

The plan's inclusion of other costs in the computation of the bonus makes it particularly suitable for organizations where these costs are significant components of the cost structure. But, there might be a downside to this positive feature if it leads to complex computations. However, this problem could be overcome by improved communication to help make the plan more understandable to employees.

Unlike the Scanlon Plan, not much has been published on the effectiveness of the Rucker Plan. From the structure and the process of the plan it can be inferred that the results will not differ greatly from those of the Scanlon Plan. In fact, the proponents of the plan claim that ". . . the reward aspect of the gainsharing program is only one-third of the program: the other two, equally important, are feedback of results to employees (and further information sharing) and involvement/participation of employees in productivity-increasing activities" (Wallace and Fay 1988, 262).

Improshare Plan

Purpose

Developed in the mid-1970s by Mitchell Fein, the Improshare Plan was initially designed for the sole purpose of improving productivity through industrial engineering work measurement principles. Today, the plan incorporates a participative management approach. Its underlying philosophy is that employees and management have a common interest in jointly improving productivity and sharing equally in the gains from such improvement.

Design and Implementation Process

Since the plan uses industrial engineering work measurement principles, the design process is dependent on the experts who develop the engineered or estimated data. Employee participation will therefore be low compared with what it is in the Scanlon and Rucker plans. However, organizations that now adopt the plan tend to adopt it along with other high-involvement strategies such as quality control circles. The focus of these organizations, it would appear, is also on encouraging participative management (Lawler 1986a).

Bonus Formula and Distribution Scheme

The bonus formula measures productivity by the use of engineered time standards as expressed by the number of direct labour hours required to produce one unit of the product during the established base period. This time standard is then applied to the production output in the base period to arrive at the estimated total labour hours required for that output. A ratio of the actual labour hours worked on the base-period output to the estimated total labour hours required provides the base productivity factor, which is used to derive the Improshare standard hours. The Improshare standard hours are then used as the base for computing the bonus.

If the actual labour hours of the plan period are less than the Improshare hours, then employees qualify for a bonus. The output data for the bonus computations include only products of acceptable quality. The bonus share of each employee is related to the employee's base salary.

Example

This example is adapted from Aft (1985). The ABC Company determines that the monthly production of the previous two years is typical, and decides to use the average 2,000 units produced over the past two years as the base. The engineered estimate of the direct labour hours required to produce each unit is 8 hours. Therefore, the estimated total labour hours required to produce the 2,000 units would be (2,000 × 8 h) = 16,000 hours. The company has 100 employees who worked a 40-work week to produce the 2,000 units a month. The actual labour hours worked would be (100 × 40 × 4) = 16,000 hours.

Hence the Base Productivity Factor of the company would be

$$\frac{\text{Actual Labour Hours Worked}}{\text{Estimated Total Labour Hours Required}}$$

$$= \frac{16{,}000}{16{,}000} = 1.00$$

The Improshare Standard is

Base Productivity Factor × Engineered Direct Labour Hours

= (1.00) (8 h) × 8 hours

In the first month of the plan period, 2,200 units were produced by 100 employees working a total of 16,000 hours. The Improshare Earned Hours for this production are

(Units Produced) × (Improshare Standard Hours)

(2,200 × 8)

= 17,600 hours

The Hours Gained were

(Improshare Earned Hours − Actual Earned Hours)

(17,600 − 16,000)

= 1,600 hours

The bonus hours gained are shared 50/50 between the employees and the company. Therefore, the employee share of the bonus hours gained will be (1,600 × .50) × 800 hours.

The Employees' Bonus will be

$$\frac{\text{Bonus Hours Gained}}{\text{Actual Earned Hours}} = \frac{800}{16{,}000} = 5\% \text{ for each employee}$$

Thus, Emilia Donato will receive in the first month of the plan period an Improshare bonus amounting to 5 per cent of her salary for that month.

Managing Change

Improshare has a well-designed mechanism for change, which is triggered when improvements in productivity exceed 160 per cent, and also when it can be demonstrated that these improvements are attributable to changes in technology or equipment (Henderson 1989).

An Assessment of the Improshare Plan

The use of engineered or estimated data to establish base standards makes the Improshare Plan suitable for new organizations. It is also suitable for organizations whose past production experience is not a reasonably reliable indicator of future operations and therefore cannot be used to develop base standards that equitably assess and reward productivity improvements.

CONDITIONS THAT FAVOUR GAIN-SHARING PLANS

In addition to the critical strategic issues that must be addressed in the design and implementation of gain-sharing plans, Lawler (1981) recommends that the organization pay attention to conditions that are specifically conducive to making gain-sharing plans effective. Some of these conditions are the capacity of the market to absorb the increased output, the overtime history, and commitment and leadership from management. The almost immediate result of a gain-sharing plan is improvement in productivity. If the increased output cannot be absorbed by the market, then no revenue will flow to provide for the plan payments. On the contrary, improved productivity might even lead to lay-offs. There is also the consideration of the history of overtime in the organization. If there was considerable paid overtime before the plan was installed, employee earnings from the plan should at least equal the amount of overtime that was previously being earned. Otherwise, employees may resort to actions that will restrict output, thus defeating the purpose of the plan. The most important condition is that of commitment and leadership from top management and a willingness to be open and honest with employees on all matters relating to the operations that have an impact on the bonus determination and pay-out. Management's commitment to the plan will also be demonstrated by its willingness to respond to employees' requests for the support and training that will enable them to improve their effectiveness. Any indifference to such requests will affect the plan operations.

SUMMARY

This chapter reviewed the major types of individual incentive and gain-sharing plans, which are designed primarily to motivate the attainment of a predetermined end result. The individual incentive plans that were examined were the piece-rate, the standard-hour, and sales commissions and bonuses. There are several variations of these plans, but the underlying rationale is essentially the same, that is, to motivate the attainment of a predetermined end result. The piece-rate plan is activated by the production of the targeted output. The standard-hour plan rewards improvements in efficiency above the established standard. Sales commissions and bonuses operate more like the piece-rate plan. The effectiveness of these plans depends not only on the plan mechanics and formula, but also on such critical process issues as the setting of specific and realistically difficult goals, employee involvement, change mechanisms, provision for circumstances beyond the employee's control, and supervisor-worker relations characterized by a high degree of trust. The effectiveness of group incentive plans also depends on a similar set of conditions. However, special attention should be paid to decisions on critical strategic and process issues in the design and management of group gain-sharing plans. These issues are the design process, bonus determination and distribution, and the change/modifications management process. The descriptions of the Scanlon, Rucker, and Improshare plans illustrate how these issues have been dealt with in the more popular gain-sharing plans. These descriptions also remind us that participative management is inherent in gain-sharing plans. The other conditions that are conducive to the effectiveness of gain-sharing plans are the capacity of the market to absorb the increased output and, most importantly, the commitment and leadership of management.

KEY TERMS

gain-sharing plan
group incentive plan
Improshare plan
piece-rate incentives
standard-hour plan
the task-and-bonus approach

REVIEW AND DISCUSSION QUESTIONS

1. Identify the similarities and differences between
   a) the Taylor Plan and the Merrick Plan
   b) the Halsey, Rowan, and the Gantt plans
2. The discussion in the chapter has identified seven conditions that contribute to the effectiveness of individual incentive plans. Why are these conditions critical to the effectiveness of the plans?
3. Review the descriptions of the Scanlon, Rucker, and Improshare plans. Which one of these plans has best addressed the critical design and implementation issues?
4. What are some of the conditions which favour gain-sharing plans?
5. After Will Walters, Jr., had obtained his M.B.A., he joined the family toy manufacturing business, Funcrafts Limited, as the assistant plant manager. He was perplexed to find that the Flying Frisbee Toy assembly line had for some time produced a constant 250 kits a day. Further enquiry revealed that although no targets were ever set, the employees were questioned whenever production fell below 250 kits. He learnt from a student he employed last summer under a federal Challenge grant that production routinely slowed down after lunch and picked up later so that the 250 kits were produced just before closing time. Will is thinking of an incentive plan and seeks your advice on (*a*) the factors he should consider; (*b*) the type of plan — individual or group.

CASE: THE ELUSIVE REWARD

Sharon Rogers became an account representative for a company that produced software packages. An established supplier to large business organizations, the company planned to enter a new market — small businesses.

Larger organizations accepted the products because their employees were familiar with the concepts involved. Employees of smaller businesses did not fully understand or appreciate the concepts underlying the products. Sharon's task was formidable, but she felt confident that she could manage, because she was assured that the customer service department would provide the necessary technical support by developing related sales and user-training materials. Also, the orientation programme for new users included a comprehensive four-day sales seminar that helped bring her academic knowledge and training (a McGill B. Com. with concentration in Management Information Systems) into a proper business focus.

Sharon was assigned a sales quota of $250,000 for the first year — one-half of the average sales quota for an account representative in the established large-business market. She had not anticipated that the quota would be so high, considering the nature of the product and the market.

Sharon found the starting salary of $25,000 to be low, but had accepted the job because of the generous bonus plan applicable to those who met the quota. This was Sharon's first full-time job. In her summer jobs, she always opted for challenging assignments and completed them quite successfully.

The report for the first quarter showed that Sharon's sales were far below the targeted figures. Although she had performed all the required behaviours, such as prospecting, demonstrating, and follow-up, these just did not translate into sales. Naturally, she was concerned that at her present rate of sales she might not make her annual quota.

It was now abundantly clear to her that her customers, the small businesses, did not fully appreciate the potential of her products. She proposed a package of new sales materials to favourably influence the customer acceptance of the products. Action on the proposal was delayed because of objections from the controller's office: the costs involved had not been budgeted.

For three months, Sharon's enthusiasm for the job was one long roller-coaster ride. She felt good about her job and took pride in her work, but she felt dejected when her efforts were not successful and wondered whether the attractive bonus package would ever be a reality. She even began to experience nagging doubts about her ability to do the job.

Three more months went by, and the situation became even more bleak for Sharon. Her sales figures did not improve, although she continued to perform her tasks as well as, if not better than, any other account rep. Her frustrations were aggravated by the failure of the customer service department to develop the needed new sales materials. She discovered that each support (staff) function in the company is a profit centre, evaluated on the basis of its contribution to the activity that brings in the largest profit. Such a practice rewards the customer service department for paying attention to clients from the large-business sector and to ignore those in the small businesses.

SOURCE: Based on Hurwich and Moynahan (1984).

Discussion Questions

1. What is the likely effect of the bonus plan on Sharon Rogers?
2. Evaluate the bonus plan in the light of the conditions that contribute to the effectiveness of incentive plans.
3. What changes (short-term and long-term) to the bonus plan would you recommend in this case? Why?

Chapter 10

Job Analysis and Job Evaluation: Internal Equity I

CHAPTER SYNOPSIS

This chapter addresses the issue of internal equity in the compensation system, and the techniques and processes that ensure the incorporation of internal equity in the compensation system. The primary thrust of the chapter is job evaluation (its techniques, methods, and processes), which enables the organization to develop a job structure. The effectiveness of the job evaluation programme is dependent on job descriptions that accurately reflect the content and contribution of the job. Hence, the chapter will also discuss the methods of job analysis, which generates the information used to develop job descriptions and job specifications.

LEARNING OBJECTIVES

- To define internal equity.
- To identify the sources of the value of a job.
- To understand why internal equity plays a predominant role in the design of a compensation system.
- To define job analysis, and to explain its important link to the job evaluation programme.
- To describe job analysis methods and to discuss their advantages and disadvantages.
- To identify the basic contents of a job description statement.
- To define job evaluation, and to understand its role in the compensation system.
- To describe the methods of job evaluation, and to discuss their advantages and disadvantages.

- To understand that the job evaluation process has a decisive impact on internal equity.
- To develop strategies for employee involvement in the job evaluation process.

INTRODUCTION

The concept of equity or fairness lies at the heart of the compensation system. Previous chapters — more specifically Chapter 4 — explored the elements and the process that contribute to employees' perceptions of the equity or fairness of a reward. There are three types of equity: personal (or individual), internal, and external. Chapters 8 and 9 discussed the methods and processes by which a compensation system can ensure personal equity. This chapter focuses on internal equity. The questions to be addressed are: What is internal equity? What role does it play in the design of a compensation system? What tools (techniques, methods) and processes are used in order to ensure the internal equity of a compensation system?

INTERNAL EQUITY

WHAT IS INTERNAL EQUITY?

"Internal Equity is a fairness criterion that requires employers to set wage rates for jobs within companies that correspond to the relative internal value of each job" (Wallace and Fay 1988, 17). Neither employers nor employees quarrel with this definition *per se*. Several questions, however, arise: What precisely is meant by the *value* of a job? What is the source or basis of this value? There are a variety of views on job value. According to some of these views, the value of a job should reflect (*a*) the sociocultural values of a society; (*b*) the value of the product or service it creates; (*c*) the investment in education, training, and experience required for the job; (*d*) the position of the job in the organizational hierarchy.

In practice, organizations have traditionally focused on the *content* and the *contribution* of the job in determining its value. Job content refers to the knowledge, skills, ability, experience, and effort required on the job, which constitute the job specifications. For example, a job that requires its holder to have a college degree will, other things being equal, have a higher job value than a job that requires only a high school diploma. The job content of the former is judged to be greater than the job content of the latter. The contribution of the job refers to its contribution to the economic value of the product or service, or its contribution to the attainment of the objectives of the work unit or of the organization, expressed in terms of profits, production, or some similar measure. In an oil-exploration company, a geologist would ordinarily be considered to be contributing more to the organizational objectives than the company's accountant. As a result, the geologist's job will be viewed as having more value, even though the investment in professional education and training for both jobs may be similar.

The Role of Internal Equity in the Design of a Compensation System

A consideration of two cases will help to explore this question. In case 1, similar jobs in Company A are not paid similar wages; some jobs are paid more than others. In case 2, the jobs in company A are paid less than similar jobs in company B. In which of the two cases will inequity be perceived to be greater? Greater inequity will be experienced in case 1 than in case 2, primarily because in case 1, employees believe that they have a better knowledge of the situation and conditions in their own organization and hence feel more confident in assessing the outcomes/inputs ratios — their own as well as those of the reference source — with relatively greater accuracy. This is not to say that external equity — the condition of case 2 — is not important. External equity, which is discussed in Chapter 12, is also crucial to the design of a compensation system. In fact, wages in the external labour market considerably influence an organization's pay structure and policies.

However, the major limitation to using the external labour market as *the* frame of reference in designing a compensation system is the issue of comparability. One aspect of this issue is: How comparable are the data of wage surveys collected from other organizations? The answer depends upon how identical the jobs in a company are in comparison with the jobs in the surveyed organizations. Usually the jobs, although having the same or similar titles, are different, in terms of both the job content and the job's contribution to organizational objectives. As discussed in the previous section, both job content and contribution are significant factors in determining the value of a job to the organization.

Another aspect of comparability (or lack of it) is that the survey data are an assortment of wages from companies participating in the survey. "Assortment" is emphasized because the wages of each company result from that company's decisions, which are based on such considerations as business strategies, industry practices, number of employees in a specific job category. The wage data will also incorporate the company's decisions on cost-of-hiring adjustments, merit pay based on performance, and seniority considerations. If some of the participating companies in the survey are unionized, their wage structure will reflect the dynamic of their unique labour-management relations.

In view of the preceding discussion, it is clear that internal equity will play a predominant role in the design of the compensation system. The major compensation item that is particularly affected by internal equity is base pay. When employees perceive internal inequity in base pay, they experience a drop in valence. As expectancy theory predicts, a drop in valence results in a lower motivational force. Consequently, base pay will not have the intended motivational impact. The resulting loss to the organization can be severe when it is recalled that an organization's investment in base pay constitutes a substantial portion of its financial resources. Futhermore, a demotivated workforce cannot guarantee the effective utilization of the physical and material resources of the organization; much less can the workforce be expected to be creative, innovative, and committed to the organization. The decision to ensure internal equity is, in effect, a strategic decision that contributes to the efficient and effective utilization of the physical, financial, and human resources of the organization.

TOOLS AND PROCESSES FOR ENSURING INTERNAL EQUITY

The primary process for determining the value of a job relative to the other jobs in the organization is *job evaluation*. To evaluate a job, one must have adequate data about the value of the job, about the similarities and differences upon which pay differentials are constructed. The collection of these data is done through the process of *job analysis*. This chapter first reviews the different methods of job analysis and then discusses the methods and processes of job evaluation systems. Some organizations, it should be noted, first decide on a job evaluation system, so that the job analysis, which follows, yields the data required to evaluate the jobs. Traditionally, however, job analysis has preceded job evaluation because the data collected from job analysis are used for several purposes besides job evaluation. Some of these purposes are

1. developing job descriptions and job specifications for recruitment and selection;
2. identifying the critical job behaviours and objectives for performance appraisals;
3. developing training programmes;
4. developing career paths and providing the counselling inherent in career planning programmes;
5. identifying job tasks and work-flow processes for designing or redesigning a job.

JOB ANALYSIS

WHAT IS JOB ANALYSIS?

Job analysis is the process of collecting information about a job. This process is conducted systematically with a view to gathering information about the tasks, duties, responsibilities, working conditions, desirable job behaviours, and competencies. Stated differently, the process attempts to collect data on

1. what is done on the job, that is, the tasks and operations involved;
2. how the job is done, that is, the behaviours that must be demonstrated on the job;
3. under what conditions the job is done, that is, the physical and social environments in which the job has to be done;
4. and the knowledge, skills, and abilities (KSAs) needed by the employee to do the job.

The data that result from a job analysis are presented in the form of a job description, which also includes a statement of job specification. This statement spells out the knowledge, skills, and abilities needed for the job.

THE PROCEDURE AND THE METHODS OF JOB ANALYSIS

The job analysis process is successful in collecting the necessary information when there is unbiased input from at least those employees directly involved in the performance of the job, namely, the job incumbent and the supervisor. So that the trust and the willingness required for the free flow of information can be generated, certain preparatory steps are necessary. First, all employees must be informed of the plans to conduct a job analysis programme. The communication must include the reasons for such a programme and an assurance that the job incumbent will have an opportunity to review and react to the data collected about his/her job before such data are translated into a definitive description of the job. The communication should also seek employees' cooperation and active participation in the programme. In a unionized organization, it is essential to seek the cooperation and involvement of the union.

Second, job analysts should prepare themselves to see the job in its proper perspective, and to understand its nature. Preparation is greatly aided by a review of the existing job descriptions and of the organization chart, which shows the job's location and relationships. A tour of the work site gives the analyst a good idea of the working conditions and the social and technical context of the job. Third, a decision must be made on the choice of the job analysis method. The analyst can pick from a variety of methods, both conventional and quantitative. The following subsections review the procedure and the merits and demerits of these conventional methods: interview, questionnaire, observation, and diary/log. Among the quantitative methods, the focus will be on the most popular, the position analysis questionnaire (PAQ).

Interview

The job analyst interviews both the job incumbent and the supervisor. If the target job has a large number of positions, it is more productive to interview the most knowledgeable worker; it is advisable to interview the employee selected by the employees to represent them. Employees must be assured of an opportunity to review the collected data for accuracy and validity. The interview should focus on job information relating to the major tasks, their importance and frequency of performance; and the tools, equipment, machines, and related material and financial resources of the job. In addition, the worker may be asked to provide information on two specific categories of tasks: (1) tasks the employee is now performing, but which the employees believes are not appropriate or efficient for him/her to be performing; (2) tasks not now being performed by the employee, but which the employee believes would contribute to enhanced performance if they were part of the job. Answers to these two questions will be invaluable when job redesign is considered.

The interview method, which is time-consuming and expensive, is most useful for managerial and professional jobs. For other jobs, the interview is effective when it is necessary to clarify the data acquired through other job analysis methods. For the successful use of the interview method, job analysts recqgnize the necessity of a structured interview format, competence in communication skills and interview techniques, and a sound knowledge of the work flow. They also recognize that they must have the complete trust of the job incumbent if they are to obtain data that are accurate and valid. Before writing up the job description, the collected data should be reviewed with the job incumbent and the supervisor.

Observation

This method is probably the oldest job analysis method. Frederick Taylor's scientific management movement had its beginnings in observation, which was later performed with a stop watch. In this method, the analyst observes, from a suitable vantage point, a complete work cycle of the job, and records the tasks and behaviours that are performed. The collected data are then reviewed by both the incumbent and the supervisor. The effectiveness of this method depends upon the observation of a complete work cycle of a job, which is not feasible for most jobs. Hence, the usefulness of the method is limited to certain factory and clerical jobs where the work cycle is short and repetitive.

Questionnaire

In this method, the job incumbent responds to a questionnaire that calls for brief responses, preferably through yes/no responses and the checking off of a scale. The questions generally relate to the nature of the work tasks/behaviours performed, the tools and the machinery used, working conditions, job challenges, requirements, and principal accountabilities. Depending upon the verbal capabilities of the respondent, a few open-ended questions are useful. The scale is a useful device for obtaining for each job task or behaviour described in the question the frequency of its performance and its degree of importance.

The questionnaire method has the advantage of being inexpensive, and its standardized format facilitates mathematical analysis. The job incumbent's participation, relative to the other methods, is greater. Such participation is conducive to a greater acceptance of the findings by the incumbent. The method is not without its share of problems, notably those related to the verbal abilities of the employee, such as the ability to read, understand, and respond to the questions. The questionnaire method is generally not suitable for employees with minimal reading or writing skills. In addition, the analyst must watch for responses that exaggerate the responsibilities and the complexities of the tasks in an attempt to depict the job as being more valuable than it really is. To probe such responses, the interview method may be used as a follow-up.

Diary/Log

The job incumbent is requested to keep a record of the activities/tasks as they are performed weekly, monthly, or quarterly. The analyst then reviews these records to get a picture of the job. Such a record is useful provided the analyst can be sure that it is a faithful description of the activities/tasks performed on that job. The job incumbent needs to be diligent and self-disciplined to maintain a continuous and reasonably accurate record of the job tasks and activities. For this reason, this method is considered appropriate primarily for professionals and managers. Even in these jobs, the analyst is well advised to supplement the information through interviews and questionnaires.

The Position Analysis Questionnaire (PAQ)

The PAQ is one of the more popular quantitative methods of job analysis (Ghorpade 1988). The questionnaire is a "worker-oriented" inventory, so-called because it contains statements of the behaviours (job elements) demonstrated by workers in a wide variety of jobs. The

Position Analysis Questionnaire has a total of 187 job elements or statements of job behaviours, which are grouped into six major divisions: information input, mental processes, work output, relationships with other persons, job context, and other job characteristics (McCormick 1979).

TABLE 10.1
THE SIX MAJOR DIVISIONS OF THE POSITION ANALYSIS QUESTIONNAIRE

Division	Illustrative Job Behaviours	Examples
Information input	Using senses, other sources, to access information	Social worker listens to and observes the client.
Mental processes	Planning, making decisions, processing information	Social worker evaluates client's file and decides on a course of action.
Work output	Performing physical activities, using equipment and various devices	Social worker uses the computer to store and process client information.
Relationships with others	Communicating, supervising, instructing, coordinating	Social worker discusses clients with professionals.
Job context	Performing job under stressful conditions	Social worker deals with uncooperative clients.
Other job characteristics	Working shifts/regular schedule, on a temporary or permanent basis, etc.	Social worker operates on a flex-time schedule.

Table 10.1 provides some illustrative job behaviours with examples in each division.

The job incumbent is required to review each statement of behaviour (job element) and respond to it in terms of

- whether the behaviour applies to the job;
- how important the behaviour is to the effective performance of the job;
- the amount of time the worker spends on this behaviour relative to the total time spent on the job;
- the degree of complexity of the behaviour or its level of difficulty.

For statements of behaviours that involve work devices (tools, equipment), the job incumbent is required to indicate the extent of their use on the job.

The PAQ provides a standardized format for quantifying the responses of job incumbents; its process is integrated and computer-supported. These job data are then subjected to statistical procedures, such as factor analysis, to develop a profile for each job — a procedure that allows for meaningful comparisons across jobs in a fairly objective manner. More pertinent to the compensation specialist is PAQ's potential usefulness in job evaluation programmes. Studies have found that the data generated by the questionnaire can predict job worth with a fair degree of accuracy (McCormick 1976).

There are, however, several limitations to the PAQ. To begin with, the PAQ has reduced the enormous variety of job behaviours performed on the job to a fixed set of 187 statements, which it assumes ought to exist on the job. In reality, there are many behaviours performed on the job that cannot be validly identified with the standardized behaviours listed in the PAQ. To the extent, therefore, that the PAQ statements do not tap these behaviours, the PAQ fails to capture fully the nature of the job. Cascio (1982) points out three further limitations. First, even when the PAQ captures the behaviours of jobs and develops the job profiles, the similarities of the profiles can be misleading. For example, the profile of the police officer's job can be amazingly similar to that of the homemaker. Both jobs incumbents would respond affirmatively to behaviour statements about detecting, trouble shooting, and handling emergencies. Nevertheless, there are significant and substantial differences in the tasks of these jobs. Moreover, the PAQ focuses on job behaviours and ignores job outcomes. Behaviourally, one job may have elements in common with those of another job, but the difference in their outcomes can be enormous.

Second, because a proper response to the PAQ requires that the job incumbent have a college-level reading ability, the PAQ is unsuitable for jobs that do not require this level of reading ability. Third, the content of the PAQ statements of job behaviours are inappropriate for professional and managerial jobs. However, the Professional and Managerial Position Questionnaire (PMPQ) developed by the PAQ researchers might address this last limitation (Henderson 1989). The PMPQ is designed specifically for the jobs of managers, professionals, scientists, engineers, and teachers.

Compared with conventional methods of job analysis, the PAQ and other quantitative methods provide the job analyst with a more rational and systematic approach to making judgements about job data. However, these methods do not relieve the analyst of the need and the responsibility for making judgements, because no objective method, technique, or approach exists that can replace rational judgement (Dunnette, Hough, and Rosse 1979).

Job Description and Job Specifications

The data gathered from job analysis are used to develop a job description, a document that informs the employee in clear, precise, and understandable terms what his/her job is, what he/she is expected to do. In other words, this document describes the job that must be done and specifies the qualifications (knowledge, skills, abilities, experience) the holder must possess to do the job. The job description usually contains the following sections (Henderson 1989):

1. Identification: provides information relating to job title, pay grade, location, and so forth.
2. Summary: spells out the major functions/activities that enable the reader to identify and differentiate these functions/activities from those of other jobs. Generally, the summary includes the major responsibilites of the job. A set of about four to seven responsibilities is sufficient to describe a job adequately.
3. Responsibilities: identifies the primary reasons for the existence of the job. Stated differently, if these responsibilities are not carried out at an acceptable level, the consequences to the work unit will be serious enough to require remedial action from management. Responsibilities may be ranked by sequence of occurrence or by importance. For each responsibility there should be listed a set of duties that describes not only what is done but also why and how it is done. A set of about three to seven duties is usually sufficient to describe a responsibility. The duties establish the foundation for the setting of job specifications and performance standards.
4. Accountabilities: describes the major results expected in the satisfactory performance of the responsibilities, and may also stipulate responsibility for the different resources assigned to the job.
5. Specifications: provides the qualifications (knowledge, skill, ability, experience) the incumbent should bring to the job for performance at the acceptable level. In addition, the specifications section details information on the context of the job, for example, supervisory controls and working conditions. This section contributes significant information for decisions in the job evaluation process. Sometimes, this portion of the information is spelt out in a separate document entitled Job Specifications.

The job description is an indispensable document in human resource management. It serves the needs of manpower planning, recruitment and selection, training and development, career planning, job design, and compensation. The information provided in it is the principal source upon which judgements will be made about the value of the job. It is the critical starting point for the job evaluation process. Errors and biases that lead to an inadequate or incorrect job description will result in an incorrect value of the job. In fact, as will be seen in the next chapter, job description is a major source of gender bias, which produces pay inequity.

JOB EVALUATION

What Is Job Evaluation?

Job evaluation is the process of determining the value of a job *within* an organization relative to all the other jobs in that organization. The job value, so derived, becomes the foundation for establishing pay differentials among the jobs in the organization. In specific terms, job evaluation is expected to contribute to the compensation programme in the following ways (Dunn and Rachel 1971):

- by providing a basis for establishing money rates for each job;
- by resolving differences on job values and job rates in a logical and systematic manner;
- by creating definite and equitable value differentials for each job relative to all the other jobs in the organization;
- by placing new or redesigned jobs into the job structure;
- by providing useful data for activities such as wage and salary surveys, labour negotiations, compliance with pay equity laws;
- by identifying a ladder of career progression.

Methods of Job Evaluation

There are basically four methods of job evaluation. These are *ranking, classification, point method,* and *factor comparison method*. This section discusses each method separately in terms of its procedure, its advantages and disadvantages, and the conditions under which it could be considered to be most effective. The section concludes with a discussion of the similarities in, and differences between, these methods.

Ranking

In this method, jobs are ranked according to their value, from the most valuable to the least valuable. What is the basis of the ranking? The job as a whole is considered, using some factor that is believed to be a valid source of value. In practice, however, the "factor" is one person's judgement of what is believed to be of value to the organization.

The rank ordering of jobs can be done by simple ranking, alternation ranking, and paired comparisons. In simple ranking, the jobs are ranked from the most valuable to the least valuable on the basis of some criterion. In alternation ranking, the most valuable job is selected, removed from the list of jobs to be considered, and placed at the top of the job structure. Of the remaining jobs, the least valuable job is selected, removed from the list of jobs to be considered, and placed at the bottom of the job structure. The next most valuable job is then selected, and then the next least valuable. The alternation process of selecting the next most valuable and then the next least valuable continues until all the jobs have been selected and placed in the job structure.

In the paired-comparison method, each job is compared with every other job, and a judgement is made on which of the jobs in the pair that is being compared has a higher ranking. That job that receives the greatest number of "higher ranking" judgements is the most valuable job in the job structure. The other jobs are then arranged below this most valuable job according to the number of "higher ranking" judgements received in the paired comparison.

The advantages of ranking are that it is simple, inexpensive, and practical. Ranking is suitable for small organizations, which do not have a wide variety of jobs and where the number of jobs is not large. The jobs are usually well known in a small organization, and there is an implicit recognition of which are the more valuable jobs. Ranking has several disadvantages. First, the evaluator's knowledge of all the jobs must be more than superficial. Even then, rank order is not an accurate measure of worth, because the evaluator can easily be influenced by his/her knowledge of the person who holds the job. As a result, the rank assigned might, in effect, be a judgement of the job incumbent rather than of the value of the job itself. Second, the differentials between the ranks occupied by the jobs are presumed to be equal; often, they are not.

Classification

The job classification method involves placing jobs in pre-established classes. Each class bears a description relating to such factors as education, responsibility, level of difficulty, and public contact. The classes are then arranged in an ascending order, from the most simple to the most complex in terms of the factors used to describe the classes.

For example, suppose an evaluator decides to develop a classification system using the factors of nature of work (in terms of simple vs. complex, and easy vs. difficult), responsibility for subordinates (exercising vs. not exercising supervision), and customer contact. In this classification, the lowest class will be

> Simple, easy work; does not exercise responsibility for subordinates; no customer contact.

The highest class will be

> Complex, very difficult work; exercises responsibility for subordinates; maintains contact with customers.

The other classes will fall in between the lowest and the highest classes and will contain varying amounts of these three factors such that the next higher level class has relatively more of one or two of these factors. The highest class has the most of each factor.

The evaluator then reviews the description of the job that is to be evaluated, and places the job into the class that best matches the job description. The job structure, then, is the order of the jobs as given by their place in the classes. The job value is determined by the job's placement in the predetermined series of classes. When the classification system is used, a separate classification is developed for the different occupations that exist in the organization, for example, managerial, professional, clerical, operational.

Classification is an improvement over the ranking method in that the evaluation judgement is based on a set of criteria that are clearly, logically, and coherently established. Within each occupation, the classification generally reflects the hierarchy that is implicity accepted by employees in that occupation. Another advantage is that the hierarchy given by the classification system for each occupation becomes the basis of a career ladder for the jobs in that occupation.

There are several disadvantages to the classification method of job evaluation. To begin with, there is the difficulty of developing the classes — more specifically, the description or definition of each class. The descriptions of the classes are arranged logically in a gradually ascending order from the most simple to the most complex in terms of the factors used. That being so, how is it possible to assess the relative worth of a job that requires a little of one factor described in the class (such as "exercising supervision for subordinates") and a great deal of another factor (such as "customer contact"), whereas another job may require just the opposite, more of "exercising supervision for subordinates" and less of "customer contact." The classification system has difficulty coping with the fact that there is a need to balance the factors in order to ensure that, in the ultimate analysis, jobs of equal total value are treated as such. The classification method also has the problem of "forced fit." This occurs when a job that more properly belongs between two established classes has to be forced into one of these two classes because the in-between class does not exist in the classification system.

The very nature of the classification method requires each occupational group to have its own classification system. This creates an insurmountable problem when interoccupational comparison becomes necessary. Very few persons in an organization are knowledgeable, wise, and impartial enough to know what each occupational class or group contributes to the attainment of the organizational goals and objectives, much less to measure the relative contributions and importance of the responsibilities and duties of each occupational group. This difficulty with the classification method takes on a more serious dimension when the issue of equal pay for work of equal value needs to be addressed. As will be discussed in Chapter 11, pay equity laws in Canada mandate that the pay rates of female-dominated jobs be the same as those of male-dominated jobs when these jobs are equal in value. The determination of whether equal pay for work of equal value exists in an organization necessitates a single job evaluation system for all occupational groups.

The Factor Comparison and Point Methods

As a preparation for considering each of these methods, two concepts will be explored: (1) compensable factors, and (2) benchmark or key jobs. Both these concepts are necessary features of the factor comparison and point methods.

Compensable Factors

Compensable factors are those characteristics of a job that are believed to be important for the organization. Therefore, the organization will be willing to pay for them. Their presence in the job gives the job its value. Table 10.2 lists the compensable factors used in one job evaluation system, known as the Factor Evaluation System (FES), developed by the U.S. government in the mid-1970s. In this system, there is a total of nine compensable factors: knowledge required by the position, supervisory controls, guidelines, complexity, scope and effect, personal contact, purpose of contact, physical demands, and work environment. An organization that adopts the FES job evaluation system is saying that it regards these nine factors to be important determinants of the values of its jobs. As will be seen later in this chapter, not all the nine factors are of equal importance; they are weighted differently. In general, however, the more of these factors a job has, the greater will be its value and, consequently, its pay.

In order for the proper value differentials to be developed among the jobs of an organization, the compensable factors must be common to all jobs, and they must be describable and quantifiable. However, the more "common" a factor is to a wide variety of jobs in the organization, the more abstract it will tend to be. As a result, only with difficulty will it be described and quanitified adequately enough to be of use in a job evaluation system. The more specific a factor, the more it can be described and measured in order to capture the unique characteristics of a job. At the same time, the specific factor will have limited usefulness, because its description will be too narrow to cover a wide variety of the jobs. Hence, it will not be applicable to all the jobs in the organization. The compensable factor needs to be both "abstract" (common) and "specific." To reconcile these apparently conflicting needs, job evaluation systems have had recourse to expressing the factor in terms of three

Table 10.2
Factor Evaluation System Factors, Weights, and Levels

Factor	Points for Factor	Value of Factor as Percentage of Total (Weight of Factor)	Number of Levels	Points for Each Level
Knowledge required by the position	1,850	41.3%	9	50, 200, 350, 550, 750, 950, 1250, 1550, 1850
Supervisory control	650	14.5%	5	25, 125, 275, 450, 650
Guidelines	650	14.5%	5	25, 125, 275, 450, 650
Complexity	450	10.0%	6	25, 75, 150, 225, 325, 450
Scope and effect	450	10.0%	6	25, 75, 150, 225, 325, 450
Personal contact	110	2.5%	4	10, 25, 60, 110
Purpose of contact	220	4.9%	4	20, 50, 120, 220
Physical demand	50	1.1%	3	5, 20, 50
Work environment	50	1.1%	3	5, 20, 50
Total	4,480	99.9%		

Source: Richard Henderson, *Compensation Management: Rewarding Performance*, 5th ed., © 1989, p. 200. Reprinted by permission of Prentice-Hall, Englewood Cliffs, New Jersey.

categories — universal factors, subfactors, degrees (or levels). The universal factor is relatively abstract (for example, the factor of skill) and hence can be applicable to a wide variety of jobs. The subfactors are subsets of universal factors that have the characteristic of making the universal factor more specific; for example, job knowledge, education, training, experience are subfactors of skill. Degrees (or levels) further define the subfactors and indicate the specific amount of the factor that is required in the performance of the job.

As an example of the use of factors and degrees, consider the first factor of the Factor Evaluation System: "knowledge required by the position." This factor appears to be universal, that is, broad enough to cover all the jobs in the organization. But, it is too broad to permit a meaningful differentiation between jobs. For this reason, the FES provides a description of this factor in a subfactor that spells out in some detail the content envisaged by the universal factor of "knowledge required by the position." In this subfactor, "knowledge required by the position" is defined as:

> The nature and extent of information or facts which the workers must understand to do acceptable work (e.g., steps, procedures, practices, rules, policies, theories, principles, and concepts) and the nature and extent of the skills needed to apply those knowledges. To be used as a basis for selecting a level under this factor, a knowledge must be required and applied. (Henderson and Wolfe 1985, 108)

The subfactor, as defined above, is much more specific, yet it is not specific enough to allow for capturing the differences between jobs whose knowledge requirements can range from the very simple to the very complex. To further differentiate on this factor, the FES has developed degrees or levels of the subfactor.

As can be seen in Table 10.2, this subfactor, knowledge, has nine levels. For illustrative purposes, only the first and ninth levels are reproduced.

> Level 1-1:
> Knowledge of simple, routine, or repetitive tasks or operations which typically includes following step-by-step instructions and requires little or no previous training or experience. (Henderson and Wolfe 1985, 108)
> Level 1-9:
> Mastery of a professional field to generate and develop new hypotheses and theories. (Henderson and Wolfe 1985, 109).

Level 1 and level 9 define the two ends of the broad spectrum of the subfactor. Levels 3 to 8 define the variations in knowledge as the levels proceed from the simple to the complex. Degrees or levels are the most specific, and for this reason, each level may require a description that fills several paragraphs.

The total number of compensable factors varies according to the system used. An effective system should have at least the following four factors: *skill, effort, responsibility, working conditions*. Note that compensable factors are not what the job incumbent may possess. Rather, these are characteristics required for the job to be done. Therefore, a job-content-based evaluation system will use the compensable factors and completely disregard the job incumbent, either the additional knowledge, skills, and abilities the individual may possess, or the individual's performance level. The focus in the job-content-based evaluation system — unlike that in the person-based job evaluation sytem referred to in Chapter 6 and discussed in some detail later in this chapter — is only on the KSAs that are determined in the job specifications as necessary for the job. Compensable factors will be effective in a job evaluation system if, in addition to their inherent characteristics, they are job related. For this reason, they must be supported by data developed from a well-conducted job analysis programme. Both employees and management must accept and support the use of the compensable factors. Recall the discussion of internal equity where the sources of job value were considered and the conclusion made that job value ought to take into account both the job content and the job contribution. To say that the compensable factors should be job related and acceptable both to employees and to management means that compensable factors should be consistent with both job content and job contribution.

Why are compensable factors important to job evaluation? Compensable factors allow the process of job evaluation to be consistent, uniform, and objective. They also contribute to an increased understanding of the process. When a job is assigned a value, the compensable factors enable one to probe why and to be satisfied that the process is not the result of the whim and caprice of the evaluator but is based on some objective criteria. Of course, understanding is increased *only* if the system is not too complicated, a point that will be considered again in discussing the administrative requirements of the job evaluation programme.

Benchmark or Key Jobs

Benchmark or key jobs are those jobs in the organization that serve as reference points or anchors from which to get a sense of the values of other jobs. The contents of key jobs do not change as drastically as the contents of non-key jobs. Because of this stability, the contents of key jobs are well known, and usually there is considerable agreement between employees and management about the nature and contents of these jobs. Moreover, there is general agreement about the pay rates of these jobs and the pay differentials that exist among the key jobs. Another important characteristic of key jobs is that such jobs (i.e., with these contents) exist in a fairly large number of organizations; hence, the external labour market regards them as reference points (anchors) for wage determination.

The Point Method

Also known as the *point rating* and *point factor* methods, the point method is the most widely used method of job evaluation. It evaluates a job by reference to an evaluation system that assigns point values to a set of compensable factors. The Factor Evaluation System outlined in Table 10.2 is an example of the point method of job evaluation. A job is evaluated on each factor and the appropriate points are assigned. The total value of the job is determined by adding up the points assigned to each compensable factor.

The following is a procedure for developing and implementing a point method job evaluation system. The Factor Evaluation System (FES) is used to illustrate the different steps of the procedure.

1. Decide on the compensable factors, keeping in mind the characteristics of compensable factors. The FES has chosen nine factors (see Table 10.2). The number and the type of factors should fit the needs of the organization, that is, enable the organization to properly identify the similarities in, and the differences between, jobs.
2. Decide on the maximum number of points in the entire system. There is no specific "good" number to use. The number chosen should be easy to work with and large enough to allow for differentiations between and within factors. The FES has a total of 4,480 points.
3. Decide on the weights to be assigned to each factor. The weight is influenced by a judgemental assessment of how important each factor is to the organization. As a practical measure, percentages can be used initially, so that all the weights add up to 100 per cent. Allocate the points to the factors on the basis of the weights. In Table 10.2 can be seen the weights of each factor and the points, out of the total 4,480 points, allocated on the basis of these weights.
4. Define each factor in detail by using a scale of degrees (levels). There is no optimal number of degrees, and all factors need not have the same number of degrees. The primary consideration is the spread from the simplest level to the most complex level of the factor; the greater the extent of this spread, the greater the number of degrees. Generally, the factor that has the greatest assigned weight will have more degrees than the factor with a lesser assigned weight. Thus, in Table 10.2, "knowledge required by the position" has been assigned the highest weight (41.3 per cent), and it also has the highest number of levels (nine). Distribute the points to the degrees in each factor. In Table 10.2, the last column shows the points assigned for each of the nine levels; the lowest level has 50 points, and the highest

level has 1,850 points. The range seems justified on the basis of the description of these two levels (1-1 and 1-9) presented earlier.

5. Validate this system by applying it to the key jobs. To do this, evaluate the key jobs on each factor and determine the total point value of the key jobs. Assess the validity of the values by checking for consistency between the differentials as determined by the job evaluation system and the differentials that are known to exist between the key jobs. The nature of key jobs is such that the differentials are well known and accepted in the organization. If an inconsistency is detected (i.e., the job values obtained do not reflect the known and accepted differentials between key jobs), review the judgements made on each factor of the job evaluation system. It might also be that the content of a key job has undergone a change to the extent that it can no longer be considered a key job. If this is so, the job should be excluded from this validation process.
6. After the system has been validated, use it to evaluate the other jobs in the organization.
7. Develop a job structure, that is, arrange the jobs in the descending order of their point values. Review for any obvious discrepancies or inconsistencies. Investigating and resolving these inconsistencies may require a review of the judgements that were made on each factor of the job evaluation system. Sometimes, the review will raise questions about the adequacy of the information provided by the job analysis and the job description that preceded the job evaluation programme.
8. Provide an appeal process that gives employees the opportunity to have the results for their jobs reviewed and explained to them. This step will be discussed later in the chapter.

The point method has several advantages. It has an objective basis, inasmuch as the judgements are made rationally by reference to compensable factors that are job related, and are weighted and defined in a manner that is acceptable to both employees and management. The mechanism and the process of the point method is conducive to greater reliability and consistency in judgements. The point values of the job structure provide differences in value between jobs, and also indicate the magnitude of the differences. For example, if job A has 200 points and job B has 400 points, the point method permits the reasonable inference that job B is two times more valuable than job A. The point method allows the job structure to be converted into a pay structure. However, since it is constructed without reference to the external labour market, it is free from the pay-rate fluctuations of the external market. Once developed, the point method is easy to use.

The disadvantages are that it is time consuming and expensive to develop, and that one can sometimes be faced with the situation of having to "force fit" a job into the predetermined fixed factor levels. However, such force-fitting is not as serious as in the classification method, because the system of levels for each factor permits the development of a range (scale) that suits the needs of the organization. Also, the subsequent adjustments of these levels are relatively easier in the point method. Nevertheless, an important question remains: In view of the fixed factors and fixed scales, can it be validly assumed that all the jobs have the same relationships relative to these factors? Also, the results must be validated by employee perceptions with regard to the equity of the results. Employee perceptions of the validity of the method, including its process, are critical, and some suggestions to ensure employee perceptions of equity are discussed later in the chapter.

The Factor Comparison Method

This method was developed by Eugene Benge in 1926 to respond to a need for a job evaluation system that could adequately evaluate a wide diversity of jobs (Benge 1984). In this approach, the key jobs are compared to identify their relative differences in value. The comparison is first based on the ranking of key jobs on each of the chosen compensable factors. The ranking indicates the importance (value) of the job on each factor. The jobs are also compared on the basis of the allocation or apportionment of the market rate of each key job to the compensable factors. The two comparisons together provide a basis for developing a "key scale with anchor points," which is then used to evaluate the other jobs in the organization, and to compute their pay rates. The factor

TABLE 10.3
FACTOR COMPARISON METHOD: FACTOR-BASED RANKING

	Compensable Factors				
Key Jobs	**Skill, Knowledge, Experience Requirements**	**Mental Ability Requirements**	**Responsibility**	**Physical Demands**	**Working Conditions**
Job A	1	3	5	6	6
Job B	6	4	1	1	3
Job C	4	1	3	5	2
Job D	5	6	4	2	4
Job E	3	5	6	3	1
Job F	2	2	2	4	5

NOTE: 1 = highest rank.
SOURCE: Adapted from Wallace and Fay (1988), 208.

comparison method is a relatively complex procedure. The steps that follow go into some detail to help illustrate the procedure.

1. Select the key jobs.
2. Decide on compensable factors, keeping in mind the characteristics of compensable factors. The number and the type of factors should permit the proper identification of the similarities in, and differences between, the key jobs.
3. Rank each key job by its importance on each factor (see the example in Table 10.3). This ranking gives an indication of the value of each job in terms of the amount of the factor the job has. The more of the factor the job has, the greater will be its value.
4. For each key job, allocate its pay (market) rate to each of the factors (see the example in Table 10.4). The allocation or apportionment of the pay rate reflects the importance of the factor for the job. Thus, the more important the factor is for the job, the larger will be the amount of the pay rate allocated to that factor.
5. Rank each job on the basis of the pay allocations (see the ranks in parentheses in Table 10.4).
6. Compare the two rankings (see Table 10.5). Investigate the jobs where there are discrepancies between the two rankings. The ranking of a job on the basis of the amount of the factor it has and on the basis of the allocation of pay rate ought to coincide, because the determination and allocation of the pay of a factor should reflect the importance of that factor. The rankings may not coincide for two reasons:
   a) Errors in judgement may have been made during the ranking process. If this is the case, the rankings should be reviewed and corrected.
   b) The pay rate is high because of market conditions. For example, in Table 10.5, there is a difference in the rankings of job B in the factor of skill, knowledge, experience requirements. The higher rank based on pay allocation suggests that the pay rate was pushed up by a labour shortage. Market pressure on the job rate suggests that the job is not a key job and therefore should be removed from this process.
7. Establish the final job evaluation scale, placing the key jobs under each factor and beside the job value expressed in dollars (see Table 10.6). The key jobs placed in this scale serve as anchor points against which other jobs can be evaluated.
8. Place the other jobs in the final scale under each factor, using the key jobs as guides. For example, to evaluate job X and compute its pay rate, begin with the first factor (skill, knowledge, experience requirements) and assess that job X is between key jobs E and F. After a review of the job descriptions (of jobs E, F, and X),

Table 10.4
Factor Comparison Method: Allocation of Pay to Each Factor and Pay-Allocation-based Ranking

Key Jobs	Compensable Factors					Pay Rate per Hour
	Skill, Knowledge, Experience Requirements	Mental Ability Requirements	Responsibility	Physical Demands	Working Conditions	
Job A	$4.80 (1)	$5.10 (3)	$1.20 (5)	$0.90 (6)	$0.75 (6)	$12.75
Job B	$4.65 (2)	$3.75 (4)	$6.75 (1)	$3.60 (1)	$1.35 (3)	$20.10
Job C	$3.15 (5)	$6.75 (1)	$3.75 (3)	$1.80 (5)	$1.65 (2)	$17.10
Job D	$1.20 (6)	$1.20 (6)	$1.65 (4)	$3.30 (2)	$1.05 (4)	$ 8.40
Job E	$3.45 (4)	$3.15 (5)	$0.90 (6)	$2.85 (3)	$3.90 (1)	$14.25
Job F	$4.35 (3)	$5.40 (2)	$4.35 (2)	$2.40 (4)	$0.90 (5)	$17.40

Note: Figures in parentheses represents pay-allocation-based ranking: 1 = highest rank.
Source: Adapted from Wallace and Fay (1988), 209.

Table 10.5
Factor Comparison Method: Comparison of the Factor-based and Pay-Allocation-based Rankings

Key Jobs	Compensable Factors									
	Skill, Knowledge, Experience Requirements		Mental Ability Requirements		Responsibility		Physical Demands		Working Conditions	
	Rank based on		Rank based on		Rank based on		Rank based on		Rank based on	
	Factor	Pay	Factor	Pay	Factor	Pay	Factor	Pay	Factor	Pay
Job A	1	1	3	3	5	5	6	6	6	6
Job B	6	2	4	4	1	1	1	1	3	3
Job C	4	5	1	1	3	3	5	5	2	2
Job D	5	6	6	6	4	4	2	2	4	4
Job E	3	4	5	5	6	6	3	3	1	1
Job F	2	3	2	2	2	2	4	4	5	5

Source: Adapted from Wallace and Fay (1988), 211.

Table 10.6
Factor Comparison Method: Job Evaluation Scale

Value of Job ($)	Compensable Factors				
	Skill, Knowledge, Experience Requirements	Mental Ability Requirements	Responsibility	Physical Demands	Working Conditions
0.00					
0.15					
0.30					
0.45					
0.60					
0.75					A
0.90			E	A	F
1.05					D
1.20	D	D	A		
1.35					B
1.50					
1.65			D		C
1.80				C	
1.95					
2.10					
2.25					
2.40				F	
2.55					
2.70					
2.85				E	
3.00					
3.15	C	E			
3.30				D	
3.45	E				
3.60				B	
3.75		B	C		
3.90					E
4.05					
4.20					
4.35	F		F		
4.50					
4.65	B				
4.80	A				
4.95					
5.10		A			
5.25					
5.40		F			
5.55					
5.70					
5.85					
6.00					
6.15					
6.30					
6.45					
6.60					
6.75		C	B		
6.90					
7.00					

Source: Adapted from Wallace and Fay (1988), 212.

conclude that job X is closer to job F than it is to job E. Then assess job X relative to job F, and decide to place it at the job value slot of $4.05 for skill, knowledge, experience requirements. Continue this process and place job X on each of the other factors. Add up the dollar values at which job X was placed in each factor to obtain the pay rate for job X.

The factor comparison method has several advantages. Like the point method, it makes explicit the compensable factors it uses as the criteria for evaluating jobs. In addition, by using the wage rates of benchmark jobs, it has the unique capability of linking external market pay rates to internal work-related factors. And because the method uses a scale of degrees of worth for each compensable factor, it can determine the dollar value of each job.

The major disadvantage of the method is that it is too complex and is often difficult to explain to the employees, especially because of the high degree of subjectivity involved in the allocation of pay rates across the compensable factors. The factor comparison method is the least popular job evaluation method; not more than 11 per cent of organizations use it (Wallace and Fay 1988). Since key-job pay rates are used as a critical feature in the method, there is the unstated assumption that these jobs themselves are free from wage inequities that might otherwise contaminate the process. This assumption may not be realistic. The advantage of the method's unique capability to provide a linkage to the market can also become a serious disadvantage, especially in a dynamic economy when wage fluctuations are high. In such an environment, constant changes in the market will necessitate a continuous updating of job and wage structures.

The factor comparison method provides the conceptual foundations and the framework for the Hays System (Bellak 1984), a customized job evaluation system used by a large number of organizations worldwide.

The Four Methods: Similarities and Differences

In both the ranking and the factor comparison methods one whole job is compared with another whole job. The difference is that the ranking method does not use a specific criterion to make this job-versus-job comparison. The factor comparison method uses well-defined compensable factors. The classification and point methods are similar in that both compare the job, not with another job, but with a set of standards. The difference is that the standards of the classification method are not defined in as great detail as they are in the point method. Also, the classification method does not provide a quantitative measure of the value of the job and the nature of the differentials between the key jobs. The point method provides a numerical measure of the value of the job that also expresses the relative worth of the differentials between the key jobs.

In terms of simplicity, the ranking method is the most simple and the factor comparison method is the most complex. The other methods fall in between. The point method has the highest acceptance rate because it is relatively easier to understand and also because the subjective judgements involved tend to be minimized by the use of detailed factor levels. The ranking and factor comparison methods have the lowest acceptance among employees. On the consideration of cost, the ranking method is the least expensive, followed by the classification method. The point and factor comparison methods tend to be expensive, particularly because of the developmental work that is involved.

On balance, the point method emerges as the best of the four methods.

ADMINISTERING THE JOB EVALUATION PROGRAMME

From the discussion so far, it is clear that despite any claims of objectivity that might be made, there is considerable subjectivity in the judgements that are required in all four methods. Even the most acceptable point method calls for judgements at practically every stage, from the development of the point system right up to its application in evaluating jobs.

To begin with, the point method uses the data collected from job analysis. The entire process of job analysis involves a variety of subjective judgements. In fact, the litigation generated by pay equity legislation has uncovered a variety of gender biases in the development and interpretation of job description documents. Decisions on the choice of compensable factors are fraught with subjective judgements; so are decisions on the weights assigned to the factors and to the definition of the levels of each factor. The application of the system to specific jobs is essentially an exercise in subjective judgements.

The purpose of the job evaluation system is to ensure internal equity. Given the high degree of subjectivity in even the best method available, the need for high trust on the part of the employees affected is crucial. Otherwise, their acceptance will be seriously compromised and they will not perceive the results to be equitable. The eventual consequence of employee perceptions of inequity with regard to the huge expenditure of base pay is that this deployment of resources will not have the desired motivational effect. Not only will the dollars expended on base pay be wasted, but also the effort put in by demotivated employees may be far too feeble to achieve the organizational objectives. Hence, a sound administration of the job evaluation programme should include efforts and strategies to ensure the employee perception that, although the job evaluation process has several subjective features, the organization is doing its utmost to see that judgements are made in a manner that is as rational and bias-free as possible.

The primary strategy in a sound job evaluation administration programme is *involving* employees right from the inception of the programme. If the organization is unionized, the union should be brought on board from the beginning. A usual way to ensure employee participation is to establish a job evaluation committee with representatives of employees and management, and to entrust this committee with the entire programme. The training of committee members is crucial; this training should include any technical training that is necessary as well as the development of interpersonal skills. The latter skills will enable committee members to cope effectively with the differences and disagreements that are inevitable in the deliberations of a committee.

The other critical strategy is to provide a mechanism and a process for appeal. Such a structure and process will help to rectify genuine mistakes and will give the committee an opportunity to get feedback on their work and to gain acceptance for the job structure. More importantly, the existence of such a structure and process gives the employees adequate participation and control over the process, thus helping to assure them of equity in the process.

Although the preceding remarks focus on employee involvement in job evaluation, a similar philosophy of employee involvement in the job analysis process is necessary. As stated earlier, the data from job analysis are the basis for job evaluation. Employees' perceptions of equity will be enhanced when they can see that they also have an input into the collection of data on their jobs.

DEVELOPING A JOB STRUCTURE

The end product of a job evaluation process is a job structure, which arranges all the jobs in a descending order of the total job evaluation points. When a job evaluation system uses compensable factors, the job structure also displays for each job the points assigned to the compensable factors. The job structure can be viewed as the organization's snapshot or statement of job values. The job structure not only shows the similarities in, and the differences between, jobs, but it also becomes the indispensable basis for the development of the pay structure, which is discussed in Chapter 12. As such, it is the foundation of internal equity. Given the necessity for the organization to ensure internal equity, no effort should be spared to make sure that the process of job evaluation, and the process of job analysis that precedes it, are conducted with care, competence, and integrity.

SUMMARY

Internal equity requires that pay rates reflect the relative value of jobs in terms of their content and contribution to the organization. Job analysis and job evaluation are the two processes used to determine the value of jobs. Job analysis generates the data on the job's content and contribution, and job evaluation processes this information to identify the similarities in, and differences between, jobs and to determine the values of jobs. The chapter discussed the procedures, as well as the advantages and disadvantages, of the four conventional methods of job analysis: interview, questionnaire, observation, and diary or log; and also the structured, quantitative method of the Position Analysis Questionnaire (PAQ). Although each method is useful under its own appropriate set of circumstances, these methods may be used more effectively in combination. The chapter also discussed the format for a job description, which puts together in a meaningful manner the data generated by job analysis and becomes the primary source of information for decisions in the job evaluation process.

The chapter identified the purposes of a job evaluation system, and examined the procedures, as well as the advantages and disadvantages, of job evaluation methods: ranking, classification, point method, and factor comparison method. The point method and the factor comparison method use compensable factors, which give them a more objective basis for determining job value. Of these two methods, the point method is the most popular with organizations that use formal job evaluation systems. The chapter concluded with a discussion of the need to involve employees in both job analysis and job evaluation, and with some strategies for employee involvement. A critical element of internal equity is employee perceptions, and employee involvement is absolutely indispensable for ensuring that these perceptions correspond with the reality.

KEY TERMS

benchmark (or key) jobs
classification method
compensable factors
factor comparison method
job analysis
job description
job evaluation
job specifications
job structure
job value

point method
position analysis questionnaire (PAQ)
ranking method

REVIEW AND DISCUSSION QUESTIONS

1. Define internal equity. What role does internal equity play in the design of a compensation system?
2. What is job analysis? In what specific way does job analysis serve the design and management of the compensation system?
3. What considerations should be kept in mind when choosing a job analysis method?
4. Some job analysts prefer the interview method, others prefer the questionnaire method, and still others prefer both. Explore the advantages and disadvantages of these methods, and explain how job analysts might use both methods.
5. The job evaluation programme can be said to be one of the pillars that support the compensation structure. Do you agree? Why?
6. Compare and contrast the four job evaluation methods.
7. "Given the high degree of subjectivity in even the best method available, the need for high trust on the part of the employees affected is crucial." What strategies would you propose to ensure that employees accept the conclusions of the job evaluation programme?

EXERCISE 10.1: DETERMINING THE APPROPRIATENESS OF JOB ANALYSIS METHODS

Objective

To acquire an understanding of which job analysis method is appropriate to collect the job content data.

Procedure

1. The class is divided into groups of five or six participants.
2. Working individually, each participant reviews the preparatory steps and the job analysis methods listed in the worksheet (Table 10.1.1) and decides on the appropriateness of these for the jobs listed in the adjoining columns.

   The decision can be indicated by a check mark in the job column; do this separately for each job. A preparatory step/a job analysis method may be used for more than one job if it is judged to be appropriate, but be prepared to justify all decisions.
3. Share your individual decision with your group. As a group, arrive at a consensus. Make sure the group spokesperson records the group consensus, together with the reasons for any irreconcilable differences.
4. Each group reports its decisions.
5. Discussion will follow each presentation. In exploring the appropriateness of a job analysis method, consider the characteristics of the method and the ultimate objectives of job analysis.

Table 10.1.1

Worksheet for Determining the Appropriateness of Job Analysis Methods

PREPARATORY STEPS AND JOB ANALYSIS METHODS	Manager	Laboratory scientist	Automobile mechanic	Travelling salesperson	Administrative assistant	Assembly-line operator
Communication						
Review of organization chart						
Review of existing job descriptions						
Tour of job location						
Interview methods						
Interviewing supervisor						
Interviewing job holder						
Observation method						
Questionnaire method						
Diary/log method						

EXERCISE 10.2: JOB EVALUATION

Objective

To experience some of the activities of job evaluation, and to become aware of the importance of the process issues involved in a job evaluation programme.

Procedure

1. The class is divided into groups of five to six participants. Each group functions as a job evaluation committee of the Tinkerman Corporation (see Chapter 1). The task of the committee is to evaluate two jobs (see the job descriptions in Table 10.2.1), using the job evaluation system (see Table 10.2.2). The job evaluation system consists of four compensable factors: knowledge, decision making, responsibility for contacts, supervision. For the purpose of this exercise, the committee will evaluate the jobs on only one factor, knowledge.

2. Working individually, each participant studies the job evaluation manual and, consistent with its guidelines, determines the points to assign to the two jobs; do this one job at a time.

3. Share your decisions with your group. As a group, arrive at a consensus. Make sure the group spokesperson records the reasons for any differences that cannot be reconciled.

4. On completion of the job evaluation activity, the group discusses the following questions:

   a) Reflecting on the group discussions, identify the basis or reasons for the initial differences in the points assigned to the job.

   b) How were the differences reconciled?

   c) If you were in charge of the job evaluation programme, what process would you use to form a job evaluation committee? What guidelines would you propose for the committee to follow?

   d) What are some of the other administrative and process issues that you will consider?

   e) Were you satisfied with the job descriptions? What further information would you seek? What method(s) would be most appropriate for obtaining this information?

TABLE 10.2.1
JOB DESCRIPTIONS — JOB A AND JOB B

JOB A

Writes, tests, and implements new programs. Corrects and modifies existing programs. Develops the information required to create a new application. Analyses the collected information and suggests definition and design of the application. Plans the project on the basis of workload requirements. Develops the database requirements for the planned application. Prepares documentation and trains users on the new application. Involves the computer operations team to maintain and handle the new application.

Knowledge: Computer programming and processing techniques; computer theory and practices; management information systems.

JOB B

Performs accounting work in accordance with generally accepted accounting principles, including cost accounting activities. Maintains financial and statistical records, including petty cash. Prepares budget variation reports and bank reconciliation statements. Reviews revenue projections and operating costs. Provides information on financial procedures and accounting requirements. Trains and supervises subordinates.

Knowledge: Principles, procedures, and practices of general and cost accounting; computerized accounting procedures; legal requirements; office systems and practices.

Discuss bases of diff → they r resolved

c) Methods of job analysis : PAQ - statements of job behaviors
- standardized format : reduces biases
: used to develop job description

find one new 956-6118

594-

Table 10.2.2
Job Evaluation Plan

The plan combines point rating (an analytical, quantitative method of determining the relative value of positions) and factor comparison (a method that requires factor-to-factor comparisons on each position). All methods of job evaluation require the exercise of judgement and the orderly collection and analysis of information in order that consistent judgements can be made. This method facilitates discussion and the resolution of differences in determining the relative worth of jobs.

Point Values

The maximum point value assigned to each factor reflects its relative importance. Point values have also been assigned to the degrees of the factors.

Factor Weights

Knowledge	350	—	35%
Decision making	350	—	35%
Responsibility for contacts	150	—	15%
Supervision	150	—	15%
	1,000		100%

The minimum point values for knowledge, decision making, and responsibility for contacts are one-fifth of the maximum value, except for supervision.

FACTOR	FACTOR WEIGHTS	
	Minimum	Maximum
Knowledge		
Education and experience	70	350
Decision making	70	350
Responsibility for contacts	30	150
Supervision	—	150

FACTORS

The combined factors do not describe all aspects of positions. They deal only with those characteristics that are useful in determining the relative value of positions. Four factors are used in this plan. All the factors have more than one dimension and have been defined in terms of two or three related elements.

Knowledge	Education Experience
Decision making	Scope for decisions Impact of decisions
Responsibility for contacts	Nature of contacts Persons contacted
Supervision	Level of employees supervised Number supervised

Table 10.2.2—*Continued*

KNOWLEDGE

Rating Scale — Education and Experience

This factor is used to measure the amount of education and related practical experience required to perform the duties of the position.

Education

Refers to the level of academic or other formal training required to provide the basis for the development of the skill and the knowledge needed in the position.

Experience

Refers to the minimum related administrative knowledge and skill needed to carry out the duties of the position.

Notes to Evaluating Committee

In selecting the degree of the *experience* element, consideration is to be given to the length of time needed to develop the specialized knowledge and the general administrative knowledge required to carry out the duties of the position. General administrative knowledge is gained through experience in such responsibilities as

- formulating ideas and expressing them orally or in written form.
- carrying out studies and preparing reports on specific aspects of existing or proposed activities.
- making critical analysis of methods and procedures with a view to recommending improvements.
- planning programmes or work to meet the requirements of the department or organization served and the plans of action developed to achieve them.
- performing advisory duties that require a knowledge of objectives of the organization served and the measures evolved to achieve them.
- supervising and directing staff.

In selecting the degree of the *education* element, the second degree is to be assigned to positions where there is a clear requirement for specialized formal training beyond completion of secondary school education, for example, two to three year programmes at the CEGEP or community college level.

The third degree is to be assigned if there is a clear requirement for a general university degree with a particular field specialization of courses of similar length and difficulty leading to membership in required associations, for example, R.I.A., C.G.A., etc.

The fourth degree of the *education* element is to be assigned when the duties of the position

1. require university graduation in a specialized field, or
2. require understanding and appreciation of the principles and concepts of two or more specialized fields for which knowledge is normally acquired through university training and which are directly associated with the duties performed, or
3. require systematic study and analysis of complicated general problems and their solution by the application of specialized knowledge acquired through extensive post-secondary school study or training rather than through experience.

(In positions with duties that are in categories 2 or 3, the incumbents will not necessarily be university graduates.)

Continued on next page

TABLE 10.2.2—*Continued*

KNOWLEDGE RATING SCALE — EDUCATION AND EXPERIENCE

Experience Requirement	Education Requirement			
	A Secondary School	B Specialized CEGEP Training	C Post CEGEP Specialized Training of General Degree	D Degree that Provides Training in Required Job Skills
	If specialized experience is a requirement, add 25 points.			
1 Up to and including 2 years	45	65	90	120
2 Up to and including 4 years	65	90	120	170
3 Up to and including 6 years	90	120	170	235
4 More than 6 years	120	170	235	325

SOURCE: Department of Human Resources, McGill University.

CHAPTER 11

PAY EQUITY LEGISLATION: INTERNAL EQUITY II

CHAPTER SYNOPSIS

The previous chapter examined internal equity as it ought to exist in the compensation system so that all employees perceive the system to be fair and equitable. This chapter looks at internal equity as mandated by pay equity laws in Canada. Specifically, the chapter reviews such salient features of pay equity laws as applicability, enforcement mechanisms, and implementation procedures. Because of their restrictive focus, pay equity laws can produce unintended effects that impinge adversely on fundametal human rights and moral justice. This chapter also addresses some of these neglected issues in pay equity laws and their effects.

LEARNING OBJECTIVES

- To define and distinguish the three meanings of *pay equity*.
- To identify the major differences in the pay equity laws in Canada.
- To describe the mechanisms and processes involved in the development of a pay equity plan.
- To understand the sources of gender bias in job analysis and job evaluation procedures, and to develop strategies for eliminating or reducing gender bias.
- To understand the moral foundation of equity, and to explain, in the context of pay equity, the concept of equity as a natural right.
- To understand the effects of pay equity laws on the norms of moral justice.

INTRODUCTION

Pay equity has been hailed as an idea whose time has come — at least in

Canada, where 10 out of 13 jurisdictions have enacted laws that prohibit pay distinctions between male and female jobs of equal or comparable value. Advocates of pay equity see it as a historic vindication of women's rights as they struggle for equality in the workplace. Critics have assailed it for the reason, among others, that it ignores the realities of the market. This chapter will approach pay equity from two angles: first, by considering the salient features of pay equity laws in Canada, including some of the procedural issues in their implementation; and second, by discussing some neglected issues and the inequities resulting from such neglect.

THE SALIENT FEATURES OF PAY EQUITY LEGISLATION

This section will first consider the legal definition of pay equity and briefly review the history of pay equity legislation in Canada. Then the chapter will examine the salient features of pay equity laws, and discuss the procedural issues relating to compliance with these laws.

WHAT IS PAY EQUITY?

The concept of pay equity has evolved over time. Pay equity was originally understood as "equal pay for equal work." Employees, whether they are male or female, who do identical jobs should be paid the same. For example, a male school teacher should be paid the same salary as a female school teacher. Pay differentials, if any, should be only for reasons of performance, experience, and seniority. The concept of equal pay for equal work was generally accepted in the workplace — although some employers who accepted the principle nevertheless paid men a higher pay rate than women because of their belief that the earnings of a man were the principal source of income for the family.

However, changes in traditional roles (as husbands and wives become joint income providers for the family), the influence of the feminist movement, and the increasing participation of women in the workforce brought about a re-definition of pay equity. It began to be seen as "equal pay for similar or substantially similar work." According to this definition, employees, whether they are male or female, who do similar work should be paid the same. Thus, the job of cleaner, predominantly held by women, was seen to be similar to the job of janitor, predominantly held by men, and should therefore be paid the same as the job of janitor.

This change in the definition of pay equity was only a transitional phase to the present understanding of pay equity, which is "equal pay for work of equal value." According to this concept, employees, whether they are male or female, who do different work but whose work is of equal value to the organization should be paid the same. For example, if it can be demonstrated that the job of clerk IV and the job of construction supervisor are of equal value to their employer, these jobs should be paid the same. In the United States, the concept of equal pay for work of equal value is generally referred to as the concept of "comparable worth." Pay equity laws in Canada incorporate the definition "equal pay for work of equal value." These laws limit the applicability of this definition only to situations of inequity that are experienced by female employees in female-dominated jobs. This restricted use of the concept is a major limitation of Canadian pay equity laws.

The History of Pay Equity Legislation in Canada

In 1951, Ontario enacted the Ontario Female Employees Fair Remuneration Act, which mandated that all female employees who do work that is "substantially similar" to that of male employees should be paid the same as the male employees. In 1972, Canada signed the International Labor Organization Convention of "equal pay for work of equivalent value." Quebec incorporated this convention into its Charter of Human Rights and Freedoms in 1976. The federal government included the concept in the Canadian Human Rights Act in 1977. After a short lull, from 1977 to 1985, a spate of pay equity laws followed: Manitoba (1985); Yukon (1986); Ontario (1987); Prince Edward Island, Nova Scotia, and Newfoundland (1988); New Brunswick (1989); and the Northwest Territories (1990). Although British Columbia has not yet enacted a pay equity law, it recently (11 September 1990) introduced a $40-million, four-year pay equity programme for government employees, to be implemented through negotiations with public-sector unions.

Selected Provisions of Pay Equity Laws

All pay equity laws have essentially the same objective, that is, to redress the pay inequities experienced by employees in a female-dominated job when the pay rate of this job is lower than that of a male-dominated job of equal value. There are differences, however, in the way that different jurisdictions seek to achieve this objective. First, there are differences in the applicability or coverage of these laws. Some of the laws apply only to employees of the government that has enacted the law. Other laws extend coverage to employees of municipalities, school boards, universities, and crown corporations. The federal, Quebec, and Ontario pay equity laws also apply to employees of private-sector organizations. Second, there are differences in the enforcement mechanism. In some jurisdictions, the pay inequity redress process is activitated only after aggrieved employees file a complaint. Other jurisdictions take a proactive approach; in this approach employers are required to institute a pay equity plan that identifies inequities and initiates measures to correct them. One such plan is described later in this section. The pay equity laws of Ontario and Prince Edward Island have adopted both approaches — the complaint-driven as well as the proactive.

The third area of differences in pay equity laws relates to the issue of *gender predominance*. The main thrust of pay equity laws is to redress the pay inequities that result when female-dominated jobs and male-dominated jobs are of equal value, but the former are paid at a lower rate than the latter. A criterion is needed for determining which jobs are female-dominated and which jobs are male-dominated. Some pay equity laws stipulate that a job is dominated by a gender when the employees of that gender constitute 70 per cent of the total incumbents of that job in the organization; other laws place the criterion at 60 per cent. According to the Ontario and New Brunswick laws, a job is female-dominated when 60 per cent of its incumbents are women; and a job is male-dominated when 70 per cent of its incumbents are men. Quebec and Yukon have not specified any criterion for determining the gender predominance of a job. Ontario plans an amendment to cover situations "where there are no male classes with which to compare female job classes" (Human Resource Management in Canada 1991, 96.1).

The fourth area of differences is the limits placed on the cost to the employer of correcting pay inequities. Pay equity laws that require employers to be proactive in identifying and redressing pay inequities generally stipulate that the resulting pay adjustments each year shall not exceed 1 per cent of the employer's payroll. The exception is Nova Scotia, which requires proactive enforcement but does not specify a limit to the cost of pay adjustments for correcting inequities. The pay equity laws that have a complaint-driven enforcement mechanism have not specified a limit to the cost of pay adjustments that result from pay inequities. As Weiner and Gunderson (1991) suggest, a limit on costs for the complaint-driven mechanism is not necessary, because the case-by-case approach is less likely to place a severe financial burden on the employer in any one year. On the other hand, the proactive approach to enforcement requires a pay equity plan that identifies at one time all the necessary pay adjustments, and making all those adjustments can be a heavy financial burden for an organization in one year.

Table 11.1 summarizes the provisions of pay equity laws in Canada in respect of coverage, enforcement, gender predominance, and the limits on the cost of resolving inequities.

THE PAY EQUITY PLAN

The pay equity laws of each jurisdiction stipulate their own implemen-

Table 11.1
A Summary of Selected Provisions of Pay Equity Laws in Canada

Coverage:	Public sector	:	Covered by all laws
	Municipalities, school boards, universities	:	Covered by all laws, except New Brunswick
	Crown corporations	:	Covered by all laws, except Yukon and New Brunswick
	Private sector	:	Covered only by Federal, Quebec, and Ontario laws
Enforcement:	Complaint-driven	:	Federal, Quebec, Yukon
	Proactive	:	Nova Scotia, New Brunswick, Manitoba
	Both	:	Ontario, Prince Edward Island
Gender predominance:	70% F; 70% M	:	Federal, Manitoba
	60% F; 70% M	:	Ontario, New Brunswick
	60% F; 60% M	:	Prince Edward Island, Nova Scotia
	Not specified	:	Quebec, Yukon
Cost limits for resolving inequities:	Case-by-case basis	:	Federal, Quebec, Yukon
	1% of payroll/year	:	Manitoba, Prince Edward Island, New Brunswick, Ontario
	No limit specified	:	Nova Scotia

Source: Adapted from Weiner and Gunderson (1990).

tation mechanisms and processes. The Pay Equity Act of Ontario is the most comprehensive in terms of its coverage; it is applicable to both the public and private sectors. Ontario's law also provides for both forms of enforcement mechanisms, the complaint-driven as well as the proactive. Hence, it may be instructive to describe the implementation mechanism of Ontario's Pay Equity Act in order to illustrate a systematic process for correcting pay inequities. The description that follows is based on Ontario's pay equity guidelines (Pay Equity Commission 1989b). The critical implementation steps are these:

1. The organization determines the extent and the form of employee involvement in the process. For unionized organizations, the Pay Equity Act envisages a negotiated process. Non-unionized organizations are free to involve their employees. Failure to involve employees, however, can seriously undermine the effectiveness of the implementation process.
2. The organization determines the female job classes and the male job classes. A female job class (also referred to as a female-dominated job class) is one in which 60 per cent of the job incumbents are female. A male job class (also referred to as a male-dominated job class) is one in which 70 per cent of the job incumbents are male.

3. The organization selects a gender-neutral system for determining the job classes that are of equal value. The criteria used for the comparison should include skill, effort, responsibility, and working conditions. Essentially, this step refers to a job evaluation system that is free of gender bias. Chapter 10 discussed the different job evaluation systems. Of these, the point method is generally the preferred system. Certain decisions in the operation of this method (i.e., in the job analysis and job evaluation processes) may introduce gender bias. This concern is dealt with in the next section.
4. The organization applies the job evaluation system, and determines the female and male job classes that are comparable. The Pay Equity Act has specified a sequential comparison process for this purpose.
5. The pay rate of the female job class is then compared with the pay rate of the comparable male job class. The pay rate, for this purpose, includes the value of the benefits.
6. The necessary pay adjustments are then determined. Pay adjustments result only when the pay rate of the female job class is lower than the pay rate of its comparable male job class. When the pay rate of the female job class is found to be higher than the pay rate of its comparable male job class, the Pay Equity Act does not require that the pay rate of the male job class be adjusted upward. Futhermore, when pay adjustments are made, all employees in the female job class, male as well as female, are eligible for these adjustments.
7. The major items of information generated in the previous steps are communicated to employees through the posting in the workplace of a pay equity plan, developed in a prescribed format. The posting of the plan gives employees an opportunity to review it and to file their objections. In non-unionized organizations, the objections should be filed within 90 days of the posting of the plan. In unionized organizations, the agreement of the union constitutes the approval of the plan by the employees.
8. After the objections have been appropriately dealt with, the organization proceeds to making the pay adjustments. As indicated earlier, the total cost to the employer is limited to a maximum of 1 per cent of the payroll.

THE ISSUE OF GENDER BIAS IN JOB ANALYSIS AND JOB EVALUATION

The discussion in Chapter 10 underscored the fact that the mechanics and procedures in job analysis and job evaluation involve a considerable degree of subjectivity, which leaves room for bias that vitiates the process. This section examines the sources of gender bias in job analysis and job evaluation, and some strategies for minimizing gender bias in these processes.

Gender Bias in Job Analysis

The first major source of gender bias in job analysis derives from perceptual errors and biases that occur in the collection of data and the writing up of job descriptions. The human perceptual process does not function like a video camera that documents events faithfully. Rather, it is a subjective process influenced not only by the properties and characteristics of objective reality but also by the observer's personality, past learning, motivation, and expectations. In these subjective elements lies the potential for inaccuracies and biases as a person observes, selects, organizes, and interprets reality. The job analyst is obviously susceptible to these biases. For example, in collecting data on the job of a secretary, the major focus might be on the typing activity, which is more salient because it is more audible and visible. As a result, activities that are not as conspicuous (e.g., planning, organizing, screening the manager's telephone calls and visitors) are either ignored or assigned less importance. When these activities are ignored or are not properly emphasized in the job description, they do not receive the credit they deserve in the job evaluation process.

The expectations of the job analyst can also result in a misleading job description. When this bias operates, the job analyst will see what he/she expects to see. A good example of this bias is the influence of job titles. To the job analyst, the job title provides the first and immediate source of information on the job. Reliance on this information alone can lead to an erroneous emphasis in the job description if the job content has, in fact, undergone change. In some clerical jobs — predominantly held by women — the title of clerk still continues, but the job content might include several administrative duties.

The second major source of gender bias in job analysis results from sociocultural factors. The different ways in which men and women have been socialized can influence the ways in which they describe their jobs. For example, women are expected to be "self-effacing," and men, "self-enhancing." Consequently, when women are asked to describe their jobs, they are likely to do so in a modest manner, and their manner will influence the importance assigned to the job in the job evaluation process. A similar phenomenon has been observed with regard to workers from non-western cultures; they are reluctant to "market" themselves and their legitimate accomplishments.

To address gender bias in job analysis, the organization should devote time and effort to preparing for this programme. The nature of this preparation has been discussed in Chapter 10. It can be re-emphasized that the objective of the job analyst is to see the job in its proper perspective and to understand its nature. The attainment of this objective is greatly facilitated by the use of multiple sources of information, for example, review of the organization chart and existing job descriptions, a tour of the job site to observe working conditions, and a study of the social and technical context of the job. Just as important as choice of job analysis method is the use of a standardized format for collecting and describing data. Without such a standardized format, the choice of what is critical in a job is left to the discretion of the analyst. Both the type and the extent of job details tend to be recorded in an inconsistent manner. Such an approach can result in inadequate or incorrect descriptions of jobs, particularly of female jobs, because many of these jobs are not as specific in terms of job tasks as are blue-collar manufacturing jobs. When a standardized format is used for describing the job of teacher, for example, the job analyst can tap the various tasks of the job, the environment in which these tasks are done, and the education, skills, and experience needed for the job.

Gender Bias in Job Evaluation

The source of gender bias in job evaluation systems that use the point method comes mainly from the choice, the weights, and the definition of compensable factors. Perceptual errors and biases creep in when the point method is used, but not as extensively as when the ranking or classification method is used. Most of the traditional job evaluation systems were designed and developed for blue-collar jobs, which are predominantly held by males. Further, the interpretation of the definition of compensable factors was in the context of manufacturing operations. The examples used in the following discussion are drawn from the November 1989 *Newsletter* published by Ontario's Pay Equity Commission (Pay Equity Commission 1989a).

The first reason for gender bias is that both the choice and the definition of compensable factors ignore the nature of the tasks and activities of female jobs. For example, the compensable factor of responsibility is usually defined to mean responsibility for things like equipment, machinery, products, finances. In most female jobs (teacher, nurse) the primary responsibility is for people. When this substantive difference is ignored by the job evaluation system, the system operates to the disadvantage of female job incumbents. Second, the definition of the compensable factor may not be wide enough to capture adequately the specific characteristics of female jobs. For example, the factor of working conditions might include a definition such as "standard office conditions." Most female jobs, clerical and secretarial, are performed inside a building, in an office. However, conditions in an office are not necessarily standard for all the office jobs. The manager's office environment might be pleasant, but his/her secretary's environment might be exposed to dust, dirt, distractions from people and traffic, and noise from telephones and machines. The job analyst may assume that the "standard office conditions" are pleasant and free from the toxic fumes and temperature extremes of the factory and will therefore not give such conditions much weight in terms of job evaluation points. As a result, predominately female office jobs will not earn many points under the working conditions factor when compared with male-dominated blue-collar jobs.

The perceptual bias of stereotype creeps in when the requirements of the job are assessed in terms of the preconceived attributes of the female. Weiner and Gunderson (1990) provide interesting examples of the inconsistent manner in which the stereotypes operate. Because men are believed to be physically stronger than women, it is assumed that male jobs will require the exertion of physical effort. Therefore, male jobs get credit for the physical effort needed on a job, whereas female jobs do not, although the jobs of nurses involve the exertion of such physical effort as the lifting of patients and prolonged standing. On the other hand, the female-dominated job of institutional supervisor of a home for the mentally retarded was not given credit for the mental and physical effort involved in the job, because it was believed that the work of caring for children is "natural to women" and therefore does not need to be compensated.

The basic strategy that an organization should use in addressing the issue of gender bias in job evaluation is to adopt a single job evaluation system. The compensable factors should be chosen, weighted, and defined with one objective — to adequately tap the content and contribution of female as well as male jobs. Some factors may favour male jobs and other factors may favour female jobs (Weiner and Gunderson 1990). For example, in the factor of skill, the subfactor of knowledge of machinery, tools will favour male jobs; the subfactor of typing and keyboarding will favour female jobs. Similarly, in the factor of working conditions, the subfactor of physical hazards will favour male jobs, and the subfactor of monotony will favour female jobs. As was discussed in Chapter 10, the organization should also ensure proper attention to the process issues that guarantee employee involvement.

SOME NEGLECTED ISSUES IN PAY EQUITY LAWS

This section deals with some of the neglected issues in pay equity laws and the inequities that result from such neglect. The specific issues to be examined are the moral foundation of pay equity, the psychological underpinnings of equity, and the effects of pay equity laws.

EQUITY AND MORAL RIGHTS

In its fundamental sense, equity means fairness, or fair treatment. Interestingly enough, only human beings qualify for this type of treatment. No one speaks of treating an object fairly or unfairly. An object may be used improperly, inefficiently, and even ineffectively but not inequitably or unfairly. Objects do not have the capacity to be fair or unfair; neither do organizations, which are abstract entities. Equity is the unique and exclusive characteristic of human relationships, and is produced by the conscious decisions of the parties to that relationship. It can therefore be said that only human beings can act in a fair or unfair manner and only human beings can be the recipient of what they perceive to be fair or unfair treatment.

Human beings seem to grow up with a sense of fairness. "That's not fair" is perhaps one of the earliest and most frequently used expressions in a growing child's vocabulary. The literature and history of societies in every culture and age are filled with accounts of fair and unfair dealings and relationships. There may be cultural differences in the content or the mode of determining equity, but the existence of the notion of equity is not in doubt. Is this sense of equity merely a matter of temperament, or the result of the socialization process, or does it reflect one of the fundamental qualities of the *nature* of the human being? To explore the substantive basis of equity, one must examine the underlying assumptions that people make when they say that they are being treated fairly or unfairly in an exchange relationship. At the very root of all equity-related perceptions is the individual's belief, well founded or baseless, that he/she has certain rights in that relationship. Equity is experienced when these perceived rights are respected. When these rights are not respected, the individual experiences inequity.

Individuals develop their awareness and understanding of their rights from a variety of sources. The most visible source of rights is the laws of the land, which are referred to as positive law. For example, a landed immigrant has the right to hold a paid job in Canada, and a visitor to Canada does not have this right. This right is conferred or denied by the relevant Canadian statute. Another category of rights is moral rights. These are not contained in a legislative statute, but are the rights referred to as *natural rights, human rights*, or (historically) the *rights of man*. The justification of human rights is that they flow from the very nature of the human person. Jacques Maritain observed: "The human person possesses rights because of the very fact that it is a person, a whole, a master of itself and its acts, and which consequently is not merely a means to an end, but an end, which must be treated as such"(quoted in Cranston 1987, 1-16). For example, the right to life and the right to freedom are basic and essential to the very survival of human beings. "There is a very ancient Western tradition of belief both in the reality of natural law — a law higher than the edicts of princes — and of the universal rights that this law confers on all rational, sentient beings. . . . They are not rights that are conferred exclusively on its members by a particular society. They are universal. . .inherited, so to speak, with men's humanity itself" (Cranston 1987, 1-17). Beliefs and values in the non-western traditions also reflect these basic natural rights.

The right to be treated fairly and equitably is founded on the notion of natural rights. This notion constitutes an important element of justice, which, according to Aristotle, is the virtue of giving each his/her due. It is also at the very essence of distributive justice, which is concerned with "the apportionment of privileges, duties, and goods in consonance with the merits of the individual and in the best interest of society" (*Webster's Third New International Dictionary*, s.v. "distributive justice").

Pay equity, then, is not a question of an individual's mere whim, or even of desire. Equity is a natural human aspiration for justice; and pay equity, as one variant of equity, does not need to be justified by an appeal to the majesty of a legislative pronouncement. Having established a firm foundation for pay equity, this chapter will first consider the psychological processes that contribute to the development of individuals' perceptions of pay equity, and will then consider pay equity legislation to determine the extent to which it is consistent with pay equity perceptions.

Equity Theory of Human Motivation and Pay Equity Laws

The understanding of the psychological processes of equity that follows comes from Adam's (1965) work on the equity theory of human motivation. According to this theory, feelings of equity or inequity are generated by the individual's perceptions of his/her outcomes-inputs ratio and the outcomes-inputs ratio of the person with whom the individual compares himself/herself. When the ratios are perceived to be equal, the individual regards the outcomes to be equitable and is satisfied with them. When these ratios are perceived to be unequal, the individual regards the outcomes to be inequitable or unfair and is dissatisfied with them.

This brief statement of equity theory underscores the critical role of social comparison in the development of equity perceptions. Further, the development of perceptions of pay equity is not the exclusive characteristic of any one employee or even of one group of employees. Each and every employee forms perceptions of pay equity and experiences its consequences. Hence, pay equity legislation, if it is to be true to the moral imperatives of justice and the psychological processes discussed above, should address pay inequities that are experienced by all individuals and groups in the workplace. Unfortunately, the objective of pay equity laws in Canada is to remedy *only* the inequity experienced by those female employees who hold female-dominated jobs. This exclusive focus on gender discrimination neglects similar interests and concerns of native peoples, the handicapped, and visible minorities, who, along with women, are designated as the protected groups under employment equity laws that seek to prevent discrimination against these groups in the matter of employment. Consequently, the inference seems justified that society's preoccupation with pay equity is motivated by purely political considerations. "The importance society is attaching to pay equity corresponds with the emergence of women in the labor force. The rise of the feminist movement and the increasing percentage of working women have been the two major factors driving the concern for wage comparability" (Kovach and Millspaugh 1990, 92).

EFFECTS OF PAY EQUITY LAWS

Changes in the demographics of the labour force and in the norms relative to the role of women in our society gave women immense political clout. Any politician who tried to resist such power would be committing political suicide. Therefore, although the politicians' rush to climb on the pay equity bandwagon is understandable, the sectoral emphasis of pay equity legislation, which ignores the moral imperatives at the very foundation of a just and stable society, cannot be condoned. A society that ignores fundamental ethical considerations in its social policies does so at its own peril. First, solutions that are prompted primarily by political expediency or ideological considerations often cause the rights of one group to be unjustly preferred to the legitimate rights of individuals and other groups. Second, the biases inherent in political and ideological movements usually prevent the rational and objective consideration of all the relevant aspects of the issue. As a result, the solutions are only temporary and superficial, and do not fully address the issue and its ramifications. Both these observations are applicable to pay equity legislation. The following subsections discuss its neglect of individuals and other employee groups who are also victims of pay discrimination in the workplace, and then considers the deleterious effects of a superficial approach to pay equity.

No one can deny that the inequities experienced by female employees as a consequence of intended or unintended pay discrimination by employers need to be redressed. One can, however, question the wisdom of focusing only on gender discrimination to the neglect of discrimination against other protected groups under employment equity, for example, visible minorities, who might also experience pay inequity. In fact, the neglected groups now have to cope with a double inequity, the pay inequity inherent in systemic discrimination against these groups, and the inequity that results when legislators prefer to remedy the inequities of one group and ignore the similar inequities of other groups in the same workplace.

Effects on Visible Minorities

Numerous studies have documented systemic employment discrimination against visible minorities (Jain 1984). Recently, a survey on employment discrimination in Canada by the Canadian Recruiters Guild (1988) found that 94 per cent of the recruiters surveyed had discriminated on the basis of colour, and 90 per cent felt that they or their organization would not be able to defend their selection decisions in court. How does employment discrimination translate into pay inequity? The individual who is discriminated against in hiring can be unfairly deprived of his/her legitimate right to work and to earn an income. Or, the individual can take a low-paying job that does not fully utilize his/her knowledge, skills, and abilities, and the organization will gain benefits from that individual's experience and qualifications far in excess of the pay and benefits given to an individual.

Table 11.2, which is based on 1986 census data from Statistics Canada, provides information on this point in respect of the South Asian visible minority group relative to the Canadian population. South Asians, who constitute 1.3 per cent of the Canadian population, have a higher labour force participation rate (78 per cent against the Canadian rate of 66 per cent); and more South Asian males than Canadian males are in professional occupations (18 per cent versus 13 per cent). However, there is a considerable difference in earned incomes. According to one source (Statistics Canada 1989), the South Asian male earned, on the average, $23,279 a year as against the Canadian average of $30,500, a gap of 24 per cent. The South Asian female earned $12,247 a year as against the Canadian average of $19,200, a gap of 36 per cent. According to another source (White and Nanda 1989), no income gap exists between South Asian and Canadian males, and between South Asian and Canadian females. There should be a gap — the average income of South Asians ought to be higher than that of Canadians, because the data show that, relative to the Canadian population, South Asians are better educated, and have a higher labour force participation rate, and more of them are in professional occupations.

The third way in which systemic employment discrimination translates into pay inequity provides one possible explanation for the earnings gap. It is not uncommon for immigrants from the developing countries to be started on a lower pay scale because their work experience outside Canada, and especially their educational qualifications, are not recognized as being on a par with Canadian work experience and educational

Table 11.2

Data on the South Asian Visible Minority Group Relative to the Canadian Population on Selected Characteristics: Age, Education, Participation in Labour Force, and Professional Occupations

Selected Characteristics	South Asians			Canadians		
	Males	Females	Both	Males	Females	Both
• Age						
* > 65 years	—	—	3%	—	—	10%
* < 15 years	—	—	30%	—	—	22%
• Education						
* University graduates	25%	17%	21%	11%	8%	10%
• Participation in labour force of adults > 25 years	89.9%	65.6%	78%	79.4%	53.6%	66%
• In professional occupations	18%	—	—	13%	—	—
• Earned income						
* Source[1]	$23,279	$12,247	—	—	—	—
* Source[2]	$30,100	$19,200	—	$30,500	$20,000	—

SOURCE: Statistics Canada 1986 Census data.

[1] Statistics Canada (1989), 7-9.
[2] White and Nanda (1989), 1.33-1.39.

qualifications. This is especially the case with professionals whose salary is related to completed years of schooling. A good example is the evaluation system adopted by the Quebec Department of Education for its teachers. Under this system, a teacher's salary is directly related to his/her *scolarité,* that is, total number of years of schooling. Thus, a teacher who studied in Quebec and holds a bachelor's degree will be credited with 16 years, computed as follows: high school, 11 years; CEGEP, 2 years; undergraduate studies, 3 years. A teacher who studied in India and holds a bachelor's degree will be credited with a total of 14 years. The rationale for discounting the Indian degree is that undergraduate work in Indian universities is judged to be of inferior quality. At the present rate, the pay differential between 16 years and 14 years schooling is about $3,750; that is, the teacher with 14 years schooling will receive $3,750 less in pay per year, despite the fact that the job content, the teaching load, the performance standards, and every other aspect of working conditions are identical for both teachers. The only way to make up for the loss of the two years' undergraduate work of an Indian university is to do a master's degree in a Canadian university. The implication is that 2 years of graduate work in Canada is equivalent to 2 years of undergraduate work in India.

The refusal to recognize the professional qualifications of visible minority immigrants produces insidious inequities. The sheer necessity of survival drives these immigrants into low-paying jobs often totally unrelated to their profession. The professional skills and expertise of the individual begin to atrophy, and self-esteem diminishes. Society also suffers from the significant economic costs of underutilization: lower national output, labour market inefficiency, higher inflation, and excessive welfare and penal system costs (Agarwal 1986).

The preceding discussion is not intended to denigrate the societal value that seeks to right the wrongs of pay discrimination practices. The point, rather, is that the issue of pay equity can be justly addressed only when it is viewed in the broader perspective of human rights and employment. Unfortunately, the discussion of employment equity seems to be restricted to hiring, when it should also include the organization's human resource policies and practices in hiring, compensation, promotion, training and development — in a word, all those activities that impinge on the employee's human rights in the workplace. This separation of employment equity from pay equity has had the effect of neglecting pay inequities that result from employment discrimination practices. This situation is further aggravated when the programme of legal remedies to redress pay inequities is restricted to cases of discrimination against women. The exception here is the pay equity legislation of Quebec, which covers all victims of pay discrimination. The effectiveness of the Quebec law is, however, compromised because the Quebec law is complaint-driven. Pay discrimination victims from visible minority groups cannot realistically be expected to muster the necessary fortitude to face possible reprisals that might result from their initiating a complaint and following it through. Besides, such a process is costly in time and money. Unlike the female hospital workers who recently won, through their union's efforts, a 10-year back-pay pay-equity fight with the federal government (*The Gazette*, 1 May 1991), visible minorities do not have the numerical strength that would draw unions to direct attention and resources to redressing their plight.

The pay inequity experienced by visible minorities will grow as their numbers increase. Changing demographics suggest a sizeable upward shift in the labour force from these groups. For instance, it has been estimated that by 2015 Canada will need about 500,000 immigrants per year just to maintain a population of 26 million (Perry 1983). At a recent conference, University of Montreal demographer Jacques Henripin is reported (*The Gazette*, 1 May 1991) to have estimated that because of its declining birth rate, Quebec will need an immigrant inflow of about 100,000 per year. If present trends are any indication, most of these immigrants will be from Africa, the Near and the Far East, and Asia. Canada's pay equity laws need to be reviewed so that new Canadian citizens will receive the fair and equitable treatment that is the avowed objective and guiding principle of the country's social policies and programmes.

Other Effects of Pay Equity Laws

Canadian pay equity laws have other effects. First, these laws provide relief *only* to employees in female job classes that are found to be underpaid in comparison with male job classes of equal value. The inconsistency here is that both female and male employees in female job classes benefit when the pay rate of the female job class is lower than that of the male job class, but female and male employees in a male job class would get no relief should it be discovered that their pay rate was lower than that of a female job class. Second, the implementing mechanisms provide for a special status and role for labour unions. Hence, the principle of equity becomes what the political process of collective bargaining makes it out to be.

Third, the determination of the pay inequity of female job classes specifically ignores the market and relies heavily on the job evaluation system to determine the job's value to the employer. This approach has two major difficulties. One difficulty relates to the task of developing a job evaluation system whose compensable factors are weighted and defined in a sufficiently abstract manner to cover the variety of jobs and are at the same time specific enough to capture the unique features and characteristics of each job. This difficulty could perhaps be overcome by a focus on job classes — and by the ingenuity, patience, and goodwill of all concerned. The second difficulty — the task of coverting into dollars the job values derived from the job evaluation system — cannot be adequately resolved if market forces are ignored.

The value of a job to an organization is determined by both its value-in-use as well as its value-in-exchange. The former is assessed internally, in the context of the organization's objectives, through the job evaluation system. The latter is the "price" of the job and is a function of the demand for and supply of labour. Adam Smith ([1796] 1950) cautioned his readers not to confuse these two meanings of value. In this context, Gold (1983) cites Ehrenberg, who estimated that the price of mowing a lawn was about $4 an hour, and the price for baby-sitting was about $1.50 an hour, and added: "It's strange, when you think about it, because your children are a lot more important to you than your lawn" (p. 60). Rather than a conspiracy of male chauvinists to raise the wages of lawn-mowers and to keep down the wages of baby-sitters, this is a simple case of demand and supply, which determines the price of each job regardless of whether it happens to be male-dominated or female-dominated.

The market system is not perfect, but it is the best mechanism in our society for allocating resources available in relative freedom. The experience of alternative systems has shown that the market system is also a relatively more efficient way of allocating resources. The requirements of pay equity interfere with the free operation of the market in determining pay and allocating human resources. The consequences of such interference is best illustrated in a scenario by Gold (1983). Suppose that a job evaluation system gives equal points to the jobs of high school math teacher and of home economics teacher; suppose also that the former is a male-dominated job and the latter is a female-dominated job. Assume that a job develops in the training department of a business organization and that this job is ideally suited to math teachers. The organization attracts them with higher pay. Under pay equity, this action creates consequences for both the business organization and the school. If the trainer's job in the business organization is male-dominated, the pay rate of comparable female jobs in that organization will also have to be raised. The school might also have to raise the pay of the math teachers to retain them, and when it does this, pay equity will require that the pay rate of comparable female-dominated jobs also be raised. Thus, in both situations, pay equity results in inefficient resource allocations, because it pushes up the pay rates of even those jobs where the supply of labour would allow the jobs to be filled at lower rates.

Conclusion

In 1980 the issue of pay equity was discussed at a conference on race and sex equality in the workplace at McMaster University, with these results: "At the conceptual level, they [the workshop participants] all agree on the principle of equal pay for work of equal value. At the operational level, they all indicate, implicitly or explicitly, that problems lie ahead" (Agarwal 1980, 48). Not only have the operational issues not been resolved, but the principles of natural law have been compromised by pay equity laws that have mushroomed in the last five years in response to strong political pressures. No one can or will quarrel with the principle of pay equity. However, any pay equity plan and action strategy must be guided by a pay equity policy that is founded on, and reflects a strong commitment to, the moral imperatives of justice. These moral imperatives demand that pay equity laws transcend gender discrimination and address the pay inequities of all employee groups in the workplace consistent with the rights of employers and with due regard to the interests of society as a whole.

To summarize, the main points of the issues that have been neglected in pay equity laws are these: (1) pay equity policies, plans, and action strategies must be driven by ethical human-rights considerations rather than by political considerations; (2) pay equity should be treated as an integral part of the more comprehensive employment-equity issue; (3) both the job evaluation system and market forces should be allowed to play a role in the implementation of pay equity programmes in organizations.

SUMMARY

This chapter reviewed the meaning of the concept of pay equity from "equal pay for equal work," through "equal pay for similar work," to its present statutory definition of "equal pay for work of equal value." After a thumbnail sketch of the history of pay equity legislation in Canada, the chapter examined the salient features of pay equity legislation. Most laws cover public-sector employees. Ontario's law is the most comprehensive — its coverage also extends to private-sector employees. Enforcement mechanisms are either complaint-driven or proactive. Some jurisdictions, such as Ontario, include both mechanisms and prescribe a format for a pay equity plan. The gender-predominance criterion for determining female-dominated and male-dominated job classes ranges from 60 to 70 per cent, and most jurisdictions limit the cost of pay equity adjustments to 1 per cent of the total payroll. The chapter identified in the job analysis and job evaluation processes the sources of gender bias that can cause pay inequities for incumbents in female-dominated jobs, and suggested strategies for eliminating or reducing this bias.

Ironically enough, pay equity laws intended to redress pay inequities can themselves produce pay and other inequities. This issue was explored with reference to the moral foundations and the psychological underpinnings of pay equity. The undesirable effects of pay equity laws were then identified. These undesirable effects came about because legislators ignored ethical considerations in responding to political pressures to create pay equity laws.

KEY TERMS

complaint-driven enforcement
equal pay for equal work
equal pay for similar work
equal pay for work of equal value
equity
female-dominated job class
gender bias in job analysis
gender bias in job evaluation
male-dominated job class
moral rights
pay equity
proactive enforcement
value-in-exchange
value-in-use

REVIEW AND DISCUSSION QUESTIONS

1. Explain the differences in the following concepts: "equal pay for equal work," "equal pay for similar work," and "equal pay for work of equal value."
2. Explain how the basic natural rights of an individual constitute the firm foundation of equity.
3. Which of the job evaluation methods discussed in Chapter 10 provides the best approach for achieving the objectives of pay equity? Why?
4. Using examples from your own (and others') observations and experiences (including case reports), discuss the sources of gender biases in job analysis and job evaluation procedures.

EXERCISE: THE PAY EQUITY DEBATE

Objective

To explore the pros and cons of pay equity.

Procedure

1. Divide the class into groups of four to five participants.
2. Assign to half the groups the role of advocates of pay equity and to the other half the role of critics of pay equity.
3. Each group discusses the arguments relating to its assigned role. See Statement A for some of the typical arguments.
4. Class debate: Teams of advocates and critics, composed of a representative from each of the groups, debate the pros and cons of pay equity.

Statement A

Advocates of pay equity argue as follows:

- Sex discrimination in the labour market is the major reason why women workers earn less than men, as evidenced by the following decisions of the Canadian Human Rights Commission (1984):
  — Female nurses in federal penitentiaries in the Atlantic Region were paid less than male technicians although they performed the same tasks and were better qualified;
  — The predominantly female clerical and factory workers at the Atomic Energy of Canada's Glace Bay plant in Nova Scotia performed job tasks that were equal in value to those of the male workers at the plant, but the women workers were paid less than the men.
  — Federal government librarians (predominantly female) were paid less than historical researchers (predominantly male) for work of equal value.
  — The jobs of male paramedics and female nurses and X-ray technicians at Canadian National Railways involve work that is equal in value, but the paramedics are paid more than the nurses and X-ray technicians.
- Gender bias in job analysis and job evaluation procedures operates to produce a lower pay for female jobs.
- The sexist socialization process inherent in our societies is the principal cause of occupational segregation that results in lower labour market pay rates for predominantly female jobs.

Critics respond as follows:

- The earnings gap is not due to discrimination in the labour market but to occupational segregation, which is largely the result of free choice exercised by women.
- The dollar value of a job is not determined by the intrinsic worth of the job but by the forces of the marketplace. Failure to recognize this reality could eventually jeopardize the competitiveness of Canadian businesses.
- "As long as women are free to become plumbers and prefer to become secretaries instead, they have no right to demand plumbers' pay for secretaries' work" (Gold 1983, 94).

CHAPTER 12

SALARY SURVEYS AND PAY STRUCTURE: EXTERNAL EQUITY

CHAPTER SYNOPSIS

This chapter builds on the job structure developed in Chapter 10. The focus of this chapter is on designing a pay structure that reflects the differentials in the job values inherent in the job structure. The chapter discusses the sources of pay rates, and the issues and methods involved in salary surveys, which provide the major input in developing a pay structure. The chapter then examines the issues and procedures of designing a pay structure, including the pay level policy, the pricing of the job structure, and the constructing of pay grades and ranges. The chapter concludes with a discussion of salary administration policies for dealing with salary cases that fall outside established pay grades.

LEARNING OBJECTIVES

- To identify the internal and external factors that influence the setting of pay rates.
- To define the *relevant external labour market*, and to identify its dimensions.
- To explain the purpose of a salary survey and to identify its contents.
- To describe the processes and methods of conducting a salary survey.
- To discuss the advantages and disadvantages to the organization of conducting its own survey compared with acquiring market data from third-party surveys.
- To understand typical procedures in the analyses of survey data.

- To identify the major pay level policies, and to discuss the rationale and criteria for the choice of a pay level policy.
- To describe the procedural steps in pricing a job structure.
- To discuss the basic approaches to constructing a pay structure.
- To describe the procedural steps in the construction of pay grades and ranges, and to explain the purpose of pay ranges.
- To explain the reasons for salary cases that fall outside the salary structure, and to recommend appropriate salary administration policies for dealing with these cases.

INTRODUCTION

Chapter 10 developed a job structure that was based on considerations of internal equity. The job structure provided an indication of the value of the jobs to the organization. The job evaluation system used in determining job values was based on compensable factors defining the content and the contribution of the job. The next step is to develop a pay structure that corresponds to the job structure. In other words, the dollar values assigned to a job should reflect the job's relative position in the overall job structure, and also the differentials in job values. For a pay structure to be developed, three decisions are necessary: a decision on the sources or bases for pay rates; a decision on the collection of pay data; and a decision on the architectural features of the pay structure, that is, its pay grades and pay ranges. The chapter begins with a discussion of the considerations that underlie the sources for pay rates; explores the relevant labour market that is the source of pay data; and discusses the methods and techniques for collecting and analysing these data. The chapter then describes the process of designing a pay structure, with a special focus on the choice of a pay level policy, and the number of pay grades and pay ranges. The objective of all the decisions and activities that lead to a pay structure is to maintain the relationship between internal equity and external equity, as expressed in the organization's compensation philosophy. Finally, the chapter discusses salary administration policies for dealing with individual salary cases that fall outside established pay grades.

THE SOURCES OR BASES OF PAY RATES

What are the sources or bases of pay rates? That is, how do organizations establish the dollar values or the prices of jobs? Several considerations enter the job pricing process. Because salaries and wages constitute a substantial portion of operating costs, an organization views the pay structure largely in terms of its effects on cost structure. Hence, the ability of the organization to bear the cost becomes the critical determinant in job pricing. In this context, it is useful to recall the discussion in Chapter 2, which argued that a consideration of business strategies and product life cycle stages is a useful and even necessary starting point in reward design. Business strategies and product life cycle stages provide the compensation specialist not only with an overall sense of direction, but also with information on the likely availability of resources and the optimal allocation of these resources. Organizations whose operations are highly labour-intensive are relatively more sensitive to labour costs, and this sensitivity to labour costs becomes an important determinant in the pricing of jobs. Pay rates high enough to deprive an organization of its competitive edge can seriously affect its survival.

External considerations are equally important in the setting of pay rates. Foremost among these are the job rates prevailing in the external labour market. As was noted in Chapter 1, the first two major behavioural objectives of the compensation system of an organization are (1) to attract individuals with the knowledge, ability, and talent demanded by specific organizational tasks; and (2) to retain valued and productive employees. To attain both objectives, organizations compete with one another, and this competition translates into the demand for labour in the external labour market. The availability of people with the required knowledge, skills, and abilities constitutes the supply of labour in the external market. The interaction of demand and supply establishes pay rates in the labour market. When employees in an organization find that their pay rates do not compare favourably with pay rates in the external labour market, they will, other things being equal, experience external inequity. And when they do, the organization's ability to attract and retain employees is seriously impaired.

Although external equity is relevant and important for employees, employee perceptions of it are generally not based on the precise information and the strongly held convictions that employee perceptions of internal equity are based on. Perceptions of internal equity are more firmly based because employees have a more accurate knowledge of the job content, the job contribution, and the outcomes received — for their own job as well as the jobs of their peers, with whom the equity comparison is being made. In the case of external equity, employees realize that a meaningful comparison is not possible, because even if the job titles are the same, considerable differences exist in the job content and job contribution, the compensation philosophy, and the total compensation mix. Yet, employees in an organization do develop a sense of whether external equity exists or does not exist. The compensation programmes in organizations where their friends and relatives work are frequently a topic of conversation. Other sources of information are media reports of union wage settlements, and publications of professional associations that report the results of compensation surveys of the members of these associations.

Employees are concerned about external equity and do form perceptions about it. These perceptions, although often based on hearsay, can and do affect decisions to join or to stay on in an organization. Organizations will recognize this fact and initiate specific actions to make the pay structure consistent with the demands of external equity. What are these specific actions? First, the organization decides on the relevant external labour market and collects data on pay rates from this market. Then, it constructs a pay structure based on the job structure and the data from the external labour market in accordance with its pay policy. The sections that follow examine the methods, techniques, and processes involved in the actions that organizations take to ensure the external equity of the pay structure.

THE RELEVANT EXTERNAL LABOUR MARKET

The pay data from the external labour market are collected through salary surveys. Before proceeding to consider the methods and techniques used in salary surveys, it is necessary to discuss the issues involved in choosing the relevant labour market.

Traditionally, organizations treated the industry as the relevant external labour market. The high mobility of employees in some jobs across industries has forced compensation specialists to reconsider the traditional focus on industry-relevant comparisons alone. Can alternative criteria be developed for determining the external labour market of an organization? The preceding discussion argued that external equity is a critical determinant of the organization's ability to attract and retain the employees it needs. From this argument can be derived a general guideline for assessing which external labour market is relevant and appropriate: An organization's relevant external labour market is any other organization in any geographic area from which the organization's employees are drawn, and to which its employees are likely to move. Exit interviews, conducted systematically and with tact, can be a good source of information about companies that have succeeded in attracting employees away from the organization.

Several dimensions of the external labour market should be considered, for example, geographic area, the nature of the jobs, the size of the companies, and the nature of the industry. A review of the organization's present workforce in an occupational group might reveal that its employees are drawn from a certain geographic area, say a radius of 30 kilometres. This fact would suggest the geographic boundary of the organization's labour market for that occupational group. The geographic boundary varies according to the nature of the jobs or of the occupational groups. For instance, for office, production, and maintenance employees, the boundary might be a local market within a radius of 30 to 40 kilometres; for professionals and managers, the boundary might well extend beyond the regional to the national, or even the international, geographic area. A good example of the latter is the oil exploration industry, which draws professionals from an international pool.

The size of the organization and, more particularly, the nature of its industry bear considerably upon the organization's capacity to pay. An organization aims to be competitive not only to attract and retain employees but also to manage its costs in such a manner that it does not surrender its competitive edge. As will be discussed later, these considerations are also critical when actual survey data are analysed to determine what is the *typical* market rate for a job. For instance, the pay rate of a company that employs only 1 engineer could not be considered the typical rate for a company that employs 20 engineers, because the cost impact of pay decisions is obviously different for the two companies.

SALARY SURVEYS

After a decision has been made on the external labour market that is relevant and appropriate to the organization, data are collected from the market through salary surveys. This section examines what a salary survey is, and what methods and techniques are used in collecting pay data. The next section will discuss those issues in data analysis that are critical for selecting the data to be used in the design of a pay structure.

WHAT IS A SALARY SURVEY?

Just as job evaluation is an essential and useful tool for ensuring internal equity, so is the salary survey an essential and useful tool for ensuring external equity. The salary survey provides information on the typical or "going" pay rate for a job. As discussed earlier, different labour markets exist for different jobs in an organization. Therefore, although a typical or going rate is spoken of, in reality there are a variety of rates, as revealed by not just one survey but by different surveys that tap the appropriate labour markets. The survey provides the organization with the data needed to develop a pay structure consistent with its pay level policy, that is, to lead, lag, or meet the market.

The data usually collected in a survey are the job title, the average or median pay rate, the number of employees in the job, the pay grade, the highest and lowest actual pay, the compa-ratio, and the starting pay rates. These items of information are necessary for assessing the comparability of the data, which will be considered later in discussing the analysis of the survey data. For now, brief comments on these items will suffice. The job title gives some indication of the job match, but it will always be considered along with the description of the job. The median pay is a better statistic than the average pay, because it disregards the influence of the extreme pay data — the very high and the very low pay rates. The number of employees in the job allows for the appropriate weighting of the pay data in order to better determine comparability. The pay grade (that is, the minimum, the midpoint, and the maximum) provides an indication of the company's intent of the range of pay for that job. However, the highest and the lowest actual pay are a better indicator of the market. The compa-ratio is an arithmetical measure used in the analysis of survey data. Essentially, it is an index of the relationship of the actual pay to a predetermined point in the pay grade, usually the midpoint of the grade. Information on starting pay rates is helpful for entry-level jobs.

SALARY SURVEY APPROACHES AND METHODS

There are basically two approaches to salary surveys: (1) the organization conducts its own surveys; (2) the organization acquires surveys conducted by third parties.

Conducting Own Survey

Some organizations conduct their own surveys because they can then focus on the external labour market that is relevant to them and can thus obtain the data that best meet their needs. The assumption here is that the organization has the competence and the resources to undertake this task efficiently and effectively. Critical to the successful conduct of the survey are decisions that relate to the selection of the companies and the jobs to be included in the survey, and the selection of the methods for ensuring the relevancy and comparability of the survey data.

The issue of the selection of the companies is also known as the determination of the survey sample. The general guideline for determining the survey sample is that the organization should include all companies from which it draws its employees and to which its employees will likely go when they leave the organization. The companies will be different for different employee groups — managerial, professional, production, maintenance, office, and technical. The analysis of the relevant labour markets for these groups will help identify such characteristics as industry, size, and geographic area, which should be considered in determining the composition of the survey sample.

What are the considerations for deciding on the type and the number of jobs that should be covered by the survey? The jobs selected for inclusion in the survey should be benchmark jobs that fairly represent the different occupational categories and salary levels. It is also useful to include entry-level jobs and those jobs that pose particular problems for the organization. These problems might be a difficulty in attracting qualified applicants, or an unusually high turnover rate. The characteristics of benchmark jobs have been identified in Chapter 10. For the purpose of the survey, extra attention should be paid to making sure that the content of benchmark jobs is relatively stable; otherwise, the comparability of the survey data will be compromised. Of course, these jobs should exist in reasonable numbers in the companies participating in the survey.

With regard to the number of jobs that should be included in the survey, theoretically, the greater the number, the more comprehensive the survey data will be. In practice, however, the quality of survey data can be adversely affected if too many jobs are included. This is so for two reasons. First, the survey return rate may be reduced because participating companies might resent the effort required to respond to a large number of jobs. Second, even if the return rate is satisfactory, the quality of the data may suffer; participating companies may fail to make the effort required and may provide incomplete or inaccurate information. It is therefore prudent to include only those jobs that are absolutely essential. In most surveys, the job sample constitutes about 25 to 30 per cent of the jobs in an organization (Wallace and Fay 1988).

The survey methods for obtaining data that are relevant and comparable are (1) the key job matching method; (2) the occupational survey method; (3) the job evaluation method (Henderson 1989). The procedure for each method is briefly outlined.

1. The Key Job Matching Method

The organization identifies the key jobs, and selects one from each job category or class series and from each organizational level. The key jobs thus selected represent the different organizational functions and levels. A brief job summary of each job is written up and sent to the organizations selected to participate in the survey, along with a request for the following information on similar jobs in their organizations: rates of pay, pay ranges (minimum, midpoint, maximum in each range); the number of employees in each range; and the job evaluation method used.

This method has limitations when the job has unique features that aggravate the task of matching. The negative effects of this limitation can be minimized by requesting that the respondent organizations review the job descriptions and assess the job match on a scale of poor to perfect match.

2. The Occupational Survey Method

The organization sends the participants a job summary of each of its occupational groups — accounting, operating, engineering, and so forth. The participating organizations are requested to identify their comparable occupational groups and to furnish for each group information relating to the pay range (minimum, midpoint, maximum) for each class, and the number of employees in each class.

The advantage of this method is that the respondent reports on objective data because it is not required to match jobs but simply to report the data that exist for the occupational groups in its company. This method has been found to elicit information on many more jobs than have been received under the key job matching method. However, there still remains the critical task of forming judgements on the comparability of the occupational groups on which the data are received.

3. The Job Evaluation Method

In this method, the organization sends to the survey participants a list of its benchmark jobs and their corresponding job evaluation points. The participants are asked to identify similar jobs with the identical job evaluation points in their companies, and to provide for these jobs the pay information, that is, the pay ranges (minimum, midpoint, maximum) and the number of employees in each range.

This method appears to be the best in that the matching issue is the least problematical. Nevertheless, even in identical job evaluation methods, the subjectivity that is inherent in the job evaluation process can still produce substantial differences in the resulting job evaluation points.

The successful conduct of a survey depends on the conditions mentioned for the effectiveness of each method, but also on the willingness of the companies to participate in the survey. Companies are generally more willing to participate if they can be assured of the confidentiality of the information they provide, and if they can have access to the information generated by the survey. In the interest of confidentiality, the data are shared in a manner that does not reveal the data of the individual companies participating in the survey.

Acquiring Surveys of Third Parties

Organizations that do not have the resources to conduct their own surveys acquire the surveys conducted by such third parties as governments, professional associations, and private consultants.

The surveys of government agencies are often not useful, because the labour markets covered may not be relevant or appropriate. Also, there is the problem of obsolescence resulting from the time lag between the collection and the publication of the data.

The surveys of professional associations are useful so long as the problems of *job match* can be overcome. Some professional associations provide data that are used in the development of *maturity curves*. These are graphical representations of the salary data of the members of a professional group (e.g., engineers) arranged on the basis of years of experience or years since receiving a degree. Maturity curves can serve as a frame of reference that an organization can use for determining its relative position in the labour market (Dunn and Rachel 1971).

The surveys conducted by consultants have advantages and disadvantages. On the one hand, these are not time-consuming and are relatively inexpensive provided the organization is a participant in the survey. The large number of participants contribute statistical soundness. The data are generally well summarized. On the other hand, the participating organizations do not get to select the jobs they might be interested in, and are unable to identify the data of the individual respondent organizations that have contributed to the survey. Such identification is useful in determining the job match. The participating organizations also do not get to control what data are collected and often find themselves inundated by both relevant and irrelevant data.

Before this section is concluded, the issue of employee involvement in the process of salary surveys should be raised. Whether an organization conducts its own survey or acquires third party surveys, the ultimate objective of a survey is to generate information demonstrating that external equity exists in the compensation system. If the compensation sytem is found to be inequitable relative to the external labour market, the survey information provides a rational and systematic basis for restoring external equity. The key to employees' perceptions of external equity is their trust in both the process and the information it generates. Employees can have legitimate concerns about the comparability of the companies, the jobs, and the data relating to pay. An important way of addressing these concerns is to involve employees in the salary survey process from the very beginning, including the selection of the jobs and the companies to be surveyed, as well as the choice of the survey methods. The effectiveness of compensation techniques, to the extent that they impinge on employee perceptions of equity, is greatly enhanced by involving employees in their design and implementation.

Techniques of Data Collection

The major preoccupation of salary survey methods is to assure the job match and the resulting comparability of data. Once the method has been decided upon, a decision is made on the choice of technique(s) for collecting data. Data can be collected by means of the telephone, mailed questionnaires, personal interviews, and a conference of the participants.

The telephone is useful when the job can be easily identified by the respondents and the survey is not too extensive, both in terms of the number of jobs and the detail of the data that is needed. The telephone technique permits an immediate check for the job match and the comparability of data.

The mailed questionnaire is the most popular technique used in collecting survey data. Although it can be quite efficient, returns can be poor, especially when the survey instrument is a lengthy questionnaire.

The personal interview is the most favoured technique if the respondent is willing to take the time for it. It readily resolves the question of job match and, as a result, enhances the comparability of the data. It also relieves the respondent of the clerical work that is entailed in the questionnaire technique.

A conference of all the participants works well if the participating organizations share common interests and problems. It has all the advantages of the personal interview as far as resolving the questions of job match and data comparability is concerned. The effective use of a conference is often impeded by a lack of common interests and by the logistics of getting together at a mutually convenient time and location.

A Critique of Salary Surveys

Even though surveys are a useful tool for ensuring external equity, organizations appear to be reluctant to participate in them. Some companies complain that there are too many requests for surveys; for example, one firm in a single year received about one hundred requests to participate in a salary survey. Moreover, there is the issue of usefulness. The statistical analysis needed to make the data useful is severely hampered by poor comparability, many restraints on information disclosure, an inadequate sample size, and poorly designed questionnaires that are full of ambiguous questions.

Another criticism that is frequently levelled against the salary survey is that it encourages the "leapfrogging" effect. As organizations work towards catching up with the market, they may eventually, it is argued, fuel inflationary pressures in the economy.

While these criticisms cannot be completely ignored, the fact remains that salary surveys are needed to provide the linkage between internal and external equity. In the ultimate analysis, pay contributes to inflation only when it is not commensurate with productivity. The more appropriate compensation strategy for combating inflation is a greater focus on performance-based pay that is equitably designed and managed. The response to these criticisms is not to discard salary surveys but to make greater efforts to improve job match and comparability.

Analysis of Survey Data

The objective of a survey is to provide data that enable the organization to develop a pay structure that is consistent with external equity. This objective imposes the obligation of using only the data of market jobs that best match the organization's jobs. Survey data should therefore be subjected to a rigorous review to make sure that they are accurate and that only those data are selected that fairly reflect the labour market rates of survey jobs. There are typical analytical procedures for reviewing the survey data. This discussion of the procedures refers to "ABC's job(s)" to mean the job(s) of the organization that is conducting the survey; and the term "market job(s)" to mean the corresponding job(s) in the organization's external market. The first question to be addressed is this: How good is the match between ABC's jobs and the market jobs? To answer this question for each job, ABC compares its job descriptions with those of the market jobs. If the comparison indicates that the match is acceptable, then the jobs are comparable, and there is no need to adjust the survey data. If the match is not acceptable, then the jobs are not comparable, and the survey data must be adjusted. The data are adjusted through the technique of "survey levelling" (Milkovich and Newman 1990), which in effect reduces both jobs to a level playing field to facilitate comparison. According to this technique, the survey data are multiplied by a factor to bring them in line with ABC's job value. For example, suppose the analysis suggests that ABC's job A has slightly less value than the market job; say the value of ABC's job is about 85 per cent of the value of the market job. The survey data will be multiplied by .85. If the market job pay is $30,000, and ABC's job is determined to be 85 per cent of the value of the market job, the market pay rate of ABC's job will likely be ($30,000 x 85 per cent) = $25,500.

After having assessed the comparability of the jobs, ABC analyses the pay data. Not all companies pay the same rate. Each company's pay rate reflects the company's assessment of the relative content and contribution of all the jobs in the company. The pay rate also reflects other factors, such as the pay level policy, employee performance, the age and the tenure of employees, and the number of employees in the job. ABC can expect pay rates to vary among companies, but does need to know the extent of the variation or the dispersion of the data. Widely dispersed data indicate companies with considerable differences in pay level policies. The dispersion is measured by the spread between the highest and lowest pay rates. Suppose the data for job A show the lowest average salary to be $28,000 and the highest average salary to be $36,000. The ratio of $28,000 to $36,000, which is .78, indicates the dispersion, and vice versa.

Another statistical procedure for analysing the data is the distribution of the pay rates. A normal distribution suggests a certain degree of consistency in the data; hence, the data are useful. A distribution that is not normal suggests inconsistencies in the data, which may indicate variations in pay level policies. The frequency distribution also makes it possible to identify the extreme values. For example, 12 companies provided information on the average salary for job A:

Company	*$*
1	28,000
2	29,200
3	31,000
4	29,500
5	30,500
6	31,070
7	31,000
8	30,000
9	36,000
10	28,300
11	28,500
12	30,600

The average salary of job A in all companies except company 9 is in the range of $28,000-31,070. Company 9 is outside the range with an average salary of $36,000. Should ABC retain this extreme value? Does it reflect the market rate for job A? To address these questions, ABC must probe the average salaries of the other survey jobs in company 9. If the average salaries of the other survey jobs are also high, then ABC can conclude that company 9 does not reflect the market rate for job A. On the other hand, if the average salaries of the other jobs in company 9 are not high, then its salaries might well reflect the market rates. The extreme difference in the salaries for job A might be that this job in company 9 does not match job A in the other companies, nor does it match ABC's job A. However, before ABC decides to eliminate company 9, it should review its job description of job A to verify the goodness of the job match. If there is a good match, then ABC should retain the data from company 9, and reconsider the data from the other companies as far as job A is concerned. If the job match between ABC's job A and company 9's job A is poor, then ABC should eliminate the data of company 9.

The analysis of the survey data also involves judgements on the choice of the available data. Should ABC choose the mean or the median pay rates? Should ABC weight the mean or the median by the number of employees in the job? Generally, the mean is chosen, but when its value is distorted by extreme values, the median is the preferred statistical measure of central tendency. Whichever measure is chosen, it is advisable to weight it by the number of the employees in the job in order to get a truer picture of the market rate.

The different procedures that have been described enable the compensation specialist to include only those companies whose pay rates are more likely to reflect the market rate for the surveyed jobs. After such decisions have been made in respect of the data for all the surveyed jobs, the compensation specialist will have prepared the ground for the next series of procedures that are necessary for the design of the pay structure.

DESIGNING THE PAY STRUCTURE

There are three major steps in the design of a pay structure. First, the organization decides on a pay level policy. Second, the organization carries out the statistical procedures that relate the data from the relevant external labour market to the organization's job structure in accordance with the organization's pay level policy. Finally, the organization constructs a pay structure — the pay grades and pay ranges.

PAY LEVEL POLICY

The objective of all the decisions and activities that lead to a pay structure is to maintain the relationship between internal equity (as expressed in the job structure) and external equity (as expressed in the data from the relevant external labour market). This pay relationship can be established at a variety of levels. The first decision is to choose to establish the pay structure in one of three categories of levels: (1) *above the level* that exists in the market; or (2) *at the level* that exists in the market; or (3) *below the level* that exists in the market. That is, the organization decides *to lead, to match,* or *to lag* the market. The second decision is to determine more specifically by *how much* the pay structure will be above or below the market. The compensation specialist also has the option of combinations; for example, paying above the market for part of the year and then paying below the market for the rest of the year (i.e., lead/lag); paying below the market for part of the year and then paying above the market for the rest of the year (i.e., lag/lead); matching the market first and then leading later in the year (i.e., match/lead), and vice versa.

Decisions on the organization's market position are strategic and should merit a place in the organization's compensation philosophy (as discussed in Chapter 6). The rationale for a choice of position — lead, match, or lag the market — is provided by the organization's compensation objectives.

If the organization wants to be certain that it will attract and retain employees with a high level of competence and ability, it will follow a lead policy. Why are employees attracted by a lead policy? Higher pay creates a higher valence because, other things being equal, a greater amount of pay is more instrumental in satisfying needs. Valence will also increase because, by leading the market in the pay level, the organization is saying that it wants the best workforce and is suggesting that its employees are its vital and most valued resource. Through rigorous selection procedures, the organization also makes sure that only the best are hired, and employees feel that they belong to an elite group. The desire to be members of an elite group is a powerful force that attracts employees, and it also has a substantial influence on the retention of employees. Generally such a policy will contribute to high pay satisfaction provided that the processes of the compensation system that ensure internal equity in pay determination are functioning properly. The organization must reckon, however, with high labour costs that result from a lead policy. Some organizations are able to withstand the effects of high costs because of increases in labour productivity and, more particularly, because of the competitive edge they gain as a result of the innovation and creativity of their employees. The mere fact of paying high salaries does not, of course, guarantee high labour productivity nor does it automatically lead to innovation. Other organizations are able to contain labour costs because of efficiencies in their cost structure, or because they are able to pass on these costs to consumers without jeopardizing their competitive position.

The preceding discussion suggests that organizations that follow a lag policy will have difficulty in attracting and retaining competent employees. Although this would appear to be the case, one cannot generalize, because of the many factors that go into the decision to join and to stay on in an organization. Many organizations offer reward items other than pay to attract the employees they need. For example, Spar Aerospace Limited in the suburbs of Montreal attracts exceptionally brilliant and competent scientists and engineers because of the challenging work the company provides, which is on the cutting edge of space technology. University faculties attract competent researchers because they offer opportunities to work with people who have established themselves in a particular area of study. Other organizations attract employees by their location — sylvan surroundings, a peaceful and safe neighbourhood, proximity to a good school. In the matter of retention, satisfaction or dissatisfaction with pay is not the only reason why employees stay with or leave an organization. Environmental factors (such as family responsibilities and the availability of jobs) do compel employees to stay on even though they may be dissatisfied with pay. Although pay is an important item, it is only one element of the compensation mix of base pay, incentives, and benefits. Organizations have been successful with a compensation mix that is determined by their product life cycle and business strategies.

Organizations adopt the policy of matching the market because they wish to be competitive in the external labour market in order to attract and retain the workforce they need. A match policy will generally not have the high labour costs associated with a lead policy. Ultimately, however, the effectiveness of this policy will depend on the composition of the organization's compensation mix, which will be influenced by the organization's business strategies and the life cycle stages of its products.

The choice of a pay level policy is a critical strategic issue in compensation. The organization's business strategies, the economics of the relevant external labour market, and the impact of labour costs on the total cost structure of the organization must be considered in developing a compensation mix of base pay, incentives, and benefits that will help achieve the objectives of the organization's compensation system. Therefore, the decision of the pay level policy cannot be divorced from the decision on the compensation mix.

Pricing the Job Structure

The procedure of pricing the job structure is an attempt to relate the survey data of the relevant external labour market to the organization's job structure, in accordance with its pay level policy. The resulting pay structure will express the internal equity of the job structure in terms of the relevant external labour market. This procedure would be relatively simple if the jobs that existed in the organization also existed in the market because, in that case, all that would be necessary would be to determine the market rates for these jobs and, depending upon the pay level policy, apply those rates to the jobs in the organization. In reality, however, this simple procedure is not applicable, because the jobs in the market, despite the similarity in their titles, are rarely identical to the jobs in the organization. It is therefore necessary to use key or benchmark jobs to function as the medium through which the job structure is related to the market by means of the statistical procedure of regression analysis. The major steps in this procedure are as follows:

1. The job descriptions of the organization's jobs are carefully compared with the job descriptions of the surveyed jobs to assess the match of these jobs. The jobs with a good and acceptable match are referred to as the key or benchmark jobs. At least three key or benchmark jobs are needed if the regression analysis is to provide good results.
2. The job evaluation points for each benchmark job are collected from the job structure, and its pay rate, from the survey data. Collecting the job evaluation points is straightforward, because each job in the job structure has only one value. This is not the case with pay rates. The survey generally provides data on a variety of pay rates for each job, for example, the average actual pay rate expressed as the mean or the median pay rate; the

lowest actual pay rate; the highest actual pay rate; the pay range in terms of the minimum, the midpoint, and the maximum. Which pay rate should an organization choose? The decision will depend on the organization's pay level policy. If the policy is to lead the market, then the highest pay rate is chosen, and an adjustment is made to reflect the percentage by which the pay structure will be above that pay rate. If the policy is to match the market, then a measure such as the mean or the median pay rate, which reflects the market average, is chosen. If the policy is to lag the market, then the lowest pay rate is chosen.

3. For the purpose of describing the process, assume that the pay level policy is to match the market. In this case, the regression analysis is conducted using the job evaluation points of the benchmark jobs and the average pay rates of these jobs in the market. The output of the regression analysis is the regression model in the form of

$$y = a + bx$$

where

- y is the predicted salary;
- a is a constant, the value of y when the job evaluation points equal 0;
- b is the slope, the rate by which the value of y will change with a change in the job evaluation points;
- x is the job evaluation points of the job for which the salary is to be predicted.

The regression analysis will also provide two other extremely important measures. These are the correlation coefficient, and the standard error of the estimate. The correlation coefficient indicates how good the "fit" of the data is. A correlation coefficient of less than .9 would indicate a poor fit, and a need to review the comparability of the data and the decisions on the job match. The standard error provides a measure of the error that is likely when the regression model is used. This measure should not exceed 1.5 to 2 per cent (Wallace and Fay 1988).

To illustrate, suppose that the Montreal Manufacturing Company (MMC) has 25 jobs. After comparing these jobs with 40 jobs from the survey data, MMC comes up with the following 6 benchmark jobs. The job evaluation points of these jobs from the company's job structure and the market median pay of these jobs are as indicated below.

Job	*Job Evaluation Points*	*Market Median Pay ($)*
A	470	1,315.47
B	270	1,194.15
C	260	941.32
D	190	906.95
E	170	742.69
F	170	832.86

The output of the regression model with these data will be

$$y = 548.29 + 1.73\,(x)$$

with a correlation coefficient of .9 and a standard error of .43.

The regression model is acceptable in terms of both the correlation coefficient and the standard error.

This regression equation can then be used to compute the pay of all the jobs in the company. Consider the following two cases:

Case I The pay of job A, which is a benchmark job, will be
Pay = 548.29 + 1.73 (job evaluation points)
= 548.29 + 1.73 (470)
= 1,361.39

Case II The pay of job J, which is a non-benchmark job with 155 job evaluation points, will be
Pay = 548.29 + 1.73 (job evaluation points)
= 548.29 + 1.73 (155)
= 816.44

The statistical procedure has helped to relate the job structure to the relevant external labour market and provided the means of converting the job structure into the pay structure. The specific manner in which this is done is discussed in the next section.

Constructing the Pay Structure: Pay Grades, Pay Ranges

There are two basic approaches to constructing a pay structure. One approach takes the job structure as it is and, using the regression model, converts the job evaluation points of each job into dollars that represent the pay of that job. Under this approach, every job with different job evaluation points will be treated differently and will, in effect, become a separate pay grade. Thus, there will be as many pay grades as there are jobs with different job evaluation points. This approach is logical and is consistent with the theory that if jobs have different point values, they are necessarily different jobs and should therefore be paid differently. In practice, this approach has many difficulties. The difference between job A and job B might be a mere 5 points. However, there may not be grounds to conclude that these jobs are so substantially different from each other that they warrant different salaries. The job evaluation process has not reached a stage of precision where a job can be said to deserve exactly 300 points. The point values assigned are judgements in a process filled with many subjective judgements that are always subject to a revision that will result in a few points more or less for the job. This approach opens the door to constant reviews. One of the realities of the workplace is that jobs do undergo minor modifications that slightly change their value. According to this approach, any pay change, however small, becomes necessary for any minor modification in a job, and the implementation of the compensation system becomes an administrative nightmare.

The other approach is to group jobs into pay grades, with each grade consisting of jobs within a certain range of point values. The next section shows how pay grades are constructed under this approach, and then discusses the advantages and disadvantages of this approach. The example of the Montreal Manufacturing Company will be used again to illustrate the mechanics of constructing pay grades. Suppose that the job structure in this company shows a range of job evaluation points from a low of 50 points to a high of 650 points. The procedural steps are as follows:

1. Subtract the lowest from the highest (650 − 50) and obtain a range, which in this example is 600 points.
2. Decide on the optimum number of pay grades. Generally, the number of pay grades has been found to be related to the categories of employees (Henderson 1989), thus:

Employee Category	*Number of Pay Grades*
Non-Exempt	12 – 16
Exempt	10 – 15
Senior Management	8 – 10

   Assume that 7 pay grades is believed to be the optimum number for the Montreal Manufacturing Corporation.
3. Given the range of 600 points and the optimum number of 7, the grade interval of 100 points is convenient and reasonable.
4. Convert the midpoint of the interval of job evaluation points of each grade (i.e., 50, 150, 250, 350, 450, 550, 650) into dollars by using the regression model: $y = 548.29 + 1.73\ (x)$. From these procedures is obtained the following table, which shows the pay

grades, the interval of the job evaluation points within each pay grade, and the midpoint of the pay grade, which was derived from the regression model.

Pay Grade	*Job Evaluation Points*	*Midpoint*
1	1 – 100	634.79
2	101 – 200	807.79
3	201 – 300	980.79
4	301 – 400	1,153.79
5	401 – 500	1,326.79
6	501 – 600	1,499.79
7	601 – 700	1,672.79

5. The pay structure is completed by constructing the pay ranges, which are the height or spread of each pay grade. The range provides the minimum and maximum of each pay grade, and it varies according to the needs of the organization for the different categories of employees. Some suggested ranges are as follows (Henderson 1989):

Employee Category	*% Spread*
Non-Exempt: Labour and Trades	up to 25%
Non-Exempt: Clerical, Technical, Paraprofessionals	15 – 40%
Exempt: First-Level Management, Administrators, Professionals	30 – 50%
Exempt: Middle and Senior Management	40 – 100%

The pay ranges of the Montreal Manufacturing Company are displayed below. On the assumption that the jobs are mainly clerical and technical, the ranges have been constructed using a spread of 15 to 40 per cent.

Pay Grade	*% Spread*	*Minimum*	*Midpoint*	*Maximum*
1	15%	590.50	634.79	679.08
2	18%	741.09	807.79	874.49
3	22%	883.59	980.79	1,077.99
4	25%	1,025.59	1,153.79	1,281.99
5	30%	1,153.73	1,326.79	1,499.85
6	35%	1,276.42	1,499.79	1,723.16
7	40%	1,393.99	1,672.79	1,951.59

Note: The grade minimum and maximum are computed as follows:

Minimum: Divide the midpoint by one, and one-half of the percentage spread assigned to the pay grade.
E.g., Pay grade 1 minimum = 634.79 ÷ 1.075 = 590.50

Or,

$$\frac{634.79}{1 + \left(\frac{.15}{2}\right)} = 590.50$$

Maximum: Add to the midpoint the difference between the midpoint and the minimum.
E.g., Pay grade 1 maximum = [634.79 + (634.79 − 590.50)]

What is the purpose of the variation in the pay ranges? Pay ranges give organizations a device for recognizing differences between employees whose jobs are in the same pay grade. These differences may be due to *experience, specialized training, performance*. Many organizations also use the pay range to recognize *seniority*. The pay ranges, then, must be tailored to the needs of the organization. Generally, pay grades at the lower end of the pay structure have smaller spreads. Jobs in these pay grades are usually entry level jobs, and organizations do not expect their employees to stay too long in these jobs; either they will be promoted to jobs in higher pay grades or they will be terminated. Therefore, these pay grades do not need a large spread. Further up in the pay structure, the opportunities for promotion are limited, and employees stay relatively longer in these jobs. The larger spread of the ranges in these pay grades permits the organization to recognize the outstanding performance of employees who cannot be, or do not wish to be, promoted. Considerable judgement — based on the accumulated experience of the desirable length of stay in the same job, on the opportunities for promotion, and on the organization's policy on performance-based pay and seniority pay — goes into the decision about how small or large the spread of the pay ranges should be.

Are there alternative ways to recognize the differences between employees whose jobs are in the same pay grade? Organizations can give cash payments separate from base pay. If this is done, the pay grade need not be used and pay ranges are not necessary. There is the need to make periodic adjustments for cost of living, which can be done by multiplying the regression model by the amount of the adjustment that is necessary. But organizations have traditionally used the pay structure to recognize the differences mentioned. There is, however, an increasing trend not to use the pay structure to recognize *performance*; instead, bonus payments are given when the required level of performance is demonstrated. When merit pay for performance is given through an increase in the base pay, it becomes a perpetual payment that recurs in future years even when performance drops. Organizations that give merit pay through a salary increase do not reduce the salary in later years when the employee's performance has dropped. To avoid this kind of situation, organizations are adopting the practice of bonus payments.

When jobs are grouped into pay grades, all the jobs with points within the interval of the pay grade receive the same pay. Thus, in the table in step 4, a job that has 205 points and another job that has 295 points will both receive the same base pay. The base pay change will occur only when the employee is promoted to a job in the next pay grade. This approach overcomes most of the administrative difficulties associated with the first approach, this is, of treating each evaluation point as a pay grade. There may still be requests for a review of job evaluation points from employees whose jobs are near the point value that begins the next pay grade. For example, in the table in step 4, an employee in a job that has 395 points might press for a review in the hope that the job will merit 401 points, and thus fall into the next pay grade. This approach also provides meaningful differences in pay rates when an employee moves from a job in a lower pay grade to a job in the next higher pay grade.

PAY STRUCTURE AND SALARY ADMINISTRATION POLICIES

A well-designed pay structure maintains the right balance between internal and external equity consistent with the organization's compensation philosophy. There are, however, situations where the individual's salary is outside the established pay ranges, either below the minimum or above the maximum of a pay grade. Often, too, a large number of employees will be bunched close to or at the top of a pay grade. In these situations, the motivating potential of the pay structure is not fully realized. This section examines the reasons for these situations and considers the appropriate salary administration policies for coping with these situations, which are referred to as "green circle," "silver circle," "red circle," "running out of range," and "shadow range" situations (Henderson 1989).

First is the situation where the individual's salary is below the minimum of the pay grade and is noted with a green circle. The reason for this situation is either a new employee or the "capping" policy of the organization. When new employees do not have the experience required for the job, they may be placed on probation and started below the minimum of the grade. As soon as the employees successfully complete their probationary period, their pay rate is raised and falls into the regular pay structure. Under the capping policy, the organization limits the salary increase to a certain amount that an employee can receive at any one time. A promotion can involve a movement from a lower pay grade to the minimum of the next higher pay grade, which can result in a substantial salary increase. The capping policy will reduce the increase to the established limit and, as a consequence, the individual's salary will fall below the minimum of the next higher pay grade. The primary reason for the capping policy is cost control. If the individual's performance continues to be satisfactory, then the next salary review will place the individual in the regular pay grade. Green circle rates are generally temporary situations.

Second are situations where the individual's salary is above the maximum of the pay grade. The silver circle, gold circle, and red circle situations fall in this category. In the case of the silver circle, employees have been receiving substantial seniority increases, which have placed them beyond the maximum of the pay grade. These increases were intended as rewards for their long tenure. Either there were no promotion opportunities or they were probably not capable of being promoted to jobs in the higher pay grades. Generally, silver circle employees are near retirement. Employees in gold circle situations are those whose performance justified merit increases that placed them above the maximum of the pay grade. Here, too, there were probably no promotion opportunities, or the employees' present knowledge, skills, and abilities were not adequate for higher level jobs. If the latter is the case, serious thought should be given to the development of these employees.

The red circle signifies a problematic situation in pay administration. The employee's salary is above the maximum of the pay grade, most probably because of a demotion from a job in a higher pay grade to a job in a lower pay grade, with the salary remaining unchanged. Another reason might be inflated merit increases, which were not justified by the individual's performance. Red circle rates are also referred to as "flagged" or "personal out-of-line differentials." The appropriate salary administration strategy in this situation is to freeze or to reduce the individual's salary. Most organizations freeze the salary until upward revisions in the pay structure bring the salary into the regular pay range.

In the third situation, running out of range, the organization finds that a large number of its employees are at the top of the range of certain pay grades. This might happen in a relatively old organization where employees of about the same age started at the same time. Limited growth opportunities might also have restricted their upward movement in the pay structure. These employees are good performers, but further increases will push them out of the pay grade. On the other hand, they will be demotivated when they find that their good performance, which brought them to the top of the pay grade, now has become an obstacle to further increases. There are long-term and short-term strategies for dealing with this situation. The long-term solution is an employee development programme to prepare them to move to jobs in the higher pay grades. In the short-term, their motivation can be maintained through cash bonuses, which do not affect the pay structure.

The case of the shadow range applies to the situation of a job rather than of an individual. In this case, there is a shortage of labour for a particular job. The excess demand relative to supply of labour pushes up the market pay rates of this job, and the organization finds itself having to pay this job more than its internal job value. Hence, the pay rate falls outside the pay grade in which the organization's job structure has placed it. Unlike the red circle case, the shadow range situation does not pay the individual more than he/she is worth. Rather, the organization's job evaluation system gives the job a lower value than does the market. An organization might be tempted to resolve this case by revising its assessment of the job's value and placing it in a higher pay grade. This is a satisfactory solution only if the job's value really justifies the higher pay grade. If it does not, then this solution will disturb the internal equity of the compensation system. A better approach is to keep the job outside the pay grade, because the market labour shortage might be a temporary phenomenon. If it is not a temporary phenomenon, then the job's evaluation should be thoroughly reviewed. Perhaps there are features of the job that are captured by the external labour market but escape the organization's job evaluation process.

The pay structure, like any other compensation technique, method, and structure, should be viewed as a means to an end. As discussed in previous chapters, the compensation system should support the business objectives and strategies of the organization. If the pay structure is treated as an end in itself, then the decisions relating to it are sure to become dysfunctional and will not contribute to the effectiveness of the organization. Adjustments to the pay structure should be understood and managed in the perspective of the compensation system as a potent instrument for achieving both the effectiveness of the organization as well as the satisfaction of the employees.

SUMMARY

This chapter dealt with the issues, procedures, techniques, and methods through which organizations strive to blend internal and external equity in the compensation system. The chapter examined the relevant external labour market, accessed by salary surveys, as an important source of pay rates. The chapter then described the methods and processes of conducting a salary survey, and considered the advantages and disadvantages to the organization of conducting its own salary survey as compared with acquiring survey data from third parties. Whether the organization decides to conduct its own survey or to buy a survey, the process issue of employee involvement should not be neglected. The chapter also examined typical analytical procedures for ensuring that the survey data are relevant and comparable for the user's situation and needs.

The job structure — in particular the job evaluation points — and the market data provide the building blocks of the pay structure. The chapter discussed the rationale and the criteria for the choice of a pay level policy, which determines the organization's position *vis-à-vis* the market. The chapter then described the procedural steps for pricing the job structure, namely, determining the job match, choosing the comparable companies and the pay data, and developing the organization's pay line through regression analysis. The chapter examined the purpose of pay grades and pay ranges, and described the procedure for constructing them.

Finally, the chapter discussed the appropriate salary administration policies for dealing with individual salary cases that fall outside the pay grades.

KEY TERMS

gold circle situation
green circle situation
job evaluation survey method
job match
key job matching survey method
occupational survey method
pay grades
pay level policies
pay ranges
pricing the job structure
red circle situation
relevant external labour market
running out of range situation
salary surveys
shadow range situation
silver circle situation
survey levelling
third-party surveys

REVIEW AND DISCUSSION QUESTIONS

1. What are the internal and external factors that influence the setting of pay rates?

2. Explain the purpose of a salary survey. What are the critical questions that should be included in a salary survey?
3. What are the advantages and disadvantages of an organization's conducting its own survey as compared with acquiring the data from third-party surveys?
4. "Survey data should be subjected to a rigorous review to make sure that they are accurate and that only those data are selected that fairly reflect the labour market rates of survey jobs." Explain the analytical procedures to be used in reviewing and selecting the survey data.
5. Discuss the rationale and the criteria for the choice of a pay level policy.
6. In the following graph:

   - Case *1, the salary is above the pay grade.
   - Case *2, the salary is below the pay grade.
   - Case *3, several salaries are clustered at the top of the grade.

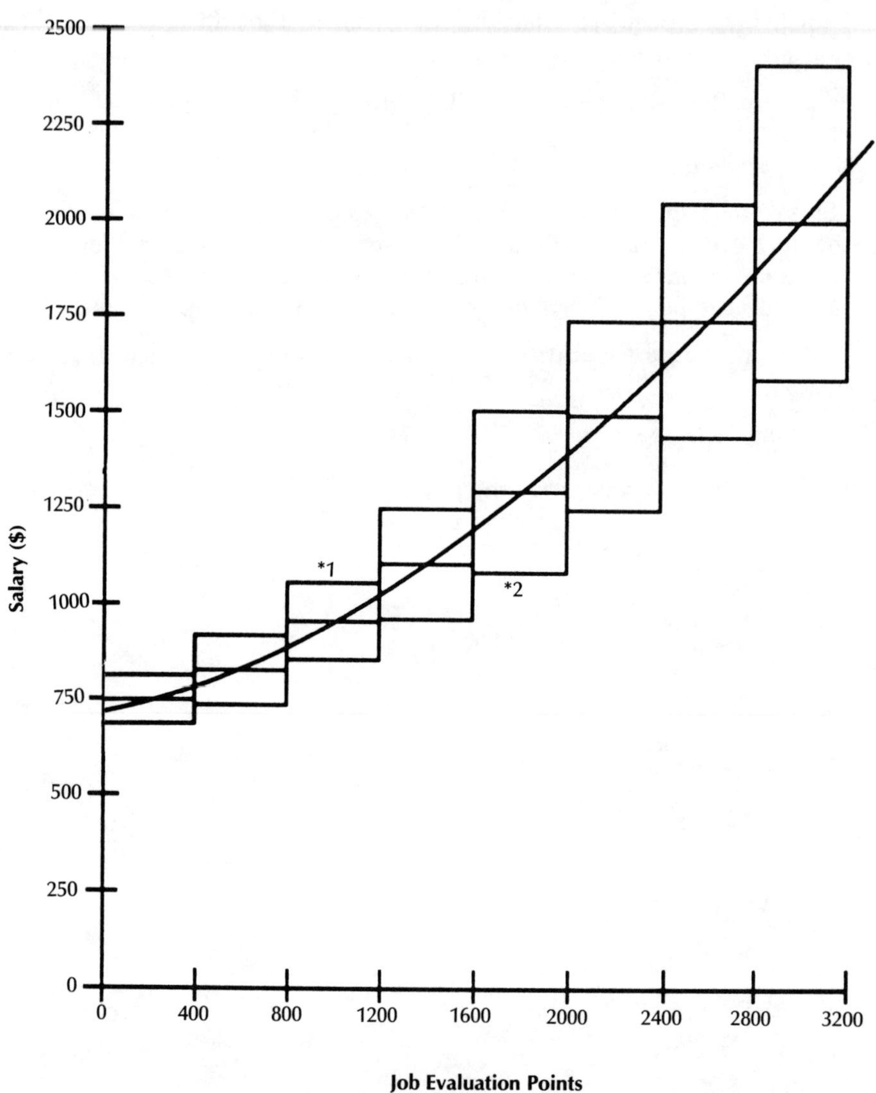

Explain the possible reasons for each of these situations. What actions would you propose for dealing with these situations?

EXERCISE: CONSTRUCTING THE PAY STRUCTURE

Objective

To construct the salary structure of the clerical and administrative staff of Beaverbrook Community College.

Data

All activities that need to be done prior to this phase (for example, developing the job structure, conducting the salary survey) have been completed. In addition, Beaverbrook's manager, salary administration, compared Beaverbrook jobs with those obtained from the salary survey and came up with five benchmark jobs. She also decided to use the market median pay of these jobs because she believes that it better reflects the market pay rates, and is also consistent with Beaverbrook's pay level policy of matching the market. The benchmark jobs and their corresponding job evaluation points and median pay are given below

Job Title	*Job Evaluation Points*	*Market Median Pay ($)*
Porter	220	772.47
Typist	390	1,013.79
Clerk	690	900.73
Secretary	910	1,213.58
Assistant Accountant	2,245	1,328.81

Procedure

1. Using the above data points, conduct a regression analysis to obtain the regression model in the form of $y = a + bx$. Most statistical software packages will let you do this on your personal computer.
2. Construct pay grades and pay ranges. Refer to the procedural steps illustrated in the chapter.

Discussion

1. Review the correlation coefficient. Is it satisfactory? If it is, identify the specific actions/judgements of the compensation specialist that might have contributed to an acceptable correlation coefficient. If it is not, indicate what aspects you would look at to improve it.
2. The compensation specialist believes that by choosing the market median pay rates, she is implementing a pay level policy of matching the market. In which sense is she matching the market, and in which sense is she not matching the market?

3. Compare your decisions on the number and the interval of points in the pay grade with the decisions of the other participants in this exercise. Discuss the reasons for the similarities and the differences.
4. Compare your decisions on the height or spread of each pay range with the decisions of the other participants. Discuss the reasons for the similarities and the differences.

CHAPTER 13
EMPLOYEE BENEFITS PROGRAMMES

CHAPTER SYNOPSIS

This chapter explores the wide variety of benefits offered to employees. Some of these benefits are legally mandatory, and others are either the result of union-management negotiations or are provided at the discretion of the employer. The chapter also examines the emerging flexible benefits approach and discusses guidelines for the design of a benefits programme.

LEARNING OBJECTIVES

- To identify the objective of a benefits programme.
- To understand the purpose, elegibility conditions, benefits, and financing arrangements of the various benefits programmes, namely, income protection programmes, reimbursed time off, and employee services and perquisites.
- To understand the rationale of the flexible benefits approach and to distinguish it from the traditional standardized benefits programme.
- To determine the essential criteria for the effective design of a benefits programme.

EMPLOYEE BENEFITS PROGRAMMES

It was remarked in Chapter 1 that employee benefits have increased both in variety and cost. In 1953–54, these programmes constituted 15 per cent of the gross annual payroll. In 1989, the cost of these programmes had climbed to 33.5 per cent of the gross annual payroll (Peat Marwick Stevenson & Kellogg 1989). Organizations are concerned to manage these costs effectively so that both the organization and its employees derive the greatest benefit from these programmes. The major focus of this chapter is therefore on critical issues in the design and management of the employee benefits programme. The chapter will first describe some programmes from the benefits categories depicted in the reward system (Figure 1.1), this is, income protection programmes, reimbursed time off, services and perquisites. The chapter will then discuss the benefits programme in the context of the model of effective reward management (Figure 1.2), which provides the objectives and the criteria for the design and management of the benefits programme.

What is an employee benefits programme? It is a planned offering of benefits designed as a component of the organization's reward system to attract and retain employees, to maintain employee morale and motivate performance, and to comply with legal requirements. An employee benefits programme also offers the organization significant tax advantages. The variety of benefits organizations offer can be grouped into three major categories: income protection programmes, reimbursed time off, and employee services and perquisites.

Many of the programmes now taken for granted are of relatively recent origin. Prior to World War II, employee benefits were restricted to work-accident compensation, and employee housing and commissary. The latter services were quite common for companies situated in remote locations. The beginnings of the present array of benefits can be traced to developments during World War II. Anticipating that shortages of personnel and materials during the war would inevitably fuel inflation and jeopardize the war effort, the government introduced wage and price controls, which prevented companies from offering higher wages to compete for a limited labour pool. Companies could, however, use deferred benefits, which did not involve a substantial current cash outlay, to retain and attract employees.

Some employee benefits programmes that have become a regular part of the compensation system of most organizations are now described.

INCOME PROTECTION PROGRAMMES

These programmes protect employees when their income is disrupted because they have lost their job; because they are unable to work due to illness, disability, or a work accident; or because of retirement. Two types of programmes are designed to achieve these objectives. The first type is the universal coverage programmes mainly funded by the federal government, such as Old Age Security (OAS) and the Guaranteed Income Supplement (GIS). Some provincial governments supplement these on the basis of a means and residence test. Neither employers nor employees are required to finance these universal benefits, which are funded from government revenues. The second type is programmes that require contributions by the employer and the employees. This chapter will focus on these programmes. Some of these programmes — Unemployment Insurance, Canada/Quebec Pension Plan, and Workers' Compensation — are required by law. Most of the larger organizations provide additional protection for their employees through private pension plans and group insurance programmes.

Unemployment Insurance (UI)

This programme was introduced in 1940 to provide income protection in the event of unemployment due to the loss of a job or a lay-off. UI does not cover employees who are on strike or have been locked out. The fundamental objective of UI is to provide financial protection in order that the individual can locate a job that suits his/her knowledge, skills, and abilities. In certain circumstances, UI enables the unemployed to pursue a specific training programme. The UI programme is administered by the federal government, and both employers and employees contribute to its funding. The premiums are tax deductible, and the benefits are treated as taxable income.

Unemployed individuals qualify for UI benefits if they have contributed during the "qualifying period," and after a "waiting period" stipulated in the UI Act. UI also pays special benefits to employees who are sick, injured, in quarantine, or on maternity leave. Some employers — notably in the automobile industry — provide supplemental unemployment benefits (SUB) to their laid-off workers. Under SUB, the laid-off worker virtually receives 95 per cent of his/her income — an attractive inducement to ride the lay-off period and return to the former employer. The SUB is an effective strategy for guaranteeing that the organization will not lose its skilled and trained workers in the event of temporary lay-offs.

How effective are the $12 billion spent on the UI programme each year? This question is the subject of continuing debate, especially when reports of abuses surface. UI is amended every now and then to improve its effectiveness. A programme of work-sharing was incorporated into UI. Under this programme, instead of laying off workers, the employer can place them in a work-sharing programme without jeopardizing their UI benefits and eligibility. Although criticized by the unions, this programme has been well received by workers (Reid and Meltz 1984).

Workers' Compensation

This benefit is provided by a Workers' Compensation Act that exists in each province and territory of Canada. Essentially, the programme covers employee injury, disability, or death caused by a work-related accident. The programme is administered by the Workers' Compensation Commission of each province and territory, and funding is through a premium collected from the employer. The rate of premium depends upon the risk factor associated with the industry. Law and accounting firms, considered to be non-hazardous workplaces, will pay a much lower premium compared with companies in the high-risk mining industry. The premium is levied on the total annual payroll, and pooled into a fund of the industry group, which is then utilized to settle claims from employees in that industry group.

This is essentially a no-fault insurance, because employee claims are settled by the Workers' Compensation Commission on the basis of an established schedule of the injury and its corresponding compensation. The liability of the employer or of the employees is not considered. However, there is now a trend to assess premiums on the basis of a company's safety record. Companies with a good safety record will be assessed a relatively lower premium. The objective here is to encourage companies to improve or maintain safe working conditions in the workplace.

Canada/Quebec Pension Plan

Introduced on January 1, 1966, the Canada Pension Plan and the Quebec Pension Plan have essentially the same features, and are portable across Canada. Both plans are administered by the government and funded entirely by a payroll tax on a portion of the total employee earnings stipulated in the regulations. This tax is then shared equally between the employer and the employee. Self-employed individuals pay the entire payroll tax. The contributions are compulsory for all employees and self-employed individuals between the ages of 18 and 65.

The plans cover retirement benefits at age 65, which amount to 25 per cent of the earnings in the previous three years. An individual whose disability prevents him/her from earning an income is entitled to a disability pension for the duration of the disability. When the individual reaches age 65, the disability pension is replaced by the retirement pension. Other benefits included in the plans are a death benefit and a benefit to the surviving spouse (of eligible age) and dependent children.

Contributions to the plans are tax deductible, and pension benefits are treated as taxable income.

Private Pension Plans

Some companies have established private pension plans to provide their employees with additional retirement benefits. These plans are tailored to suit the specific needs of the organization. The variations in plans are largely in respect of the amount of employer and employee contributions that are necessary in order to obtain the desired level of pension benefits. With regard to the contributions, an important consideration is whether the plan should be contributory or non-contributory. In a contributory plan, the employees contribute to the pension fund; in a non-contributory plan, the pension fund is financed solely by the employer. One advantage of a contributory plan is that employee contributions increase the pool of funds and a correspondingly lower level of financing is required from the company. The other advantage is that employee contributions lead to greater employee interest in the plan. The major disadvantage is that the employer does not have complete freedom and autonomy in the management of the pension fund.

In most plans, the pension income at retirement is determined by two factors: (1) the percentage for each year of service, and (2) the average earnings of the years before retirement — usually the best five years. For example, the basic pension calculation formula for the plan of Quebec Civil Service employees is as follows (CARRA 1988):

2%	×	Number of years service (max. 35)	×	Average pensionable salary for 5 best-paid years	=	Basic annual pension

In pension plans where the pension benefit is predetermined, the amount of employee contribution to the pension fund is generally fixed. But the amount of the employer's contribution depends upon the actuarial assessment of the amount needed to meet the objective of the plan, that is, the annual pension benefits that must be paid as they become due. The fixed, predetermined benefit imposes upon the employer the obligation of generating the necessary funds to pay the pension benefits.

In other plans, both employer and employee make fixed contributions to the pension fund, and this fund is invested. In these plans, the employee's pension benefit is not predetermined but depends entirely upon how well the fund's investments have performed. For the organization, a fixed contribution clearly defines its cost commitment. For the employee, there is considerable uncertainty with regard to the benefit that will be received.

In designing the pension plan, some of the other decisions relate to eligibility conditions and the date when pension benefits become due. In eligibility conditions, the issue is whether the employee is eligible to join to plan when he/she starts work or on the satisfactory completion of the probationary period. The pension benefit ordinarily commences at the "normal" retirement age stipulated in the plan. Most pension plans allow early retirement, and therefore the early drawing of pension benefits, but most do so with a penalty that reduces the pension, usually at a rate of .5 per cent per month of the period between the date of the early retirement and the normal retirement date.

The plan may also allow employees to retire at a date later than the normal retirement date. In such a case, the employee's pension benefits begin as soon as he/she reaches the normal retirement age, and the employee ceases to contribute to the pension fund from this date. Alternatively, the employee does not draw pension benefits on reaching the normal retirement age, and continues to contribute to the pension fund. The plan then allows the employee to draw a higher pension benefit when he/she actually retires. The options allowed by the plan for late retirement will depend on the organization's policy on this issue, that is, whether it wishes to encourage employees to stay beyond the normal retirement.

Another critical issue in pension plans is the employee's *vesting* rights. These are the rights of an employee to the contribution that the employer has made to the pension fund on his/her behalf. The vesting rights determine when and under what circumstances an employee has the right to benefit from the employer's contributions. This issue assumes importance in the event the employee leaves the company before retirement. In such an event, the employee has full rights to the contributions he/she has made to the pension fund. However, the rights to the employer's contributions depend upon the vesting provisions of the plan. The vesting provisions are often an effective leverage for retaining an employee. The laws of most provinces confer vesting rights when the employee meets two conditions: he or she is 45 years old and has completed 10 years of service with that employer.

There is an increasing interest in the issue of portability, which is the right to carry to the pension fund of a new employer the contributions accumulated in the pension fund of a previous employer. For example, the McGill University Pension Plan has reciprocal transfer agreements with several universities and government plans in Quebec and across Canada. Portability privileges eventually result in a higher pension benefit.

The contributions to a pension fund are tax deductible up to certain maximum limits, and the pension benefit is considered as taxable income.

Group Insurance Programmes

Many organizations find group insurance to be a relatively economic way of offering employees the benefit of income protection. Lower admimistrative costs to the insurance carrier, combined with tax advantages for the employer, make these programmes quite attractive. In addition to the cost savings, the pooling of risks inherent in group insurance programmes allows uninsurable employees to be covered. It also allows the coverage of employees in high-risk occupations. Premium rates for individual insurance policies for these employees would be prohibitive. Group insurance programmes offer income protection in the event of disability or death. Under the group disability insurance plan, employees are protected against income disruption resulting from long-term disability that is not attributable to their occupation. Separate coverage for non-occupational disability is necessary for two reasons. First, the Workers' Compensation programme discussed earlier covers only work-related disability. Second, non-occupational disability coverage is a useful supplement for the low disability pension benefit received under the CPP/QPP. The amount of the disability benefit depends upon the policy negotiated with the insurers and can vary from 66 2/3 per cent to 80 per cent of the employee's salary. The benefits begin after a waiting period ranging from 120 to 180 days, and end when the employee returns to work or reaches retirement age.

Group life insurance serves to continue income to the employee's survivors in the event of death. It is usually a term life insurance contract, which, unlike a whole life or cash value contract, requires the insurer to pay the insurance benefit (i.e., the amount insured) only in the event of death. Since term life insurance does not include an investment component, the premiums are considerably lower than for whole life or similar life insurance policies. Group life insurance policies may include a survivors' benefit plan. Under such a plan, the beneficiary who receives a lump-sum payment on the death of the employee may opt to convert this into a continuing monthly income to provide for the employee's survivors. Some benefit packages also include a "dependents' life insurance." Under this plan, the amount insured is payable, on the death of the insured dependent, to the employee, the employee's spouse, or the dependent's legal heirs.

Group life and disability insurance programmes are generally sold by insurance companies as a package that includes health insurance. The health insurance component, as described later, covers prescription drugs, private hospital rooms, ambulance services, dental care, and so forth. Most group life and disability insurance plans are contributory, that is, the employee pays some or all of the premiums.

The major design issue in group insurance programmes is whether employees should contribute (contributory plan), or whether these plans should be financed entirely by the employer. When employees contribute to the plan, they add resources that enable the plan to provide a much higher level of benefits. The process involved in a contributory plan results in better employee appreciation of the costs. The process also makes employees more willing to cooperate in the cost control of the plan. In a non-contributory plan, the employer has greater control over the administration of the plan, an advantage of dubious value.

In most cases, the group insurance programme is for the employees of a single organization. However, several employers in an industry can pool together to buy a group insurance policy, as is the case in the construction and small retail sectors. In the construction industry, workers change employers as projects come to an end; a small retailer just does not have the numbers to profit from a group insurance policy (McPherson and Wallace 1985).

REIMBURSED TIME OFF

Time off includes all the work breaks the employee is permitted, such as lunch and coffee/tea/smoke breaks, annual vacations, national/religious holidays, personal holidays, sick leave, maternity/paternity and adoption leave, jury duty. Some of these benefits are mandated by law. A good reference source for these is Labour Canada's annual publication *Labour Standards in Canada* (Labour Canada 1986). Other benefits are either negotiated with the union or provided at the discretion of the employer.

Most Canadian jurisdictions stipulate a minimum paid annual vacation of two weeks. However, many organizations offer more than the minimum. The vacations entitlement is related to years of service. Generally, it is four weeks for 9 to 12 years of service, and five weeks for 15 to 20 years of service. Some collective agreements provide for four weeks for 6 to 9 years. In some organizations, employees with more than 25 years of service receive six to seven weeks of paid vacation. Annual vacations are intended to satisfy the employee's need for a prolonged period of rest and recreation, which, it is hoped, will enable the employee to continue at the expected performance level.

The number of paid national/religious holidays that are legally required varies in the different jurisdictions. The common holidays observed in most provinces include New Year's Day, Good Friday, Victoria Day, Canada Day, Labour Day, Thanksgiving Day, Christmas Day, and Boxing Day. Additional holidays may be observed in each province, for example, Saint-Jean-Baptiste Day in Quebec. Employees who are required to work on these days are entitled to premium pay varying from 2 to 2 1/2 times the regular pay.

Paid "personal days" is another form of reimbursed time off in many organizations. The entitlement varies from 2 to 5 days, and is intended to give employees an opportunity to meet personal, family, and social obligations. In some organizations, flex time arrangements become a useful alternative for meeting some of these obligations.

Most organizations offer paid sick leave programmes, but the entitlements and conditions differ considerably. Some allow up to 10 days of sick leave a year, which can neither be accumulated nor cashed if unused. To prevent the abuse of this benefit, some organizations require a medical certificate to support the request for this leave. As was discussed in Chapter 7, for this benefit programme to be effectively administered, the first day of absence should not be paid and the accumulation of unused sick leave should be permitted. Often organizations buy insurance policies to cover the costs of this benefit.

Maternity leave is now a legal entitlement in almost all Canadian jurisdictions. Paternity leave, on the other hand, is a legal entitlement only in the federal jurisdiction and in some provinces. Some of the larger organizations provide paternity and adoption leave. During these types of leave the employee retains all rights and benefits, including the accrual of seniority rights.

It is legally obligatory for organizations to provide time off for employees who are called to perform jury duty. Many organizations pay for such leave of absence. Sabbaticals or educational leaves for managers are becoming increasingly popular in many organizations. The Polaroid Corporation has an innovative time-off programme called the "rehearsal retirement" programme (McGrath 1988). Any employee can take advantage of this programme, but it is mostly used by those near retirement. Under this programme, an employee can take time off for three months to explore such options as hobbies, starting his/her own business, volunteer work, and relocating. At the end of the three months or even before that the employee can return to his/her job. Alternatively, if the employee has discovered a viable option, then he/she is free to retire immediately to work on this new interest. Rehearsal retirement not only provides retirement options but also counselling and the opportunity to make the transition into retirement smooth and graceful.

Employee Services and Perquisites

There is an infinite variety of employee services and perquisites. Some of the more common employee services and perquisites are health insurance plans, educational assistance, subsidized cafeterias, recreational facilities and programmes, parking privileges, discounts on company products, and credit unions.

Private health insurance plans are intended to supplement government funded medicare benefits, that is, to provide for costs not covered by government plans. Typically, these health insurance plans cover supplementary hospital and medical costs, health costs outside Canada, prescription drugs, private duty nursing and emergency ambulance services, vision and hearing care, and dental care. In most organizations, these plans are contributory, although there are wide variations in the sharing of the premiums between the organization and the employees. Cost control is maintained through deductibles, co-insurance, and benefit maximum. The higher the deductible, the lower the cost of the premiums. For a family plan, such a deductible is about $25 per year; that is, the employee bears the first $25 of the claims he/she has submitted in a year. In co-insurance, the employee is reimbursed only about 80 per cent of the claim; the non-reimbursed amount is borne by the employee. The third cost-control mechanism, benefit maximum, stipulates that the total claims paid in a year shall not be above a specified maximum.

The components of the educational assistance programme vary in different organizations. Some organizations reimburse tuition fees and the cost of course materials. Others also provide time off and tuition loans for employees who pursue a programme of study. Sometimes the assistance is limited to job-related study programmes and includes paid time off. In some organizations, educational assistance is also extended to employees' dependents.

Subsidized cafeterias are quite common in large organizations. So are recreational facilities and programmes, including hockey, bowling, and softball teams. Often the recreational programme takes the form of subsidized memberships in fitness clubs. Discounts on company products are popular in organizations that manufacture or market consumer goods and services. For example, retail store employees can buy products at special discounts; similarly, financial institutions provide their employees with mortgage loans at reduced interest rates. Large organizations also provide facilities for employee credit unions. The convenient feature of this service is the payroll deduction, which is also used for savings and stock purchase plans.

Managers and executives have their own set of perquisites or "perks," which include a company car, club memberships, the payment of a spouse's travel expenses when the spouse accompanies the employee on company business, tickets to the theatre and related cultural events.

Some emerging employee services and benefits are employee assistance programmes (EAPs), day care, and flex time. Although the focus of EAPs is primarily on alcohol and drug rehabilitation, EAPs now also include employee counselling on stress, burn-out, and related conditions.

With the increasing participation of women in the workforce, day-care services are now a much-sought-after benefit. Some organizations provide day-care facilities at the workplace. These are run either by the company itself or by an independent organization. On-site day-care facilities give user-employees much peace of mind. They have also proved to be beneficial to the employer in terms of reduced absenteeism and turnover, and as a competitive advantage in hiring (Paull 1986; *Financial Post*, 18 October 1986). In other organizations, this benefit takes the form of an allowance to help employees defray their day-care costs.

Flex time gives employees the freedom to determine the time when they will begin and end the work day, provided they put in the required total hours of the work day. It is understood that the freedom implicit in this programme is not exercised in a manner that jeopardizes the efficient and effective fulfilment of job objectives. Hence, the flex-time system stipulates a period of "core hours" during which all employees should be present. Outside of the core hours, employees can schedule their own starting and quitting times. In some companies, employees maintain the same schedule for a week or more. In other companies, a greater variation is allowed.

Flex time promotes favourable employee attitudes (job satisfaction, organizational commitment). Employees now have larger blocks of time available for leisure or for personal, family, and social obligations, and the absenteeism that was previously necessary to meet these personal needs is eliminated. Flex time also gives employees greater control over their jobs. Often the logistics of flex-time scheduling require that employees learn the other jobs in the work unit to ensure its uninterrupted operation. As a result, flex time can lead to job enrichment. The effects of flex time on performance range from no change to positive effects (Pierce et al. 1989). The establishment of narrow core hours would contribute to the success of flex time, but the feasibility of narrow core hours depends upon the processes and the operations of the work unit. The flex-time system cannot succeed without employee involvement in its design and implementation. The effect of flex time is, to some extent, a move towards employee self-management. Therefore, its success will also depend upon the cooperation and support of middle management.

Flex time is not suitable for work units in which the work process or technology creates interdependent jobs. Some of the other disadvantages of flex time are increased administration costs and the administrative difficulties that arise when the flex-time schedule conflicts with legislation relating to overtime pay and rest periods.

THE FLEXIBLE BENEFITS APPROACH

Traditionally, organizations have offered their employees a standardized benefits program. This approach is still used in most organizations. However, several factors are making organizations question the wisdom of this approach. There are questions about whether the benefits programme addresses the needs and preferences of the employees. For example, older employees have greater preferences for pensions, and employees with children prefer health insurance plans. Moreover, a standardized benefits programme often duplicates the coverage for employees whose spouses have similar coverage with their employers. If employees do not value the programme, the organization is not effectively deploying the enormous resources it invests in the standardized benefits programme. For these reasons the flexible benefit or the cafeteria-style approach is gaining popularity.

Under a flexible benefits programme, the organization decides on a "core" coverage, which includes the absolute minimum for life insurance, medical, disability, pensions, vacations, and so forth. These are compulsory for all employees. In addition, the organization offers a "flexible dollar allowance," which employees can utilize to acquire more life insurance or medical or disability or other benefits according to their needs and preferences. By trading in other benefits, employees can increase the flexible dollar allowance. For example, employees of Noranda Inc. can trade their vacation time for additional life insurance or long-term disability benefits. Employees of Canadian General Tower have similar flexibility (Gibb-Clark 1991). Employees can even cash the unused portion of the flexible dollar allowance.

There are concerns that employees might trade away such critical benefits as life insurance and leave their families unprotected. Likewise, they might cash all their vacation time and be exposed to the risk of burn-out for lack of time off. The compulsory core coverage of the flexible benefits approach can and should be designed to provide the needed safeguards. Noranda Inc. places restrictions on the trade of vacation time, making a minimum of vacation time obligatory for all employees; this minimum depends upon the employee's vacation entitlement.

The flexible benefits approach has the advantage of meeting individual needs and preferences. It also gives employees a better understanding and appreciation of the benefits, and this understanding leads to a more effective utilization of the programme. Increased autonomy in the choice of benefits results in a more positive attitude towards the organization, and this positive attitude can influence retention behaviour. The major disadvantages relate to costs. First, the costs of benefits generally tend to be about 5 per cent higher than in the traditional approach (*The Globe and Mail*, 24 June 1991). Second, there are the costs of installing and implementing the system. Finally, there is the potential that inequity may arise when the increased costs of one benefit plan require that more resources be allocated to it than to the other plans. On balance, however, the advantages outweigh the disadvantages.

GUIDELINES IN DESIGNING THE BENEFITS PROGRAMME

The description of benefits programmes shows that there are not only many types of benefits, but there are also several variations in each type. However, all benefits have one feature in common. They are elements or components of the organization's compensation system. Therefore, the model of effective reward management (Figure 1.2) provides a useful framework for developing guidelines to design the benefits programme. As was discussed in Chapter 2, the organization's external and internal environments, which influence the development of the total compensation system, will also influence the design of the benefits programme. Some of the specific design determinants are the business strategies of the organization and its capacity to pay, the internal work culture of the organization, the legal requirements in a benefits programme, and the philosophy and objectives of the compensation system.

More critical to an effective design, however, is ensuring that the programme meets the test of saliency, valence, and contingency. As was seen in Chapter 4, a compensation item will be effective in motivating the desired work behaviour when employees perceive it to be salient, valued, and contingent upon the desired behaviour.

Employees will perceive benefits to be salient when these benefits are properly communicated. Benefits can be communicated through booklets, meetings, and personalized statements. Booklets that summarize the key features and provide details in a readable format are the most effective means of communicating the benefits programme. Employees retain these as a reference source for consulation when needed. Meetings help to further clarify the information in the booklets and to answer questions that may arise. Personalized benefit statements, which highlight the benefits that have accrued to the employee as well as projected future benefits, are effective in increasing the saliency of the benefits and, as a result, can serve to influence retention behaviour. Some organizations use audio-visual presentations, which are also informative, but these can be expensive. The key to increasing saliency is to present the information so that it is easy to understand, and to include information on the content, the mechanics, and the change procedures of the benefits plans. If these things are done, the employee is not confronted with any surprises as he/she begins to take advantage of the benefit.

Benefits should be valued by employees. In this respect, the flexible benefits or cafeteria-style benefits programme is a much better approach than the traditional standardized benefits programme. The freedom of the employee to choose those benefits that meet his/her needs and preferences is a critical feature that increases the valence of the benefits. Employee participation in the design and implementation of the benefits programme will also help to increase saliency and valence. The valence of a compensation item is also determined by employee perceptions of internal and external equity. Employee involvement from the very inception of the design process, including the benefits survey process, will contribute to feelings of the fairness and equity of the programme.

The benefits programme should be contingent on the desired work behaviour. This consideration should be reflected in the design of the programme. Chapter 7, in discussing absenteeism, illustrated how a sick leave benefits programme could be dysfunctional in producing unintended, undesirable behaviours. For many benefits, the primary contingent work behaviour is that of retention. Exit interviews can be useful in assessing the effectiveness of the benefits programme — or parts of it — in influencing retention behaviour. The action programme discussed in the next chapter can be used to identify those items of the benefits programme that are deficient in this respect; the action programme also proposes specific measures for improving the effectiveness of such items.

SUMMARY

This chapter explored the various benefits programmes offered by organizations. The discussion focused on three major categories: income protection programmes, reimbursed time off, and employee services and perquisites. The typical programmes in each category were discussed in terms of objective, eligibility conditions, benefit provisions, financing arrangements, and advantages and disadvantages. Some of these programmes are mandated by law, and others are either negotiated between union and management or provided at the discretion of the employer. The discussion of flexible benefits or cafeteria-style benefits showed that such a benefits programme has several advantages over the standardized benefits programme currently offered by most organizations. In conclusion, it was noted that a benefit can be said to be effectively designed only when it is perceived by employees to be salient, valent, and contingent on the desired work behaviour.

KEY TERMS

employee benefits programme
employee services and perquisites
flexible benefits programme
income protection programme
reimbursed time off
standardized benefits programme

REVIEW AND DISCUSSION QUESTIONS

1. Refer to the benefit items in the income protection programmes, reimbursed time off, and employee services and perquisites categories. Which compensation objective(s) would be served by each benefit item? Why?
2. Distinguish between the traditional standardized benefits programme and the emerging flexible benefits approach. What are the factors that weigh in favour of the flexible benefits approach?

3. What are the key design and administration issues in the following benefits programmes?

   - Pension plan
   - Group insurance (life and disability) plan
   - Dental insurance plan

4. Although there are a variety of employee benefits, yet each benefit should meet certain essential criteria if it is to be effective. What are the criteria? Why are they essential?

EXERCISE: EVALUATING A BENEFITS PROGRAMME

Objective

To use the framework of the model of effective reward management to evaluate a benefits programme.

Procedure

1. Prior to this exercise, participants are asked to collect information on employee benefits programmes from organizations of their choice. It is desirable that this information include at least one item from each of the three major categories: income protection programmes, reimbursed time off, employee services and perquisites.
2. Divide the class into groups of three to four participants.
3. Each group reviews the employee benefits programmes collected by its members. The review should
   a) evaluate the likely effectiveness of each programme in the light of the guidelines in designing the benefits programme discussed in the chapter; and
   b) explore what aspects of the programmes they might design and/or implement differently, and the reasons for these changes.
4. Each group then shares its findings with the class. The class discussion that follows at this stage should focus on the reasons for the similarities and differences between employee benefits programmes in different organizations.

PART IV
MANAGING THE COMPENSATION SYSTEM

CHAPTER 14

MANAGING THE COMPENSATION SYSTEM

CHAPTER SYNOPSIS

This chapter discusses the administrative process of the salary budget, which has traditionally been used to manage the compensation system, along with techniques for ensuring its internal and external equity. The chapter also focuses on two emerging issues in compensation management: (1) person-based pay, and (2) evaluating the effectiveness of compensation systems. The chapter explores person-based pay through the practices of *multi-skilling* and *knowledge-based pay*. To evaluate the effectiveness of the compensation system, the chapter discusses an *action programme* that identifies ineffective reward items and proposes strategies for improving their effectiveness.

LEARNING OBJECTIVES

- To understand the meaning of *compa-ratio*, and to discuss the usefulness of the compa-ratio in evaluating the impact of salary decisions.
- To describe the *top-down* and *bottom-up* approaches to developing a salary budget.
- To define *person-based pay* and to distinguish it from *job-based pay*.
- To understand how multi-skilling and knowledge-based pay implement the basic concept of person-based pay.
- To discuss the advantages and disadvantages of person-based pay and to identify the conditions that favour it.
- To understand the rationale underlying the action programme for evaluating the effectiveness of the compensation system.
- To describe the procedural steps of the action programme and to understand the purpose of each step.

- To understand the analytical procedures used in the action programme.
- To develop competence in analysing the results of the diagnostic procedure of the action programme and in recommending the appropriate corrective actions envisaged in the programme.

INTRODUCTION

In the past, the approach to managing the compensation system consisted of activities in two areas: (1) the proper implementation of compensation techniques designed to achieve the internal and external equity of the compensation system; (2) the control of the compensation system through the administrative process of the salary budget. The activities related to the first area have already been covered in detail in the previous chapters. The activities related to the second area, the salary budget, are discussed in this chapter.

Both of these areas are important, but an exclusive focus on these areas in the past has resulted in the neglect of two vital issues in the compensation management process. The first issue relates to the evaluation of the compensation system to determine whether the system is achieving its objectives. Without a systematic and rational evaluation programme, no valid evidence is available that an existing compensation system is effective. The second issue relates to person-based pay, also known as multi-skilling or knowledge-based pay. A preoccupation with traditional compensation techniques such as the job-based job evaluation system has prevented compensation specialists from being open to this strategic compensation issue. Because the two emerging issues — evaluating the effectiveness of the compensation system and person-based pay — are critical to the strategic management of the compensation system, they are the focus of this chapter. The chapter begins with a discussion of two approaches to developing a salary budget, and then explores the issue of person-based pay. Finally, the chapter discusses the issue of evaluating compensation systems and presents an action programme for evaluating the effectiveness of the compensation system. The diagnostic procedure inherent in the programme not only identifies ineffective reward items but also proposes specific recommendations for improving their effectiveness.

THE SALARY BUDGET PROCESS

The previous chapter discussed the process of developing the pay structure, and also the pay adjustments that are necessary when employees' salaries fall outside their respective pay grades. This chapter now considers the process of developing a salary budget for an organization. The major compensation decision in the budget relates to the overall salary increase the organization can afford. In other words, the budget is the organization's salary level policy statement for the budget year.

Before the approaches to developing a salary budget are considered, it is helpful to dwell briefly on the concept of the compa-ratio, a useful device for providing meaningful information on the impact of salary decisions. This information enables the compensation specialist to assess salary decisions relating to an individual employee as well as to groups of employees. The compa-ratio is also used to develop salary budgets. Essentially, the compa-ratio relates the item to be assessed — individual or group salaries — to the midpoint of the pay grade.

When the compa-ratio is used to assess decisions on the salary of the individual employee, the formula is

$$\text{Compa-ratio} = \frac{\text{Salary of the employee}}{\text{Midpoint of the pay grade}}$$

Compa-ratios above or below 1 indicate that the individual's salary is above or below the midpoint of the pay grade. The significance of the compa-ratio depends upon the meaning assigned to the midpoint. The pay grade midpoint can be viewed as an average benchmark for salary decision criteria such as performance, tenure, and experience. The manager can assess whether the individual's salary compa-ratio reflects the individual's job performance, tenure, or experience, and then can initiate measures to address the inequities.

The compa-ratio can similarly be used to assess salary decisions on a group of employees in the same pay grade. The formula for this purpose will be

$$\text{Compa-ratio} = \frac{\text{Average salaries paid}}{\text{Midpoint of the pay grade}}$$

In addition, the compa-ratio will alert the manager to movement within and across pay grades. For example, a compa-ratio considerably lower than 1 indicates relatively high turnover or new employees. A compa-ratio considerably higher than 1 indicates that a large number of employees are bunched at the top of the pay grade and suggests that not much movement is occurring across pay grades.

There are two approaches to developing the salary budget, the top-down and the bottom-up.

The Top-Down Approach

The top-down approach to salary budgeting is based on the compa-ratio. The organization decides, for the budget year, a specific compa-ratio of its total salaries paid to the total midpoints of the pay grades. From this targeted compa-ratio, the salary budget is derived.

In the top-down approach, top management decides on the salary budget for the entire organization. The budget forecast is based on four factors: (1) the organization's pay structure policy relative to the market; (2) the estimated change in the market rates expected in the budget year; (3) the organization's employee pay policy for the budget year; (4) the organization's *experience factor* relative to salary budget forecasts. Chapter 12 discussed the major pay structure policies, namely, to meet, lead, or lag the market. The following example illustrates how these factors contribute to the development of the salary budget.

Example

The Montreal Manufacturing Company (MMC) has been following the lead/lag pay structure policy relative to the market. It seeks to lead the market in the first six months of the year, and lag the market in the second six months. According to this policy, the pay structure will match the market about the middle of the year, and then lag the market until the end of the year. The other relevant data for this illustration are

- The market is expected to increase by 9 per cent.
- MMC's employee pay policy for the budget year is to meet the market at the end of the year.
- The total of the midpoints of the pay grades of MMC employees at the start of the budget year is $102,550.
- The organization's experience factor is the ratio of the budgeted or targeted compa-ratio and the actual compa-ratio at year end. The new hires, promotions, separations (voluntary and involuntary), retirements, and so forth, account for the difference between the budgeted and the actual compa-ratios. The experience factor of 102 per cent for the prebudget year is considered to be typical and therefore suitable for incorporation in the budget year salary forecast.

The MMC salary budget process for the budget year incorporates these data in the following three steps:

Step 1

Establish MMC's target compa-ratio for the budget year.

This step considers MMC's pay structure policy relative to the market, the increase in the market rate for the budget year, and MMC's employee pay policy for the budget year. The midpoints of the pay structure approximate the market. But, when the market rate is projected to increase by 9 per cent, MMC's midpoints, under its lead/lag policy, will lag by 4.5 per cent at the end of the year, with the result that employees' pay will not meet the market, as is desired by the employee pay policy for the budget year. However, if the compa-ratio is set at 104.5 per cent, the actual salaries of employees will increase by 4.5 per cent, thus fulfilling MMC's employee pay objective of meeting the market. Hence, MMC's target compa-ratio for the budget year will be 104.5 per cent.

Step 2

Moderate the target compa-ratio by the experience factor.

The target compa-ratio is multiplied by the experience factor to obtain the revised target compa-ratio:

$$104.5\% \times 102\% = 106.6\%$$

Step 3

Compute MMC's salary budget for the budget year.

The salary budget is derived from the compa-ratio:

$$\text{Compa-ratio} = \frac{\text{Total budgeted salaries}}{\text{Total midpoints of the pay grades}}$$

$$106.6\% = \frac{x}{\$102{,}550}$$

Step 3

Solving for x gives the salary budget of $109,318.30.

The Bottom-Up Approach

In the bottom-up approach, the salary budgeting process builds on the work unit's manpower plan, which is based on the projected business activities and the estimated human resource flows — new hires, promotions, and separations (voluntary and involuntary) — of the unit. The manager develops salary projections for each employee on the basis of his/her anticipated decisions relative to issues that require salary changes. Some of these issues are cost-of-living adjustment, merit increase, seniority increase, promotion, and adjustments for temporary transfers. In making these adjustments, the manager is guided by the organization's policies. For example: (*a*) the starting salaries of new hires should be 5 per cent below the minimum of the pay grade, and adjusted upward to the minimum on successful completion of the probationary period; (*b*) all salary increases resulting from promotion to a job in a higher pay grade should be capped at $5,000. Following these adjustments, the revised salaries of all the employees are added up, and become the projected salary budget of the work unit. The projected salary budgets of all the work units are consolidated to form the salary budget of the organization.

EMERGING ISSUES: PERSON-BASED PAY

Chapter 10 discussed the job-content-based job evaluation system used traditionally by organizations in designing the compensation system. The effectiveness of this approach is being questioned. Foremost among its critics is Lawler (1986), who cites several reasons why the job-content-based job evaluation system has outlived its usefulness. Its focus on right job descriptions and responsibility levels that reflect hierarchical relationships reinforces traditional bureaucratic management. The job-content-based job evaluation system measures the worth of employees in terms of their jobs — what they do in terms of the demands of the job rather than what they can do in terms of skills repertoire. Since the job value, and eventually the employee's pay, is largely based on the content of the job description, employees often "dress up" their job description to increase the value of their job. Often, too, the job evaluation system becomes an end in itself, instead of a means of supporting the organization's business objectives and strategies. Today's turbulent business environment demands a compensation system that motivates people to learn, grow and develop; that rewards them as they acquire more skills and become more flexible; and that promotes employee involvement and commitment.

The alternative approach to compensation system design, and one of the emerging compensation issues, is person-based pay (Lawler 1971, 1981; Lawler and Ledford 1985; Tosi and Tosi 1986). The effectiveness of this approach relative to job-based pay cannot be definitively established because of a lack of empirical data. However, organizations that emphasize high employee involvement have used person-based pay with considerable success (Lawler 1986; Walton 1977; Halpern 1984). This section explores person-based pay in terms of its definition, the procedures it uses, its advantages and disadvantages, and situations in which it is particularly suitable.

MULTI-SKILLING

In the person-based pay approach employees' pay is determined by the skills or knowledge they possess even though they may not use all the skills and knowledge on the job. Job content does not determine the employees' pay. Person-based pay is also referred to as multi-skilling, or as a knowledge-based pay (KNP) system. When the person-based pay approach is adopted, the organization first identifies the basic skills and knowledge that are needed for the tasks to be performed. It then develops a pay scheme that stipulates the pay rate for additional skills or knowledge that are acquired.

Generally, multi-skilling is used for manufacturing or production jobs. It is designed to encourage workers to acquire the skills needed for all the related jobs in an integrated production process. The person-based pay system of the Shell Canada Chemical Company plant in Sarnia, Ontario, provides a good illustration of multi-skilling.

On entry to the Sarnia plant, the employee's salary is $1,124 (see Table 14.1). After satisfactory completion of the basic training, as determined by appropriate tests and measures, the employee receives a raise. The employee can earn future raises by progressively acquiring proficiency in the job knowledge clusters and competency in the four modules of the specialty skill that is established for that raise. Thus, the employee with

Table 14.1
Multi-Skilling

PROGRESSION PROGRAM		
Salary $/Month**	**Process Operations**	**Speciality Skill**
	Total	Total
S1 698	10 JKCs*	40 Modules
S1 643	1 JKC	4 Modules
S1 588	1 JKC	4 Modules
S1 536	1 JKC	4 Modules
S1 483	1 JKC	4 Modules
S1 429	1 JKC	4 Modules
S1 376	1 JKC	4 Modules
S1 322	1 JKC	4 Modules
S1 269	1 JKC	4 Modules
S1 215	1 JKC	4 Modules
S1 162	1 JKC	4 Modules
Entry — S1 124	Basic Training	

*JKC — Job Knowledge Cluster
**Basis 1978 wages

Source: Norman Halpern, "Sociotechnical Systems Design: The Shell Sarnia Experience." In J.B. Cunningham and T.H. White (eds.), *Quality of Working Life: Contemporary Cases* (Ottawa: Minister of Supply and Services, 1984), 48. Reproduced with the permission of the Minister of Supply and Services Canada.

the top salary of $1,698 will have demonstrated proficiency in the 10 job knowledge clusters, and competency in the 40 modules of such specialty skills as instrumentation, electrical, pipefitting, millwrighting, and so forth. The expected level of competency is not journey level, but just enough to cope successfully with the relatively less complex situations that frequently crop up. The more complex problems are attended to by the journey-level workers. An employee who has completed all or part of the job knowledge clusters and specialty skill modules would be in a job that does not use all the acquired competencies, but the salary rate of the employee would nevertheless be based on the acquired competencies.

Training and testing programmes are critical to a successful multi-skilling system. Supervisors and employees are generally involved in these programmes.

KNOWLEDGE-BASED PAY

Unlike a multi-skilling system, where skills are acquired in related jobs, a knowledge-based pay system rewards the acquisition of in-depth knowledge of a job or of knowledge greater in a job than is required. Its focus might also be increased specialization or expertise in the same job, rather than the acquisition of knowledge of other jobs. Jobs of research scientists illustrate well this focus on the acquisition of in-depth knowledge and expertise, because such acquisition generally increases the likelihood that individuals will become more innovative and productive in their work. Another illustration of knowledge-based pay is the system used by several public school boards for its teachers. The Montreal Catholic School Commission, the largest single school board in Canada, pays its teachers on the basis of *scolarité,* that is, the total number of years of schooling. For example, a teacher who holds a bachelor's degree will ordinarily be credited with 16 years of schooling, computed as follows: 11 years for high school, 2 years for CEGEP (the college-level program in Quebec), and 3 years for undergraduate studies. For every additional 30 university credits in a recognized certificate, diploma, or degree programme acquired by the teacher, he/she receives an additional year of schooling, which entitles him/her to a salary raise. However, there are no differences in the teaching job of teachers. It is quite common for multi-sections — say of Grade 9 Canadian history — to be taught by teachers whose years of schooling ranges from 15 years to 20 years.

The underlying rationale for multi-skilling and knowledge-based pay systems is that such systems increase employee productivity and satisfaction, and make employees more valuable to the organization. Specific advantages and disadvantages have been identified (Lawler and Ledford 1985; Tosi and Tosi 1986) for the person-based pay systems.

The advantages mainly relate to a flexible workforce that has a better understanding of the strategies and operations of the organization, and increased involvement and commitment. When the workforce is flexible, the production process does not experience the disruptions that might be caused by employee absenteeism. A flexible workforce is also better prepared to adapt to technological and production process changes. Because of multi-skilling, employees are better informed and more knowledgeable about their own tasks as well as of those of the work unit. They are also more involved in the problem-solving and decision-making activities of the work unit. A person-based pay system gives employees an opportunity to get an overview of the entire operation. Jobs in such a system tend to be relatively high on skill variety, task identity, task significance, autonomy, and feedback. Consequently, as discussed in Chapter 5, employees will experience the critical psychological states of meaning, responsibility, and knowledge of work results, which produce high internal work motivation. The resulting increased involvement and commitment will also make employees more alert to spot opportunities for innovation in their work unit.

The disadvantages of the person-based pay are increased labour and training costs, reduced productivity during the learning periods, and the negative effects of unfulfilled expectations. Increased labour and training costs are to a considerable extent offset by increased productivity, a reduced level of staffing, and the substantial benefits that accrue from a flexible, motivated, and committed workforce. The issue of reduced productivity during the training period has several aspects. First, production will be affected while the employee is away on training. Second, since the system rewards the acquisition of skills, some employees acquire additional skills without giving themselves the time to practise them and develop the high level of competence that can only come from practice. This issue, however, may be more a criticism of the implementation of the person-based pay system than of the system itself. Organizations can address this issue by requiring that employees not be permitted to acquire an additional skill unless they have spent a period of time on the job practising the previously acquired skill, and developing a certain level of competence in it.

The negative effects of unfulfilled expectations can be quite serious and need to be properly managed. One of these effects is the *topping out* effect (Lawler 1981). The topping out effect is produced when employees have acquired all the possible skills and are now earning the top pay. The system does not provide an opportunity for earning further increases in salary. For example, when a Shell Canada Chemical Company employee in Sarnia becomes proficient in the 10 job knowledge clusters and the 40 specialty skill modules, he/she will feel frustrated if there are no opportunities for further salary raises or career progression. Another negative effect occurs when changes in technology render certain skills obsolete.

Appropriate strategies to cope with these negative effects are a well-designed career-development plan and a gain-sharing plan. Employees also experience frustration when they do not have opportunities to use their skills; the skills may atrophy. To address this situation, the person-based pay system should develop a sound job rotation programme.

On balance, the advantages of a person-based pay system significantly outweigh the disadvantages. However, organizations will be able to reap the full benefits of a person-based pay system only when the beliefs and values of management are consistent with the underlying philosophy of the person-based pay system. The person-based pay system works best when management genuinely believes that its employees have high growth needs, and that they seek and can handle challenge, autonomy, and responsibility. Management recognizes that in a state of frequent and turbulent changes, the organization can respond effectively to new opportunities and challenges only when its employees are afforded opportunities for growth and development. Hence, the job design will include enriched jobs and autonomous work teams. The person-based pay system is the appropriate reward strategy for organizations with such a participative work culture.

EMERGING ISSUES: EVALUATING THE EFFECTIVENESS OF THE COMPENSATION SYSTEM

Because the mere design and implementation of a compensation system is an incomplete process without a programme for evaluating its effectiveness, this section discusses the issue of evaluating the effectiveness of the compensation system.

"When you pay your employees, do you get a fair return for your investment?" "How do you know?" If these questions are posed of today's managers, the chances are that they will consider them to be irrelevant or regard them as mysteries too obscure to resolve. Yet, these managers routinely subject their organization's capital and operating costs to an array of rigorous analyses to determine whether the target rates of return are being obtained. They will also ensure that the variances are studied and investigated, and an appropriate plan of action is initiated for achieving the desired goals.

Logically, the compensation package should be subjected to the same searching cost-benefit analysis. In absolute dollars, the compensation package involves a considerable cash outflow. In relative terms, too, the cash outflow is significant — often more than 50 per cent of the total costs of the organization and, in many service industries and public-sector organizations, as high as 80 per cent. Why then do managers treat compensation costs differently? The answer to this question can be traced to managers' understanding of how pay and benefits affect work motivation.

There was a time when business and industry designed compensation programmes to pay only for what was produced. Such programmes — pioneered by Frederick Taylor, the father of scientific management — were widespread from around the turn of the century until World War II. As was discussed in Chapter 3, these programmes were based on the belief that money was a prime motivator of people's work efforts. In such a context, managers could properly be expected to assess whether their compensation programmes did, in fact, motivate employees to the extent and in the direction established by the organization.

However, after World War II, the belief that money was a prime motivator of performance was seriously challenged. By the 1960s, behavioural scientists with humanistic orientations, notably Herzberg and McGregor, began to argue that people do not work mainly for money but for ego-need gratification and self-fulfillment. Using these motivational assumptions, Herzberg's two-factor theory divided rewards into two categories, intrinsic and extrinsic. The theory claimed that intrinsic rewards (responsibility, autonomy, feelings of accomplishment) were the only real motivators of work behaviour. Extrinsic rewards (pay, benefits, working conditions) were consigned to a secondary role; these rewards were needed to prevent dissatisfaction with one's job, but they had no positive influence in motivating performance.

If pay and benefits do not motivate performance, then it is only logical for managers to shrug off these rewards as an expense — an expense that is necessary but is not specifically designed to influence and improve work behaviour. Hence, the management of these rewards, despite the outlay involved, does not become a major concern of managers. However, an examination (Chapter 3) of the intrinsic-extrinsic dichotomy in rewards management found that the theory is conceptually flawed, and that the empirical findings contradict its motivational assumptions. The theory also ignores the fact that a reward, intrinsic or extrinsic, will influence and improve work behaviour as long as it is valued by the recipient and received as a consequence of that behaviour.

This fact has been recognized by the expectancy theory model, which offers a better explanation of work behaviour and also provides the compensation specialist with a sound theoretical framework for designing the reward system and evaluating its effectiveness (Chapter 4). In this text, the discussion of the design of the compensation system has been consistently rooted in the constructs of the expectancy model. Whatever has been considered — the design of the base pay, merit pay, incentives and gain-sharing, benefits, or even the non-economic elements of the compensation system such as job design — the basic question pervading the design process has been this: Will the employee perceive the item as *salient, valued,* and *contingent on the desired behaviour*?

The constructs of expectancy theory provide the basis of a diagnostic procedure for evaluating the effectiveness of the compensation system. This diagnostic procedure can be used to evaluate each item of the compensation programme and to recommend design changes that will improve its effectiveness. Because this diagnostic procedure is inextricably linked to compensation system design, it is more appropriately designated an *action programme* for designing and administering the reward system, and for evaluating its effectiveness. Discussion of the action programme will first focus on its rationale and procedural steps, and then on its use, as illustrated in a study of the effectiveness of the reward system in a Canadian corporation.

AN ACTION PROGRAMME

Rationale

The rationale underlying the action programme is as follows:

1. In designing its compensation programme, the organization intends that each component of the programme will elicit a specific set of behaviours from its employees to further the overall goals of the organization.
2. The intended set of behaviours will be realized only to the extent that each component of the programme is perceived by the employee as salient, valuable, and contingent on producing the intended set of behaviours.

The critical test of the effectiveness of the compensation programme is a comparison of the intended set of behaviours for each component of the programme with employee perceptions of that component in terms of valence, contingency, and saliency.

Procedural Steps

The procedural steps of the action programme are presented schematically in Figure 14.1.

Step 1

Develop a list of all the rewards the organization offers its employees. The list should include rewards that involve cash payments and benefits (the economic compensation items) and those that do not involve any payments, such as autonomy and challenging assignments (the non-economic compensation items).

Step 2

Decide on the purpose of *each* reward that is listed. The purpose should

Figure 14.1
Managerial Action Programme for Assessing and Designing a Reward System

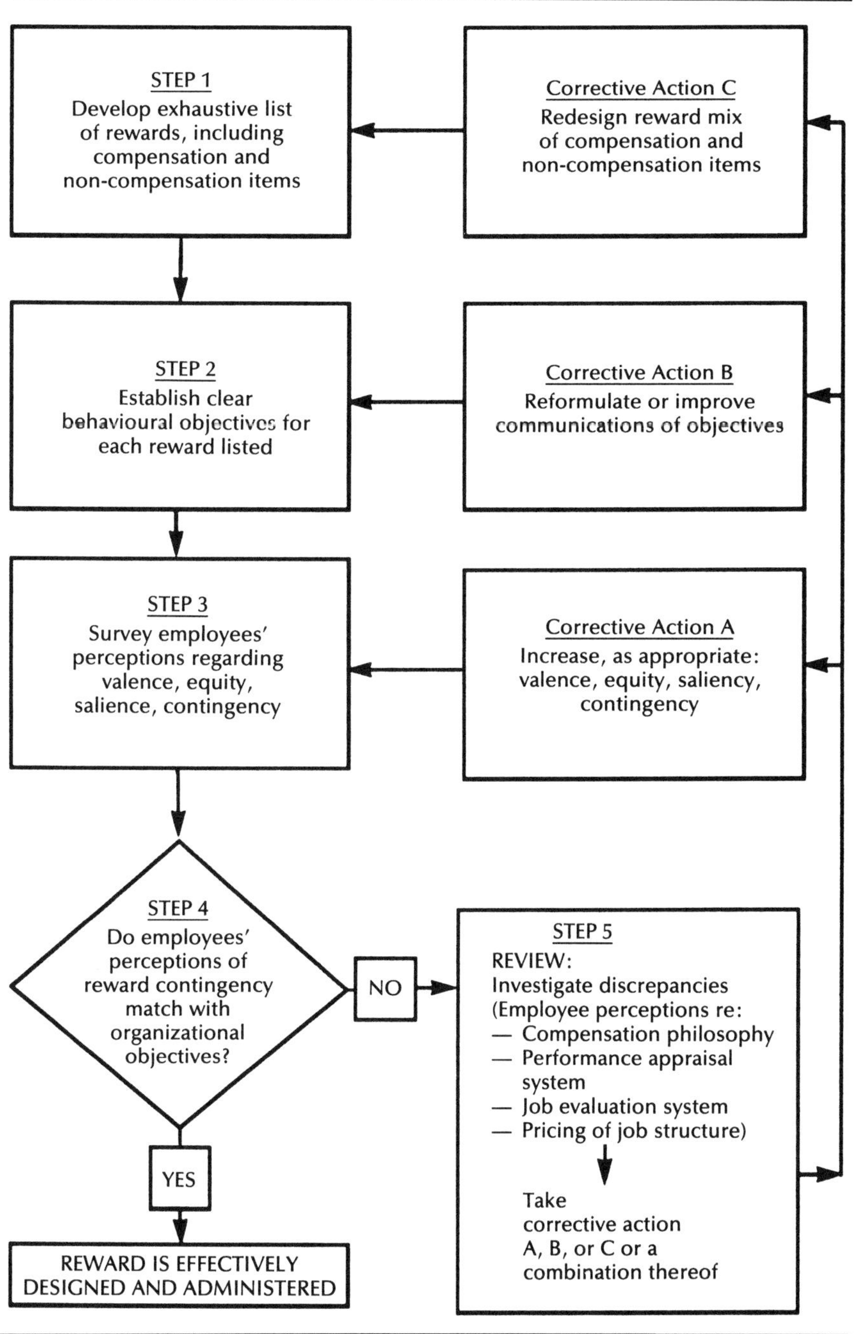

be expressed in behavioural terms, so that the realization of the purpose can be objectively assessed. Experience suggests that organizations frequently choose from among the following five major behavioural objectives:

a) to attract individuals with the knowledge, ability, and talents demanded by specific organizational tasks;
b) to retain valued, productive employees;
c) to motivate regular attendance and a desired level of performance;
d) to promote attitudes conducive to loyalty and commitment to the organization, to high job involvement, and to job satisfaction; and
e) to stimulate employee growth that will enable the employee to accept more challenging positions.

Objectives such as these become the target behaviours, which, the organization expects, will be elicited by the rewards it offers. A reward may be intended to elicit more than one behaviour. If this is so, the targeted behaviours for a reward must be prioritized to clearly reflect the intentions of the organization. For example, if the reward "merit pay" is intended to motivate the retention, performance, and growth of employees, then management ought to set priorities for these behaviours. It may accord priorities in terms of high for performance, medium for growth, and low for retention. The priorities spell out the *type* and the *extent* of the behaviour that which management expects the reward to generate. Management will also state, at this stage, its beliefs about the extent to which the rewards are perceived by employees to be salient and valent.

The decisions made in this step of the programme will clearly state the purpose management has in mind for each reward. In other words, management makes a conscious, deliberate choice of what it wishes to achieve by each reward. Thus, the targets for returns on investment in the reward programme are definitively established. Against these targets the reward system will be evaluated.

Step 3

Conduct a survey of the employees to find out how they perceive each reward. The survey seeks to identify two sets of employee perceptions: (*a*) perceptions relating to reward saliency, valence, and contingency with reference to the target behaviour; and (*b*) perceptions of the personal, internal, and external equity of the compensation system. Data on the latter set of perceptions are collected through questions on employee perception of the fairness of compensation policies, practices, and procedures relative to the performance appraisal system, the job evaluation system, and the pricing of the job structure. The first set of perceptions provides feedback on the effectiveness of each reward. Both sets of perceptions aid in the diagnostic investigations of step 4 of the action programme.

For example, suppose management had decided that the primary goal of the reward of promotion is to motivate employees to superior job performance, and this reward is therefore made contingent on superior performance. Also suppose that the survey results indicate that employees perceive promotion to be highly valuable (because it satisfies their strong esteem needs, and is perceived as equitable because it is based on a performance appraisal system acceptable to employees); highly salient (because its existence and the conditions for awarding it have been frequently communicated); and based on outstanding performance. The findings suggest that there is complete congruence between the objectives of the organization and the perceptions and expectations of the employees. Consequently, management can conclude that its design and administration of the reward of promotion will be effective in eliciting the behaviour established for it.

On the other hand, suppose the survey results for this same reward indicate just the opposite: promotion is not seen by the workers as valuable, salient, and contingent. In this situation, promotion will be a meaningless reward for employees and will not produce the job behaviour intended for it by management.

Step 4

Examine the findings of the survey and investigate those rewards where the perceptions of employees relative to behaviour-reward contingency, saliency, and valence are different from those established by the organization. Such discrepancies or lack of congruence imply that the reward is not attaining the objective intended for it by management. Clues to the causes of the discrepancies will come from survey results about employee perceptions of reward valence and saliency and about employee perceptions of the fairness of compensation policies and practices.

The following situations, which use the reward of promotion as an example, show how the discrepancies revealed by the survey results could indicate that employees do not perceive promotion to be valuable, or salient, or contingent on performance.

a) *Employees do not perceive promotion to be a valuable reward.* If the results show that this reward is administered in an equitable manner, and the reward saliency is high, then there can be two reasons why employees do not value the reward of promotion. The first reason is that employees lack the ability needed in the higher level job; if further investigation find this to be the case, then training is recommended. The second reason is that employees do not have a desire for enhanced self-esteem and are happy with their present jobs; if this is the case, counselling may help, followed by training. Finally, employees may perceive that the reward is administered inequitably and hence will not value it. The remedy in this case is to remove the inequities through corrective measures in the form of performance appraisals and peer evaluations. If the inequities in awarding promotions are not real but are only perceived as such, then improved communication and the development of a climate of trust should help.

b) *Employees perceive promotion to be a valuable reward, but the reward saliency is low.* This situation can only be resolved by better and more frequent communication of the performance-based promotion policy.

c) *Employees do not see promotion as contingent on superior performance.* For a reward system to be effective, the contingency link must be clearly and unambiguously communicated in words and, more importantly, in deeds. If employees are not aware of the appropriate contingent behaviour for a specific reward, that reward may influence a different set of behaviours that could be counterproductive to the ones intended by management. For example, suppose the promotion policy makes promotion contingent on superior performance. But it is common knowledge that, in practice, only employees who socialize or get along well with their supervisors are promoted. In this situation the contingency link between superior performance and promotion will be severed. What is more insidious is that the practice conveys that the way to the top is through indulging in ingratiating or similarly dysfunctional behaviour.

For reasons beyond management's control it may not be feasible to alter employee perceptions of a reward by the recommended action or by another appropriate action. It may also happen that, because of legislation or contractual obligations, a particular reward cannot be made contingent on a behaviour intended for it by management. In these circumstances, management will change the behavioural objective to one that reflects the reality of the situation.

Step 5

The final, and most vital, step in the action programme is *review*. This consists of reformulating the reward package objectives or redesigning the reward system or both, on the basis of the diagnosis of the present reward system. Employee perceptions of the personal, internal, and external equity of the compensation system are significant input to the review process. These data will point to the specific policy, technique, and process (i.e., compensation philosophy, performance appraisal, job evaluation, pricing the job structure) that needs to be modified. These modifications will be the vehicle for corrective actions A, B, and C identified in Figure 14.1. At this stage, a great deal of learning takes place, as management reflects on the perceptions and expectations of its employees and their impact on organizational goals. It is also a time for important decisions, time for management to respond, not in a reactive mode but more in a proactive stance that considers how best the reward system can be creatively employed to cope with the new challenges that constantly confront a dynamic organization. Although review is the final step, yet it is also an ongoing process that enables management to keep on top of the situation at all times.

As shown in Figure 14.1, the implementation of these steps requires regular monitoring of reward attributes and appropriate response to the feedback. The next section illustrates the entire process involved in the programme.

Illustration of the Action Programme

A study that used the procedures of the action programme tested the effectiveness of the compensation programme of a group of senior managers of a Canadian corporation.

Methodology

1. For each of the organization's 23 rewards (which included both economic compensation items such as pay and vacation and non-economic compensation items such as participation in decision making, sense of belonging, and challenge) the compensation specialist was asked to indicate

- the targeted behaviour under the categories of retention, performance, and growth; and
- the priority accorded to the targeted behaviour in terms of high, medium, and low. The priorities designate the type and the extent of the behaviour that management expects will be generated by the reward. If a particular behaviour was not targeted for a reward, the compensation specialist responded with a "not applicable" for that behaviour. The compensation specialist had the option of assigning equal priorities to the targeted behaviours if such were management's expectations for the reward. The status of the compensation specialist's position in the management hierarchy of this organization qualified him to reflect adequately the organization's priorities for the compensation programme. These are summarized in Table 14.2.

Table 14.2
Summary of Reward Costs, Organizational Priority for Targeted Behaviours, and Employee Perceptions of Rewards

Reward Item	Cost of Reward as % of Total Compensation Costs	Organizational					Employees' Perceptions				
		Priority for the Targeted Behaviours of			Belief of Reward's		Reward Contingent on			Reward's	
		Retention	Performance	Growth	Saliency	Valence	Retention	Performance	Growth	Saliency	Valence
Company pension	12 %	High	Medium	Low	High	High	High	Low	Low	Low	Low
Post-retirement ins.	0.11%	High	Medium	Low	High	High	High	Low	Low	Low	Low
Medicare	0.28%	High	Medium	Low	High	High	Medium	Low	Low	Low	Medium
Term life insurance	0.72%	High	Medium	Low	High	High	Medium	Low	Low	Low	Medium
Dental plan	0.50%	High	Medium	Low	High	High	Medium	Low	Low	Low	Medium
Long-term disability	1 %	High	Medium	Low	High	High	Low	Low	Low	Low	Medium
Blue Cross plan	0.44%	High	Medium	Low	High	High	Medium	Low	Low	Low	Medium
Health insurance	3 %	High	Medium	Low	High	High	Medium	Low	Low	Low	Medium
Pay	77.95%	Medium	High	Low	High	High	Medium	High	High	High	High
Salary increases	4 %	Medium	High	Low	High	High	Low	High	High	Low	Medium
Job security	—	High	Medium	Low	High	High	Medium	Medium	Medium	Low	Medium
Personal challenge	—	Low	High	Medium	High	High	Low	High	High	High	High
Job variety	—	Low	High	Medium	High	High	Low	High	High	Low	High
Recognition	—	Low	High	Medium	High	High	Low	High	High	Medium	High
Achieving organizational goals	—	Medium	High	Low	High	High	Medium	High	High	Medium	Medium
Personal growth and development	—	Medium	High	Low	High	High	Medium	High	High	High	Medium

TABLE 14.2 — *CONTINUED*

Reward Item	Cost of Reward as % of Total Compensation Costs	Organizational					Employees' Perceptions				
		Priority for the Targeted Behaviours of			Belief of Reward's		Reward Contingent on			Reward's	
		Retention	Performance	Growth	Saliency	Valence	Retention	Performance	Growth	Saliency	Valence
Pride in work	—	High	Medium	Low	High	High	Medium	High	High	Low	Medium
Sense of belonging	—	High	Medium	Low	High	High	Medium	Medium	High	Medium	Medium
Participation in decision making	—	Low	Medium	High	High	High	Medium	High	High	High	High
Sick leave	— NA	High	Medium	Low	High	High	High	Low	Low	Low	Medium
Vacation pay	— NA	High	Medium	Low	High	High	High	Low	Low	Low	Medium
Free rail transportation	— NA	Medium	High	Low	High	High	Low	Low	Low	Low	Low
Educational financial aid	— NA	Low	Medium	High	High	High	Low	Low	Low	Low	Low

2. Discussions with the compensation specialist revealed that management believed that the employees were fully aware of the rewards and the contingencies involved in earning them. Management also believed that the employees placed a high value on the rewards offered by the organization. The reward system therefore operated on the assumption that each reward was perceived by the employees to be highly salient and valuable. Hence, the values assigned to saliency and valence by management were high.

3. The employees were surveyed to obtain, for each of the 23 rewards, their perceptions about whether the reward was contingent on retention, performance, and growth; was salient; and was valued. The median of employee perceptions was categorized as high, medium, or low for each reward item. The cost of each monetary and in-kind reward item was obtained as a percentage of the total cost of all such rewards. These data are presented in Table 14.2.

(*Note*: The instrument utilized in this study did not include questions for determining the extent to which employees were aware of and perceived the fairness of the compensation policies and practices relating to performance appraisals, job evaluation, and the pricing of the job structure. Information on these issues would enable the compensation specialist to focus on some of the specific causes of the ineffectiveness of the reward system.)

Analyses

So that the perceptions of the compensation specialist could be compared with those of the employees for each reward item, it was necessary to reduce them to a common unit of measurement. This was done by calculating two sets of three scores representing the reward's saliency, valence, and contingency. One set of scores was derived from the responses of the compensation specialist and expressed the organization's expectations and beliefs about the reward; the other set of scores was derived from employee perceptions. For saliency and valence scores, the responses of the compensation specialist and the employees, categorized as high, medium, and low, were assigned factor values of 1.00, 0.70, and 0.30 respectively.

For reward contingency, the targeted reward contingency value (TRCV) and the perceived reward contingency value (PRCV) were calculated. The TRCV combines the organizational priorities for the targeted behaviours of a reward. The PRCV combines the employees' perceptions of the contingent behaviours for a reward. For a reward item that involves a direct money or in-kind payment, the targeted and perceived reward contingency values were weighted to reflect the appropriate costs of the reward. The computation of these scores (TRCV and PRCV) is illustrated below.

For Reward Items Involving Direct Money or In-Kind Payments

The computation for this category of rewards is illustrated using the data from Table 14.2 for the reward item *company pension*.

a) Compute the TRCV by combining the targeted behaviours for company pension with the cost of company pension, expressed as a percentage of the total cost of the compensation package. This is done in two steps:

(1) Assign a factor value to the priority accorded to the targeted behaviours: 1.00 for high, 0.70 medium, and 0.30 for low, and 0.00 for not applicable. For company pension, the assigned factor value will be

Item	*Targeted behaviours*	*Priority accorded*	*Assigned factor value*
Company pension	Retention	High	1.00
	Performance	Medium	0.70
	Growth	Low	0.30

(2) Multiply the cost of company pension by the assigned factor values to obtain the targeted reward contingency value, as follows:

Item	*% of Total cost*	×	*Assigned factor value for targeted behavior*	=	*Targeted reward contingency value*
Company pension	12	×	1.00 (for retention)	=	12
	12	×	0.70 (for performance)	=	8
	12	×	0.30 (for growth)	=	4
Targeted reward contingency value (TRCV)				=	24

The TRCV of 24 represents a standard that the organization expects to attain for company pension if employees do in fact perceive this reward to be contingent on the behaviours targeted for it.

b) Compute the *perceived reward contingency value* (PRCV) by combining the perceived behaviours for company pension with the cost of company pension expressed as a percentage of the total compensation costs. This is also done in two steps:

(1) Assign factor values to employee perceptions of the contingent behaviours for each reward item: 1.00 for high, 0.70 for medium, 0.30 for low. For company pension, the assigned factor value will be

Item	*Targeted behaviours*	*Perceived contingency*	*Assigned factor value*
Company pension	Retention	High	1.00
	Performance	Low	0.30
	Growth	Low	0.30

(2) Multiply the cost of company pension by the assigned factor values to obtain the perceived reward contingency value, as follows:

Item	*% of Total cost*	×	*Assigned factor value for targeted behaviour*	=	*Targeted reward contingency value*
Company pension	12	×	1.00 (for retention)	=	12
	12	×	0.30 (for performance)	=	4
	12	×	0.30 (for growth)	=	4
Perceived reward contingency value (PRCV)				=	20

For Rewards That Do Not Involve Money or In-Kind Payments

The computation of the targeted and perceived reward contingency values (TRCV and PRCV) for this category is illustrated below using the data from Table 14.2 for the reward *personal challenge*.

a) Compute the TRCV by assigning a factor value to the priority accorded to the targeted behaviours for each reward item: 1.00 for high, 0.70 for medium, 0.30 for low, 0.00 for not applicable. For personal challenge, the assigned factor value will be

Item	*Targeted behaviours*	*Priority accorded*	*Assigned factor value*
Personal challenge	Retention	Low	0.30
	Performance	High	1.00
	Growth	Medium	0.70
Targeted reward contingency value (TRCV)			2.00

b) Compute the PRCV by assigning a factor value to employee perceptions of the contingent behaviours for each reward item: 1.00 for high, 0.70 for medium, 0.30 for low. For personal challenge, the assigned factor value will be

Item	*Targeted behaviours*	*Perceived contingency*	*Assigned factor value*
Personal challenge	Retention	Low	0.30
	Performance	High	1.00
	Growth	High	1.00
Perceived reward contingency value (PRCV)		=	2.30

Table 14.3 shows the two sets (organization's and employees') of scores for each reward. These reward attributes have a multiplicative, motivational effect on the recipient of the reward; hence, the significance of the product of each set of scores. The product of the organization's set of scores denotes the *intended effectiveness* of each reward; whereas the product of the employees' set of scores denotes the *actual effectiveness* likely to result from employee perceptions of each reward.

Table 14.3
A Comparison of the Intended and the Actual Effectiveness of Rewards

Reward Item	Organizational Score: Targeted Reward Contingency Value (TRCV) ×	Saliency (S) ×	Valence (V) =	Intended Effectiveness	Employees' Score: Perceived Reward Contingency Value (PRCV) ×	Saliency (S) ×	Valence (V) =	Actual Effectiveness	Action to Retain/ Modify*
Company pension	24.00	1	1	24.00	20.00	0.3	0.3	1.80	Modify
Post-retirement ins.	0.22	1	1	0.22	0.18	0.3	0.3	0.02	Modify
Medicare	0.56	1	1	0.56	0.36	0.3	0.7	0.08	Modify
Term life insurance	1.44	1	1	1.44	0.94	0.3	0.7	0.20	Modify
Dental plan	1.00	1	1	1.00	0.65	0.3	0.7	0.14	Modify
Long-term disability	2.00	1	1	2.00	0.90	0.3	0.7	0.19	Modify
Blue Cross plan	0.88	1	1	0.88	0.57	0.3	0.7	0.12	Modify
Health insurance	6.00	1	1	6.00	3.90	0.3	0.7	0.82	Modify
Pay	155.90	1	1	155.90	210.47	1	1	210.47	Retain
Salary increases	8.00	1	1	8.00	9.20	0.3	0.7	1.93	Modify
Job security	2.00	1	1	2.00	2.10	0.3	0.7	0.44	Modify
Personal challenge	2.00	1	1	2.00	2.30	1	1	2.30	Retain
Job variety	2.00	1	1	2.00	2.30	0.3	1	0.69	Modify
Recognition	2.00	1	1	2.00	2.30	0.7	1	1.61	Modify
Achieving organizational goals	2.00	1	1	2.00	2.70	0.7	0.7	1.32	Modify
Personal growth and development	2.00	1	1	2.00	2.70	1	0.7	1.89	Modify
Pride in work	2.00	1	1	2.00	2.70	0.3	0.7	0.57	Modify
Sense of belonging	2.00	1	1	2.00	2.40	0.7	0.7	1.18	Modify
Participation in decision making	2.00	1	1	2.00	2.70	1	1	2.70	Retain
Sick leave	2.00	1	1	2.00	1.60	0.3	0.7	0.34	Modify
Vacation pay	2.00	1	1	2.00	1.60	0.3	0.7	0.34	Modify
Free rail transportation	2.00	1	1	2.00	0.90	0.3	0.3	0.08	Modify
Educational financial aid	2.00	1	1	2.00	0.90	0.3	0.3	0.08	Modify

*For illustrative examples, refer to the section Implications of the Results.

Implications of the Results

The theoretical foundation for this diagnostic tool postulates that the targeted set of behaviours will be realized only to the extent that each reward item is perceived by the employees as valuable, salient, and contingent on the targeted behaviours. Therefore, a comparison of the two sets of scores (Table 14.3) helps identify the relative motivational effectiveness of each reward, highlights the specific reasons why a given reward has reduced effectiveness, and provides clues for appropriate intervention to increase the effectiveness of the reward.

The next sections discuss the implications of the findings in Table 14.3 in respect of the reward items involving direct money and in-kind payments, and then in respect of the reward items that do not involve such money payments.

Rewards Involving Money and In-Kind Payments

In this category of rewards, discussion will focus on company pension and pay. For the reward of company pension, there is a glaring disparity between intended effectiveness (24) and actual effectiveness (1.80). This indicates that the organization is not achieving the targeted rate of return on its investment in the reward of company pension. The TRCV is 24, the PRCV is 20. This suggests that the employees perceive the reward as being contingent on behaviours to an extent less than that anticipated by the organization.

A closer examination of Table 14.2 shows that this disparity in reward contingency can be traced to the targeted behaviour of job performance. The priority accorded to this behaviour by the organization was medium, but employee perceptions that this reward was contingent on performance were low. Employees saw a weak link between deferred pension benefits and present job performance. If the organization still intends that the reward of company pension should have a moderate effect on performance, it should devise some form of *performance-based deferred compensation* that could be seen by the employees as eventually making a significant impact on the pension payout. If such a method is not possible or desirable, the organization must lower the priority accorded to this targeted behaviour.

From Table 14.3 it can be seen that this reward is not highly salient to employees, nor is it highly valued by them. Therefore, the organization should take steps to raise the saliency and valence of company pension. One way to increase a reward's salience is to communicate to employees periodically the salient features of the reward programme. In the case of company pension, information on how improved performance can lead to a *faster accumulation* in the fund, resulting eventually in a much *higher payout*, will increase the valence of company pension.

For the reward of pay, the intended effectiveness (156) is considerably lower than the actual effectiveness (210). This indicates that the organization has exceeded the targeted rates of return on its investment in this reward. Since employees perceive pay to be both highly salient and valued, the primary reasons for the motivational effectiveness of pay can be traced to the reward contingency. The TRCV is 156, the PRCV is 210.47. This suggests that the employees perceive the reward as being contingent on the targeted behaviours to an extent much greater than that anticipated by the organization. From Table 14.2 it can be seen that employees perceive pay to be moderately contingent on retention and highly contingent on performance (exactly as targeted by the organization), but also as highly contingent on growth, which was not the priority accorded to it by the organization; the organization had accorded growth a low priority. Since pay functions as a powerful motivating influence in promoting the behaviours of retention, performance, and growth, this reward and the manner in which it is administered should be retained.

The other reward items in this category (money and in-kind payments) can be similarly investigated and appropriate plans of action considered.

Rewards Not Involving Money and In-Kind Payments

For this category of rewards, discussion will focus on the rewards of participation in decision making and achieving organizational goals.

The motivating effect of *participation in decision making* has exceeded the organization's expectations, as can be seen from the actual effectiveness value of 2.7 as against the intended effectiveness value of 2.0. Since both the organization and the employees perceive this reward to be highly salient and valued, the primary reason for the added motivational effectiveness can be traced to the reward contingency. The TRCV is 2, as against the PRCV of 2.7. This disparity suggests that the employees perceive this reward to be contingent on the targeted behaviours but to an extent greater than that anticipated by the organization. From Table 14.2 it can be seen that the employees perceive this reward's contingency to be high on growth, exactly as targeted by the organization. The employees perceive the reward to be also highly contingent on job performance and moderately contingent on retention, whereas the organization had accorded performance a medium priority and retention a low priority. Participation in decision making is an effective reward in generating the behaviours of retention, performance, and growth in the right direction. It should therefore be retained.

For the reward *achieving organizational goals*, there is a disparity between the intended effectiveness (2.0) and the actual effectiveness (1.3). This disparity indicates that the motivational impact of the reward is less than was expected by the organization. The reason for this disparity is not in the reward contingency scores (PRCV of 2.3 as against the TRCV of 2.0), which show that employees perceive this reward to be contingent on the targeted behaviours to an extent greater than that anticipated by the organization. Rather, the disparity is in employees' perceptions of saliency and valence, which is medium, in contrast to organizational expectations that the reward is highly salient and valuable to the employees. The organization should initiate measures to increase both the saliency and the valence through the effective communication of the potential benefits of this reward.

Rewards that do not involve money or in-kind payments are generally received by employees as they perform the tasks of their job. In such task-related rewards, the reward contingency is automatically perceived as the tasks are performed. Hence, the perceived reward contingency value of these rewards will generally be high. But employee perceptions of the saliency and the valence of these rewards may not be high unless the organization takes specific steps to bring about increases in the saliency and valence. Any interventions in task-related rewards call for actions to increase employee perceptions of the saliency and valence of these rewards.

All the other rewards in this category can be similarly investigated and action plans initiated to modify the reward — its design and/or its administration — suitably.

Conclusion

An organization's investment in its employee compensation programme is always at a level that cries out for innovative approaches that will ensure a reasonably fair return. The action programme is an approach that transforms the manager's role from that of a passive, helpless observer of enormous compensation expenditures to an active, confident manager who makes deliberate, conscious decisions on behavioural objectives for each reward item. By using the action programme, the manager can evaluate the effectiveness of the reward system by subjecting it to the same rigorous analysis that is routinely employed on other operating costs.

The programme also serves as a diagnostic tool. As the manager probes a reward item whose targeted objective is not being realized, the data provided by the analysis will reveal specific reasons why the objective is not being realized. The reasons then become the basis for the appropriate remedial interventions. The weighting procedure of each reward by its relative cost is a useful mechanism in helping managers to focus their efforts on those rewards for which the cost-benefit consideration is the most significant.

The action programme can be implemented with relatively little effort and expense. However, its successful implementation presupposes three essential conditions. First, management must accept its responsibility to obtain a fair return on its compensation expenditures. Second, management must be committed to designing and administering the reward system in a manner which ensures that employees clearly perceive the rewards to be valuable, salient, and contingent on the targeted behaviours. Third, management must be willing to review the reward system continuously and to modify it, as necessary, in the light of organizational goals and employee perceptions relative to valence, saliency, and contingency.

Most organizations today believe, and rightly, that the employee compensation programme is an investment in its most valuable resource. Implementing the action programme will bring the organization a step closer to realizing the tremendous potential of that investment.

SUMMARY

This chapter considered three issues in managing the compensation system: the traditional administrative process of the salary budget, and the emerging issues of person-based pay and evaluating the effectiveness of the compensation system. The procedures involved in the top-down and the bottom-up approaches to developing a salary budget were described. The multi-skilling and knowledge-based pay forms of person-based pay were explored, the advantages and disadvantages of person-based pay were examined, and the conditions that would favor person-based pay as an alternative strategy in compensation management were identified. Finally, an action programme to evaluate the effectiveness of the reward items was considered in detail. As shown in the description of the action programme and illustrated by data from its use in a Canadian corporation, the programme not only identifies ineffective reward items but also proposes specific remedial measures for improving their effectiveness. It must be emphasized that the programme's success depends upon management's recognition that enormous compensation expenditures are an investment rather than an expense. Furthermore, management must be committed to managing the reward system in a manner which ensures that employees clearly perceive the rewards to be valued, salient, and contingent on the targeted behaviours.

KEY TERMS

action programme for evaluating employee compensation
actual effectiveness of rewards
bottom-up approach to budgeting
compa-ratio
intended effectiveness of rewards

knowledge-based pay
multi-skilling
perceived reward contingency value (PRCV)
targeted reward contingency value (TRCV)
top-down approach to budgeting

REVIEW AND DISCUSSION QUESTIONS

1. The following table provides information on tenure, performance rating, and compa-ratio of the six clerks in the sales department of Omega Products Limited.

Name	*Compa-ratio*
Suzy	.95
Frank	1.10
Richard	1.20
Joann	.85
Harry	1.23
Chantal	.90
Angela	.80

   What might these compa-ratios mean? What areas would you wish to probe further? Why?

2. Which approach to budgeting salaries — top-down or bottom-up — would you prefer? Why?
3. Distinguish between person-based pay and job-based pay.
4. What are the advantages and the disadvantages of person-based pay?
5. Explain the underlying rationale of the action programme for evaluating the effectiveness of the compensation system.
6. Would the action programme be suitable for all organizations? Why or why not?

CASE: GETTING THE MOTIVATIONAL BANG FROM THE COMPENSATION BUCKS

The young, dynamic president of the Canadian Transportation Company is rather uneasy about the costs of the compensation package — about 70 per cent of the total operating costs. It is not that she grudges the bill. In fact, she takes pride in being the leader in innovative compensation practices in the industry. But she does want to get her money's worth. All business expenditures (except for compensation) are rigorously reviewed to determine whether the targeted rates of return are achieved, and appropriate corrective actions are initiated. Mindful of this concern, the compensation specialist administered the diagnostic instrument of the action programme (described in the chapter) to the middle managers. Tables 14.1.1, 14.1.2, and 14.1.3 show the findings in respect of four reward items. The compensation specialist seeks your advice, specifically:

- to interpret these findings and to explain their significance relative to the effectiveness or ineffectiveness of these items;
- to propose concrete remedial actions, where necessary.

Table 14.1.1

Summary of Organizational Priority for Targeted Behaviours and Employee Perceptions of Rewards

REWARD ITEM	Organizational					Employees' Perceptions				
	Priority for Targeted Behaviours			Beliefs of Reward's		Reward Contingent on			Reward's	
	Retention	Performance	Growth	Saliency	Valence	Retention	Performance	Growth	Saliency	Valence
Merit pay	High	High	Medium	High	High	Medium	Medium	Medium	Medium	Medium
Vacations	High	Low	Low	High	High	Medium	Low	Low	Medium	High
Educational assistance	Medium	Medium	High	High	High	Low	Low	Low	Low	Medium
Interesting work	High	High	High	High	High	High	High	High	High	High

Table 14.1.2
Employees' Responses to the Question Whether the Rewards Are Fairly or Not Fairly Administered

Reward Item	Administered: Fairly	Administered: Unfairly	Undecided
Merit pay	50%	33%	17%
Vacations	100%	—	—
Educational assistance	67%	11%	22%
Interesting work	78%	5%	17%

Table 14.1.3
Employees' Responses to the Questions on Performance Appraisals Policies and Practices

QUESTIONS	RESPONSE (on 6 point scale) Strongly Disagree = 1 Strongly Agree = 6
My performance is periodically evaluated	5
I am aware of the criteria on which my performance is evaluated	2
My supervisor consults with me in determining the job objectives on which I will be evaluated	3
My supervisor is in constant dialogue with me, coaching me to achieve my job objectives	2
My assessment of my performance is generally in agreement with my supervisor's assessment of my performance	2
My performance plays an important role in determining the rewards I will receive	3
Although I put in more time and effort and generally achieve more of the job objectives than my peers, yet I am paid the same as my peers	5

References

Abella, Judge Rosalie Silberman. (1984). *Equality in Employment: A Royal Commission Report — General Summary*. Toronto: Commission on Equality in Employment.

Adams, J. S. (1965). "Injustice in Social Exchange." In *Advances in Experimental Social Psychology*. Vol. 2, edited by L. Berkowitz. New York: Academic Press.

Aft, Lawrence S. (1985). *Wage and Salary Administration: A Guide to Job Evaluation*. Reston, Va.: Reston Publishing Co.

Agarwal, Naresh. (1980). "Equal Pay for Work of Equal Value." In *Race and Sex Equality in the Workplace: A Challenge and an Opportunity*, edited by Harish C. Jain and Diane Carroll. Ottawa: Minister of Supply and Services Canada.

_______. (1986). "Economic Costs of Employment Discrimination." In *Is There a New Canadian Industrial Relations?* Proceedings of the 23d annual meeting of the Canadian Industrial Relations Association, Winnipeg.

Balkin, David B., and Gomez-Mejia, Luis R. (1987). "Towards a Contingency Theory of Compensation Strategy." *Strategic Management Journal* 8:169–82.

Bellak, Alvin O. (1984). "Specific Job Evaluation Systems: The Hay Guide Chart-Profile Method." In *Handbook of Wage and Salary Administration*, edited by Milton L. Rock. New York: McGraw-Hill.

Benge, Eugene J. (1984). "Specific Job Evaluation Systems: The Factor Method." In *Handbook of Wage and Salary Administration*, edited by Milton L. Rock. New York: McGraw-Hill.

Canadian Human Rights Commission. (1984). *Equal Pay Casebook 1978–1984*. Ottawa, Ont.: Canadian Human Rights Commission.

Canadian Recruiters Guild. (1988). "Employment Discrimination in Canada." *The Human Resource* (August-September).

CARRA. *See* Commission administrative des régimes de retraite et d'assurances.

Cascio, W. (1982). *Applied Psychology in Personnel Management*. Reston, Va.: Reston Publishing Co.

Chadwick-Jones, J. K., C. A. Brown, and N. Nicholson. (1973). "Absence from Work: Its Meaning, Measurement, and Control." *International Review of Applied Psychology* 22:137–55.

Clegg, J. W. (1983). "Psychology of Employee Lateness, Absence, and Turnover." *Journal of Applied Psychology* 65:467–73.

Commission administrative des régimes de retraite et d'assurances. (1988). *An Investment for the Future: RREGOP, TPP, CSSP*. Quebec: Services des communications, CARRA.

Conger, J. A., and R. N. Kanungo. (1988). "The Empowerment Process: Integrating Theory and Practice." *The Academy of Management Review* 13:471–82.

Cranston, Maurice. (1987). "What Are Human Rights." In *Human Rights and Freedoms in Canada*, edited by Mark L. Berlin and William F. Pentney. Toronto: Butterworths.

Davis, L. E., and A. B. Cherns. (1975). *The Quality of Working Life*. Vol. 2, *Cases and Commentary*. New York: Free Press.

Deci, E. L. (1972). "The Effects of Contingent and Noncontingent Rewards and Controls on Intrinsic Motivation." *Organizational Behavior and Human Performance* 8:217–29.

Dubin, R. (1956). "Industrial Workers' Worlds: A Study of the Central Life Interests of Industrial Workers." *Social Problems* 3:131–42.

Dunn, J. D., and Frank M. Rachel. (1971). *Wage and Salary Administration: Total Compensation Systems*. New York: McGraw-Hill.

Dunnette, M. D., L. M. Hough, and R. L. Rosse. (1979). "Task and Job Taxonomies as a Basis for Identifying Labor Supply Sources and Evaluating Employment Qualifications." *Human Resources Planning* 2(1).

Dyer, L., and D. F. Parker. (1976). "Classifying Outcomes in Work Motivation Research: An Examination of the Intrinsic-Extrinsic Dichotomy." *Journal of Applied Psychology* 60:455–58.

Ellig, B., ed. (1985). *Compensation and Benefits: Design and Analysis*. Scottsdale, Ariz.: American Compensation Association.

Fein, M. (1976). "Motivation for Work." In *Handbook of Work, Organization, and Society*, edited by Robert Dubin. Chicago: Rand McNally College Publishing Co.

———. (1974). "Job Enrichment: A Reevaluation." *Sloan Management Review* 15(2): 69–88.

Financial Post, The. (1988). "Day Care Becoming Management Issue: On-Site Centres Latest Addition to Modern Office." 18 October: 43.

Flowers, Vincent S., and Charles L. Hughes. (1973). "Why Employees Stay." *Harvard Business Review* (July-August): 49–60.

Formbrun, C. (1982). "Environmental Trends Create New Pressures on Human Resources." *Journal of Business Strategy* 3(1): 61–69.

Freedman, Robert J. (1986). "How to Develop a Sales Compensation Plan." *Compensation and Benefits Review* (March-April): 41–48.

Frost, Greenwood and Associates. (1982). *The Scanlon Plan Today*. Lansing, Mich.: Scanlon Plan Associates.

Gazette, The (Montreal). (1980). "Absenteeism Is '10 Times Costlier Than Strikes.'" October 14: 54.

_______. (1990). "Prospects at Ste. Thérèse." April 17.

_______. (1991). "Women Win Pay-Equity Fight: Ottawa Paid Hospital Workers Less Because of Sex — Tribunal." May 1.

Ghorpade, Jai. (1988). *Job Analysis: A Handbook for the Human Resource Director*. Englewood Cliffs, N. J.: Prentice-Hall.

Gibb-Clark, Margot. (1991). "Flexible Benefits Let Employees Tailor Coverage." *The Globe and Mail* (Toronto) 24 June: B4.

Gillespie, J. J. (1948). *Free Expression in Industry*. London: Pilot Press.

Gold, Michael Evan. (1983). *A Dialogue on Comparable Worth*. Ithaca, N.Y.: ILR Press, Cornell University.

Gupta, A. K., and V. Govindarajan. (1984). "Business Unit Strategy, Managerial Characteristics, and Business Unit Effectiveness at Strategy Implementation." *Academy of Management Journal* 27:25–41.

Guzzo, R. A. (1979). "Types of Rewards, Cognitions, and Work Motivation." *Academy of Management Review* 4:75–86.

Hackman, Richard J., and Greg R. Oldham. (1980). *Work Redesign*. Reading, Mass.: Addison-Wesley.

Halpern, Norman. (1984). "Sociotechnical Systems Design: The Shell Sarnia Experience." In *Quality of Working Life: Contemporary Cases*, edited by J. B. Cunningham and T. H. White. Ottawa: Minister of Supply and Services.

Henderson, R. I. (1989). *Compensation Management — Rewarding Performance*. 5th ed. Englewood Cliffs, N.J.: Prentice-Hall.

Henderson, R. I., and Michael N. Wolfe. (1985). *Workbook for Compensation Management: Rewarding Performance*. Reston, Va.: Reston Publishing Co.

Herman Miller. (1987). *See* "Participative Management at Herman Miller: An Innovative Strategy for Action."

Herzberg, F. (1966). *Work and the Nature of Man*. Cleveland, Ohio: World Publishing.

_______. (1968). "One More Time: How Do You Motivate Employees?" *Harvard Business Review* (January/February): 53–62.

Herzberg, F., B. Mausner, and B. B. Snyderman. (1959). *The Motivation to Work*. New York: Wiley.

Hofer, C. W. (1975). "Toward a Contingency Theory of Business Strategy." *Academy of Management Journal* 18:784–810.

Hofstede, G. (1980a). *Culture's Consequences: International Differences in Work-Related Values*. Beverly Hills, Calif.: Sage Publications.

_______. (1980b). "Motivation, Leadership, and Organization: Do American Theories Apply Abroad?" *Organizational Dynamics* 9(1): 42–62.

Human Resource Management in Canada. (1991). "Ontario Expands Pay Equity Program." *Report Bulletin No. 96* (February): 1–16. Scarborough, Ont.: Prentice-Hall.

Hurwich, Mark R., and John K. Moynahan. (1984). "Designing Sales Compensation Plans to Keep Pace with Fast Moving High-Tech Markets." *Management Review* 73(4): 57–61.

Jaeger, A. M., and R. N. Kanungo. (1990). "The Need for Indigenous Management in Developing Countries." In *Management in Developing Countries*, edited by A. M. Jaeger and R. N. Kanungo. London: Routledge.

Jain, Harish C. (1984). "Racial Discrimination in Employment in Canada: Issues and Policies." In *South Asians in the Canadian Mosaic*, edited by R. N. Kanungo. Montreal: Kala Bharati.

Johns, Gary. (1980). "Did You Go to Work Today?" *The Montreal Business Report* (Fourth Quarter): 52–56.

Kanungo, R. N. (1975). "Managerial Job Satisfaction: A Comparison between Anglophones and Francophones." In *Canadian Industrial Relations*, edited by S. M. A. Hameed. Toronto: Butterworths.

———. (1980). *Biculturalism and Management*. Toronto: Butterworths.

Kanungo, R. N., and J. Hartwick. (1987). "An Alternative to the Intrinsic-Extrinsic Dichotomy of Work Rewards." *Journal of Management* 13:751–66.

Kanungo, R. N., and M. Mendonca. (1988). "Evaluating Employee Compensation." *California Management Review* (Fall): 23–29.

Kovach, Kenneth A., and Peter E. Millspaugh. (1990). "Comparable Worth: Canada Legislates Pay Equity." *Academy of Management Executive* 4(2): 92–101.

Labour Canada. (1986). *Labour Standards in Canada*, 1986 edition. Ottawa: Minister of Supply and Services Canada.

Lawler, E. E. (1966). "Managers' Attitudes Toward How Their Pay Is and Should Be Determined." *Journal of Applied Psychology* 50:273–79.

———. (1971). *Pay and Organizational Effectiveness*. New York: McGraw-Hill.

———. (1972). "Secrecy and the Need to Know." In *Readings in Managerial Motivation and Compensation*, edited by M. Dunnette, R. House, and H. Tosi. East Lansing: Michigan State University Press.

———. (1973). *Motivation in Work Organizations*. Monterey, Calif.: Brooks/Cole.

———. (1977). "Reward Systems." In *Improving Life at Work*, edited by J. R. Hackman and J. L. Shuttle. Santa Monica, Calif.: Goodyear.

———. (1981). *Pay and Organizational Development*. Reading, Mass.: Addison-Wesley.

———. (1986a). *High-Involvement Management*. San Francisco, Calif.: Jossey-Bass.

———. (1986b). "What's Wrong With Point-Factor Job Evaluation." *Compensation and Benefits Review* 18(2): 20–28.

Lawler, E. E., and J. R. Hackman. (1969). "The Impact of Employee

Participation in the Development of Pay Incentive Plans: A Field Experiment." *Journal of Applied Psychology* 53:467–71.

Lawler, E. E., and G. D. Jenkins. (1976). "Employee Participation in Pay Plan Development." Unpublished technical report to the Department of Labor, Ann Arbor, Michigan, cited in *Pay and Organizational Development*, edited by E. E. Lawler. Reading, Mass.: Addison-Wesley.

Lawler, E. E., and Gerald E. Ledford. (1985). "Skill-based Pay: A Concept That's Catching On." *Personnel* September: 54–61.

Lawler, E. E., A. M. Mohrman, and S. M. Resnick. (1984). "Performance Appraisal Revisited." *Organizational Dynamics* (Summer): 20–35.

Lewin, Kurt. (1935). *A Dynamic Theory of Personality*. New York: McGraw-Hill.

Locke, E. A., and J. F. Bryan. (1968). "Goal-Setting as a Determinant of the Effect of Knowledge of Score on Performance." *American Journal of Psychology* 81:398–406.

Locke, E. A., and G. P. Latham. (1984). *Goal-Setting: A Motivational Technique That Works!* Englewood Cliffs, N.J.: Prentice-Hall.

Locke, E. A., K. N. Shaw, L. M. Saari, and G. P. Latham. (1981). "Goal-Setting and Task Performance: 1969–1980." *Psychological Bulletin* 90: 125–52.

Luthans, Fred. (1989). *Organizational Behavior*. 5th ed. New York: McGraw-Hill.

Luthans, F., and W. E. Reif. (1972). "Does Job Enrichment Really Pay Off?" *California Management Review* 15:30–36.

———. (1973). "Job Enrichment: Long on Theory, Short on Practice." *Organizational Dynamics* 3:30–43.

Maslow, Abraham H. (1954). *Motivation and Personality*. New York: Harper.

McCormick, E. J. (1976). "Job and Task Analysis." In *Handbook of Industrial and Organizational Psychology*, edited by M. D. Dunnette. Chicago: Rand McNally and Company.

———. (1979). *Job Analysis Methods and Applications*. New York: AMACOM.

McGrath, Karen. (1988). "Polaroid Workers Able to Picture Retirement." *The Globe and Mail* (Toronto) 28 January: B1–B2.

McGregor, D. (1960). *The Human Side of Enterprise*. New York: McGraw-Hill.

———. (1966). "The Human Side of Enterprise." In *Leadership and Motivation: Essays of Douglas McGregor*, edited by W. G. Bennis and E. H. Schein with C. McGregor. Cambridge, Mass.: MIT Press.

McPherson, David L., and John T. Wallace. (1985). "Employee Benefit Plans." In *Human Resource Management in Canada*. Scarborough, Ont.: Prentice-Hall.

Miles, Raymond E., and Charles C. Snow. (1984). "Designing Strategic Human Resources Systems." *Organizational Dynamics* 13(1): 36–52.

Milkowich, George T., and Jerry M. Newman. (1990). *Compensation*. Homewood, Ill.: Richard D. Irwin.

Miner, J. B. (1980). *Theories of Organizational Behavior*. Hinsdale, Ill.: Dryden Press.

Morgan Guaranty Survey, The. (n.d.). "Rising Absenteeism." Morgan Guaranty Trust Company of New York.

Morrison, E. E. (1966). *New Machines and Modern Times*. Cambridge, Mass.: MIT Press.

Neibel, B. (1976). *Motion and Timestudy*. Homewood, Ill.: Richard D. Irwin.

Ng, Ignace. (1989). "The Effect of Vacation and Sickleave Policies on Absenteeism." *Canadian Journal of Administrative Sciences* 6(4): 18–26.

Panchatantra. Translated from the Sanskrit by Arthur W. Ryder (1949). Bombay: Jaico Publishing House.

"Participative Management at Herman Miller: An Innovative Strategy for Action." (1987). Proceedings of the Ecology of Work: Improving Productivity and the Quality of Work Life, Tenth Anniversary Conference, Washington, D.C., June 24–26. Northwood, N.H.: NTL Institute and the OD Network.

Paull, Jay. (1986). "How to Boost Productivity — Put a Nanny on Your Payroll." *Canadian Business* (March): 122–23.

Pay Equity Commission. (1989a). "Assessing the Gender Bias of Your Point Factor Job Evaluation System." *Newsletter* 1(9): 1–7. Toronto: Government of the Province of Ontario.

———. (1989b) *Pay Equity Implementation Series # 15* (January): 15.1–15.7. Toronto: Government of the Province of Ontario.

Peat Marwick Stevenson & Kellogg. (1989). "Employee Benefit Cost in Canada." Toronto: Peat Marwick Stevenson & Kellogg.

Perry, D. (1983). "Employment Equity: A Means to Organizational Effectiveness." In *Human Resources Management in Canada*. Vol. 2. Scarborough, Ontario: Prentice-Hall.

Pierce, Jon L., John W. Newstrom, Randall B. Dunham, and Alison E. Barber. (1989). *Alternative Work Schedules*. Toronto: Allyn and Bacon.

Quinn, James B. (1988). "Strategies for Change." In *The Strategy Process: Concepts, Contexts, and Cases*, edited by James B. Quinn, Henry Mintzberg, and Robert M. James. Englewood Cliffs, N.J.: Prentice-Hall.

Reid, Frank, and Noah Meltz. (1984). "Canada's STC: A Comparison with the California Version." In *Short-Time Compensation: A Formula for Work Sharing*, edited by R. MaCoy and M. V. Morand. New York: Pergamon Press.

Rock, Milton L., ed. (1984). *Handbook of Wage and Salary Administration.* New York: McGraw-Hill.

Rotter, J. B. (1966). "Generalized Expectancies for Internal vs. External Control of Reinforcement." *Psychological Monographs* 80(1): 1–28.

Sathe, Vijay. (1985). *Culture and Related Corporate Realities: Text, Cases, and Readings on Organizational Entry, Establishment, and Change.* Homewood, Ill.: Richard D. Irwin.

Scheflon, K. C., E. E. Lawler and J. R. Hackman. (1971). "Long-Term Impact of Employee Participation in the Development of Pay Incentive Plans: A Field Experiment Revisited." *Journal of Applied Psychology* 55:182–86.

Schein, E. H. (1985). *Organizational Culture and Leadership.* San Francisco: Jossey-Bass.

_______. (1988). "Innovative Cultures and Adaptive Organizations." Working Paper, Sloan School of Management, Massachusetts Institute of Technology, Cambridge, Mass.

Schneller, George O., IV, and Richard E. Kopelman. (1983). "Using Incentives to Increase Absenteeism: A Plan That Backfired." *Compensation Review* 15(2): 40–45.

Schwinger, P. (1975). *Wage Incentive Systems.* New York: Halsted.

Shapiro, W. Jack, and Mahmoud A. Wahba. (1978). "Pay Satisfaction: Empirical Test of Discrepancy Model." *Management Science* 24(6): 612–22.

Simon, H. A. (1957). *Administrative Behavior.* New York: Free Press.

Smith, Adam ([1796] 1950). *An Inquiry into the Nature and Causes of the Wealth of Nations,* edited by Edwin Cannan. Vol. 1. London: Methuen.

Statistics Canada. (1989). *Dimensions: Profile of Ethnic Groups.* Ottawa, Ont.: Minister of Supply and Services Canada.

Staw, B. M. (1984). "Organizational Behavior: A Review and Reformulation of the Field's Outcome Variables." *Annual Review of Psychology* 35:627–66.

Taylor, F. W. (1911). *The Principles of Scientific Management.* New York: Harper.

Tilles, S. (1966). "Strategies for Allocating Funds." *Harvard Business Review* 44:72–80.

Tolman. E. C. (1932). *Purposive Behavior in Animals.* New York: Century.

Tosi, Henry, and Lisa Tosi. (1986). "What Managers Need to Know about Knowledge-based Pay." *Organizational Dynamics* 14(3): 52–64.

Treece, James B. (1990). "Here Comes GM's Saturn: More Than a Car, It Is GM's Hope for Reinventing Itself." *Business Week* April 9: 56–62.

Vroom, V. H. (1964). *Work and Motivation.* New York: Wiley.

Wallace, Marc J., and Charles H. Fay. (1988). *Compensation Theory and Practice.* Boston: PWS-Kent.

Walton, R. E. (1977). "Work Innovations at Topeka: After Six Years." *Journal of Applied Behavioral Science* 13:422–33.

Weiner, Nan, and Morley Gunderson. (1990). *Pay Equity: Issues, Options and Experiences*. Markham, Ont.: Butterworths.

White, P. M., and A. Nanda. (1989). "South Asians in Canada." *Canadian Social Trends*. Autumn. Ottawa: Statistics Canada.

Whyte, W. F., ed. (1955). *Money and Motivation: An Analysis of Incentives in Industry*. New York: Harper.

Winpisinger, W. W. (1973). "Job Satisfaction: A Union Response." *AFL-CIO American Federalist* 80:8–10.

INDEX

Abella Royal Commission on Equality in Employment, 2
Absence, casual, 165, 166
  and overtime, 167–68
Absenteeism
  attendance-outcomes expectancy, 161–62
  effects of, 156
  effort-attendance expectancy, 159, 160, 161
  employee assistance programme, 163
  flex time, 163
  involuntary, 159, 161
  job context satisfaction, 164–65
  and job design, 164
  job factors related to, 157–58
  measuring, 166–67
  methods of controlling, 163–68
  personal factors related to, 157
  and positive rewards, 167–68
  reasons for, 158–62
  reducing through rewards, 156–68
  sanctions, using, 165–67
  shorter work week, 163
  time preference for, 158
  transportation facilities, 164
  valence of outcomes, 162
  voluntary, 161, 166
  and work group norms, 161, 162
Accident insurance, 79
Achievement needs, 219
Action programme, 352
  illustration of, 357–66
  procedural steps, 352–57
  rationale, 352
Adams, J. Stacy, 65
Age, and absenteeism, 157
Analyzer strategy, 30, 31, 32
Anti-Inflation Act, 9
Autonomy, 113, 115

Base pay, 7–8, 32, 33
Benchmark jobs, 253, 300, 301, 309–11
Benefits. *See* Employee benefits programme
Benge, Eugene, 256
Blue Monday index, 166
Bonus, 8, 24, 215, 314–15
Business strategies, 29–32, 297
  Analyzer, 30, 31, 32
  Defender, 30, 31
  Prospector, 30, 31

Cafeteria, subsidized, 332
Cafeteria-style benefit plans, 108
Canada Labour Code, 11
Canadian Pacific, 32
Cardinal River Coal Mine, 25
Career ladders, 135
Car pools, 164
Carrot approach to compensation, 48
Carrot and stick approach to compensation, 47
Centralized compensation system, 139–40
Classical approach to job design, 110
Classification of jobs, 248–50, 262
Coffee breaks, 79
Communication, and performance-pay linkage, 184
Comparable worth, defined, 275
Company car, 10
Company discount, 10
Compa-ratio, 299, 300, 343
Compensable factors
  gender bias in determining, 280–81
  in job evaluation, 250, 252–53
Compensation
  defined, 2
  economic. *See* Economic compensation system
  and job satisfaction, 4

Compensation — *continued*
- non-economic. *See* Non-economic compensation system
- organization objectives, 4
- process issues in, 128
- strategic issues in, 128

Compensation mix, and product life cycle, 32–35
Compensation model, 12–16
Compensation philosophy, 129–31
- components of, 130–31

Compensation system
- and business strategies, 30
- evaluating, effectiveness of, 350–66
- open vs. closed, 197–98
- and turnover, 169
- types of equity, 66

Complaint-driven enforcement, pay equity, 275, 276
Computerization, 24
Consumer Price Index, 9
Content theories of work motivation, 46–56, 64
- defined, 46
- Herzberg's two-factor theory of reward classification, 49–56
- human relations, 48–49
- scientific management, 47–48

Contingency approach to job design, 111–14
Cost-of-living adjustment (COLA), 9
Core job characteristics, 112–13, 164

Day-care centres, 163, 332
- in workplace, 163

Decentralized compensation system, 139–40
Defender strategy, 30, 31
Dental plans, 10
Descriptive assumptions, 28, 29
Disability insurance, 9, 328–29
Discrepancy theory, 95
Dissatisfaction, pay
- and absenteeism, 161
- consequences of, 103–107
- and employee turnover, 169, 171
- external environmental factors, 106
- job content factors, 106
- job context factors, 105–106
- Lawler's model of, 104, 105

Economic compensation system, 7–10
- base pay, 7–8
- benefits, 9
- cost-of-living adjustment (COLA), 9
- incentive plans, 8
- merit pay, 8

Economic conditions, 22–23
Economic man concept, 111
Education, and absenteeism, 157
Educational assistance programme, 332
Effort, defined, 181–82
Effort-performance expectancy, 67
- determinants of, 68, 69–71
  - actual situation, 70
  - communication from others, 70
  - past experiences in similar situations, 70
  - self-esteem, 70–71

Employee assistance plans, 10, 163, 332
Employee benefits programme, 9–10, 33, 35, 323–36
- cafeteria-style, 108
- flexible approach, 333–34
- guidelines in designing, 334–36
- income protection programmes, 9, 324–33
- reimbursed time off, 9–10
- services and perquisites, 10
- standardized, 333

Employee discounts, 332
Employees
- classification of, 11
- involvement in decision making, 145–50
- participation in designing incentive plans, 217
- satisfaction. *See* Satisfaction
- turn-ons-plus, 107
- turnovers, 107

Employment discrimination, and pay equity, 285–88
Energy and Chemical Workers Union, 25
Enriched job, 113
Environment
- and absenteeism, 164
- and compensation system, 21–22, 23
- employee turnover, 171

external. *See* External environment
internal. *See* Internal environment
Equal pay for equal work, 274
Equal pay for similar work, 274
Equal pay for work of equal value, 274
Equity theory of human motivation, 64, 65–66, 95–96, 100–101, 283–84
social comparison, 96
European market, 23
Exempt employees, 11
Exit interview, 298
Expectancy theory, 64, 66–82, 94
basic elements of, 67
contingency, 77
effort-performance expectancy, 67
equation, 74–75
model, 69
perceived skill, 77
performance-outcome expectancy, 67–68
process of, 74–77
salience, 77
valence of outcome, 67, 68
Expectancy theory model
and absenteeism, 159–62
empirical support for, 77–80
and employee turnover, 170–73
implications for reward management, 80–82
and process issues of compensation, 133
External environment, 22–27
economic conditions, 22–23
government regulations, 24–25
sociocultural, 25–27
technological changes, 24
union expectations, 25
External equity, 66, 137, 138, 239. *See also* Salary surveys
and pay rates, 297–98
Extrinsic rewards, 50–56

Factor comparison method of job evaluation, 256–61, 262
Factor Evaluation System, 250–56
Family obligations
and absenteeism, 157, 159
and employee turnover, 171
Female-dominated job class, 275, 276, 288
Fixed income, 34
Flex time, 163, 332–33
Free Trade Agreement, 21–22
Frequency index, 166
Fulfilment theory, 95

Gain-sharing plan(s)
bonus formula, determining, 222
conditions favouring, 231–32
costs to be used, 222
frequency of payment, 223
gains to be shared, 222–23
Improshare Plan, 8, 229–31
maintaining participative process, 223
modifications to, 223
process used to set up plan, 221–22
Rucker Plan, 227–29
Scanlon Plan, 222, 224–26
Gantt Plan, 214
Gender bias, 278–79
in job analysis, 279–80
in job evaluation, 280–81
Gender predominance, 276
General Motors (GM), 24, 25
Gold circle situation, 316
Government regulation, 24–25
Green circle situation, 315
Gross Domestic Product (GDP), 24
Guaranteed Income Supplement (GIS), 324

Hackman/Oldham job characteristics model, 111–14, 115
Halsey 50-50 Method, 214
Hawthorne experiments, 48
Health insurance plans, 331
Herzberg, Frederick, 49
Hewlett-Packard, 31
Hierarchy of needs theory (Maslow), 49, 50
High flyers, 33
Human relations movement, 48–49
social man concept, 48
Human resource management, 30
Hygiene factors, extrinsic rewards as, 50, 51

Illness, and absenteeism, 159
Improshare Plan, 8, 229–31
Incentive pay, 32, 33, 34
under scientific management, 47

Incentive plans, 8, 32–33
  group, 220–32. *See also* Gain-sharing plans
    conditions favouring effectiveness of, 220
  individual, 212–20
    conditions favouring effectiveness of, 216–20
    and incentive pay, 218
    measuring performance objectives, 218
    modifying, 217
    nature of task, 219
    piece-rate plan, 212–13
    sales commissions and bonuses, 215
    side-effects of, 219–20
    standard-hours plan, 213–14
    time standard, 216–17
    valuing money, 218–19
  objectives of, 220
Income, and absenteeism, 158
Income protection programmes, 9, 324–33
  Canada/Quebec Pension Plan, 326
  employee services, 331–33
  group insurance, 328–30
  private pension plans, 326–28
  reimbursed time off, 330–31
  unemployment insurance, 325
  workers' compensation, 325–26
Individual equity, 66
Inflation, 9
  impact on organizations, 22
Information system, and level of aggregation, 188
Insurance, group plans, 328–30. *See also* Accident insurance; Disability insurance; Health insurance plans; Life insurance; Medical insurance; Unemployment insurance
Interest rates, high, and inflation, 22
Internal environment, 23, 27–35
  business strategies, 29–32
  internal work culture, 27–29
  product life cycle, 32–35
Internal equity, 66, 137, 138
  and base pay, 240
  and compensation system design, 239–40
  defined, 238–39
  and pay rates, 297
Interpersonal rewards, 10
Intrinsic rewards, 10, 50–56, 78
  and job motivation, 50–51

Job analysis, 240
  defined, 241
  diary/log, 243
  gender bias in, 279–80
  interview, 242
  observation, 242–43
  Position Analysis Questionnaire (PAQ), 243–45
  procedure and methods, 241–42
  questionnaire, 243
Job content, 238–39
Job contribution, 239
Job description, 245–47
Job design, 110–17
  and absenteeism, 164
  classical approach to, 110
  combining tasks, 114
  contingency approach to, 111–14
  core job characteristics, 112–13, 164
  economic man concept, 111
  establishing client relationships, 116
  forming natural work units, 114–15
  growth theories of, 111
  implications for reward management, 117
  job characteristics model, 112–14, 115
  opening feedback channels, 116
  process of, 114–17
  self-actualizing man concept, 111
  theoretical approach to, 110–14
  vertically loading the job, 116
Job enrichment programmes, 55
Job evaluation, 240
  administering programme, 262–63
  appeal of, 263
  benchmark jobs, 253
  classification, 248–50, 262
  compensable factors, 134–35, 250, 252–53
  defined, 247
  factor comparison method, 256–61, 262
  gender bias in, 280–81
  methods, 247–62
  in pay equity determination, 288–89
  person-based vs. job-content-based, 134–35
  point factor, 131, 254–56, 262

ranking, 247–48, 261–62
Job feedback, 113, 115
Job match, salary surveys, 302
Job performance
behaviours, 180–82
defined, 180–81
role of pay in increasing, 183–85
Job safety, and absenteeism, 158
Job security, and absenteeism, 165
Job specifications, 245–47
Job structure, developing, 263–64
Jury-duty leave, 9, 331

Key jobs, 253
Key scale with anchor points, 256
Knowledge-based pay, 348–50

Labour legislation, 24–25
Lawler, 64, 67
Legal holidays, 330
Level of aggregation
defined, 186
determining, 187–91
Lewin, Kurt, 64
Life insurance, 329
Lincoln Electric Company, 31
Locus of control, internal/external, 28, 29
Lotteries
attendance, 167
for punctuality, 168
Loyalty, and absenteeism, 158, 162

Male-dominated job class, 276, 288
Management
descriptive assumptions about human nature, 28, 29
prescriptive assumptions about guiding principles of conduct, 28, 29
Theory X model of, 29
Maslow, Abraham, 49, 50
Maternity leave, 9, 331
Medical insurance, 9
Merit pay, 8, 212, 314–15
determining, 194–95
employee involvement in, 197–98
frequency of, 196–97
salary increase vs. one-time bonus, 193–94
Merit raise, 143–44
Merrick (piece-rate) Plan, 213

Motivation
and compensation, 4
consequences of neglecting, 94–95
equity theory of, 64, 65–66, 283–84
expectancy theory of, 64, 66–82
and intrinsic/extrinsic rewards, 50–52, 50–56, 78
myths about, 52–56
job enrichment programmes, 55
and motives, 45
theories, 45–46
content. *See* Content theories of work motivation
process. *See* Process theories of work motivation
work redesign model, 55
Motivation model (Lawler), 64
Multi-skilling, 346–48

Needs
deficiency, 50, 51
growth, 50, 51
hierarchy of (Maslow), 50
self-actualization, 50
Non-economic compensation system, 10–11
seven dimensions of, 10
Non-exempt employees, 11

Old Age Security (OAS), 324
Organizational culture, 8
and performance appraisal, 202–203
Organizational stressors, 164
Organizations
behavioural objectives, 11–12
cultural dimensions of, 26–27
Defender-type, 31
entrepreneurial, 30
high-tech, pay mix in, 34–35
internal work culture, 27–29
objectives of, and compensation programme, 4
Organization size, and level of aggregation, 188–89
Outcome-input ratio, 65, 74
Overtime
and absenteeism, 167–68
and tardiness, 168

Paternity leave, 9, 159
Pay, performance-based and job performance, 183–85

Pay equity, 2
comparable worth, 25
defined, 274–75
legislation
adjustments, cost of, 276
applicability of, 275
effects of, 284–85
enforcement of, 275–76
and equity theory of human motivation, 283–84
gender predominance, 276
history, Canada, 275, 277
and moral rights, 282–83
plan, 276–78
visible minorities, effects on, 285–88
Pay Equity Act (Ontario), 277–78
Pay grade, 299, 300
Pay rates
external equity, effect on, 297–98
and internal equity, 297
relevant external labour market, 298–99
sources or bases of, 296–98
Pay relationships
external, 4
internal, 4
Pay secrecy, 142–45
effects of, 142–44
Pay structure
capping policy, 315–16
designing, 307–15
pay grades, 311–12, 314, 315
pay level policy, 307–309
and pay ranges, 312–14
pricing job structure, 309–11
and salary administration policies, 315–17
sources or bases of pay rates, 296–98
Pension plans, 9
Canada/Quebec, 326
portability, 328
private, 326–28
vesting rights, 328
Perceived reward contingency value, 360
Percentage time-lost index, 166
Performance, defined, 180–81
Performance appraisal, 181
formal appraisal review, 201
goal-setting theory, 199
and information system, 188
monitoring performance, 200–201
and performance-based rewards, 198–203
personal traits, using, 201–202
preconditions for effective, 202–203
process, 199–202, 204
subjective vs. objective measures, 195–96
trust, and, 189–90
Performance-based deferred compensation, 364
Performance-based pay, issues in, 185–98
Performance-based rewards, 181
employee involvement in design and administration of, 197–98
length of payout period, 196–97
level of aggregation, 186–91
information system, 188
size, 188–89
technology, 187–88
trust, 189–90
union status, 190
merit pay, determining, 194–95
number of pay plans, 191–93
objectives of, 182–83
salary increase vs. one-time bonus, 193–94
subjective vs. objective performance measures, 195–96
Performance-outcome expectancy, 67–68
determinants of, 71–72
actual situation, 71
attractiveness of outcomes, 72
belief in locus of control, 72
communication from others, 71
effort-performance expectancies, 71–72
past experiences in similar situations, 72
Perquisites, 10, 332
Personal days, paid, 330
Personal equity, 238
Personal growth rewards, 10
Personal equity, 66
Person-based pay, 346–50
knowledge-based pay, 346, 348–50
multi-skilling, 346–48
Person-based job evaluation, 134, 135
Person-related variables, and job satisfaction, 98
Piece-rate plan, 212–13
sales commissions, 215

Point method of job evaluation, 254–56, 262
Position Analysis Questionnaire (PAQ), 243–45
Prescriptive assumptions, 28, 29
Proactive enforcement of pay equity, 276
Process issues in compensation, 128, 142–50
  communicating the system, 142–45
  involving employees in decision making, 145–50
  role in compensation design and administration, 150–51
Process theories of work motivation, 64
  equity theory, 64, 65–66
  expectancy theory, 64, 66–82
Product life cycle, 32–35, 297
  pay mix in stages of
    decline, 33
    growth, 33
    limitations of approach, 35
    maturity, 33
    renewal, 33
    stability, 33
    start-up, 32
Productivity
  and COLA, 9
  defined, 181
  performance appraisal, 200
  rate of, 22–23
Professional memberships, 10
Prospector strategy, 30, 31

Quality of Working Life programme, 25, 165

Ranking, of jobs, 247–48, 261–62
  alternation, 247–48
  paired comparisons, 248
  simple, 247
Red circle situation, 315, 316
Regression analysis, 309–11
Rehearsal retirement programme, 331
Relevant other, 74
Retirement benefits, 79
Reward(s)
  actual effectiveness of, 362
  to employees, 5, 6
  employees' perception of, 78–79, 262
    dimensions of, 79
    generality, 79
  Herzberg's two-factor theory of classification of, 50
  intended effectiveness of, 351–52, 362
  interpersonal, 10
  intrinsic/extrinsic, 50–56, 78
  mediation of reward criterion, 53, 54
  performance-based. *See* Performance-based rewards
  personal growth, 10
  productivity, 181
  saliency of, 74
  satisfaction with. *See* Satisfaction
  task criterion, 53–54
  used to reduce absenteeism, 156–68
  used to reduce tardiness, 168
  used to reduce turnover, 169–74
Reward system, 7
  and business strategies, 29–30
  compensation model, 12–16
  defined, 5
  economic compensation, 7–10
  objectives of, 11–12
Rowan Plan, 214
Rucker Plan, 8, 227–29
Running out of range, 315, 316–17

Salary, defined, 7–8
Salary budget process, 342–46
  bottom-up approach, 345–46
  top-down approach, 343–45
Salary surveys
  benchmark jobs, 300, 301
  choosing external labour markets for, 138–39
  conducted by organization, 300–302
  critique of, 304
  data-collection techniques, 303–304
    conference, 304
    personal interview, 304
    questionnaire, 304
    telephone, 303–304
  defined, 299–300
  determination of survey sample, 300
  job evaluation method, 302
  job match, 302
  key job matching method, 301
  maturity curves, 302–303
  occupational survey method, 301–302

Salary surveys — *continued*
relevant labour market for, 298–99
return rate, 301
by third parties, 302–303
Sales commissions, 215
Sanctions
for controlling absenteeism, 165–67
measurement problem, 166–67
side-effects of, 167
Satisfaction
context-related variables, 101–103
discrepancy theory, 95
equity theory, 95–96
fulfilment theory, 95
guidelines for enhancing, 107–109
Hackman/Oldham job characteristics model, 111–14, 115
job context, and absenteeism, 164–65
and job design, 110–17
job evaluation system, 108
job-related variables, 99–100, 102
Lawler's model of, 95, 96, 98
models of, 95
monitoring, 108
with non-economic outcomes, 109–17
open pay system, 109
pay, determinants of, 96–98
person-related variables, 96, 98, 102
referent-other-related variables, 100–101, 102–103
Saturn car project, 24, 25
Scanlon Plan, 8, 31, 222, 224–26
Scientific management, 47–48, 110
economic man concept, 47, 111
Self-actualizing man concept, 111
Seniority, 314
Shadow range situation, 315, 317
Shell Canada Chemical Company, 25
Shift work, and absenteeism, 158
Sick leave, 9
Sick leave policy, 330
and absenteeism, 158, 161–62, 165
Sickness insurance, 79
Sick pay, 79
Silver circle situation, 315, 316
Size of work groups, and absenteeism, 157–58
Skill level, and absenteeism, 157
Skill variety, 112, 115
Social comparison, 103, 109, 283
and equity theory, 96
and pay equity, 283–84
Sociocultural environment, 25–27
cultural dimensions, 26
Standard-hours plan, 213–14
Stereotypes, 281
Strategic issues in compensation, 128
balancing mechanistic and process issues, 131, 133
centralization vs. decentralization, 139–40
choice of compensation mix, 141–42
choice of external labour markets for salary surveys, 138–39
compensation philosophy, 129–31
compensation system as end or as means to end, 136–37
internal vs. external equity, 137–38
job-content-based vs. person-based evaluation system, 134–35
performance vs. seniority, 140–41
role in compensation design and administration, 150–51
Supervision, and absenteeism, 158
Survey data, analysing, 304–307
Survey levelling, 305

Tardiness
and overtime, 168
using rewards to reduce, 168
Targeted reward contingency value, 360
Task-and-bonus system, 215
Task identity, 112, 115
Task significance, 112, 115
Taylor, Frederick, 47
Taylor (piece-rate) Plan, 213
Technological changes, 24
Technology and level of aggregation, 187–88
Texas Instruments, 31
Time off, reimbursed, 9–10
Time span of discretion, 99
Time standard, incentive plans, 217
Tolman, Edward, 64
Topping out effect, 349
Transportation, and absenteeism, 159, 161, 164
Turn-ons, 107
Turn-ons-plus, 107
Turnover, 107

annual rate, computing, 173
effort-stay expectancy, 171
and internal-external equity, 173–74
methods of controlling, 173–74
stay-outcomes expectancy, 171–72
using rewards to reduce, 169–74
valence of outcomes, 172
Two-factor theory of reward classification (Herzberg), 49–57

Unemployment insurance, 9
Unions
as external environment, 25
participation in incentive plans, 217
and pay equity, 288
and performance-based rewards, 190
United Auto Workers (UAW), 25

Vacations, 9, 79, 330
Vacation policy, and absenteeism, 158
Valence of outcomes, 67, 68
determinants of, 73–74
equity of outcome, 74
instrumentality of outcome, 73
Value-in-exchange of a job, 289
Value-in-use of a job, 289
Visible minorities, 284
and pay equity, 285–88
Vroom, Victor, 64, 66

Wage history, 101–102, 103
Wage surveys, and internal equity, 239
Wages, defined, 7
Work culture, internal, 27–29
descriptive/prescriptive assumptions, 28–29
Schein's three-level model, 27
Work motivation. *See* Motivation
Worker's compensation, 9
Work ethic, and absenteeism, 162
Work group norms, and absenteeism, 164–65
Work redesign model, 55
Worst-day index, 166